ROUTLEDGE LIBRARY
CULTURAL STU

Volume 6

OTHERNESS AND THE MEDIA

OTHERNESS AND THE MEDIA

The Ethnography of the Imagined and
the Imaged

Edited by
HAMID NAFICY AND TESHOME H. GABRIEL

Routledge
Taylor & Francis Group

LONDON AND NEW YORK

First published in 1993 by Harwood Academic Publishers

This edition first published in 2017
by Routledge
2 Park Square, Milton Park, Abingdon, Oxon OX14 4RN

and by Routledge
711 Third Avenue, New York, NY 10017

Routledge is an imprint of the Taylor & Francis Group, an informa business

© 1993 Harwood Academic Publishers GmbH

British Library Cataloguing in Publication Data
A catalogue record for this book is available from the British Library

ISBN: 978-1-138-69145-2 (Set)
ISBN: 978-1-315-45997-4 (Set) (ebk)
ISBN: 978-1-138-69950-2 (Volume 6) (hbk)
ISBN: 978-1-138-69952-6 (Volume 6) (pbk)
ISBN: 978-1-315-51517-5 (Volume 6) (ebk)

Publisher's Note
The publisher has gone to great lengths to ensure the quality of this reprint but points out that some imperfections in the original copies may be apparent.

Disclaimer
The publisher has made every effort to trace copyright holders and would welcome correspondence from those they have been unable to trace.

OTHERNESS AND THE MEDIA

THE ETHNOGRAPHY OF THE IMAGINED AND THE IMAGED

Edited by

Hamid Naficy

and

Teshome H. Gabriel

harwood academic publishers

USA • Switzerland • Australia • Belgium • France • Germany • Great Britain •
India • Japan • Malaysia • Netherlands • Russia • Singapore

Harwood Academic Publishers

820 Town Center Drive
Langhorne, Pennsylvania 19047
United States of America

Post Office Box 90
Reading, Berkshire RG1 8JL
Great Britain

Private Bag 8
Camberwell, Victoria 3124
Australia

3-14-9, Okubo
Shinjuku-ku, Tokyo 169
Japan

58, rue Lhomond
75005 Paris
France

Emmaplein 5
1075 AW Amsterdam
Netherlands

Christburger Str. 11
10405 Berlin
Germany

Some of the articles appearing in this book were originally published in volume 13, numbers 1-3 of the journal *Quarterly Review of Film and Video*.

Contents

Introduction to the Series

Studies in Film and Video is a series of multi-authored volumes exploring, in some depth, particular topics in film, television, and video studies. As with *Quarterly Review of Film and Video,* the journal out of which the series emerged, the work published will focus on areas of research that are among the most pressing for the current study of culture: studies of gender, race and sexuality of representation; critical inquiries into postcolonial and cross-cultural media practices; explorations of new critical or theoretical dimensions in media studies; research on the function and effects of new technologies on global image cultures. The books of this series will enlarge and clarify current understandings of film and video culture during an era of their dramatic reconfiguration.

Introduction — Consuming the Other

This anthology on otherness and the media has been prompted by the proliferation of recent writings, both academic and popular, emanating from various disciplines. These writings have centered on issues of "difference," "diversity," "multiculturalism," "representation" and "postcolonial" discourses. They have generated intense interest not only because such issues and discourses question existing canons of criticism, theory, and cultural practice but also because they suggest a new sense of direction in theorization of difference and representation.

The anthology first appeared in a different form as a special triple issue of *Quarterly Review of Film and Video* (volume 13, numbers 1-3, 1990). The response of readers was so enthusiastic that the issue sold out very quickly, prompting its emergence in book form. What you have in your hands now is a revised version which contains two additional original contributions on the discourse of otherness. These essays and other modifications substantially strengthen this collection.

It has been obvious for quite some time that certain metaphors long held as apt descriptions of America no longer hold sway. The metaphors of the "melting pot" with its implication of homogenization of differences and otherness or the "salad bowl" and the "unmeltable ethnics" with their connotations of benign pluralism and coexistence of differences, evoke ideologies of conformity and affirmation. These have proved untenable in actuality. In the late 1980s and early 1990s major corporate establishments (academic and business), particularly in North America, fell into a sudden paroxysm of interest in otherness and in institutionalization of "diversity," "pluralism," and "multiculturalism." Like all high fevers this too will break quickly! By highlighting consensus and parity, these efforts tend to co-opt differences and to elide histories — as though the brutal enslavement of peoples, the ruthless massacre of Others, the dislocation and disenfranchisement of gendered minorities and marginal populations can be erased in the interest of some putative equality. These consensual efforts also tend to paper over the "essential" diversity and conflictual relationships that exist among various social forces, ethnicities, nationalities, and postcolonial scatterings. We speak of putative equality because the end result of such a *construction of diversity* and difference is the democratization of consumption and not of representation. Corporatism nurtures the fundamental transformation that postmodernism is ushering in whereby conscientious citizen is replaced with carefree consumer. Some logic would have it that if not equal under the law we can be equal as consumers of products and ideas.

Whatever the metaphor, the crisis of capitalism, the collapse of communism and the bipolar superpower world order, and the infusion into North America of othered populations — diasporaic immigrants, exiles, emigrés, expatriates, evicted, homeless, and the undocumented — have reawakened [in] difference and enhanced dialog across cultures and geographies. Not least of the contributions of these formerly othered, subaltern people has been their persistent and increasingly effective effort not only to critique the status quo but also to open up new discursive spaces. It seems to us that we are entering now not only a third but a multiple discursive and cultural space — a slipzone of practices in the arts, literature, popular culture, cinema, and television — where all kinds of resistive hybridities, syncretism, and mongrelizations are possible, valued. Such practices of critical theory have gained credibility within the academe as well as in certain sectors of society at large. Critical discourses within existing relations of production continue to be subjected to the operation of dominant hegemonies which tend to want to capture ideologically and economically both the threat and the allure of the other and its discursive strategies. Co-opting differences, effacing histories and conflictual relations of forces, multinational corporatism tends to map out alterity as mere difference to be consumed only as style. It is in this light that we must view the sudden feverish love affair with pluralism, otherness, and diversity. It now appears as if the issue is no longer to capture the means of production, or to gain control over the means of representation, but to pose as question representation itself.

As concerned intellectuals we cannot afford but to continue to resist relentlessly the co-optation and appropriation of discourses. But since we are always already situated in place and in time we cannot escape the phenomenon of being positioned in culture and in ideology. Furthermore, because all of us are engaged in a continual process of constructing others as subjects, need we not put into question also our own subjectivity and, for that matter, the whole notion of the constitution of the "subject" itself.

Theorizing difference, location, and subjectivity tends to reverse the process of stressing, celebrating, or appropriating difference and turns the other upon itself, thus returning it to its "[in]appropriate" condition and place — as unfitting, unbelonging, unfixed excess.

What of this unfitting, unbelonging, unfixed excess? For instance, in the present crisis of Middle East war and the "stories" of other wars, theories of postcoloniality are problematized. We are faced with an inability to "name" both the "new" in the New World Order and the "post" in postcoloniality. This is because this new condition in politics and discourse appears to be both different from and similar to the "old" colonial and bipolar world orders. Hence, the need to place postcoloniality itself into question and the "post" into quotation marks.

To examine the boundaries of difference is to acknowledge the relations of difference as the relations of power. The discourse of the other is not solely involved in the bashing of the canon as it is usually construed, it is rather engaged in a different practice of discourse. In fact, this other discourse acknowledges the inherent dynamics of the canon to deconstruct itself and it thrives on the interstices and the cracks of the canon. Thus, this volume focuses on a range of illuminating examples of cultural practices about otherness far and wide. We have brought together a number of established and emerging intellectuals and scholars with diverse interests and approaches. Among them: autobiographical musings and theorization of spectatorship (Trinh T. Minh-ha) and of naming and cultural trends (Martin Blythe); close textual reading and ideological analysis of nation and narration in African cinema (Philip Rosen); new ethnographic writings about the poetics of resistance (Smadar Lavie); cross-cultural readings of films (Scott Nygren); investigation of subnational cinemas (Marvin D'Lugo); postcolonial readings of feminism (Christine Anne Holmlund); critiquing Orientalist representations of race and gender (Ella Shohat); deploying local knowledge in analysis of representations of race on mainstream television (Herman Grey); theorization of liminality, of displacement, and of exilic television (Hamid Naficy); an appraisal of the evolution of tendencies and theories of third cinema and third world media (Robert Stam); and a critical evaluation of a decade of Latin American film scholarship both in English and indigenous languages (Ana López). Two new thought-provoking essays have been added: one interrogates the cultural economies of music and the ethics of identity and difference (Iain Chambers), while the other explores the in-between sites of ruin, memory, and the other (Teshome H. Gabriel).

We hope that our intervention will have contributed to an understanding of the multiple discursive space to which we have referred. In the end, however, our concern goes beyond the categories of race, ethnicity, class, gender, and national origin as the defining elements of the notion of otherness. To essentialize these categories biologically is detrimental, to ignore or belittle their import politically is even more damaging.

Consuming the other is a continual process of yearning — for meaning, for those qualities which the dominant order has exiled or lost, and for the certainties that ideologies provide in a world that is increasingly uncertain and unpredictable. Since this yearning is never fulfilled, the other remains forever alluring (and threatening). But, it derives its allure not from an essential authenticity, moral absolutism, or some higher knowledge but from its own shifting nomadic sensibilities. The other tends to thrive on the ambiguities and the limits of language. The only lasting and promising discourse, therefore, is that which is incomplete, provisional, and of a research nature. To fix a phenomenon like the other by defining it is simply to engage in weakening or arresting its potentialities. The other creates simultaneously both its own conditions of possibility and its own conditions of impossibility. The other is disorder.

Hamid Naficy
Teshome H. Gabriel

Displacing Limits of Difference: Gender, Race, and Colonialism in Edward Said and Homi Bhabha's Theoretical Models and Marguerite Duras's Experimental Films

Christine Anne Holmlund

Increasingly, radical literary and film critics, anthropologists, sociologists, political scientists, philosophers, historians, and others are exploring, exposing, and exploding the ways colonial and post-colonial discourses represent racial and sexual others as monolithically and inalterably different from a subject defined as Western, white, and male. Working with a wide range of intellectual traditions, often testing them against personal experiences, Third World critics like Edward Said and Homi Bhabha critique dominant representations of racial and/or ethnic difference. In *Orientalism*, for example, Said deconstructs racist stereotypes as the products of Orientalist dogmas. Part of a much larger project involving what may be termed the creation of a practical political theory, Said's focus here is on how Western colonial discourses, including modern mass media, promulgate rigid dichotomies of racial/ ethnic difference. In a smaller body of work, Bhabha insists on the psychic ambivalence that underpins and necessitates the compulsive repetition of colonial racist stereotypes. Drawing on Lacanian psychoanalytic theory and post-Althusserian Marxism, he looks at how stereotypes function for both the colonizer and the colonized and, unlike Said, engages to some extent sexual as well as racial difference.

From other angles, but often using similar techniques and strategies, a number of Western feminist critics insist on the need to view sexual difference as a complex and shifting dialectic of projections, idealizations, and rejections. Like Said, and, in other ways, Bhabha, they view difference as constituted intersubjectively in discourse, and draw on shared experiences to subvert patriarchal and imperialist conceptions of identity and authority.

Problems nonetheless remain. Said on the whole ignores the *female* racial other in his analyses of Orientalism, and thus, despite his support for feminist projects elsewhere, perpetuates in *Orientalism* the patriarchal definitions of women as "lamentably alien" which he seeks to critique.[1] Bhabha, though more sensitive to "the complexity of the question of gender difference,"[2] nevertheless chooses to treat racial difference as *equivalent* to sexual difference when he posits the racial stereo-

CHRISTINE HOLMLUND *is an Assistant Professor of French at the University of Tennessee where she regularly teaches in the Cinema Studies and Women's Studies Programs. She has written articles on lesbian and feminist theory and film. She is working on a book about Sylvester Stallone and Arnold Schwartzenegger.*

type and the sexual fetish as analogous psychic operations. As a result, he, too, has difficulty articulating sexual difference *with* racial difference when he discusses colonial stereotypes.[3]

Those Western feminist critics who focus exclusively or primarily on sexual difference and/or assume that women constitute a coherent category for analysis fall into a reverse trap. Third World feminists like Gayatri Spivak, Chahandra Mohanty, and Marnia Lazreg criticize them for appealing to a timeless, universal, and idealized "sisterhood" of women. In effect, because these Western feminists fail to account for differences of class, race, and ethnicity while they nonetheless still consider Third World women as an ill-defined and separate bloc, they become tacitly complicit with Orientalist strategies. At times they even, in Lazreg's words, engage in "a search . . . for the sensational and the uncouth . . . which reinforces the notion of difference as objectified otherness."[4]

In what follows I want to displace the limits of these various theoretical and critical models and thereby open a space for the simultaneous articulation of sexual and racial/ethnic difference. In the first two sections of this paper I will return to the general theoretical paradigms Said and Bhabha propose. Using the insights of Third World and Western feminist critics and others, I will argue that feminism and women cannot be taken for granted or subsumed within general and generically male models of difference. I will not, however, go so far as to propose jettisoning Said and Bhabha's inclusive models; on the contrary, my goal is to indicate how they may be strengthened when interrupted and challenged by feminist voices.

Throughout this article, I will also ask how and where Said and Bhabha's theoretical models may be used to analyze cinematic representations of otherness. Both Said and Bhabha concern themselves primarily with realist texts: Said examines nineteenth century novels, traditional ethnographic narratives, travelogues, and the like,[5] while in "The Other Question . . ." and "Difference, Discrimination and the Discourse of Colonialism," Bhabha addresses cinema directly, discussing Stephen Heath's reading of Orson Welles' *Touch of Evil*.[6]

What happens, however, to these theories when they are applied to non-realist movies or when they are interrogated by feminist voices? As touchstone for my evaluation of the paradigms Said and Bhabha profer I will, in a third part of this essay, measure their models against three of Marguerite Duras's experimental films marked by her childhood experiences in French colonial Indochina: *India Song* (1975), *Son Nom de Venise dans Calcutta désert* (1976) and *Les Mains négatives* (1979).[7] Duras's films, I will argue, offer a unique and virtually untapped opportunity to discuss how colonial and post-colonial discourses represent racial and sexual difference, for two main reasons. First, in these films, and elsewhere,[8] Duras speaks from a perspective lacking in most discussions of colonialism: that of the white female colonizer sympathetic to yet separate from male and female racial others. "This is what not lying is," she says.[9] Hers is a voice not usually heard from in discussions of colonialism. As anthropologist Paul Rabinow notes: "strangely enough, the group in the colonies who have received the least attention in historical and sociological studies are the colonists themselves."[10] All too frequently the binary opposition colonizer/colonized inhibits examination of what Gayatri Spivak calls "the heterogeneity of 'Colonial Power,' " at the same time that it masks the roles women play, whether as colonizers or as colonized.[11] In Duras's films, however, both the shared experiences Said and Lazreg call for as alternatives to Orientalism *and* the deep ambivalence Bhabha unmasks structure the interactions among Third World and female characters and narrators.

Second, because Duras's films are made in conscious opposition to Hollywood cinema,[12] separating voices from images in multiple and unexpected ways, they facilitate critiques of the ideological operations of mainstream films. Usually non-white or female others are positioned as visibly and unalterably different and as silenced, excluded from language. Unheard, these others are seen as weaker and more primitive, yet as threatening and powerful as well. In those cases where the racial, colonial, or national other is actually heard in mainstream films, her or his speech is usually an incomprehensible babel, part of the background, a block of sound.[13] Because we cannot understand her or him, we are sure that s/he is relatively unimportant. Only to the degree that s/he adopts the language of the dominant culture is s/he granted "the status of speech as an individual property right."[14]

In mainstream film in general, then, visible difference not only justifies discrimination against and oppression of the Other, it makes such discrimination and oppression seem necessary. In Duras's films, in contrast, women and non-whites speak, but often without being seen. As a result, the importance of fantasy and language, not just, or simply, sight, in the construction and perception of difference is highlighted. The emphases both Said and Bhabha place on vision and the visible are called into question, and must be adjusted accordingly.

My intention is not, however, to revere avant-garde film practice as radical while dismissing Hollywood film as reactionary. Duras's reduction of the image track in favor of the sound track is by no means solely a progressive strategy to be universally or automatically adopted. Clearly her decision to make avant-garde films severely limits who can and will see her cinema, but in itself this does not preclude her film practice from constituting a form of political cinema. A more serious objection is the fact that, far more than Duras's earlier, more descriptive novels, the same exotic and essentialist clichés Lazreg objects to in Western feminist theory are still to be found in these films, because they fail to situate sexual and racial/ethnic differences within larger historical contexts.

In conclusion, therefore, I will argue that critical and feminist theory have as much to learn from the problems of Duras's films and the blind spots in Said's and Bhabha's general models as from the solutions all three, though differently, suggest. As each is used to interrogate the others, however, the limits to how we think about ourselves and others can be displaced, and, hopefully, reworked, making it easier to discuss and evaluate the ways sexual and racial/ethnic difference are interwoven, in cinema and society.

I

Of all the recent studies dealing with the construction and functioning of racial/ethnic stereotypes in colonial and imperialist discourse, Edward Said's *Orientalism*, a critique and analysis of two centuries of Western writings about the Orient, has no doubt had the most wide-ranging impact. Scholars in fields ranging from anthropology to art history to philosophy find Said's concern with representation and reality, knowledge and power, challenging and troubling, often at one and the same time.[15] Though Said identifies three interdependent Orientalisms—an academic discipline comprised of specialists who write or teach about the Orient; a style of thought "based upon an ontological and epistemological distinction between 'the Orient' and 'the Occident' " and premised on a conception of difference as exteriority; and "a corporate institution for dealing with the Orient"[16]—the second has provoked the most debate. For Said, dichotomous thought seems a priori to underpin cross-cultural representation, though he insists that "this . . . does not mean that the division between Orient and Occident is unchanging, nor that it is simply fictional."[17] On the contrary, time and again he locates the source and raison d'être of Orientalism's ongoing popularity in politics, arguing that Orientalist discourse channels and organizes the fascination and threat posed by the unknown for purposes of domination.

Because what Said calls the "dogmas of Orientalism" motivate and legitimate racial discrimination in much the same ways patriarchal stereotypes define and manipulate sexual difference, they are worth recapitulating here. Said characterizes them as follows: the first is "the absolute and systematic difference between the West, which is rational, developed, humane, superior, and the Orient, which is aberrant, undeveloped, inferior"; the second, "abstractions about the Orient . . . are always preferable to direct evidence drawn from modern Oriental realities"; the third, "the Orient is eternal, uniform, and incapable of defining itself"; and the fourth, "the Orient is at bottom something either to be feared . . . or to be controlled."[18]

Briefly, Said discusses connections made in nineteenth century writings between Orientalist dogmas and sexual stereotypes: "the Oriental was linked . . . to elements in Western society (delinquents, the insane, women, the poor) having in common an identity best described as lamentably alien." In passing he also acknowledges that "Orientalism . . . encouraged a peculiarly (not to say invidiously) male conception of the world."[19] Nonetheless, for the most part, women's voices and the question of sexual difference are subsumed or ignored in Orientalism. Even though Said critiques nineteenth century Orientalism as "an exclusively male province" which "viewed itself and its subject matter with sexist blinders,"[20] he does not recognize his own failure to integrate gender into his analyses. Women and sexual difference do not, as Gayatri Spivak points out, represent just one more area to be studied. Rather, sexual difference defines men as well as women: "woman's voice is not one voice to be added to the orchestra; every voice is inhabited by the sexual differential."[21]

Because Said sidesteps sexual difference throughout Orientalism, "we" and "they" function all the more as dichotomies, all the less as dialectics. Though in Covering Islam Said does discuss disagreement in what he calls "communities of interpretation," if without mentioning gender, in Orientalism (as George Marcus and Michael Fischer argue) he "acknowledges no motives of the West other than domination, no internal debates among Westerners about alternative modes of representation. . . . Most tellingly he acknowledges no political or cultural divisions among the subject people he is allegedly defending."[22] Here cultural texts are viewed as coherent, not contradictory, entities, and colonial discourse emerges as monolithic and seamless once more.

The consequences of Said's decision to analyze Orientalist discourses as an ideological bloc wherein "no dialectic is either desired or allowed"[23] are profound:

because he sees no alternatives in the past, he can suggest no alternatives for the present.[24] Admittedly, the silencing of the voices of racial and sexual others imparts an ideological purity to Said's argumentation and affords him a space of pure truth from which to criticize false representations. Though Said insists it is not his intention to suggest "that there is such a thing as a real or true Orient,"[25] frequently in *Orientalism* the "real" does seem to remain opposed to and outside of "representation," with the result that difference is once again reified, not explored. Nor is the possibility that what we think of as "different" and "familiar" might be shifting in today's world—where, as James Clifford puts it, "difference is encountered in the adjoining neighborhood, [and] the familiar turns up at the ends of the earth"[26]—adequately considered. Instead, the historical and geographical specificity of Orientalist discourses disappears under an avalanche of synchronic analysis knotted around the second of the three Orientalisms: thought in oppositions.[27] Though stereotypes, as Sander L. Gilman makes clear, are "inherently protean, the product of history . . . and culture,"[28] the very force of Said's argumentation perversely reinforces a view of them as rigid and unchanging.

With all its problems and contradictions, however—indeed, in some senses, because of them—Said's model has much to offer film studies. His discussion of the relationship between representation and reality and his vehement engagement with issues of text and context are provocative, for all their flaws. His recognition of the importance of the mass media in shaping and perpetuating current versions of Orientalism tempers the ahistoricism which results from his concentration on synchronic, not diachronic analysis. Moreover, his discussions of how racial/ethnic difference is constructed in literary, anthropological and bureaucratic texts support claims made by film critics like Robert Stam and Louise Spence that:

The magic carpet provided by [the] apparatuses [of TV and film] flies us around the globe and makes us, by virtue of our subject position, its audio-visual masters. It produces us as subjects, transforming us into armchair conquistadores, affirming our sense of power while making the inhabitants of the Third World objects of spectacle for the First World's voyeuristic gaze.[29]

Nevertheless, critics interested in examining the ways films articulate racial/ethnic and sexual difference may find the weaknesses in Said's analysis of cross-cultural representation in *Orientalism*—his failure to examine contradictions within texts or dissimilarities between texts; his blindness to differences within the subject, within the group, and over time—as instructive as the strengths. We may well want to ask how Said's generalizations about Orientalism need to be filtered through and read against the paradigms of sexual difference refined over the years by feminist film theorists. How, for example, do spectators who are not Western white males interact with film texts? Do Western white males always react to texts in only one way? Do they really find stable points of identification, as the passage quoted above by Stam and Spence would seem to suggest? What to make of textual contradiction? How to approach different kinds of texts? Do representations of racial/ethnic and sexual difference change over time? Should struggles around representation undertaken by filmmakers, audiences, or critics be formulated, as Said suggests, in terms of "personal, authentic, sympathetic, humanistic knowledges,"[30] or should they be struggles *against* representation?[31] Is there a third alternative? How can we think differences with, and against, each other?

II

Homi Bhabha's discussions of racial/ethnic stereotypes, sexual fetishes, and colonial discourse represent attempts to engage with and continue Said's analyses. Like Said, Bhabha views "the question of the 'colonial' in literary [and cinematic] representation" as political, "fundamentally a problem of the signification of historical and cultural difference."[32] But unlike Said, Bhabha tries to demonstrate the interconnections, not just the oppositions, between the colonial subject and the colonized other. Instead of Said's unchanging dichotomies of difference addressed to a unitary subject in control of a unitary other, Bhabha proposes viewing the fixity of racial/ethnic stereotypes as "a form of knowledge and identification that vacillates between what is always in place, already known, and something that must be anxiously repeated."[33]

For Bhabha, as a result, far more than for Said, stereotypes function as both phobias and fetishes, the co-presence of fear and desire betraying a fundamental ambivalence and split within both the colonial subject and the colonized other. Access to power and knowledge on the part of individual members within these groups is, of course, disproportionate, functionally over-determined by what Bhabha calls "the 'play' of power within colonial discourse and the shifting positionalities of its subjects." By "positionalities" Bhabha understands the reinforcing and contradictory effects "class, gender, ideology, different social formations, varied systems of colonization, etc." have on people. Bhabha maintains such contradictions and reinforcements are crucial to the exercise of power within colonial discourse,[34] but he does not develop this observation, preferring to explore textual contradiction and "the *processes of subjectification* made possible (and plausible) through stereotypical discourse."[35]

Benita Parry describes Bhabha's strategies in terms which clearly mark his departure, following Fanon, from a conception of the "Other" as the opposite of "Self" towards an "'Otherness' of the Self."[36] On the one hand, she says, Bhabha "decentre[s] the native as fixed, unified through showing how colonialism's contradictory mode of address constituted an ambivalently positioned colonial subject"; on the other hand, she argues, he also "make[s] known the devious techniques of obligation and persuasion and the native's collusion and resistance."[37] Importantly, therefore, and unlike Said, Bhabha does not see power or discourse as located solely or securely in the hands of the colonizer. On the contrary, he charges that such a "suggestion . . . is a historical and theoretical simplification."[38] Grounds for intervention in and subversion of colonial discourse appear in consequence, and Said's conception of difference as exteriority is replaced by a view of difference as boundary and pressure.[39]

Moreover, because Bhabha insists on the heterogeneity and vulnerability of colonial discourse, he is more open than Said is to examining racial/ethnic difference in conjunction with sexual difference. In "Difference, Discrimination and the Discourse of Colonialism" and "The Other Question," he postulates an analogy between the sexual fetish, as described by Freud, and the racial stereotype. In each case, Bhabha argues, fantasies of an original similarity—to paraphrase him: "All people have penises" . . . / "All people have the same skin/race/culture"—coexist with fears of lack and difference—"Some do not have penises" . . ./"Some do not have the same skin/race/culture."[40] As Bhabha explains it, the sexual fetish and the racial stereotype function to recognize and disavow difference, at one and the same time, and thereby ensure the continuation of "normal" sexual relations and "normal" political relations, respectively. In the case of the sexual fetish, some men are able to recognize yet ignore women's sexual difference and the threat of castration it poses for them by substituting a fetish object (the woman's leg or foot, for example) for her lack of the penis. In the case of the racial stereotype, the colonial Subject acknowledges yet denies the Other's racial difference and the threat it represents to his or her white skin privilege by reducing the Other to skin color. As Fanon says in *Black Skin, White Masks*, racial inferiority is "epidermalized," for the Black as well as for the White.[41] Formulated in this way, both the racial/ethnic stereotype and the sexual fetish thus center around visible difference, though, as Bhabha notes, "the fetish of colonial discourse . . . is not like the sexual fetish a secret."[42]

The pertinence of Bhabha's analysis for a critique of mainstream films organized around a scopic regime of voyeurism and fetishism is undeniable: small wonder that he begins his discussion with Welles's *Touch of Evil*, arguing that Heath's reading of visible difference in the film focuses too exclusively on sexual difference. Like Said, Bhabha begins by saying that "orientalism very generally is a form of *radical realism*,"[43] but then shifts the focus of Said's analysis from content and form to address. For Bhabha the "reality effect" produced by realist novels or films cannot be opposed by images which are "more true," in the sense of more mimetically faithful to an underlying and pre-given "reality." Neither, however, can they simply be replaced by anti-realist strategies.[44] Within Bhabha's framework, therefore, I would argue, the spectator of mainstream *and* avant-garde film is not a priori a Western white male, secure in his position of authority; rather, multiple viewing positions exist, none of them stable, and none of them a priori associated with either avant-garde or mainstream texts.

But though Bhabha improves on Said's discussions of literary and cinematic representations of racial/ethnic and sexual difference, his emphasis on vision leads him to gloss over the importance of language in Fanon's accounts of the relationship between colonizer and colonized. His description of skin as "the most visible of fetishes,"[45] for example, narrows considerably Fanon's use of the term. As Stephan Feuchtwang observes, for Fanon "the body . . . is not an obvious body. . . . The skin is also a kind of psychic interface. It is a skin of reactive transmission between two organisations, the psychic and its 'environment.' "[46] For film study especially, it is important that "vision" and/or "the visible" not be understood so literally that they obscure the roles sound and speech play in the construction and perception of difference.[47]

But Bhabha's concentration on "vision" and "the visible" poses a second, more serious, problem, as well. Even when read as metaphors for psychic interactions, the decision to posit racial/ethnic difference as *analogous* to sexual difference invariably makes it hard for Bhabha to think the two categories together and against each other, with the result that, once again, the voices of women as colonizers and colonized are distorted or silenced.[48]

Bhabha's repression of sexual difference in the first of what he labels the two "primal scenes" in Fanon's *Black Skin, White Masks* is a case in point. Bhabha retells Fanon's story as follows: "On one occasion a white girl fixes Fanon in a look and word as she turns to identify with her mother. . . . 'Look, a Negro . . . Mamma, see the Negro! I'm frightened. Frightened. Frightened.' " Bhabha analyzes this scene in Freudian/Lacanian terms: "[T]he subject turns around the pivot of the 'stereo-type' to return to a point of total identification. The girl's gaze returns to her mother in the recognition and disavowal of the Negroid type."[49]

In the original French, however, the child is not a girl, but a boy.[50] One wonders first why Bhabha misreads Fanon in this way, then why he offers no analysis of the overlay of sexual threat he has added by having a white girl confront a black man. When Bhabha charges in a postscript to his foreword to Black Skin, White Masks that Fanon portrays white women in ways "which often collude with their cultural stereotypes and reduce the 'desire' of sexuality to the desire for sex, leaving unexplored the elusive function of the 'object' of desire,"[51] why does Bhabha himself similarly conflate sex and sexuality? Why, too, when he specifically criti-cizes Fanon for overlooking the woman of color, does he do so as well?

Although Bhabha's rereading of Fanon through Lacan shifts the former's "politics of nationalism" to a "politics of narcissism" and thereby "opens up a margin of interrogation that causes a subversive slippage of identity and authority,"[52] it also, as Benita Parry charges, "dehistoricizes Fanon's revolutionary moments."[53] Though, unlike Said in Orientalism, Bhabha acknowledges and discusses strategies and agents of resistance in all his analyses—he examines, for example, the potential threat of the native elite,[54] describes the subversive use of mimicry and hybridiza-tion,[55] and speaks of the colonized's doubled vision and his return of the colonizer's look[56]—his reliance on the generalizing, ahistorical model of psychoanalysis com-plicates the project he has set himself of evaluating cultural otherness within specific historical contexts.[57]

As we return once more to film studies, now with the oversights, not just the insights, of Bhabha's work in mind, it seems evident that the theoretical paradigms within which we work must be shifted, repeatedly, as Jane Gaines, Gina Marchetti, and others have recently shifted them, in order to account for the complexity and specificity of the articulation of sexual and racial/ethnic difference at distinct mo-ments in time.[58] The look must neither be fetishized, valued over the voice, nor locked into an unchanging and fundamentally Western psychoanalytic model. If "the unitary voice of command" Bhabha deconstructs is truly to be "interrupted by questions that arise from . . . heterogeneous sites and circuits of power,"[59] it is imperative that women's voices, sexual difference and sexuality not be bracketed, as Bhabha brackets them, until all "their implications for colonial discourse" have been worked through.[60]

In order to explore in more depth how we might approach cinematic representa-tions of sexual and racial/ethnic difference, I will now turn to three of Marguerite Duras's films about colonialism and imperialism which center on women, as colonizers and colonized, characters and narrators. In the introduction to this third, and final, section of my paper, I will first suggest why these films are so rarely discussed with reference to the representation of racial/ethnic difference, then sketch how they might be used to critique and extend Said's analyses of Oriental-ism and Bhabha's theory of colonial discourse. I will then look at each film in turn, and ask whether and how Duras's experimentation with sounds and images may be said to inhibit or perpetuate sexual and racial/ethnic stereotypes. In conclusion, I will come back once more to the over-arching questions Said, Bhabha, and Duras all pose about power, knowledge, and colonial discourse, and summarize what their various responses may suggest for an alternative political cinema and for an alternative understanding of sexual and racial/ethnic differences.

III

Duras's experiences as a female child in French colonial Indochina resonate throughout her literary and cinematic oeuvre, providing the basis for a politics of marginality which she translates into the very shape of her texts, separating sounds from images and overlapping and/or splitting characters and narrators. In interviews she has said repeatedly that because her family was poor (her father died when she was young, leaving the family dependent on the mother's meager earnings as a teacher of Vietnamese children—the lowest position in the French foreign education system),[61] she considered herself far more Vietnamese than French: "This misery, I knew it very well. We were closer to the natives than to the whites."[62] Her childhood awareness of colonial oppression and her sense of identification with the Vietnamese were so acute they provided her with the impetus to write: "We had close to hand . . . colonialism in its most caricatural, abject form. And, because of my mother's profession, we had the good fortune to be relegated to the ranks of the natives. That is why I have written . . . . : I was not part of the milieu of important functionaries, I looked at them. That is why, subsequently, I have been able to write, to raise the question of all that that covered up."[63]

Given the importance of Duras's experiences of colonialism and discrimination based on sexual, racial/ethnic, and class differences, it is surprising that so few American critics have acknowledged, let alone analyzed, her films from this angle. While there are excellent and varied readings of individual films in relation to women, sexual difference, and femininity, little work has been done, to my knowledge, on them as examples of or limits to colonial discourse.[64] In their analyses of Duras's texts, Western feminists have drawn on psychoanalytic models of sexual difference and applied them universally and cross-culturally, viewing female characters of all nationalities, races, and classes as, in Chahandra Mohanty's words, "an already constituted and coherent group with identical interests and desires."[65] Racial/ethnic difference has dropped out of sight. It seems as if, at least where Duras's scholarship in the States is concerned, feminist criticism too must face Said's charge that: "The literary-cultural establishment as a whole has declared the serious study of imperialism and culture off limits."[66]

Yet *India Song*, *Son Nom de Venise dans Calcutta désert* and *Les Mains négatives* clearly transcribe Duras's childhood memories of colonialism, and obviously entwine racial/ethnic and sexual difference. In both *India Song* and *Son Nom de Venise* echoes and reflections among the characters mitigate and permute the negative attributes Said notes Orientalist dogmas accord racial/ethnic others. Using different image tracks but virtually identical sound tracks, the two films tell the same story of love, death, and madness. The narrative we hear revolves around the same three key figures: the French Ambassador to Calcutta's glamorous wife, Anne-Marie Stretter, who kills herself at the end of the film for "reasons that exist outside her";[67] the

French Vice-Consul to Lahore, dismissed from his post for shooting lepers in the streets, mad with love for Anne-Marie Stretter; and, finally, a sterile, insane, Laotian beggar woman who has followed Anne-Marie Stretter from Indochina to Calcutta.[68]

The short film *Les Mains négatives* tells another story altogether: the age-old tale of a man's love for a woman. Here a woman's voice speaks as both a male character and a female narrator. Unlike *India Song* or even *Son Nom de Venise*, the image track, composed of outtakes from another feature length film, *Le Navire Night* (1979), has nothing at all to do with the sound track. For the most part we see travelling shots of early morning Paris in the late 1970s. Occasionally African Blacks on their way to work as street sweepers and a few white women Duras says are Portuguese maids are visible.[69]

In all three films, therefore, though differently in each case, sexual and racial/ ethnic differences are linked, and Western and Oriental women's voices are privileged. Sexual difference is not subsumed under a general discussion of Orientalism, as in Said's model, nor simply equated with racial/ethnic difference, as in Bhabha's paradigm. Moreover, because in all three films, sounds, not images, organize the narrative, it is difficult to use visible difference to legitimate power, as Bhabha contends colonial discourse does, and hard to believe that film representation in any way equals reality. What Kari Hanet says of *Hiroshima, mon amour* is true of these films as well: "[T]he effect of reality, . . . of the visual code, is played against a verbal code, whose relation with it is neither relay nor anchorage, but incompatibility."[70] For spectators familiar with Duras's work as a whole, this incompatibility is particularly striking, because the juxtaposition of visual and verbal codes takes place not only within a single text, but from film to film and/or from book to play to film, as Duras obsessively reworks the same skeletal stories of difference and desire.

Yet, as I will argue throughout the textual analyses of these films which follow, Duras's application of modernist narrative strategies to film is not necessarily radical. Rather, her movies about colonialism are challenging precisely because they are ambivalent, evoking rather than representing reality, and thereby suggesting other ways of hearing and seeing sameness and difference. On the one hand, Duras's experimentation with sounds and images—the confusion of author, narrators, and characters, the multiplication of voices and their separation from images, the repetition and reduction of narrative elements—makes it hard to tell who is speaking and in what capacity. The very concept of a stable identity, so often invoked to legitimate power relations, is splintered, rendered incoherent. On the other hand, however, Duras's film fictions also reinforce racist and sexist stereotypes, because they function on a mythic plane where historical specificity has no place, much as is the case in Hollywood films. Clichés of Orientalism remain throughout Duras's oeuvre, and are particularly prevalent in *India Song* and *Son Nom de Venise*; indeed, one might even argue that they are exacerbated in these films.

The multivalent meanings which can be attributed to Duras's representations of racial/ethnic and sexual difference are especially apparent in *India Song*. Of all three films, it has been the most widely distributed and the most hotly debated. Of all three films, too, it is the most permeated by nostalgia for colonial society, despite its oblique critiques of British India and despite its reworkings of how otherness and identity are seen and heard. Set in colonial India in the late 1930s, *India Song* evokes a closed and claustrophobic world of languor, decadence, and decay. Yet though the disjunction between images and sounds and the importance of female and foreign voices vastly complicates the dichotomies of difference so often encouraged by mainstream film, the two separate camps Said describes—colonizers and colonized, whites and Asians—are nonetheless still present. Material differences between colonizers and colonized emerge from the alternation of interior and exterior shots in the first two sections of the film. (The third section is set entirely inside the Prince of Wales hotel). The rooms of the Embassy are filled with expensive objects (jewels, champagne glasses, chandeliers, Second Empire armchairs, evening gowns, and the like), in stark contrast to the deserted park outside. Periodically, offscreen voices associate the space beyond the outside we see with the starving masses of India, heat, and humidity. Because what Marie-Claire Ropars-Wuillemier calls "exotic clichés . . . set in place by Occidental culture"[71] are repeated, the Orient is once again positioned as exteriority and absence.

As the film progresses, however, the outside the camera gradually unveils to us— the empty park, deserted tennis courts, an abandoned bicycle, crumbling statues— suggests the precariousness of the Empire's power more than it does the inferiority and helplessness of India. Indeed, in this film India is almost entirely absent. As Ropars-Wuillemier notes: "By an apparent paradox, the more India is named, perpetuated by the voices in mental images which traditionally accompany it, the more representation of it is refused: the film never leaves the Embassy grounds or the palace."[72]

Duras's refusal to show India means that the film's stereotypes are evoked more through sounds and language—the cries of birds, the barking of dogs, the murmur of fishermen's voices—than through sight. In effect, the only Indian we see is a turbaned servant who appears at the beginning of the film to light incense in front of a picture of Anne-Marie Stretter, and then later briefly reappears carrying trays filled with drinks. Like Hollywood characterizations of colonized peoples, he is silent, his only function being to serve.

The Laotian beggar woman, in contrast, is pure sound. She is never seen, but compared to the male servant, she is far more important. Nameless, faceless, she is a mythic figure representative of the Orient in general: for Duras her only social identity is "madness, general madness, madness due to hunger, misery."[73] Lacking all specificity, accorded the most negative of attributes, she seems the epitome of the bad Oriental Said describes. Yet her crazy laughter and incomprehensible speech punctuate the entire film and haunt both the film's narrators and its characters. For Duras, her verbal presence and visual absence are profoundly subversive. As she puts it: "The Embassy is a leaking ship. Leprosy enters everywhere with the song of the beggar woman."[74]

India Song's reworkings of film representations of racial/ethnic and sexual difference and its ambivalence towards colonial power are particularly manifest in the beggar woman's association with Anne-Marie Stretter. Their paths, the offscreen voices say, have crossed repeatedly. As females and foreigners (Venitian and Laotian, respectively), both are marginal figures in British colonial society. Anne-Marie Stretter, too, is ill, "stricken with a leprosy of the heart." Two female narrating voices describe her and the beggar woman in sentences which begin with indeterminate pronouns or lack subjects altogether, making it even harder to tell to whom they are referring.[75] In the context of a film about colonialism, this undermining and transposition of identities acquires a particular resonance, linking the Empire with decay and death and the Orient with beauty and grace, and evoking the fantasized identity of origin which Bhabha maintains the racial stereotype usually represses. For these reasons, no doubt, despite her initial critiques of the film's clichés, Ropars-Wuillemier ultimately interprets the movement of *India Song* as one which counters notions of pre-fixed difference, incorporating instead in every colonial character "the trace of the other, and in every other the trace of the same."[76]

Colonial power is further distanced and refracted during the central Embassy reception sequence. There the European characters are filmed solely as reflections in mirrors or together with their reflections in mirrors. Throughout the film the movements of Anne-Marie Stretter and her male entourage are slow, frozen, always somehow "off," the result of the actors acting while listening to a recording of the spoken scenario.[77] When their voices are heard, they are not synchronized with their movements. Barely distinguishable voices of other Europeans constitute a background babel of sound, much as "native" voices do in mainstream colonial films.[78] Long takes, slow pans and dollies, the ever noticeable framing in windows, doors, and mirrors restrict the sphere of action still further. On the sound track the narrating voices—there are several, not just one—are multiplied and also interrupted by the ill-defined characters' voices. As a result, the power and control mainstream films usually assign to a single male narrator is countered, and attention is focused on audible differences in gender and nationality.[79]

In many ways *India Song* thus dissolves and subverts colonial power and presence, situating it as already past, acknowledging Western ambivalence and internal differences among colonizers, even insisting at one point on European feelings of culpability ("The suicides of Europeans which increase with the famines from which they never suffer. . . . Somewhere inside oneself . . . that guilt of the Occidental"). Nonetheless, of all Duras's films, it also remains the most sympathetic to colonialism. Duras admits that *India Song* shows "a bourgeoisie in perdition, but rendered innocent . . . by the passion I have for it."[80] The simple elegance of the costumes and the restrained luxury of the interior sets gratify the eye, as the slow rhythms of the voices and composer Carlos Alesia's blues, waltzes, fox trots, and rumbas enchant the ear. The virtual absence of specific historical references and the constant confusion of geographical space move the narrative as a whole toward myth and fantasy and away from reality. As Elizabeth Lyon says, "the geographical and historical notations make of *India Song* a dated scene [. . .], a frame in which subjectivity and history meet in the scene of the fantasy."[81] Only near the end of the film do the narrating female voices position the love story they tell within the context of world events: the year is 1937; they say, in China war is raging, the Russian Revolution has failed, and the Congress of Nuremberg has just taken place. Despite the final pan in close-up of a map of Indochina, the film's geographical references are usually more than vague; they are out and out false. Calcutta is not, for example, on the edge of the Ganges, nor is it the capital of India.[82] Duras's attribution to colonial British India of her childhood experiences in French Indochina, like Alesia's transposition to India of the ballroom music of his youth in Argentina, further mythologize representation.[83]

Unlike Said, however, Duras believes that myth expresses misery better than realism does, saying that without myth "I could only show [misery] in fragments, in disorder and to my way of thinking in a less convincing fashion."[84] The question *India Song* poses, *because of* its ambivalence to colonialism, is thus the question of whether and how to construct alternative representations of difference. In Ropars-Wuillemier's words, "does India present itself as an object to be read—the figure of an unnameable, unrepresentable History—or as a tool for writing—as the historical sign of a writing which would attempt to break with signs and History?"[85] Clifford asks much the same question with respect to Said's analyses of Orientalism as structuring thought as a series of oppositions: should the struggle against Orientalism be towards more accurate representation or should it be against representation altogether?

India Song offers no clear cut answers. Visible difference and specific historical referents are occasionally invoked, though they are more often contradicted or replaced by audible difference and/or myth. *Son Nom de Venise dans Calcutta désert* provides a more unequivocal answer, for the most part rejecting the visible representation of sexual and racial/ethnic difference altogether. Though, as I mentioned earlier, the sound tracks of both films are almost identical, in *Son Nom de Venise* fewer objects remain to be read, and no characters ever appear. While in *India Song*, the pleasure of the colonizer is never shown without death also being shown,[86] in *Son Nom de Venise* both the colonizer and the colonized are long gone: death itself is distanced. "What was begun in *India Song*, death, showing death, is finished in *Son Nom de Venise dans Calcutta désert*," says Duras of the two films.[87] Anne-Marie Stretter may already be dead at the beginning of *India Song*—the Indian servant's placing of flowers and lighting of candles and incense before her photograph suggest as much—but she is present throughout the film. Only at the end do we learn of her suicide. In *Son Nom de Venise*, in contrast, she is as absent as the beggar woman from the start. Because neither the colonial subject nor the colonized other are visible here, the categories of exterior and interior become meaningless: all is fantasmatic. As Madeleine Borgomano puts it: "*India Song* was still a ritual celebration of the memory of bodies—already given as dead . . . *Son Nom de Venise dans Calcutta désert* . . . effaces even their traces: a disincarnated universe, the voice alone takes the place of the bodies which have disappeared."[88] Ruined statues and the unexpected appearance near the end of *Son Nom de Venise* of women in modern dress without apparent connection to the narrative (offscreen male and female voices are discussing Anne-Marie Stretter's suicide) are all that remains of *India Song*'s nostalgia for beautiful bodies.[89] Even the tracings of the beggar woman's wanderings on the map at the end of *India Song* are missing from *Son Nom de Venise*'s image track, replaced by a fixed long shot of the sun setting over the ocean. Instead, offscreen the narrating voices *tell* of the beggar woman's march towards oblivion. Significantly, this is the only difference between the two films' sound tracks.

The disappearance of bodies from *Son Nom de Venise* profoundly affects the status of all the voices we hear. "The very distinction between *on* and *off* is put in question," Ropars-Wuillemier observes. "In *Son Nom de Venise* . . . voices are neither outside nor inside, they are elsewhere, absent. Are not these voices cut off from bodies . . . hypothetical voices, or voices-*if*?"[90] The tenuous separations *India Song* makes between narrators and characters are still further obliterated in *Son Nom de Venise*.

Identification with either, or with the camera, is unlikely. Because there is no action to follow, camera movements seem to stop and start for no reason. Though as in *India Song* interior spaces alternate with exterior shots, in *Son Nom de Venise* everything we see—cracks in the pavement, broken windows, shattered mirrors, decrepit balustrades, a collapsed fireplace, a deserted park, an abandoned castle filled with spider webs and dust—bespeaks death and decay.[91] In Oudart's words, "What complaisance with the colonial referent still remained in *India Song* is contradicted here by the heaviness, the baseness of the material of the images."[92] As colonial presence is replaced by absence, visible sexual and racial/ethnic differences can no longer serve as rationales for oppression.

With *Les Mains négatives* Duras reworks the questions of representation and reality, colonial discourse and otherness yet again, recycling images from *Le Navire Night* as *Son Nom de Venise* recycled sounds from *India Song*. Although the sounds and images of *Le Navire Night* are disjunctive, at least the disjointed soap opera of the loves and lies of a man and woman in 70s Paris we hear on the sound track of this film is temporally related to the images we see: streets, gardens, cemeteries, a house, and three actors in contemporary dress. In *Les Mains négatives*, however, sounds and images have nothing in common.

Les Mains négatives returns to the visual representation of racial difference which *Son Nom de Venise* refuses, showing black street sweepers in modern day Paris. In some ways the image track seems more like a documentary than it does a fiction film: what we see seems to be a "slice of life" picture of Paris in the late 1970s. Most of the film consists of travelling shots taken from a slowly moving car. Though the camera does not stop on the immigrant workers or center them in the frame, it is possible that some viewers will take these workers to be the subjects of the image track: we are all conditioned, after all, by mainstream film to focus on the human figure in the landscape. Duras herself reads *Les Mains négatives* as a film about imperialism and, in her descriptions of the shoot, says she saw these foreign workers as the victims of racism:

I suddenly found myself at 7 a.m. in a colonial mass of humanity. There was an enormous number of Blacks who were cleaning the sidewalks, the street, the gutters. There were Portuguese cleaning women—one could guess they were Portuguese cleaning women, they have their own way of walking—who came out of banks, cafés, and all these people, one knew, would disappear in the coming hour to make way for us. There you have it . . . [T]his film is given, dedicated to that humanity which peoples the great cities of the Occident in the morning. I find the film *Les Main négatives* terrible. It is a terrifying film.[93]

The sound track does not, however, offer any such commentary on the images. As a result, we may or we may not read them as Duras intends, and we may or may not view these workers as the film's subjects. Though for contemporary Western viewers *Les Mains négatives'* images are more easily placed, both historically and geographically, than are *India Song's* images, this placement does not necessarily entail a political critique.

Indeed, the female voice on the sound track proposes another subject altogether for the film: a man of unknown race who lived 30,000 years earlier. Like *Son Nom de Venise* and *India Song*, *Les Mains négatives* tells a love story: the man of the sound track is passionately in love with an unidentified woman. Here, however, unlike the earlier films, links between the love story of the sound track and the reflections on racism and colonialism of the image track are entirely missing. Instead of deconstructing racial/ethnic difference by pitting sounds against images as she does in *India Song* and *Son Nom de Venise*, in *Les Mains négatives* Duras confuses sexual difference as the categories of female narrator (Duras herself) and male character overlap and merge. By the end of the film, as a result, the labels of subject and other have no fixed meaning in relation to each other at all: each is undermined from within. Who is narrator and who or what is narrated, who looks, and who speaks is all a blur.

Given this blur, this ambiguity, how are we to evaluate Duras's experimental examinations of colonial discourse in cinema? How do the questions and answers her films propose intersect with and differ from the models Said and Bhabha offer? Do Duras's films present a clear cut, politically progressive alternative to the representations of sexual and racial/ethnic difference in mainstream films?

As I have argued, Duras's films about colonialism and imperialism often dissolve fixed categories of identity and highlight the ambivalence both the colonizer and the colonized feel towards themselves and each other. It is hard to imagine they could function to secure a Western white male spectator in a position of power. *India Song* and *Son Nom de Venise* both inscribe relationships of empathy, identification, or love between white and non-white women and men. All three films foreground female voices to an exceptional degree. Yet in *Son Nom de Venise* and especially in *India Song*, colonial clichés can still be found, though they are transmitted via sound and language and not, as is the case in the realist texts Said and Bhabha analyze, via sight. In *Les Mains négatives*, in contrast, the disjunction between sounds and images is so complete that it throws into question all representation of difference as fixed.

Duras herself describes her films as political in a characteristically provocative and paradoxical manner: "My films are political, but they don't speak of politics."[94] I would agree with her assessment: her experimentation with sounds and images does indeed offer a third alternative to the critiques of the photographic image proposed earlier by Brecht and Godard, though as an alternative it has its limits.

Brecht mistrusts images because he is oriented towards the real, the outside world: "A photograph of the Krupp factories doesn't really tell you much about those factories," he says. Godard, in contrast, emphasizes representation. As one of the characters in *Tout va bien* puts it: " A photograph is not the reflection of reality, but the reality of that reflection."[95] Duras disengages from both positions. Her idea of political cinema is to refuse to accept that the complexity of reality can in any way be directly represented by cinema:

I know nothing, absolutely nothing which is as pretentious as . . . the guy, even the exemplary militant, who . . . films a Renault assembly line and who dares tell you: there you are, what I have filmed will teach you what a Renault assembly line is. As if he could say what an assembly line is, and *as if this assembly line were to be found in these images*. . . . How to show the obscurity of the world: that is, the fact that people accept assembly lines? That they submit to them and know about them?"[96]

Duras's answer to the problem of how to construct a political cinema is therefore to *evoke* reality and question representation through sounds rather than attempt to reproduce reality through images. Her films emphasize feelings over facts, ambivalence over knowledge, opting neither simply for an "expressive subjectivity" nor for a "total unrepresentability."[97] They are, as Benoît Jacquot notes, non-didactic, "interpellating rather than addressing the spectator" as a unitary subject.[98]

Yet while Duras's avant-garde strategies may in certain instances be considered progressive, there is no guarantee that her experimental films will heighten political consciousness regarding the functioning of racial/ethnic and/or sexual stereotypes, whether in mainstream or in avant-garde film. Furthermore, these same avant-garde strategies necessarily restrict her audience and therefore can easily be over-looked by the dominant ideology. Though avant-garde interventions *may* facilitate awareness of how difference functions in mainstream films (as Bhabha says, "the recognition and disavowal of 'difference' is always disturbed by the question of its representation or construction"), it is important, I think, to remember that in Bhabha this passage refers to "the threatened return of the [colonizer's] look" by the colonized.[99] "The question of re-presentation or construction" he speaks of is not, in other words, an act which can be separated from an agent: textual strategies do not acquire meaning in a void. Anti-realism is not necessarily more politically correct than realism. To argue as much would be to fetishize the text over the spectator, as Bhabha sometimes does in his insistence on discourse, or to ignore textual contra-diction and differences in reception, as Said frequently does in *Orientalism*, or, finally, to situate naively the avant-garde spectator somewhere outside ideology, as film criticism all too often does. Any single text can be used in many different ways, and avant-garde films as well as mainstream films are organized around genre conventions.[100] Neither type of film practice is to be confused with material real-ities. Dana Polan puts it well: "[M]eaning is really social meaning, dependent on the ways one decides to relate to history, including film as historical act. . . ."[101]

To call for increased critical attention to the specific ways individual texts are used does not, however, obviate the need for general theories of representation. Even if necessarily incomplete, descriptions which address racial/ethnic and sexual differ-ence simultaneously are urgently needed. Perhaps the best way to think the two kinds of difference together is to look at "intersections of difference . . . around sexuality," as Isaac Julian and Kobena Mercer urge us to do,[102] or to see difference as undermining, though not annulling identity, and as existing, in Trinh Minh-ha's words, *"both between* and *within* entities."[103] In other words, I do not think we should a priori take "identity" to be a necessary humanistic goal, as Said does. Nor do I think we should dissolve identity altogether, as Bhabha tends to do, with the result that resistance comes to be torturously conceptualized as "the effect of an ambiva-lence produced within the rules of recognition of dominating discourses as they articulate the signs of cultural difference and reimplicate them within the deferen-tial relations of colonial power."[104] Rather it seems to me more productive to retain identity as a category to be invoked as needed, strategically, situationally. In this way it will perhaps be possible to avoid that Gayatri Spivak calls "universaliz[ing] the local." As she reminds us, "the operations of racism in the First World today are by no means homogenous," and imperialism is not identical with racism. "No good practice comes of [such reductions]."[105] Nor are women the same the world over and across time. To argue that Third World women and Western women are the same is to colonize them anew, and thereby, as Chahandra Mohanty points out, "to rob them of their historical *agency*."[106]

In the final analysis, it is not possible or desirable to give one answer to the question of how identity and difference, text and context, power and knowledge relate to resistance. This is why, throughout this paper, I have argued against positioning critical theory and textual practice, avant-garde and mainstream films, racial/ethnic and sexual difference as oppositions: they are all, I believe, best conceived as dialectics. For the limits which constitute subjectivity vary, according to where and how the boundaries defining otherness are drawn. By speaking from marginal positions to gender, race, and colonialism, Said, Bhabha, and Duras all, on different registers, displace the limits of difference. When their voices are intermingled, the possible centers of identity and agency are widened indeed.

NOTES

1. Edward W. Said, *Orientalism* (New York: Random House, 1979), p. 207. In "Orientalism Reconsidered," Said makes it clear that he considers his critique in *Orientalism* part of a larger, interventionary, endeavour. He cites a number of Third World and Western feminist scholars with approval, and, following Myra Jehlen, stresses the danger in creating monopolies of experience and knowledge. See Edward W. Said, "Orientalism Reconsidered," *Race and Class* 27, no. 2 (Autumn 1985): 1–16.

2. Homi Bhabha, "Foreword: Remembering Fanon," in Frantz Fanon, *Black Skin, White Masks*, trans. Charles Markmann (London: Pluto Press, 1986), p. xxvi; see also "The Other Question," *Screen* 24, no. 6 (November/December 1983): 18 and 23.

3. Admittedly, Bhabha *chooses* not to address sexual and class difference in his article on racial/ethnic difference, "The Other Question . . . ," and acknowledges that this choice is a "major problem." See Bhabha, "The Other Question," p. 18. My point is rather that his decision to argue by analogy necessarily inhibits, prohibits, thinking sexual and racial difference together.

4. Marnia Lazreg, "Feminism and Difference: The Perils of Writing as a Woman on Women in Algeria," *Feminist Studies* 14, no. 1 (Spring 1988): 89.

5. Said also notes, in passing, "a reinforcement [today] of the stereotypes by which the Orient is viewed" by television, film, and mass media in general. See Said, *Orientalism*, p. 26. In *Covering Islam*, a study of how the media shapes American views of the Islamic world today, he briefly mentions film as well: "[F]ilms play a role, of course, if only because to the extent that a visual sense of history and distant lands informs our own, it often comes by way of the cinema." Edward Said, *Covering Islam* (New York: Random House, 1981), p. 43.

6. Homi Bhabha, "Difference, Discrimination and the Discourse of Colonialism," in *The Politics of Theory*, ed. Francis Barker, et al. (Colchester, England: Essex University, 1982), pp. 194–211. "Difference, Discrimination and the Discourse of Colonialism" is an earlier version of "The Other Question." Though in what follows most citations will be to "The Other Question," where there are significant changes I will refer to the earlier article.

7. Although *Des Journées entières dans les arbres* (1976) also deals with colonialism, I have chosen not to analyze it in detail here because it is merely the filmed version of a realist play with the same title, not an experimental film.

8. The list of Duras's works which deal with either colonialism or imperialism is as follows: *Un Barrage contre le Pacifique* (1950), *Le Vice-Consul* (1965), and *L'Amant* (1984), all novels; *Des Journées entières dans les arbres*, a collection of short stories (1954), a play (1968) and a film (1976); *L'Eden Cinéma* (1977), a play; and *Hiroshima, mon amour* (dir: Alain Resnais, script: Marguerite Duras, 1959). I would argue that Duras's film *Nathalie Granger* (1972) also alludes to these issues: the little rebel, Nathalie, strongly identifies with the family's Portuguese maid, expelled from France because her papers were not in order.

9. Jacques Grant, "Entretien avec Marguerite Duras," *Cinéma 75*, no. 200 (July-August 1975): 109. Duras is referring here to her decision to speak from the point of view of Anne-Marie Stretter, not the beggar woman, in *India Song*. The entire cite is as follows: "If I put myself in the place of the beggar woman, I would be lying. I put myself in the place of Anne-Marie Stretter, who is, like

myself, a bourgeoise, a White woman, a woman I could have been" (translation mine, as are all subsequent translations from French to English unless otherwise indicated).

10. Paul Rabinow, "Representations Are Social Facts," in *Writing Culture: The Poetics and Politics of Ethnography*, ed. James Clifford and George E. Marcus (Berkeley: University of California Press, 1986), p. 259.

11. Angela McRobbie, "Strategies of Vigilance: An Interview with Gayatri Chakravorti Spivak," *Block*, no. 10 (1985): 9.

12. In *Les Yeux Verts*, a special issue of *Cahiers du Cinéma* which Duras edited, she says: "The phenomenal pimping of cinema by capitalism since its birth has formed four to six generations of spectators and we find ourselves before a HIMALAYA of images which constitute without doubt the biggest modern historical idiocy. Parallel to the history of the proletariat is the history of this supplementary oppression: that of its leisure fabricated by the same capitalism which enslaves it, the cinema of its Saturdays." Marguerite Duras, "Book and Film," *Les Yeux Verts, Cahiers du Cinéma* no. 312–313 (June 1980): 64.

13. See Linda Dittmar, "Dislocated Utterances," *Iris* 3, no. 1 (1985): 91–97 for an analysis of the ideological ramifications behind conventional arrangements and avant-garde and Third World rearrangements of sounds and images.

14. Mary Ann Doane, "Ideology and the Practice of Sound Editing and Mixing," in *The Cinematic Apparatus*, ed. Teresa de Lauretis and Stephen Heath (New York: St. Martin's Press, 1980), p. 52.

15. The impact of *Orientalism* is amply demonstrated by the diversity of academic fields reviewing the book. See Lata Mani and Ruth Frankenberg, "The Challenge of Orientalism," *Economy and Society* 14, no. 2 (May 1985): 174–192, for an excellent summary and analysis of the critiques raised by reviewers.

16. Said, *Orientalism*, p. 3. See also p. 20.

17. Said, "Orientalism Reconsidered," p. 2.

18. Said, *Orientalism*, pp. 300–301.

19. Said, p. 207.

20. Said, p. 207.

21. Gayatri Spivak, "The Politics of Interpretations," in *In Other Worlds: Essays in Cultural Politics* (New York: Routledge, 1988), p. 132.

22. George E. Marcus and Michael M. J. Fischer, *Anthropology as Cultural Critique* (Chicago: University of Chicago Press, 1986). p. 2.

23. Said, *Orientalism*, p. 308.

24. See Dennis Porter, "*Orientalism* and Its Problems," in *The Politics of Theory*, p. 181. For a similar critique, see also Benita Parry, "Problems in Current Theories of Colonial Discourse," *Oxford Literary Review* 9, no. 1–2 (1987): 140. In fairness to Said, I would note that in his conclusion to *Orientalism* he says that it was not his intention to offer an alternative to Orientalism. See Said, *Orientalism*, p. 325. But his constant, utopian appeals to humanism and experience as the grounds for another kind of scholarship suggest otherwise.

25. Said, p. 322. See also Said, *Covering Islam*, p. 41.

26. James Clifford, *The Predicament of Culture* (Cambridge: Harvard University Press, 1988), p. 14.

27. This lack of specificity is by no means characteristic of Said's work. See, for example, Edward Said, "An Ideology of Difference," *Critical Inquiry* 12, no. 1 (Autumn 1985): 38–58; "Zionism from the Standpoint of Its Victims," *Social Text* 1, no. 1 (Winter 1979): 7–58; and *Covering Islam*.

28. Sander L. Gilman, *Difference and Pathology: Stereotypes of Sexuality, Race and Madness* (Ithaca: Cornell University Press, 1985), p. 20.

29. Robert Stam and Louise Spence, "Colonialism, Racism and Cinematic Representation," *Screen* 24, no. 2 (January/February 1983): 4. Stam and Spence also note that the beginnings of cinema coincide with the height of imperialism (p. 6).

30. Said, *Orientalism*, p. 197.

31. See Clifford, p. 259.

32. Homi Bhabha, "Representation and the Colonial Text," in *The Theory of Reading*, ed. Frank Gloversmith (Sussex, England: Harvester Press, 1984), p. 101.

33. Bhabha, "The Other Question," p. 18.

34. Bhabha, p. 23.

35. Bhabha, p. 18.

36. Bhabha, "Foreword: Remembering Fanon," pp. xiv–xv.

37. Benita Parry, "Problems in Current Theories of Colonial Discourse," *Oxford Literary Review* 9, no. 1–2 (1987): 29.

38. Bhabha, "The Other Question," 25. This and other such statements by Bhabha lead me to disagree with JanMohamed's charge that Bhabha's insistence that power is possessed by both the colonizer and the colonized represents a conflation or circumvention of the "dense history of the material conflict between Europeans and natives." See Abdul R. JanMohamed, "The Economy of Manichean Allegory: The Function of Racial Difference in Colonialist Literature," *Critical Inquiry* 12, no. 1 (Autumn 1985): 59–60.

39. See, for example, Homi Bhabha, "Signs Taken for Wonders," *Critical Inquiry* 12, no. 1 (Autumn 1985): 152: "The place of difference and otherness . . . is never entirely on the outside or implacably oppositional. It is a pressure, and a presence, that acts constantly, if unevenly along the entire boundary of authorization. . . ." See also p. 158.

40. Bhabha, "The Other Question," p. 27.

41. Frantz Fanon, *Black Skin, White Masks*, p. 11.

42. Bhabha, "The Other Question," p. 30.

43. Bhabha, p. 23.

44. See, for example, Bhabha's discussions of images and "reality" in "Representation and the Colonial Text," pp. 98 and 105, and his critique of Stam and Spence in "The Other Question," pp. 22–23. See also "Signs Taken for Wonders," p. 151.

45. Bhabha, "The Other Question," p. 30.

46. Stephan Feuchtwang, "Fanon's Politics of Culture: the Colonial Situation and Its Extension," *Economy and Society* 14, no. 4 (Nov. 1985): 458.

47. Bhabha does acknowledge sound, but in passing. See, for example, Bhabha, "The Other Question," p. 28: "For what [Fanon's] primal scenes illustrate is that looking/hearing/reading as sites of subjectification in colonial discourse are evidence of the importance of the visual and auditory imaginary for the *histories* of societies."

48. There is, of course, the possibility that the silencing and distortion of women's voices is attributable to Bhabha's use of psychoanalysis: many feminists maintain that 'women' do not speak in psychoanalytic discourse, for 'Woman' is the unknown.

49. Bhabha, p. 28.

50. Fanon's references to the child leave no doubt as to his sex:

> —Regarde le nègre . . . Maman, un nègre! . . . Chut! Il va se fâcher . . . Ne faites pas attention, monsieur, *il* ne sait pas que vous êtes aussi civilisé que nous . . .
> [. . .]
> [T]iens, un nègre, il fait froid, le nègre tremble, le nègre tremble parce qu'il a froid, *le petit garçon* tremble parce qu'il a peur du nègre, le nègre tremble de froid, ce froid qui vous tord les os, *le beau petit garçon* tremble parce qu'il croit que le nègre tremble de rage, *le petit garçon blanc* se jette dans les bras de sa mère: maman, le nègre va me manger.

Frantz Fanon, *Peau noir, masques blancs* (Paris: Editions du Seuil, 1952), pp. 93–94. Emphases added.

51. Bhabha, "Foreword," p. xxvi.

52. Bhabha, p. xxiv.

53. Parry, p. 31.

54. Bhabha, "Difference, Discrimination and Colonial Discourse," p. 199.

55. Bhabha, "Of Mimicry and Man: The Ambivalence of Colonial Discourse," *October* 28 (Spring 1984): 126 and "Signs Taken for Wonders," p. 161.

56. Bhabha, "Signs Taken for Wonders," p. 161 and "Of Mimicry and Man," p. 129.

57. See Bhabha, "Difference, Discrimination, and Colonial Discourse," p. 204. This passage is missing in "The Other Question"—in my opinion a crucial, and an unfortunate revision.

58. See, for example, Jane Gaines, "White Privilege and Looking Relations: Race and Gender in Feminist Film Theory," *Screen* 29, no. 1 (Autumn 1988): 12–27 and Gina Marchetti, "Women Warriors in Hong Kong Cinema," a paper delivered at the Society for Cinema Studies Conference, Montreal, May 23, 1987.

59. Bhabha, "Signs Taken for Wonders," p. 158.

60. Bhabha, "The Other Question," p. 18.

61. See Jean Pierrot, *Marguerite Duras* (Paris: Librairie José Corti, 1986), p. 9.

62. Grant, p. 109.

63. Marguerite Duras, *Oeuvres cinématographiques: Edition vidéographique critique* (Paris: Ministère des relations extérieures, Bureau d'animation culturelle, n.d.), pp. 21–22.

64. As examples of discussions of sexual difference in Duras's films see: Madeleine Borgomano, *Une Lecture des fantasmes* (Paris: Cistre, 1985) and "Le Corps et le texte," in *Ecrire dit-elle*, ed. Danielle Bajomée and Ralph Heyndels (Brussels: Editions de l'Université de Bruxelles, 1985), pp. 49–62; Joan Copjec, "*India Song/Son Nom de Venise dans Calcutta désert*: The Compulsion to Repeat," *October*, no. 17 (1981): 37–52; Mary Ann Doane, "Films and the Masquerade: Theorising the Female Spectator," *Screen* 23, no. 3/4 (1982): 74–87; Stephen Heath, "Body, Voice" in *Questions of Cinema* (Bloomington: Indiana U P, 1981), pp. 176–193 and "Difference," *Screen* 19, no. 3 (1978): 50–112; E. Ann Kaplan, *Women and Film* (New York: Methuen, 1983), pp. 91–103; Elisabeth Lyon, "The Cinema of   V. Stein," *Camera Obscura*, no. 6 (Fall 1980): 7–41; Marcelle Marini, *Territoires du feminin* (Paris: Ed   ons de Minuit, 1977) and "L'Autre Corps," in *Ecrire, dit-elle*, pp. 21–48; Trista Selous, *The Other Woman: Feminism and Femininity in the Work of Marguerite Duras* (New Haven: Yale University Press, 1988); and Sharon Willis, *Writing on the Body* (Chicago: University of Illinois Press, 1987).

   Several French critics discuss *India Song* and *Son Nom de Venise* from the point of view of racial/ethnic difference and colonialism. See, for example, Mireille Amiel, "*India Song*," *Cinéma 75*, no. 199 (June 1975): 126–128; Pascal Bonitzer, "D'Une Inde l'autre," *Cahiers du Cinéma*, no. 258–259 (July-August 1975): 49–51; Jacques Frenais, "*Son Nom de Venise dans Calcutta désert*: Le Silence," *Cinéma 76*, no. 210 (June 1976): 126–128; Jacques Grant, "Entretien avec Marguerite Duras," *Cinéma 75*, no. 200 (July-August 1975); Jean-Pierre Oudart, "Sur *Son Nom de Venise dans Calcutta désert*," *Cahiers du Cinéma*, no. 268–269 (July-August 1976): 75–77; Marie-Claire Ropars-Wuilleumier, "La Mort des miroirs," *L'Avant-Scène du cinéma*, no. 225 (April 1979): 4–13 and *Le Texte divisé* (Paris: Presses universitaires françaises, 1981). For a brief discussion of the politics of *Les Mains négatives*, see Youssef Ishaghpour, *D'Une Image à l'autre* (Paris: Editions Denoël/Gouthier, 1982), pp. 288–291. Madeleine Borgomano's is the only book length study of Duras's cinema to date, but it offers a formal, not an ideological, reading of the films. See Madeleine Borgomano, *L'Ecriture filmiq .e de Marguerite Duras* (Paris: Editions Albatros, 1985).

   In contrast, as far as I am aware, except for a few interviews with Duras published in the States when *India Song* and *Son Nom de Venise* were first shown here, Linda Dittmar and Martine Loutfi are the only critics writing in English who look at Duras's films in the context of colonial discourse. See Linda Dittmar, "Dislocated Utterances" and Martine Loutfi, "Duras's India," *Literature/Film Quarterly* 14, no. 3 (1986): 151–153. As examples of interviews where the issue of colonialism is raised, see Carlo Clarens. "*India Song* and Marguerite Duras," *Sight and Sound* 45, no. 1 (Winter 1975–76): 32–35; Jan Dawson, "*India Song*: A Chant of Love and Death," *Film Comment* 11, no. 6 (Nov.-Dec. 1975): 52–55; and Michael Tarantino, "Review and Interview," *Take One* 5, no. 4 (October 1976): 42–43.

65. Chahandra Mohanty, "Under Western Eyes: Feminist Scholarship and Colonial Discourses," *Feminist Revolution*, no. 30 (Autumn 1988): 64.

66. Said, *Orientalism*, p. 13, rephrasing an interview published in *Diacritics* 6, no. 3 (Fall 1976): 38. Said makes a similar point in "Orientalism Reconsidered." See p. 13.

67. Marguerite Duras, cited in Clarens, p. 35.

68. Duras says that as a child she was fascinated by the fact that a young man killed himself for love of the "real" Anne-Marie Stretter, the wife of a career diplomat and mother of two young girls. See François Barat and Joël Farges, eds., *Marguerite Duras* (Paris: Editions Albatros, 1975), p. 85. The beggar woman came into Duras's life at age twelve, appearing on the family doorstep with a sick baby. See Clarens, p. 35 and Duras, *Oeuvres cinématographiques*, p. 21. The model for the Vice-Consul was one of Duras's adolescent friends in Paris who later became Vice-Consul to Bombay. Clarens, p. 23.

69. Marguerite Duras, *Oeuvres cinématographiques*, p. 55.

70. Kari Hanet, "Does the Camera Lie?," *Screen* 14, no. 3 (Autumn 1973): 74.

71. Ropars-Wuillemier, *Le Texte divisé*, p. 206.

72. Ropars-Wuillemier, *Le Texte divisé*, p. 206.

73. Grant, pp. 103–104. See also Borgomano, *L'Ecriture filmique de Marguerite Duras*, p. 110, citing Nicole-Lise Bernheim, ed., *Marguerite Duras tourne un film* (Paris: Editions Albatros, 1975), p. 106. Duras tells Bernheim that the beggar woman "is misery, she is the extreme limit of a state of being, a situation. . . . She is designated by her function. . . . An unbounded state of the individual."

74. Grant, p. 111.

75. For a discussion of Duras's use of indeterminate subject pronouns in *India Song* see, for example, Marie-François Grange, "Un Système d'écriture: *India Song* de Marguerite Duras," *Ça Cinéma*, no. 19 (1980): 57.

76. Ropars-Wuillemier, *Le Texte divisé*, p. 204.

77. See Dawson, p. 52. Ropars-Wuillemier speaks of the "quasi-immobility of the characters which certain shots treat as inert bodies, arranged in tableaux." See "La Mort des miroirs," p. 10.

78. Duras distinguishes five levels of voices in *India Song*: the privileged, clearly comprehensible voices of the protagonists; very clear voices which comment on the past; clear voices of the guests at the reception; lost voices which speak of India's heat and humidity; and, finally, blocks of voices from which snatches of sentences alone are comprehensible. See Grant, p. 105 and Ropars-Wuillemier, "La Mort des miroirs," pp. 8–9.

79. Duras maintains that these narrating voices do not address the spectator directly but rather "speak with each other" and "don't know they are being listened to" (Marguerite Duras, *India Song: Texte, Théâtre, Film* (Paris: Gallimard, 1973), p. 147). While this statement may accurately describe the other-worldly impression one gets from these voices, I would argue that audiences, not authors or texts, ultimately decide whether or not they are being addressed.

80. Grant, p. 110.

81. Lyon, p. 36.

82. Duras admits as much. See, for example, Duras *India Song*, p. 9 and Marguerite Duras and Xavière Gauthier, *Les Parleuses* (Paris: Editions de Minuit, 1974), p. 169.

83. See Duras, *Oeuvres cinématographiques*, pp. 27–29.

84. Grant, p. 104.

85. Ropars-Wuillemier, "La Mort des miroirs," p. 12.

86. Bonitzer, p. 50.

87. Duras, *Oeuvres cinématographiques*, p. 35.

88. Borgomano, "L'Autre Corps," in *Ecrire, dit-elle*, pp. 59–60.

89. These women are actually vaguely connected to the film narrative, for one is Delphine Seyrig (Anne-Marie Stretter), the other Nicole Hiss (one of the narrating female voices). They seem to appear more as actresses than as characters here, however.

90. Ropars-Wuillemier, "La Mort des miroirs," p. 8.

91. In the interviews which accompany the video collection of her films, Duras notes that the castle she explores in *Son Nom de Venise* was owned by the Rothchilds. Because Goering made it his residence during the war, they abandoned it. See Duras, *Oeuvres cinématographiques*, p. 36.

92. Oudart, p. 76.

93. Duras, *Oeuvres cinématographiques*, p. 55.

94. Grant, p. 111.

95. Cited in Sylvia Harvey, *May '68 and Film Culture* (London: British Film Institute, 1977), p. 71. No specific references given.

96. Grant, p. 112. In *Oeuvres cinématographiques* Duras says that "the immense misery of world cinema is to think that people are representable." See Duras, *Oeuvres cinématographiques*, p. 26.

97. The either/or choice I describe is the one Gayatri Spivak says confronts the radical intellectual in the West. See Gayatri Spivak, "Subaltern Studies: Deconstructing Historiography," in *In Other Worlds* (New York: Routledge, 1988), p. 209.

98. Domonique Noguez, "Les India Songs de Marguerite Duras," *Cahiers du 20e siècle: Cinéma et littérature*, no. 9 (1978): 147.

99. Bhabha, "The Other Question," p. 33.

100. Martine Loutfi's discussion of Duras's films is one of the few I have read which treats her cinema as part of an avant-garde *genre*. See Loutfi, p. 152. Consequently, I would argue, it avoids some of the polarities which so characterize Duras criticism: in general her films are either dismissed as boring and/or reactionary or lauded as intriguing and/or revolutionary.

101. Dana Polan, *The Political Language of Film and the Avant-garde* (Ann Arbor: UMI Research Press, 1985), p. 30. Polan also maintains that: "What cinema seems to need to be politically progressive is not to insert history into its texts, but to insert its texts into history." By positing "cinema" as a subject, however, Polan's definition simplifies the problem of political cinema. As Isaac Julian and Kobena Mercer point out, extra-textual factors like funding and distribution often determine what

pictures get made and who sees them. See Isaac Julian and Kobena Mercer, "Introduction: De Margin and De Centre," *Screen* 29, no. 1 (Autumn 1988): 4.

102. Julian and Mercer, p. 8.
103. Trinh T. Minh-ha, *Woman, Native, Other: Writing Postcoloniality and Feminism* (Bloomington: Indiana; UP, 1989), pp. 94, 95, 104.
104. Bhabha, "Signs Taken for Wonders," p. 153.
105. See McRobbie, pp. 7–8. Stuart Hall makes much the same point when he says:

> [T]here might be more to be learned from distinguishing what, in common sense, appear to be variants of the same thing: for example, the racism of the slave South from the racism of the insertion of blacks into the 'free forms' of industrial-capitalist development in the post-bellum North. . . .
>
> In part, this must be because one cannot explain racism in abstraction from other social relations—even if, alternatively, one cannot explain it by reducing it to those relations.

See Stuart Hall, "Race, Articulation and Societies Structured in Dominance," in *Sociological Theories: Race and Colonialism* (United Kingdom: UNESCO, 1980), p. 337.

106. Mohanty, p. 79.

The Bedouin, the Beatniks, and the Redemptive Fool

Smadar Lavie

Fool. Truth's a dog must to kennel; he must be whipped
   out, when the Lady Brach may stand by th' fire
   and stink . . . Prithee, nuncle, keep a schoolmaster that
   can teach thy fool to lie. I would fain learn to lie.

Lear. An you lie, sirrah, we'll have you whipped.

   William Shakespeare, *King Lear*

I

al-Billij, Dahab, Christmas night, 1985

Tourists who started flocking en masse to this spectacular South Sinai beach in the mid-1970s wished to live in the authentic conditions of a traditional Bedouin village. Upon getting off the bus, they used to ask, "Where is the Bedouin village?" So Bedouin entrepreneurs of the Mzeina tribe built this fake one and named it al-Billij, imitating the sound of the English word but only as an arbitrary proper name, with no particular significance.

Deep black sea, unusually calm. Beam of half a moon. Aluminum beach chairs half-sunk in sand. Posters of Michael Jackson and Prince glued on the plywood counters of flimsy cafés, their facades sheathed in date palm fronds so they look genuine from the outside. Some Madonna hit competing with Simon and Garfunkel's "Bridge over Troubled Water," both pouring out of raspy Mitsubishi loudspeakers. An asbestos structure dyed brownish-orange dominating the scene with its big sign: Tourist Police. Five policemen in the station, all crammed behind the small rectangular desk—more than enough protection for the fifteen tourists milling around.

"No nudity," announces the big red print, in English only, on white signs scattered along the beach more frequently than necessary. Strings of Christmas lights, interwoven among the palm fronds, twinkle like cheerful guests from another planet. After Forest and I have waited a long time in a line of three people to

SMADAR LAVIE *is Assistant Professor of Anthropology and Comparative Research in History, Culture and Society at the University of California, Davis. She is the author of* The Poetics of Military Occupation *(UC Press) and co-editor of* Creativity in Anthropology *(Cornell University Press, in press).*

23

see five policemen, our passports are stamped. We are now under the official auspices of the Tourist Police of the Arab Republic of Egypt.

It's too late to arrive as guests at the home of my adoptive Mzeini family. Not only do they live four kilometers north of here, but after the four and a half years since my last visit in 1981, I am coming with my American spouse and want to introduce him properly. Aside from these considerations, the local scene is sufficiently bizarre to attract the postmodernist scholar's curiosity.

Simon and Garfunkel have won. Madonna's loudspeaker conked out, so now we are listening only to the sound of silence.

"Let's have a cup of tea in one of those cafés," I suggest to Forest, "and then find a rental hut for the night."

"The music isn't bad," he muses, "but my first time in the Sinai Desert, I didn't expect to be celebrating Christmas."

So we stay.

"Hey, Smadar, how you doin', what's up? Who's this handsome guy with you? Remember me? I'm Şubhi." A young Bedouin approaches me from behind the café counter in a barrage in Hebrew.

I am stunned. I can't quite place this tall tanned young man with long curls down his back, costumed in a tight Speedo swimsuit and a tight tank-top bearing a faded picture of Rambo. Why on earth is he speaking Hebrew to me when he knows I am perfectly fluent in the Mzeini Arabic dialect?

After a long, nebulous moment, he smiles, revealing teeth coated by a patina of brown tar from smoking too many cigarettes. "I am the grandchild of Hajj Madᶜān the Healer, the one who lives up in Wadi Zaghara," he chatters in very fast Hebrew. "I am the son of Muhammad, and just before you went to America, when I was still a child, our family moved here from the mountains. This is my father's café."

"All right, all right, but why in Hebrew, ya Şubhi?" I inquire in Arabic, feeling hurt that he addresses me in the language of the occupier.

"English they understand a bit, but Hebrew not at all." He points his chin in the direction of the brownish-orange structure. "We could also talk in Swedish—they don't understand any Swedish either, even though they enjoy staring at the blonde Swedish women who suntan on the beach. Yok tola Svenska?"

"No, but why not Arabic?" I insist in Arabic, while Forest, who understands a bit of Swedish, tries to recover from these hybridized realities.

"Because they—they have big ears. They are snoopy about what everyone says, even someone as young and innocuous (zarūk, Hebrew) as me. I don't want any problems with them," he continues in Hebrew under his breath.

Suddenly the anthropologist realizes that the occupier of the South Sinai has changed, and therefore so has the language of oppression.

"How is business?" I ask. But Şubhi suddenly freezes. A sleepy policeman, wearing a disheveled wool khaki uniform (despite the warmth of the coastal desert winter) is patrolling around the café, a submachine gun slung over his shoulder. Nonchalantly, Şubhi raises the volume and we sink into the epic of Mrs. Robinson. When the soldier finishes patrolling around all five other flimsy cafés and the four hut clusters of the Billij, Şubhi yells at him in Hebrew, "Hey, go to hell, son of a whore!" The soldier smiles at him and waves back.

"So how is business?" I ask again in Hebrew, and the anthropologist feels very weird.

"No business," he says briskly. "No nudity, no business."

"But during the Israeli occupation, people your parents' age kept complaining that the nudes on the beach were offensive to Islam." I still feel disoriented from speaking Hebrew with this Mzeini.

"Yes, our fathers complained and made money, and complained more, and made more money. We don't get the fat tourists who come to Cairo. The kind we get have beards and backpacks, and like the freedom of the desert. For them, freedom means taking off their clothes and screwing all the women in sight. That's what they believe, and it's OK with me. I sell them things and make money, and they teach me their languages. But they don't like to be asked ten times a day where they come from, where they're going, where they've eaten, where they will sleep and with whom. The Tourist Police means no tourists."

I look around and see that the whole place is a stage set to welcome hippie trekkers or stray remnants from *Hair*. Political and personal graffiti are scratched in charcoal on the counter plywood: "Make love, not war," "Make love, not babies," "Barbara—see you in Khartoum," "John Lennon," "Nelson Mandela." Here and there are peace signs and hearts.

Ṣubḥi goes behind the counter to change the cassette. "How about 'The Beatles' Best'?" he asks us. "And what would you like to eat? Omelet? French fries? Canned tuna? Mackerel in tomato sauce?"

"Whatever," I answer listlessly. Ṣubḥi gets to work on supper and soon we smell omelets. Forest and I start singing along with the Beatles: "Michelle, ma belle . . ." Meanwhile I notice that two tourists in long Bedouin caftans, sporting blond beard stubble and sunburned to the point the Mzeini described as "roasted lobsters," have come into the café and are intently involved in a poker game with a Bedouin wearing a T-shirt and jeans. One of the lobsters turns to Forest.

"Hey man, what's happenin'? Where you guys from?" He tries to talk jive, but it doesn't come off.

"Berkeley, California," Forest answers laconically.

"I'm from San Francisco myself, the Haight." Here follows small talk about weather and politics back home. Then he says, "After traveling around the world, the only thing I miss from the good ol' USA is Christmas."

"Well, at least you got a few lights here," says Forest. And he whimsically starts singing "Jingle Bells." The two guys join in, trying to drown out the Beatles booming from the huge speakers. The Bedouin get into the spirit of the thing, clapping their hands in little circles as they would have for the *redēhi* dance.

Ṣubḥi arrives at our table with a platter bearing two cheap china plates, each with a steaming, elegantly rolled omelet stuffed with "La Vache Qui Rit" cheese, accompanied by traditional unleavened Bedouin flatbread. He meticulously sets our places with stainless steel flatware and lays the plates before us.

"S'il vous plait, monsieur, madame," he says with a flourish, then shifts to Arabic. "Eat, eat!"

"We won't unless you join us, because you are our host. But don't worry, we'll pay you anyway." So he pulls up another chair and sits down, and the three of us share the two plates of food.

"Too bad you weren't here yesterday," he says between bites of omelet. "We sacrificed a lamb for Christmas. It was a great dinner."

"We? Who's 'we?'" He has piqued the anthropologist's curiosity.

"All of us young Bedouin who work here for the tourists."

"But Christmas is for Christians," I protest the obvious.

"Look," he says, "when you Jews were here and occupied our land, we all were very devout Muslims. Even Shgētef the Fool was. From the money he made renting out his huts here, half of our mosque was built. But now things have changed. The Egyptians are here and they have brought all sorts of government teachers to show us how to be Muslim. They think theirs is the only way. So why not check out Christianity? Most of the tourists are nice people. And now they wear some clothes, of course."

The anthropologist is at first puzzled by this logic. She remembers noticing and writing in her 1978 fieldnotes that during the Israeli occupation, the more hippies there were lolling on the Sinai beaches, the more permanent mosques, built of hewn stone, sprang up around the Bedouin settlements. Perhaps a refuge from, perhaps a defense against, the non-Muslim impingement on Bedouin tradition. Then she suddenly realizes that, just as the language of the occupier has changed, so has their religion.

We slept that night on the soft sand floor of one of Shgētef's huts, under the lone beam of the half moon, with only twinkling Christmas lights for stars. Ṣubhi gave us a candle, though, saying it would be more romantic. And the deep black sea was mirror-calm—no storm, as usual, to wake us up in the middle of the night.

In the morning Shgētef arrived to collect his fee. "One dollar or two Egyptian pounds per person per night," he announced, poker-faced. Only after he got the money did he give me a big hug and tell me that the whole Mzeini settlement up north was waiting to see me and meet my husband.

When we loaded our packs and walked north on the beach toward the settlement, we noticed a freckled peachy-blonde woman dressed in cut-off pants. She also had a black kerchief tied in back of her head to imitate a veil.

"Where are you from?" I queried.

"Amsterdam."

"Why the veil?"

"I heard it helps attract a young Bedouin lover. When Israel was here, I bathed here nude, but what the guys seemed really interested in was my nose and mouth. So I'm covering them to make them more mysterious."

The anthropologist sees that the tourists are fine-tuning their longstanding efforts to go native and imitate the Bedouin, who now, in contrast, are acting like an international mishmash of all the various tourists they have had to deal with. Under these circumstances, I can see why, when I asked Shgētef "What are you doing these days?", he wryly remarked, "I'm working at being a Bedouin."

Even way out here on the beach the strains of Simon and Garfunkel float from the scratchy loudspeakers:

Slow down, you move too fast.
You got to make the morning last.
Just kicking down the cobble stones.
Looking for fun and Feelin' Groovy . . .

Doot-in' doo-doo,
Feelin' Groovy.

Got no deeds to do,
No promises to keep.
I'm dappled and drowsy and ready to sleep.
Let the morning time drop all its petals on me.
Life, I love you,
All is groovy.

II

Even though Shgēṭef was just a fool, his ironic remark, "I am working at being a Bedouin," raises unresolved existential dilemmas that the Mzeina Bedouin, a tribe of approximately 5,000 and the largest of the South Sinai Tawara intertribal alliance, had to face every day.

While the free-spirited nomadic tribes who roamed the Arabian Deserts attracted turn-of-the-century European explorers in search of exotic experiences and currently have become the nostalgic subject of ethnographic literature and films, travelers' accounts of the South Sinai tribes evoke images of less glamorous but still outlandish Bedouin. Dan Rabinowitz (1985) has recently emphasized that all nineteenth- and early twentieth-century travelers to the South Sinai, expecting to find the idealized pastoral nomads, were surprised to find only very few camels, sheep, and goats, and therefore concluded that the region was not prime pasture land (Rabinowitz 1985:216). Hence, when travelers to the Eastern Deserts were still pursuing their romantic images of free and independent nomads, travelers to the South Sinai peninsula had long since been disabused of all such naivetes. The latter travelers clearly recognized that the Ṭawara Bedouin of the South Sinai were almost totally dependent on the economic centers of the colonial powers occupying their territory: the Ottoman Turks, and later the British. By the turn of the twentieth century Ṭawara members derived much of their income from making charcoal, and also from acting as authentic travel guides for genteel pilgrims and explorers, uneasily saddled on camelback, suffering through Mount Sinai and the rest of the peninsula. They could sell the charcoal only in the faraway Nile Valley, four to fourteen strenuous days away by camel. Or they could share camel rides and walk fifteen to thirty days north to Jaffa, to hire themselves out as the cheapest of laborers to Palestinian orange grove owners. They also cultivated date palms in the desert's few oases, tended petite mountain gardens, hunted whatever the fragile desert ecology would yield, and fished along the ʿAqaba and Suez gulf coasts.

To this day, the basic fact is that the Mzeina have been in the hinterland of every occupier of the South Sinai, and therefore have had to depend for their survival on the occupier's center of power (Marx 1977, 1980; Lavie 1989, 1990; Lavie and Young 1984). In the course of the Arab-Israeli conflict of the last forty years, the South Sinai has been a political football tossed at least five times between Egypt and Israel. From the 1940s until 1952, the Sinai was governed by the Egyptian King Farouq but patrolled by British army units. From 1952 to 1956 it was under independent control of the Arab Republic of Egypt. Although the South Sinai has officially been an Egyptian territory since Ottoman times, the South Sinai Bedouin nonetheless still view the Egyptians as a foreign occupation force, now perhaps because the Egyptians, preoccupied by the tremendous problems in the densely populated Nile

Valley, have been unable to develop much sensitivity towards the idiosyncrasies of their hinterland Bedouin population. In 1956 Israel, backed by France and Britain, staging one of the last major colonial wars over the nationalization of the Suez Canal, occupied the Sinai, but a few months later returned it to Egypt, which, by then aided by the Soviets, held on to it until 1967, when it was again occupied by Israel. Following the 1973 October War, and the politics of shuttle diplomacy and Camp David, Israel again returned the Sinai to Egypt in eight stages between January 1975 and April 1982.

And throughout all this, the Mzeina Bedouin were nothing but pawns. The Egyptian, Israeli, British, American, and Soviet leaders never once consulted them or their leadership on issues of war, peace, occupation, or treaties.

This article attempts to show that the constant military occupation of the South Sinai precluded for the Mzeina the identity that both turn-of-the-century travelers' accounts and contemporary nostalgic literature or media accounts inscribed for the Bedouin: fierce romantic nomads on loping camels in the vast desert. On the contrary, given that the Mzeina were helpless objects of external political processes, I argue that their Bedouin identity could be little more than literary allegory: tribal identity appeared as moralistic, multi-layered narratives transcending the spatial and temporal boundaries of military occupation through symbolic defiance only, because for Mzeinis to openly confront any armed or unarmed occupier could mean beatings, jail, even death.

Within the tribe, only a handful of charismatic individuals had the creative capacity to allegorize the military occupation by dramatizing its humiliations and absurdities for a Bedouin audience. Yet these individuals, gifted with persuasive theatrical skills, did not perform their dramatized critiques at regular, ritual-like intervals. Only when challenged by fellow tribesmembers would a Mzeini creative individual such as the Fool evoke the allegory of Bedouin identity. The story would unfold during the fragile interstices of a tense, discontinuous conversation. Such precious moments, filling the otherwise awkward breaks within the flow of every-day conversation, temporarily reconstructed the image of the tribe for the listeners, even though the political situation that had generated the allegory remained un-changed.

This article will retrace the process by which a Mzeina allegory of Bedouin identity emerges from a performance by Shgētef, who creatively plays a character based on his identity as a Fool. Embedded in the Fool's performance is the hege-monic poetics of a culture under military occupation.

III

"Every dog has its day [to get a beating], and every place has its Fool." So goes the Mzeini saying. And the day young Manṣūr left for Zurich, to marry his love whom he had met on an cAqaba Gulf nude beach,[1] his father declared him *meshammas*, disowned from both family and tribe by the father's statement that from this day forth, his son was dead. During the week of ritual mourning that followed, the father kept repeating, "The day has come when iron talks back and the Fool rules."

Indeed, the Fool, a Mzeini character present in almost every encampment or sedentarized settlement, was the agent who expressed clearly and succinctly, though perhaps with deliberate awkwardness, the paradoxes of the local South Sinai hybridization of two contradictory cultures: the Mzeina qua traditional Bedouin, with their Islamic religion and nomadic-pastoralist ideology, and the Western culture imposed on them by international politics.

The Fool himself would usually be a reification of this hybridized juncture. He typically looked like a klutz, with a dirty patched caftan and headdress only half-tied around his head, and with uncut fingernails and beard, which the Mzeinis consider pollution. "We Bedouin are almost waterless, very poor," remarked one Fool, "so we'd better look like it."

"Don't believe him," some who were listening warned me later. "He's made lots of money since the Eilat-Sharm road was opened in 1972. He keeps it all in that khaki pouch hanging diagonally from his shoulder."

The handful of Fools I knew were talented businessmen who accumulated wealth from pioneering entrepreneurial activities. If a Fool lived in the heavily toured coastal areas, he would venture into building and renting out traditional-style Bedouin palm-frond huts to the many tourists who wanted to vacation in what they envisioned as authentic desert settings. He also sold them food, drink, and touristy simulations of traditional Bedouin attire imported from the West Bank, and later from Cairo. He was among the first to organize and market Desert Tours on Camelback, and to produce Bedouin-style celebrations for the tourists' amusement and edification. In addition the Fool would be a money changer, at better rates than the Bank, illegally converting the tourists' hard currency (preferably German marks, Swiss francs, or American dollars) into the notoriously inflation-ridden Israeli and later Egyptian currencies. In a case where the Fool lived away from the main tourist routes, he would usually be the one to win the hearts and pockets of Israeli or Egyptian developers, who conceived of him as both nonthreatening, due to his use of humor, and cheap to employ, due to his shabby appearance. So they would appoint him as a subcontractor or labor supervisor, the foreign developers' go-between in their relations with their Mzeini blue-collar laborers.

Unlike the typical Mzeini nouveaux riches, the Fool did not invest his money in conspicuous consumption of semi-dilapidated pickup trucks or jeeps. Nor did he buy fancy Japanese transistor radios and cassette recorders, or elegant Swiss watches. Rather, as Subhi stated, Fools like Shgētef generously donated the money they made to the building of hewn-stone mosques that mushroomed in all the heavily toured communities. These replaced the spaces on the rough ground made sacred by marking, with only laid-down stones or conch shells, the *miḥrāb* pointing toward Mecca. Perhaps this building of permanent mosques was a response to the presence of so many scantily-clad tourists who intruded into the everyday life of the Mzeini encampments and settlements as if visiting some sort of human zoo.

The Mzeinis repeatedly organized delegations that went to plead with the peninsula's Israeli military governor to put up signs requesting the tourists to wear bathing suits. But the military governor merely advised the Mzeinis to make the best of it and learn to enjoy the show, and refused to take any further action aside from choosing an occasional one-night stand from among the naked bodies on the beach. The Mzeinis had no choice but to acquiesce.

When the Egyptians got the ᶜAqaba Gulf Coast back in 1982, they immediately

Figure 1.   The daily coastal Israeli military patrol, Gulf of ᶜAqaba. Photo: Shalom Bar-Tal.

responded to the Bedouin request and erected those long-hoped-for signs on the South Sinai beaches. But the more signs, the fewer tourists. Every tourist also had to register with the Egyptian Tourist Police, and could be subject to occasional questioning. A few women were subjected to sexual harassment. The Egyptians also outlawed individual and spontaneous small group backpacking by putting up signs along the peninsula's asphalt roads announcing that tourists were prohibited from leaving them. Perhaps the Egyptians, fearing the desert themselves, feared also for the tourists' safety. But the Bedouin thereby lost a relatively hefty source of income. Once again they organized delegations to the governing authorities of the South Sinai, this time requesting the Egyptians to ease the no-nudity and no-hiking regulations. And once again they were instructed to make the best of the new situation, and had to acquiesce.

"I am a merchant of sins," confessed one Fool. "I sell the tourists alcohol and rent them huts where unmarried people have tabooed sex." (One of his own brothers later announced, for all but this Fool to hear, "That's why he was the first to sign up and pay the large deposit the first year the Israelis organized the holy pilgrimage to Mecca.") "In Mecca I went to see a holy man. I asked him whether selling alcohol to non-Muslims was ḥarām (taboo for Muslims) or ḥalāl (religiously permitted). He told me I should cease this at once. But what can I do instead? Make money cleaning toilets in non-Muslim hotels?"

From the remarks I heard by and about the Fool, and given his no-win situation, it is clear that, like other figures of sacred clowns or tricksters, the contradictions built into the composition of the Fool's persona were never resolved.[2] But in contrast to the textually prescribed roles of those other clowns or tricksters, the Mzeini Fool did not make his debut on the societal stage during the spatially and temporally bounded domains that characterize communal ritual performances. Rather, the Mzeini Fool, if present and only if he chose to perform, might spontaneously rise up during awkward breaks in the conversation, interrupting the spatially and temporally unbounded flow of ordinary quotidian discourse. Such fissures would occur when the conversation got stuck in a circular, reductionist argument pitting the Mzeini identity as Bedouin against the hybridizations in their identity forced on them by their local compromises with Western influences. At this point, the people might all just get up and leave the conversation circle. But sometimes a Fool could save the situation for the time being at least, bridging the textual and contextual discontinuities by embodying them in his own persona and performing a solo ritual with its own farcical logic, allegorizing his own experiences into a moral exemplar that clarified for his listeners their own identity.

The Fool had "ill-formed unity" (Handelman 1987:548): a bright, rich merchant dressed in rags and acting silly, miming the antics of those naked Others on the beach even while his audience was well aware of his conspicuous Muslim piety. His own paradoxical existence enabled him to draw for his audience a clear boundary between themselves qua traditional Bedouin, and themselves qua workers, many of whom preferred the creative, clever job of running their own enterprises marketing their culture to sinful foreigners when the only apparent alternatives were miserable unskilled jobs in similar enterprises run by their occupiers. The Fool's staging of his own paradoxes, therefore, temporarily solved the Mzeinis' contradiction between their yearning to embody their traditional Bedouin lifestyle and their reality of having to perform this lifestyle they had never really had in front of exotica-hunting tourists, whom they could not restrain into civility because they were not the ones to decide on the rules and regulations in their own land.

IV

Dahab, Spring 1978, seven years earlier

Evening at this main sedentarized oasis along the ᶜAqaba Gulf, a community of 89 nuclear households living here permanently. Dinner smells, still in the air, mingle with the salty sea breeze softly blowing among the fronds of the date trees scattered in clusters on the coastline. A mother's undulating melancholy voice, singing a lullaby, tenderly echoes the cry of the muezzin calling for the ᶜasha after-dinner prayer. Answering the call, fourteen men from the northern neighborhood's *magᶜad* enter the newly-built nearby mosque. After about ten minutes, some of them begin to go back to the magᶜad, where they sit in a circle around the embers of a small fire. The older men stay a few minutes longer for pious individual prayer. Moonlight glows on the faces of people tranquil because they have fulfilled another duty of their religious routine. The youngest of the men serves small glasses of sweet dark tea that has been heated on the embers. A quiet conversation emerges from the silence.[3]

The conversation focuses on the hippies in al-Billij, called by the Mzeinis "Batānka," a *nisba* (group name) for "Beatniks." Since the Mzeinis considered the hippies to be sort of an international clan, they gave them a group name ending in "-a," like their own clan names. They were sure that the word "Beatnik" was derived from the Arabic *nīk*, meaning, "to fuck." This made sense to them because the Mzeinis, both women and men clad in their traditional attire, observed the Batānka from close range, doing it on the beach daily.

ᶜID: By Allah, today there was such a fat, healthy girl on the beach. Did you see her? The one with that dark, skinny guy.

KHDEIR: Yes, I think I know who you are talking about. They are in Ham-ṁuda's hut, under the palms he shares with Freij.

ᶜID: Too bad she sunbathes. Her beautiful milky skin has turned red like a roasted lobster.

JUMᶜA: Yeah, she came to me asking for tobacco. I told her I smoke only *banjo*, and asked her if she would like to buy some.

The listeners grin with amusement, knowing that Jumᶜa was offering the woman cheap homegrown green tobacco, which smells very much like marijuana but of course lacks its active ingredient.

When the first Batānka arrived in the South Sinai, they asked the Bedouin for marijuana. When it became clear that the Bedouin did not know that word, the hippies resorted to the exotic term "ganja," which the Bedouin misheard and then mispronounced as "banjo." The local folk wisdom has it that one day a naked beatnik sniffed the smoke from an ordinary rolled green tobacco cigarette a Bedouin was smoking, and instead of shouting "Eureka!" he pointed and gleefully exclaimed, "Ganja! Ganja! Whereupon the Bedouin realized they had a common product with extraordinary commercial possibilities.

JUMᶜA: I sold her three cigarettes at four American bucks a shot.

The circle is sprinkled with wry smiles.

RĀSHED: I saw her too. I think she dyes her hair. Her pubic hair is black, and her hair is kind of red.

ABU-MŪSA [*muttering in dismay*]: Oh evil of disaster!

Everyone but Abu-Mūsa is snickering as if at a dirty joke, but also with embarrassment, not only because they have all seen the young woman naked, but also because she didn't follow the proper custom of removing her body hair, which the Mzeinis considered religious pollution.

ᶜID: I swear by my life, I can't figure out what she sees in that guy; he's so dark and skinny.

People laugh again. For the Mzeinis, being dark meant a person had to work hard in the sun, and being skinny meant that the person did not get enough to eat—so he was poor and ugly.

SWĒLEM: This summer the Batānka increased like the amount of rubbish they throw on the beach. They throw themselves on the sand, too—dirty.

The atmosphere sobers at this distressing reality.

JUMᶜA [*raising his voice*]: What do you want? It's their vacation. This is how they enjoy themselves. Tell me, isn't it fun to take your girlfriend, or even come by yourself—everybody's naked, and you—just pick the one you like? And with their exchange rate, a vacation like that is pretty cheap.

ABU-MŪSA [*loud*]: Pray to the Prophet! You two have turned into Beatniks. Aren't you fed up with staring at the genitals of heretic girls? Do we have to discuss it every evening here in our magᶜad by the holy mosque?

ᶜAWAYED [*louder*]: All of us are gradually joining the Batānka. Today when I was praying the noon prayer to myself near the hut I rent out in al-Billij, two guys with their uncircumcised penises dangling—tphooo [*he spits on the ground in disgust*]—and wearing only their cameras—they took pictures of me, just like that, without asking and without paying me. [*very upset, beating his hands on the air*] Who do they think we are? Their free picture show? It's bad enough they put on *their* free picture show for us all over the beach.

KHDEIR: [*just as loud, with gestures that punctuate the air*]: Other places don't have this mess that we do. People still follow the old ways. The hell with money—what kind of a life are we living?

ABU-MŪSA: [*firmly*]: Have you even seen or heard of an Arab praying right in the middle of a bunch of naked ladies and their lovers?

The anthropologist, in spite of hearing the pain in Abu-Mūsa's voice, barely manages to suppress a grin at the incongruity of this image.

ᶜAWAYED: Allah the Great! The Bedouin live in the desert, in Egypt, in Saudi Arabia, everywhere, without being touched by this pollution. Why do we have the bad luck to have to do this for a living?

ᶜID [*with deliberate calmness, to tone down the argument in tempo and volume*]: You think you got problems? Just try raising goats in this desert and see how far you get. Within a week all your money will have gone for their food. Our desert has lots of the wrong kind of grass.

ᶜId meant to end the argument with a funny pun: both pasture grass and dope were referred to by the word *hashish*. But by now, the men are so demoralized by the subject that the joke musters only a few weak smiles.

JUMᶜA [*flares up*]: We are all Batānka now. Living on as little money as they, spending no more than they do. What property do we own? Our land is all bare rugged mountains and jagged corals, good for nothing except attracting crazy tourists to dive and climb and risk their necks for the fun of it. Real Bedouin have fields and flocks. Every once in a while they go to the market and exchange some goats for [consumer] goods. But these dollars are killing us.

ᶜAWAYED [*with conviction*]: The Bedouin are people of honor. They believe in God and His Discipline. They disdain moneygrubbing!

ᶜID [*with a voice of sugar-coated poison*]: Oh yes, we all saw you yesterday haggling with those scumbags over exchange rates of Israeli and German money down to the last penny, nervously counting your sheaf of bills. Oh Great Lord, we're not like the rest of 'em, The Bedouin.

RĀSHED [*furiously jumps into the conversation*]: Who needs money anyway? The Bedouin need freedom. Let them roam around in the desert like they used to, riding their camels, singing *hejēnis* (caravan songs), courting the veiled goatherds.

SWĒLEM [*with authority*]: The Bedouin don't put their heart in money. One helps the other: the father his sons, the sons their old father, everyone their uncles and cousins. They are organized better than the Eged Corporation.

The anthropologist is startled to hear this comparison made between the classic agnatic-corporate tribe and Eged, the powerful transportation monopoly that owns and runs almost every bus in Israel and the Occupied Territories.

ABU-MŪSA [with finality]: For the Bedouin, al-damm dhamm, ma fi khramm! (The blood is protected—there are no holes).

"Al-damm dhamm, ma fi khramm" was a legal statement taken from the codex of Blood Vengeance Law. It meant that, in a social network based on blood relationship, there could not be any gaps. When such a statement was uttered in everyday discourse, it meant that the conversation had reached a moment of crisis and could no longer proceed.

All of a sudden, out of the silence following this weighty declaration, a very short, skinny, sharp-boned, and sloppily dressed figure rises, waving his hands.

"Ho!" exclaims this Shgētef, the local Fool.

The others, realizing he has not spoken yet and has something to say, turn their heads in his direction.

With all solemnity he declares, "The Bedouin pee in a squat and so do we."

After initial puzzlement, the group bursts into hearty laughter. The Mzeinis believed that squatting was the proper way Muslims should urinate in order not to become polluted with drops of urine. The Fool's remark drew a sharp line between the magᶜad and al-Billij. In that absurd context, peeing while squatting meant existing in the world as Bedouin.

After the last peals of laughter fade away, the Fool starts speaking in the calm and measured voice that signifies a shift into a story-telling mode.

"Yesterday a couple came to me. They wanted to rent one of my huts. I think they were from a kibbutz because they wore those plaid flannel shirts. But the guy looked Swedish."

"You mean, he had those devil-colored eyes?" asks ᶜId, to show he is listening attentively.

"Yes, his eyes were as green as the eyes of those accursed cats. And believe it or not, *she* was driving the car and *he* unloaded it."

The Fool stops to give his audience a chance to laugh at the ridiculous gender-role reversal of the Batānka tribe. When the Mzeinis migrated, or even just went away with the family for a couple of days to visit friends and relatives, it was the husband who loaded and drove the pickup truck, and the wife who unloaded it.

"That devilish guy shut up, and *she* haggled with me over the price of the hut, and then tried to cheat and pay less."

The Fool again pauses to let his audience savor yet another role reversal that delineates the boundaries between the Batānka and themselves.

"So finally, after all that, they took all their clothes off and went for a walk on the beach, like Adam and Eve in the Garden."

And then the Fool stands up, violating the convention of the magᶜad, and starts miming an imitation of a Batānka woman delicately prancing on the beach.

"Wait a second," he suddenly says, still jogging around the amused circle. "I forgot my tits!" He holds his open hands under the places where his size E breasts would have been, and with huge motions moves them up and down. The men crack up. The Fool stops to catch his breath, and again violates convention by wiping the sweat off his brow with the hem of his long caftan, deliberately raising it to an immodest height and revealing his undergarment.

ᶜId, the youngest among the men, whistles with his fingers, but immediately stops because of Abu-Mūsa's piercing look.

"And that Swede, he had the biggest foreskin I've ever seen in my life." And the Fool jabs his elbow into his navel and dangles his arm from side to side, using his whole forearm to represent the tourist's penis, with the hand being the huge foreskin. The men roar with laughter.

"There really is some difference between the Batānka tribe and the Mzeina tribe," chokes Jumᶜa through his guffaws.

"There is indeed a difference." agree ᶜAwayed and Khdeir.

"In the afternoon she pulled the guy by his hand from the water and shoved him into the hut. There they did all sorts of things that people never do." And the Fool mimes hugging the air, kissing it, and mouthing around it.

These gestures were all varieties of sexual foreplay foreign to the Mzeinis, though they had seen them many times on their own beach. Nevertheless they now cheerfully volunteer lots of free advice to the Fool, just as they had gotten into the habit of doing when they walked on the beach among the bodies of the Batānka.

"Hey, give her another kiss there."

"No, no, above, on her neck."

"Don't forget her navel . . ."

"And believe it or not, by the end of it all, she was on top," Shgētef proclaims.

Everyone is weeping with laughter at this final proof of the topsy-turvy world of the Batānka.

"And that's the way it is," the Fool concludes, using this formulaic statement typical of codas for solo performances.

"And that's the way it is," all the men repeat in unison.

After several moments of awkward silence, which the anthropologist is careful to record, the conversation begins to flow again. Now the topic is the prices and amount of stock on hand, of the tourists' favorite designs for Bedouin caftans and so on, as if the bitter argument had never happened.

I look around for the Fool, but it seems he has already left the circle. "Where is Shgētef?" I ask Jumᶜa, sitting on my right.

"He's already gone back to his Billij huts, to make some more money off the tourists just arriving on the evening bus."

So the Fool has walked right back into the source of all the tension played out just now on the stage of the magᶜad. But where did it go? This quirky tension-dissolver has taken it with him until his next performance.

V

In the summer of 1979, the same dispute kept arising in Dahab's northern magᶜad. The Mzeinis juxtaposed their Muslim, Bedouin identity with that of their drifting Batānka neighbors, and the Fool had to keep reassuring them in his farcical, convoluted way, that there were clear boundaries between them and their neighbors. A couple of days after one of these performances, I was sitting on the beach, leaning my back against a date palm trunk. These were the smudgy hours of dusk, when the sharp red-granite cliffs seemed to glide into the Red Sea, and be mirrored in its reddish-blue water. These were also the soon-to-be sacred moments when men washed in the tidal zone, purifying themselves for the *maghreb* prayer, while smells of poached fish, black pepper, and cumin drifted in the air. Jumᶜa and Rāshed completed their ritual purification, and seated themselves near me beneath the palms, silently waiting for the muezzin cry.

The anthropologist dropped a casual remark, as if to herself: "This Shgētef is an incredibly funny guy. I have notebooks and rolls of film full of his antics."

There were almost sixty seconds of silence—a very long pause in a regular Mzeini conversation. Then Jumᶜa said, somehow baffled: "You came all the way here just to write and picture some fool?"

After another very long pause, Rāshed slowly and carefully chose his words. "No, ya Jumᶜa," he said frankly, "Shgētef is no fool. His mind is sharp as a sword. This summer he earned more than any of the rest of us off the tourists. And if it had not been for Shgētef's generosity, we would not have our mosque. But let me tell you, ya Smadar," Rāshed went on, turning his head towards me, "at times, this Fool's mind goes with the *tarāwa* (early evening breeze). His mind and his tongue then go separate routes, and he thinks of himself as if he's one of those Batānka."

"Poor Shgētef," added ᶜAwayed, who had just joined our little group after finishing his ritual washing while half-listening to the conversation. With matter-of-fact finality he declared, "The Fool is a *fool*."

"Is *he* a fool?" Rāshed immediately responded, "*All* of us have become fools!"

"All of you? fools?" The anthropologist perked up. "What do you mean?"

"The tourists have made us into fools," Rāshed replied at once. "They photograph us, they even make movies of us. There's no mountain left they didn't climb, no wadi they didn't hike, no coral reef they didn't scuba. They want to drink our tea and eat our bread, and then complain of constipation and *we* are to blame." Then he stopped his diatribe. His deeply lined face grimaced, and he continued: "Our children, our own children, they don't know this desert, their own land, as well as some of these Batānka tourists do. They just want to hang around Eilat, and eat white bread soaked in factory milk. And all they dream of is owning Mercedes taxis and screwing in the foreign style."

There were five whole minutes of silence. In that moody limbo of the waning day, I mourned how so many romantic pasts are dissolving into the transnational future, and the anthropologist wanted me to stop being sentimental and try to rescue this disappearing culture by getting it into text.

"The Fool is a *fool*," Jumᶜa, Rāshed and ᶜAwayed said in quiet unison, and then ᶜAwayed proceeded with a slow, monotonous recitation of a traditional *gaṣīda* (poem) about the Fool, careful to note that I had turned on my cassette recorder while the men repeated the rhymed syllables.

Al-Ahabal la shāf al-deif ma yewanni,	The Fool jumps up to greet his guest,
Ya ḥasrati minno la leginā.	But each time we meet, it's the end of rest.
Damn al-dabāyeh jamb beit'ho yejanni—	Such lavish sacrifices—too much blood to clean—
Mabṣūt illi ᶜindho we-illi ḥawelā.	He thinks he makes everyone glad and free of sin.

Ya karwato tishbaᶜ al-deif watethanni!	So many guests his hospitality stuffs!
Wasamn al-mebahhar minho ganā.	Spiced ghee rivers from him gush.
Wenghab ᶜanna gheibto ma temanni!	How we'll miss him when he leaves!
Kul ḥayii yugᶜud ᶜala darbo yetaḥarrā.	But waiting on his path is all that lives.
Wanwagef ᶜindok tegūl ghazāl mit'hanni,	He tries to visit like a delicate gazelle,
Watarrad al-fagr ᶜannok weyaglaᶜ mada'ā.	Wishing poverty away from you—he throws it to hell.
Wankheito lel-molma yezarret ma yewanni	But he gives communal feasts only fearless farts
Mithel al-beᶜīr illi khabrīn ma ᶜasā.	Like those of a camel before his dinner starts.
Wala lo ma al-ḥayii min al-mahalīg hanni	All God's creatures can live without his strife
Middat ḥayāti wana mashi warrā.	But me—I'll follow his footsteps the rest of my life.

VI

Fredric Jameson (1986:68) has argued that due to the hegemonic relationships between East and West (cf. Said 1978), one of the few kinds of resistance tribal societies can mount to Western economic and political encroachment is allegorical (cf. JanMohamed 1985). A case in point is the Mzeinis, who repeatedly transmute their everyday experience of life under occupation into allegorical stories they tell only among themselves. The history of the present, what happened just yesterday or a week ago, often conceived as the impingement of an alien nation-state upon the Mzeini idealized notion of the classical Bedouin tribe, is called upon to salvage the nostalgic history of the tribal past.

And Joel Fineman notes that "allegory seems regularly to surface in critical or polemical atmospheres, when for political or metaphysical reasons there is something that cannot be said" (1981:28). The Mzeini lived-reality of the perpetual occupation of their land generates an atmosphere of continuous crisis. From the many voices presented here you can realize that, torn between economic and cultural survival (cf. Lavie and Young 1984; Marx 1977, 1980; Rabinowitz 1985), one of the few avenues for protest still open to tribal members is transmuting their experience into ongoing allegories rooted in tradition.[4] These allegories, however, have a what Walter Benjamin has termed "dialectical nature" (1985:176)—they sustain the Mzeina belief in the immortality of their collective tribal past; at the same time they repeatedly show the Mzeinis the extent to which they are entrapped within the global fluctuations of the present (cf. Jameson 1981, 1986).

Unlike other literary forms, allegories call attention to themselves as both cultural texts and the literary criticisms of those same texts (Frye 1967:89–90; Quilligan 1979:25–26). They are thus the "tropes of tropes," or "representative of critical activity *per se*" (Fineman 1981:27). In this manner allegories voice, at one and the same time, subjective and objectified representations of both the text and its many meanings. One notes that here the same ideas were unfolded, refolded and reunfolded: unfolded in the 1985 Christmas night scene, refolded in the conversation in the magᶜad followed by the Fool's story; and re-unfolded in my dusk conversation with the men a year later. Each of the three vignettes reflects on each of the others.

At the moment of what Peter McHugh termed "emergence" (1968:24–28) in the mag°ad, the Fool linked Mzeini feelings about their Bedouin tribal identity— feelings evoking eternity—to the here-and-now of naked tourists under the aus- pices of the occupying agencies. In recounting the story of the Swedish-Israeli couple's migration to the Sinai beaches—an experience of reversal and insult to Bedouin values—he fashioned it into a distanced, funny story of the present. In short, the Fool molded current events into a stylized literary form. Therefore, despite the volatile subject, both the Fool and his audience were able to grasp the account as a "traditional," authentic Bedouin story, belonging to the "once-upon- a-time" genre typical of Arab moralistic, didactic folk tales. Moreover, the Fool's experience, molded into a story, succeeded in bringing to the surface two other traditionally recognized Bedouin stories from tribal collective memory—that of the Bedouin annual migration, and that of the Poem of the Fool. Thus, the three vignettes presented here are stories within stories about stories. Such layers and layers of reflexivity evoke the feeling of being in a hall of mirrors. And mirrors, like allegories, capture the inclusiveness of timespans and the completeness of spaces (Wimsatt 1970:215–221).

During my first four years of fieldwork among the Mzeina I recorded many mundane, after-prayer conversations that developed into loud and painful argu- ments. Some of these arguments were open-ended, abruptly discontinued, and never resolved. Others ended in communal agreement accompanied by the ele- vated feeling of "communitas" (Turner 1969).

In my third year I wrote in my field diary that the latter kind of debate reminded me of a sonata form. Just like the first movement of a sonata, these conversations- cum-debates consisted of an exposition of a theme, a development phase that explored and exhausted the many variations of that theme, and then a grandiose finale, in which the original theme was recapitulated. But the Mzeina's after-prayer arguments did not match the sonata's rules of vocality: while the exposition of the argument's theme and its many explorations were multivocal, the recapitulation of the theme was performed by a solo voice. To my amazement, even though the voice was single, it had the persuasive power to tie all ends of the debate together, and thus it brought the argument to a harmonious end.

The Fool was one of the powerful soloists of these conversations-cum-debates. He demonstrated theatrical skills enabling him to play on the fact that, though Mzeina tradition is marginal to everyday life, it still defines the identity of each tribes- person. Like the "otherness" (allos) of allegories, the Fool conjoined in himself the Mzeini Self and the occupier's Other. When he chose at the spur of an angry moment to rise up and participate in the discussion, he changed the abrupt openendedness of the argument by recapitulating its major themes. Gifted with a dramatic power to persuade, Shgētef presented a summation of the argument by improvising on traditional tribal themes, poetically "adjusting" them to the present (cf. Lavie 1986, 1989, 1990).

I also recorded traditional stories and poems about Fools. This made me realize that the life of the Fool as storyteller, caught up in the present, extends beyond the lifespan of Fools as real people in real time: the Fool was both person and allegorical persona. So what in the social context allows the Fool-as-person to first move into his allegorical persona; then to communicate not only a message about himself as a particular type, but a further message about the historical context of Mzeina nomadic structure and cultural action; and then, to leave his allegorical persona and return to being a person?

Caught in the midst of what Harold Garfinkel termed "familiar scenes" (1967:35–36), Mzeini conversations gradually drifted from talking about matters of everyday life into argument. Regarding themselves as people with collective history and identity, and not only as individuals under military occupation, the factious men tried to locate both their structural and experiential essences entitling them to exist in this world as members of a Bedouin tribe (cf. Levi-Strauss 1967:271; Husserl 1962:48). But they could not succeed in discovering their tribal essence because it was nothing but something to yearn for and argue about in allegories, which can be seen therefore not as practices of tribal "archaic survival, but . . . [as] an ongoing process, politically contested and historically unfinished . . . [where] identity is conjunctural, not essential" (Clifford 1988:9, 11).

But while the men were reflecting about themselves in these essentialist terms, their routine typifications of reality became temporarily inconsistent, anomalous, and contradictory (cf. Grathoff 1970:58–61). Imbued with liminal qualities, the paradoxes immanent both in the position of the Mzeina vis-à-vis the modern world, and in the position of the Fool vis-à-vis the Mzeina, gradually surfaced. The paradoxes then penetrated both the context and the text of the men's dialogue until they were struck by their powerlessness in defining their own situation (McHugh 1968:45, 52).

At that very moment Shgētef, the person, rose up and temporarily fused himself with the persona of the Fool. Entering into the inconsistent social situation with the unintelligible shout, "Ho," and followed by his allegorized experience, this person-persona reconstructed the thematic meaning of the social context (cf. Grathoff 1970:122–130; Handelman 1981, 1986; Handelman and Kapferer 1980). The Fool was able to eliminate the previous open-ended discontinuity by transmuting the paradoxes intrinsic into the taken-for-granted, precarious realities of both the Mzeina and his pious "merchant of sins" position. Through the interplay of images, evoked by allegory of temporary make-believe linked to the immortality of the "once upon a time" textual tradition, he transcended them.

Raising up and shouting his "Ho," the temporaneous Fool transformed the men. From men acting out their familiar evening scene, they became partakers in the imposed, non-negotiable frame of the Fool's ritual/play (Handelman 1977). But in yelling out his "Ho," Shgētef was himself transformed. He constructed his ritual/play in accordance with an unambiguous notion of himself as Fool, not as a savvy entrepreneur. While the social selves (Mead 1962:140) of the men became irrelevant during the allegorical solo performance of Shgētef-the-Fool *the persona*, they were involved in the telling and interpreting of the experiences of Shgētef *the person* (Quilligan 1979:226). Hence, during the performance, every phrase was acknowledged by "expletives signaling that the images created [were] not simply understood, but [were] enhancing the listener's appreciation of the story" (Basso 1984).

In retrospect, Shgētef's frustrating experience of wheeling and dealing with the tourists became an allegory. And only then and there was he able to exert the charisma of the *traditional* Fool. The *person-Shgētef*, on the other hand, palpably expressed *the* identity of these men, one they opaquely sensed in themselves even before he artistically intruded into their familiar scene as a *persona-Fool*. Applauded by the men, the persona-Fool completed its literary mission. At that time, when someone in the audience recapitulated the story's main point, careful to emphasize that it was just a story, the audience gracefully re-transformed the Fool back to being a person. After a short pause, a fresh, businesslike conversation developed, leaving only the anthropologist baffled by its lack of all connection to the previous discourse.

Northrop Frye has argued that allegory *is* interpretation, "an attaching of ideas to the structure of poetic imagery" (1967:89–90). Jameson (1986) would add that the interplay of allegorical images affects both poetics and politics. In the Mzeina case, this interplay thus conjoins new experiences attached to the traditional structure of tribal poetics with global ideas affecting the old yet liminal political leaders of the tribe. Mzeini allegories are therefore "successful as allegory only to the extent that [they] can suggest the authenticity with which the two coordinating poles," the poetic and political, "bespeak each other" (Fineman 1981:83). The Mzeina are able to construct their identity as an "ideal type" (Weber 1949) of a Bedouin tribe through allegorical transcendence. In their stories regular people like Shgētef temporarily fuse themselves with the personae from the folkloric pantheon of tribal charismatic characters like the Fool to authentically perform allegories of mundane experience. They are at once living persons and traditional personae, residing in that peculiar limbo where the fantastic and the real coincide.

VII

al-Billij, Christmas Night, 1985

SUBHI [still in Hebrew]:
Remember Mansūr? He is in Switzerland. His girlfriend, Ursula, took him there. He can't leave because he still doesn't have a Swiss passport. So Ursula, who's now his wife, came here with a big pack of money to give to his father. But his father would not touch it. "Give me back my son," he said.

And remember Hamd? He married his Dutch girlfriend, Lizzy. She has converted to Islam. She even veils. They live in Nuwēbᶜa and have a business where they take tourists on camelback all over the place. But they don't live with the Bedouin. They don't live with the Egyptians either. They live in the middle of the road between the two.

And Rubhi? Remember him? Last week he and Ruth left for Florida. Her father bought plane tickets for them and their three children. She couldn't take it any more. The Egyptians treat all these foreign women who fall in love with us and marry us as prostitutes, and the policemen gave her a lot of grief.

And you wouldn't believe it! Mūsa, who used to call himself Mike, and started all this Beat-meets-Bedouin brouhaha—he shaved off his long hair and beard, traded his jeans for some beautiful Saudi caftans, sold his café to Shgētef, and married his own cousin, the Fool's daughter. Next year, they plan to hajj to Mecca together. When the Israelis ran the show, we tried hard to be Egyptian-style Muslims. But now, under the Egyptians, the old folks are into Saudi-style Islam,[5] and me and my buddies are goofing around with Christmas. But Mike and Shgētef are on their way to Mecca—who would have believed that?

ACKNOWLEDGMENTS

This article is based on thirty months of fieldwork carried out between October 1975 and August 1979 in the South Sinai Peninsula, and four additional shorter trips made in 1981, 1985, 1987, and 1988. The research was funded by a grant from the Ford Foundation, given to me through the Desert Research Institute in Sde Bokker, Israel, and by the Lowie fund and the Humanities Fellowship of the University of California, Berkeley. I would also like to acknowledge the Mabel McLeod Lewis Fund and the Hebrew Free Loan Association for their support during the write-up stage. Some of the materials discussed in this article have appeared elsewhere (Lavie 1984, 1989). They all appear in my book (1990). Saad Sowayan ably assisted me in translating from Bedouin Arabic into English the poem appearing in this text. Helene Knox, with her poetic gifts, helped me hone the raw poetry translation and restore to the English some of the music inevitably lost in the accurate literary translation. I also wish to thank Gerald Berreman, Stanley Brandes, Grace Buzaljco, James Clifford, Elizabeth Colson, Stephen Greenblatt, Don Handelman, Fredric Huxley, Abdul JanMohamed, Fred Kennamer, Ira Lapidus, Emanuel Marx, Forest Rouse, William Shack, and Paul Stoller for their time and many good suggestions.

NOTES

1. Generally I describe the hippies as naked, as distinguished from nude, since "nude" connotes asexuality; the tourists' shedding of clothes on the South Sinai beaches had definite sexual overtones.
2. The unresolved contradictions built into the composition of fools or tricksters are discussed in Charles (1945), Cox (1970), Crumrine (1969), Fellini (1976), Handelman (1981, 1987), Klapp (1949), Makarius (1970), Parsons and Beals (1934), Radin (1956), Stevens (1980), Werbner (1986), Willeford (1969), and Zucker (1969).
3. The reader familiar with purdah cultures—of which the Arab World is one example—may wonder why I, as a woman, appear here and throughout the paper in contexts which are primarily male. Because the South Sinai Bedouin have long been accustomed to the influx of tourists, developers, soldiers, and other Westerners, both male and female, it was not difficult to develop strong nonsexual friendships with Mzeini men. Both Mzeini men and women poked fun at my facility in moving between the genders, saying, "Smadar has the body (*jism*) and soul (*nafs*) of a woman and the logical mind (ᶜagl) of a man." They explained that I could churn yoghurt and play the flute, as well as gallop on camels and talk foreign currency rates. My time in the field was divided equally between the daily and ritual spheres of men and women. Both employed me as a go-between in romantic trysts. This would suggest that, despite my transgender mobility, I nonetheless enjoyed the trust of both.

   In retrospect, the only person to suffer from these circumstances was myself. After four years of genderless identity, my first four years in the field, it was a real struggle to regain a distinct sense of womanhood.

   Interestingly, Amal Rassam [Vinogradov] (1974), who studied the Ait Ndhir tribe of Morocco, also mentions that the men "graciously put up with [her] female presence in their *jama*ᶜas," or official gathering places (v). This despite the fact that the tribe she studied did not live in the surreal context forced upon the Mzeina, on which I elaborate in subsequent pages.
4. In the field of literary criticism, allegory is defined as a story of the present which at the same time reflects the stories of some mythical or occult past, flowing into an eternal future (De Man, 1969, 1979, 1981; Fineman, 1981; Fletcher, 1964; Greenblatt, 1981; Quilligan, 1979; Todorov, 1970; Wimsatt, 1970). It thus "heals the gap between the present and a disappearing past, which without interpretation, would be otherwise irretrievable and foreclosed" (Fineman 1981:29). Nonetheless, allegory can dance between these pasts and presents by "renouncing the nostalgia and the desire to coincide . . . establish[ing] its language in the void of this temporal difference" (De Man, 1969:191).
5. Official Islam, both in Egypt and in Saudi Arabia, is influenced by government concerns. During the

last years of the Israeli occupation (1975–1982), many old Mzeinis listened to radio programs broadcast by the al-Azhar Academy in Cairo, perhaps as a quiet protest against their scantily-clad Jewish occupiers. When it became clear to the Mzeinis that Egypt was going to be just another occupier, they switched stations and listened to Saudi religious radio broadcasts by Sheikh Bin Baz.

REFERENCES

Basso, Ellen B.
   1984   "Monological Understanding in Dialogic Discourse." Presented at the Annual Meeting of the American Anthropological Association.
Benjamin, Walter
   1985 [1963]   "Allegory and Trauerspiel." In *The Origin of German Tragic Drama*, Pp. 159–235. Translated by J. Osborne. London: Verso.
Charles, Lucille Hoerr
   1945   "The Clown's Function." *Journal of American Folklore* 58:25–34.
Clifford, James
   1988   *The Predicament of Culture: Twentieth-Century Ethnography, Literature, and Art*. Cambridge, MA: Harvard UP.
Cox, Harvey
   1970   *The Feast of Fools: A Theological Essay on Festivity and Fantasy*. New York: Harper and Row.
Crumrine, N. Ross
   1969   "Capakoba, the Mayo Easter Ceremonial Impersonator: Explanations of Ritual Clowning." *Journal of Scientific Study of Religion* 8:1–22.
De Man, Paul
   1969   "The Rhetoric of Temporality." In *Interpretation: Theory and Practice*. C. C. Singleton, ed. Pp. 173–210. Baltimore, MD: Johns Hopkins UP.
   1979   *Allegories of Reading: Figural Language in Rousseau, Nietzsche, Rilke, and Proust*. New Haven, CT: Yale UP.
   1981   "Pascal's Allegory of Persuasion." In *Allegory and Representation*. S. J. Greenblatt, ed. Pp. 1–25. Baltimore, MD: Johns Hopkins UP.
Fellini, Federico
   1976   "Why Clowns?" In *Fellini on Fellini*. Pp. 115–139. New York: Delacorte Press.
Fineman, Joel
   1981   "The Structure of Allegorical Desire." In *Allegory and Representation*. S. J. Greenblatt, ed. Pp. 26–60. Baltimore, MD: Johns Hopkins UP.
Fletcher, Angus
   1964   *Allegory: The Theory of a Symbolic Mode*. Ithaca, NY: Cornell UP.
Frye, Northrop
   1967   *Anatomy of Criticism: Four Essays*. New York: Atheneum.
Garfinkel, Harold
   1967   *Studies in Ethnomethodology*. Englewood Cliffs, NJ: Prentice-Hall.
Grathoff, Richard
   1970   The Structure of Social Inconsistencies: A Contribution to a Unified Theory of Play, Game, and Social Action. The Hague: Martinus Nijhoff.
Greenblatt, Stephen J., ed.
   1981   "Preface." In *Allegory and Representation*. Pp. vii–xiii. Baltimore, MD: Johns Hopkins UP.
Handelman, Don
   1977   "Play and Ritual: Complementary Frames of Metacommunication." In *It's a Funny Thing, Humor*. A. J. Cahpman and H. Foot, eds. Pp. 186–192. Oxford: Pergamon Press.
   1981   "The Ritual Clown: Attributes and Affinities." *Anthropos* 76(1/2):321–370.
   1986   "Charisma, Liminality, and Symbolic Types." In *Comparative Social Dynamics: Essays in Honor of S. N. Eisenstadt*. E. Cohen, M. Lissak and U. Almagor, eds. Pp. 346–359. Boulder: Westview Press.

1987 "Clowns." In *The Encyclopedia of Religion*. M. Eliade, ed. in chief. 3(547–551). New York: MacMillan.

Handelman, Don, and Bruce Kapferer
1980 "Symbolic Types, Mediation, and the Transformation of Ritual Context: Sinhalese Demons and Tewa Clowns." *Semiotica* 30(1/2):41–71.

Husserl, Edmund
1962 [1931] *Ideas: General Introduction to Pure Phenomenology*. Translated by W. C. Boyce Gibson. New York: Collier Books.

Jameson, Fredric
1981 *The Political Unconscious: Narrative as a Socially Symbolic Act*. Ithaca, NY: Cornell UP.
1986 "Third-World Literature in the Era of Multinational Capitalism." *Social Text* 15:65–88.

JanMohamed, Abdul M.
1985 "The Economy of Manichean Allegory: The Function of Racial Difference in Colonialist Literature." *Critical Inquiry* 12(1):59–87.

Klapp, Orrin E.
1949 "The Fool as a Social Type." *American Journal of Sociology* 55(2):157–162.

Lavie, Smadar
1984 The Fool and The Hippies: Ritual/Play and Social Inconsistencies Among the Mzeina Bedouin of the Sinai." In *The Masks of Play*. B. Sutton-Smith and D. Kelly-Byrne, eds. Pp. 63–70. New York: Leisure Press.
1986 "The Poetics of Politics: An Allegory of Bedouin Identity." In *Political Anthropology, Vol. 5: The Frailty of Authority*. M. J. Aronoff, ed. Pp. 131–146. New Brunswick, NJ: Transaction Books.
1989 "When Leadership Becomes Allegory: Mzeina Sheikhs and the Experience of Military Occupation." *Cultural Anthropology* 4(2):99–135.
1990 *The Poetics of Military Occupation: Mzeina Allegories of Bedouin Identity Under Israeli and Egyptian Rule*. Berkeley: University of California Press.

Lavie, Smadar, and William C. Young
1984 "Bedouin in Limbo: Egyptian and Israeli Development Policies in the Southern Sinai." *Antipode* 16(2):33–44.

Levi-Strauss, Claude
1967 *Structural Anthropology*. Garden City, NY: Anchor.

Makarius, Laura
1970 "Ritual Clowns and Symbolical Behavior." *Diogenes* 69:44–73.

Marx, Emanuel
1977 "Communal and Individual Pilgrimage: The Region of Saints' Tombs in the South Sinai." In *Regional Cults*. R. P. Werbner, ed. Pp. 29–51. London: Academic Press.
1980 "Wage Labor and Tribal Economy of the Bedouin in South Sinai." In *When Nomads Settle: Processes of Sedentarization as Adaptation and Response*. P. C. Salzman, ed. Pp. 111–123. New York: Praeger.

McHugh, Peter
1968 *Defining the Situation: The Organization of Meaning in Social Interaction*. New York: Bobbs-Merrill.

Mead, George H.
1962 *Mind, Self, and Society*. Chicago: Chicago UP.

Parsons, Elsie Clews, and Ralph L. Beals
1934 "The Sacred Clowns of the Pueblo and Mayo-Yaqui Indians." *American Anthropologist* 36: 491–514.

Quilligan, Maureen
1979 "The Language of Allegory: Defining the Genre. Ithaca, NY: Cornell UP.

Rabinowitz, Dan
1985 "Themes in the Economy of the Bedouin of South Sinai in the Nineteenth and Twentieth Centuries." *International Journal of Middle East Studies* 17(1):211–228.

Radin, Paul
1956 *The Trickster: A Study in American Indian Mythology*. London: Routledge and Kegan Paul.

Rassam [Vinogradov] Amal
1974 "The Ait Ndhir of Morocco: A Study of the Social Transformation of a Berber Tribe." Anthro-

pological Papers. Museum of Anthropology, University of Michigan, No. 55. Ann Arbor, MI: University of Michigan Press.

Said, Edward
1978   *Orientalism*. New York: Random House.

Shakespeare, William
1958   *King Lear*. Baltimore: Penguin Books.

Stevens, Jr., Philip
1980   "The Bachama Trickster as Model for Clowning Behavior." *Rice University Studies* 66(1):137–150.

Todorov, Tzvetan
1975   *The Fantastic: A Structural Approach to a Literary Genre*. Ithaca, NY: Cornell UP.

Turner, Victor W.
1969   *The Ritual Process: Structure and Anti-Structure*. Chicago: Aldine.

Weber, Max
1949   "The Ideal Type and Generalized Analytical Theory." In *The Structure of Social Action*. T. Parsons, ed. Pp. 601–610. Glencoe, IL: Free Press.

Werbner, Pnina
1986   "The Virgin and the Clown: Ritual Elaboration in Pakistani Migrant's Weddings." *Man* 21(2):227–250.

Willeford, William
1969   *The Fool and His Sceptre*. London: Edward Arnold.

Wimsatt, James I.
1970   *Allegory and Mirror: Tradition and Structure in Middle English Literature*. New York: Pegasus.

Zucker, Wolfgang M.
1969   "The Clown as the Lord of Disorder." In *Holy Laughter*. M. C. Hyers, ed. Pp. 75–88. New York: Seabury.

Gender and Culture of Empire: Toward a Feminist Ethnography of the Cinema

Ella Shohat

Although recent feminist film theory has acknowledged the issue of differences among women, there has been little attempt to explore and problematize the implications of these differences for the representation of gender relations within racially and culturally non-homogeneous textual environments.[1] While implicitly universalizing "womanhood," and without questioning the undergirding racial and national boundaries of its discourse, feminist film theory, for the most part, has not articulated its generally insightful analyses vis-a-vis the contradictions and assymetries provoked by (post)colonial arrangements of power. This elision is especially striking since the beginnings of cinema coincided with the height of imperialism between the late 19th century and World War I. Western cinema not only inherited and disseminated colonial discourse, but also created a system of domination through monopolistic control of film distribution and exhibition in much of Asia, Africa, and Latin America. The critique of colonialism within cinema studies, meanwhile, has tended to downplay the significance of gender issues, thus eliding the fact that (post)colonial discourse has impinged differently on the representation of men and women. It is between these two major theoretical frameworks that my essay is situated, attempting to synthesize feminist and postcolonial cultural critiques.

In this essay I explore Western cinema's geographical and historical constructs as symptomatic of the colonialist imaginary generally but also more specifically as a product of a gendered Western gaze, an imbrication reflective of the symbiotic relations between patriarchal and colonial articulations of difference. I emphasize the role of sexual difference in the construction of a number of superimposed oppositions—West/East, North/South—not only on a narratological level but also on the level of the implicit structuring metaphors undergirding colonial discourse. While referring to some resistant counter-narratives, I also examine the structural analogies in the colonialist positioning of different regions, particularly in sexual terms, showing the extent to which Western representation of otherized territories serves diacritically to define the "West" itself.

ELLA SHOHAT *teaches cinema and cultural studies at the City University of New York, and is the coordinator of the Cinema Studies program at the College of Staten Island/CUNY. She is a member of the Social Text Editorial Collective and is the author of* Israeli Cinema: East/West and the Politics of Representation. *Forthcoming from Routledge is* Unthinking Eurocentrism (with Robert Stam).

A) GENDERED METAPHORS

Virgins, Adams, and the Prospero Complex

An examination of colonial discourse reveals the crucial role of gendered metaphors in constructing the colonial "subaltern." Europe's "civilizing mission" in the Third World is projected as interweaving opposing yet linked narratives of Western penetration into inviting virginal landscape[2] *and* resisting libidinal nature. The early exaltation of the New World paradise, suggested for example by Sir Walter Raleigh's report—". . . a country that hath yet her mayden head, never sakt, turned, nor wrought"[3]—and by Crèvecoeur's letters—"Here nature opens her broad lap to receive the perpetual accession of new comers, and to supply them with food"[4]—gradually centered around the idealized figure of the pioneer. Linked to nineteenth century westward expansionism, the garden symbol embraced metaphors related to growth, increase, cultivation, and blissful agricultural labor.[5] At the same time, the discourse of Empire suggests that "primitive" landscapes (deserts, jungles) are tamed; "shrew" peoples (Native Americans, Africans, Arabs) are domesticated; and the desert is made to bloom, all thanks to the infusion of Western dynamism and enlightenment. Within this Promethean master-narrative, subliminally gendered tropes such as "conquering the desolation," and "fecundating the wilderness," acquire heroic resonances of Western fertilization of barren lands. The metaphoric portrayal of the (non-European) land as a "virgin" coyly awaiting the touch of the colonizer implied that whole continents—Africa, America, Asia, and Australia—could only benefit from the emanation of colonial praxis. The revivification of a wasted soil evokes a quasi-divine process of endowing life and meaning ex nihilo, of bringing order from chaos, plenitude from lack. Indeed, the West's *Prospero complex* is premised on an East/South portrayed as a Prospero's isle, seen as the site of superimposed lacks calling for Western transformation of primeval matter. The engendering of "civilization," then, is clearly phallo-centric, not unlike the mythical woman's birth from Adam's Rib.[6]

The American hero, as R. W. B. Lewis points out, has been celebrated as prelapsarian Adam, as a New Man emancipated from history (i.e., European history) before whom all the world and time lay available.[7] The American Adam archetype implied not only his status as a kind of creator, blessed with the divine prerogative of naming the elements of the scene about him, but also his fundamental innocence. Here colonial and patriarchal discourses are clearly interwoven. The Biblical narration of Genesis recounts the creation of the World; the creation of Adam from earth (*adama* in Hebrew) in order for man to rule over nature. The power of creation is inextricably linked to the power of naming—God lends his naming authority to Adam as mark of his rule, and the woman is "called Woman because she was taken out of man." The question of naming played an important role not only in gender mythology but also in colonial narratives in which the "discoverer" gave names as a mark of possession ("America" as celebrating Amerigo Vespucci) or as bearers of a European global perspective ("Middle East," "Far East"). "Peripheral" places and their inhabitants were often stripped of their "unpronounceable" indigenous names and outfitted with names marking them as the property of the colonizer. The colonial explorer as depicted in *Robinson Crusoe* creates, demiurge-like, a whole civilization and has the power of naming "his" Islander "Friday," for he "saves" his life on that day; and Friday, we recall, is the day God created Adam, thus further strengthening the analogy between the "self-sufficient" Crusoe and God (Figure 1).

The notion of an American Adam elided a number of crucial facts, notably that there were other civilizations in the New World; that the settlers were not creating "being from nothingness"; and that the settlers had scarcely jettisoned all their Old World cultural baggage, their deeply ingrained attitudes and discourses. Here the notion of "virginity," present for example in the etymology of Virginia, must be seen in diacritical relation to the metaphor of the (European) "motherland." A "virgin" land is implicitly available for defloration and fecundation. Implied to lack owners, it therefore becomes the property of its "discoverers" and cultivators. The "purity" of the terminology masks the dispossession of the land and its resources. A land already fecund, already producing for the indigenous peoples, and thus a "mother," is metaphorically projected as virgin, "untouched nature," and therefore as available and awaiting a master. Colonial gendered metaphors are visibly rendered in Jan Van der Straet's pictorial representation of the discovery of America, focussing on the mythical figure of Amerigo Vespucci, shown as bearing Europe's emblems of meaning (cross, armor, compass).[8] Behind him we see the vessels which will bring back to the Occident the treasures of the New World Paradise. In front of him we see a welcoming naked woman, the Indian American. If she is an harmonious exten-

Figure 1. Adventures of Robinson Crusoe *(1954): The Promethean master-narrative.*

sion of nature, he represents its scientific mastery.[9] Here the conqueror, as Michel de Certeau puts it, "will write the body of the other and inscribe upon it his own history."[10]

In Nelson Pereira dos Santos' *How Tasty Was My Frenchman* (*Como Era Gostoso Meu Françes*, 1970), the patriarchal discourse on the encounter between Europeans and Native Americans is subverted.[11] Partly based on a diary written by the German adventurer, Hans Staden, the film concerns a Frenchman who is captured by the Tupinamba tribe and sentenced to death in response to previous massacres inflicted by Europeans upon them. Before his ritualized execution and cannibalization, however, he is given a wife, Sebiopepe (a widow of one of the Tupinamba massacred by the Europeans) and he is allowed to participate in the tribe's daily activities.[12] In the last shot, the camera zooms into Sebiopepe's face as she is emotionlessly devouring her Frenchman, despite the fact that she has developed a close relationship with him. This final image is followed by a citation from a report on Native American genocide by Europeans, which undermines the possibly disturbing nature of the last shot.[13] If pictorial representations of the "discovery" tend to center on a nude Native American woman as metaphorizing the welcoming "new-found-land," in *How Tasty Was My Frenchman* the Native American woman is far from being an object of European discourse. Presented as linked to her communal culture and history, she herself becomes part of history. Her nudity is not contrasted with the discoverer's heavy clothing; rather, she is part of an environment where nudity is not a category. The fact that the film employs largely longshots in which characters appear nude in the performance of their banal daily activities undermines voyeurism and stands in contrast to the fetishistic Hollywood mode that tends to fragment the (female) body in close shots.[14] In her interaction with the Frenchman, Sebiopepe represents, above all, the voice of the Native American counter narrative.[15] In one scene, for example, a myth of origins prefigures the symbolic revolt of the Tupinamba. Sebiopepe begins to narrate in Tupi a Tupinamba Promethean myth concerning the God, Mair, who brought them knowledge. The Frenchman, at one point, takes over the narration and, in French, further recounts the deeds of the God, while we see him performing the divine deeds. The Whitening of the Tupinamba God on the image track evokes the Promethean colonial discourse concerning the redemption of the Natives, but here that discourse is relativized, especially since the Native American woman ends the myth in Tupi, recounting the rebellion of the people against the God, while the image track shows the destruction of the Frenchman's work. Her voice, then, recounts the tale of the people who revolted, undercutting the masculinist myth of availability, submissiveness, and redemption (Figure 2).

Graphological Tropes

The inclination to project the non-Occident as feminine is seen even in the nineteenth century Romantic depiction of the ancient Orient of Babylonia and Egypt, reproduced in films such as D. W. Griffith's *Intolerance* (1916) and Cecil B. DeMille's *Cleopatra* (1934) (Figure 3). In *Intolerance* Babylon signifies sexual excess, building on the Book of Revelation as "Babylon, the Great, the Mother of Harlots and of the

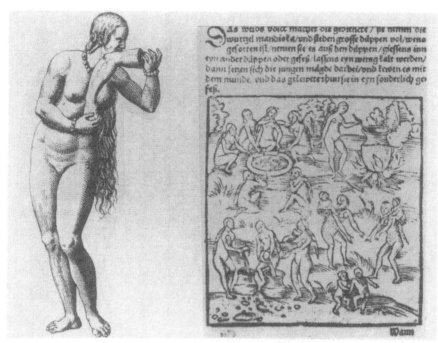

Figure 2. How Tasty Was My Frenchman *(1970): Counter narrative to the "Discovery."*

Abominations of the Earth." DeMille's *Cleopatra* explicitly expresses this view by having the sexually manipulative Cleopatra addressed as Egypt[16] and by presenting the Orient as exclusively the scene of carnal delights. The ultimate subordination of the woman Cleopatra and her country Egypt is not without contemporary colonial overtones, suggested for example in the Anglo-aristocratic "Roman" court where sarcastic jokes are made at the expense of a presumably Black Cleopatra, asserting that Rome could never be turned into the Orient, or ruled by an Egyptian. (The historically dark Cleopatra is turned by Hollywood conventions of Beauty into a European looking White woman, just as the iconography of Christ has gradually de-Semitized him.)[17] The visual infatuation with Babylon and Egypt's material abundance emphasized through a mise-en-scene of monumental architecture, domestic detail, and quasi-pornographic feasts, cannot be divorced from the intertext of colonial travel literature whose reports also obsessively recounted the details of Oriental sensual excesses (Figure 4).

Cinema, in this sense, enacted a historiographical and anthropological role, writing (in-light) the cultures of others. The early films' penchant for graphological signifiers such as hieroglyphs (in the different versions of *Cleopatra*), Hebrew script (*Intolerance*), or the image of an open book as in "The Book of Intolerance" and the marginal "notes" accompanying the intertitles (which pedagogically supply the spectator with additional information) imply Hollywood as a kind of a Western popular griot. By associating itself with writing, and particularly with "original"

Figure 3.   Cleopatra *(1934): The iconography of a feminized Egypt.*

Figure 4.   Intolerance (1916): Babylon and the pornographic intertext of travel literature.

writing, early cinema lent a pedagogical, historical, and artistic aura to a medium still associated with circus-like entertainments. (It is not a coincidence, perhaps, that Siegfried Kracauer, for example, referred to films as "visible hieroglyphs.") And by linking a new apprentice art to ancient times and "exotic" places cinema celebrated its ethnographic and quasi-archaeological powers to resuscitate forgotten and distant civilizations, a celebration implicit in the construction of pseudo-Egyptian movie palaces. The "birth" of cinema itself coincided with the imperialist moment, when diverse colonized civilizations were already shaping their conflicting identities vis-a-vis their colonizers. These films about the ancient world suggest, perhaps, a Romantic nostalgia for a "pure" civilization prior to Western "contamination." They also represent a Romantic search for the lost Eastern origins of Western civilizations, analogous to Schlieman's excavations in Troy. It is within this context that we can understand the "structuring absence"—in the representation of Egypt, Babylonia, and the (Biblical) Holy Land—of the contemporary colonized Arab Orient and its nationalist struggles.[18] Through a historiographical gesture, the films define the Orient as ancient and mysterious, participating in what Jacques Derrida in another context calls the "hieroglyphist prejudice." The cinematic Orient, then, is best epitomized by an iconography of Papyruses, Sphinxes, and Mummies, whose existence and revival depend on the "look" and "reading" of the Westerner. This rescue of the past, in other words, suppresses the voice of the present and thus legitimates by default the availability of the space of the Orient for the geopolitical maneuvers of the Western powers.

The filmic mummified zone of ancient civilizations, then, is dialectically linked to the representation of the historical role of the West in the imperial age. Reproducing Western historiography, First World cinema narrates European penetration into the Third World through the figure of the "discoverer."[19] In most Western films about the colonies (such as *Bird of Paradise* (1932), *Wee Willie Winkie* (1937), *Black Narcissus* (1947), *The King and I* (1956), *Lawrence of Arabia* (1962), and even Buñuel's *Adventures of Robinson Crusoe* (1954) we accompany, quite literally, the explorer's perspective. A simple shift in focalization to that of the "natives," as occurs in the Australian-Aboriginal *Nice Coloured Girls* (1987)[20] or in the Brazilian *How Tasty Was My French-man* where the camera is placed on land with the "natives" rather than on ship with the Europeans, reveals the illusory and intrusive nature of the "discovery." More usually, however, heroic status is attributed to the voyager (often a male scientist) come to master a new land and its treasures, the value of which the "primitive" residents had been unaware.[21] It is this construction of consciousness of "value" as a pretext for (capitalist) ownership which legitimizes the colonizer's act of appropriation. The "discovery," furthermore, has gender overtones.[22] In this exploratory adventure, seen in such films as *Lawrence of Arabia* and the *Indiana Jones* series, the camera relays the hero's dynamic movement across a passive, static space, gradually stripping the land of its "enigma," as the spectator wins visual access to Oriental treasures through the eyes of the explorer-protagonist. *Lawrence of Arabia* provides an example of Western historical representation whereby the individual Romantic "genius" leads the Arab national revolt, presumed to be a passive entity awaiting T. E. Lawrence's inspiration. (Arab sources obviously have challenged this historical account.)[23] The unveiling of the mysteries of an unknown space becomes a *rite de passage* allegorizing the Western achievement of virile heroic stature.

Mapping Terra Incognita

The masculinist desire of mastering a new land is deeply linked to colonial history and even to its contemporary companion, philosophy, in which epistemology partially modeled itself on geography. The traditional discourse on nature as feminine—for example Francis Bacon's idea that insofar as we learn the laws of nature through science, we become her master, as we are now, in ignorance, "her thralls"[24]—gains, within the colonial context, clear geopolitical implications. Bacon's search for expanding scientific knowledge is inseparable from the contemporaneous European geographical expansion, clearly suggested by his language of analogies and metaphors: "[A]s the immense regions of the West Indies had never been discovered, if the use of the compass had not first been known, it is no wonder that the discovery and advancement of arts hath made no greater progress, when the art of inventing and discovering of the sciences remains hitherto unknown."[25] And Bacon finds it "disgraceful," that "while the regions of the material globe . . . have been in our times laid widely open and revealed, the intellectual globe should remain shut up within the narrow limits of old discoveries."[26] Travelling into the indefiniteness of the ocean, the Faustian overreacher's voyage beyond the Pillars of

Hercules aims at the possibility of a *terra incognita* on the other side of the ocean. Studying topography, systematizing the paths, as Hans Blumenberg points out, guarantees that the accidents of things coming to light ultimately lead to a universal acquaintance with the world. "So much had remained concealed from the human spirit throughout many centuries and was discovered neither by philosophy nor by the faculty of reason but rather by accident and favorable opportunity, because it was all too different and distant from what was familiar, so that no preconception (*praenotio aliqua*) could lead one to it."[27] The logic of explorers from Robinson Crusoe to Indiana Jones is, in this sense, based on the hope that "nature" conceals in its "womb" still more, outside the familiar paths of the power of imagination (*extra vias phantasiae*). It is within this broader historical and intellectual context that we may understand the symptomatic image of penetration into a cave placed in a non-European land to discover that "Unknown," seen for example in the Rudyard Kipling-based *The Jungle Book* (1942), *Raiders of the Lost Ark* (1981), *Indiana Jones and the Temple of Doom* (1984), and the E. M. Forster-based *A Passage to India* (1984).

Colonial narratives legitimized the embarking upon treasure hunts by lending a scientific aura, encapsulated especially by images of maps and globes. Detailed descriptions of maps were probably inspired by the growing science of geography which determined the significance of places through its power of inscription on the map, with the compass on top as the signature of scientific authority. Geography, then, was microcosmically reflected in the map-based adventures which involved the drawing or deciphering of a map, and its authentication through the physical contact with the "new" land. Western cinema, from the earliest anthropological films through *Morocco* (1930) to the *Indiana Jones* series, has relied on map imagery for plotting the Empire, while simultaneously celebrating its own technological power—implicitly vis-a-vis the novel's reliance upon words or static drawings, and later still photographs—to illustrate vividly the topography. For example, venture-narrative films mark maps with moving arrows to signify the progress of the Westerner in his world-navigation, a practice characterizing even the recent *Raiders of the Lost Ark* and *Indiana Jones and the Temple of Doom*. By associating itself with the visual medium of maps, cinema represents itself scientifically, as being a twentieth-century continuation of Geography.

Films often superimposed illustrative maps on shots of landscapes, subliminally imposing the map's "claim" over the land, functioning as a legal document. *King Solomon's Mines* (1937, 1950, 1985), as Anne McClintock suggests in her discussion of Rider Haggard work, explicitly genderizes the relation between the explorer and the topography.[28] Menahem Golan's version, for example, reveals in the second shot of the film a small nude female sculpture engraved with Canaanite signs, explained by the archeologist to be a map leading to the twin mountains, the Breasts of Sheba, below which, in a cave, are hidden King Solomon's diamond mines. The camera voyeuristically tilts down on the female body/map, scrutinizing it from the excited perspective of the archeologist and the antique dealer. The road to utopia involves the deciphering of the map, of comprehending the female body; the legendary twin mountains and the cave metaphorize the desired telos of the hero's mission of plunder. The geology and topography of the land, then, is explicitly sexualized to resemble the physiology of a woman.

The recurrent image of the spinning globe, similarly, entitles the scientist to possess the world, since the globe, as the world's representation, allegorizes the relationship between creator and creation. Cinema's penchant for spinning globe logos serves to celebrate the medium's kinetic possibilities as well as its global ubiquity, allowing spectators a cheap voyage while remaining in the metropolitan "centers"—Lumières' location shootings of diverse Third World sites, such as India, Mexico, and Palestine being symptomatic of this visual national-geographics-mania. The spinning globe virtually became the trade-mark of the British Korda brothers' productions, many of whose films, such as *Sanders of the River* (1935), *The Drum* (1938), *The Four Feathers* (1939), and *The Jungle Book*, concerned colonial themes.[29] The overarching global point-of-view sutures the spectator into a God-like cosmic perspective. Incorporating images of maps and globes, the Jules Verne-based film *Around the World in 80 Days* (1956), for example, begins by its omniscient narrator hailing the "shrinking of the world" as Verne was writing the book.[30] The "shrinking" relates the perspective of upper-class British men whose scientific confidence about circling the world in eighty days is materialized, thus linking the development of science to imperialist control: "Nothing is impossible. When science finally conquers the air it may be feasible to circle the globe in eighty hours," says the David Niven character (Figure 5).

Science, knowledge, and technology can also be read allegorically as linked to imperial expansionism in the film's citation of Georges Melies's film *A Trip to the Moon* (*Le Voyage dans la Lune*, 1902) (based on Verne's *From the Earth to the Moon*, 1865) in which the "last frontier" explored is seen first in the imagistic phallic penetration of the rounded moon[31] (Figure 6). This imagination of the "last frontier," in a period when most of the world was dominated by Europe, reproduces the historical discourse of the "first frontier." The narrative is structured similarly to the colonial captivity narrative where the skeleton creatures carrying spears burst from the moon's simulacrum of a jungle but are defeated by the male explorers' umbrella-like guns which magically eliminate the savage creatures. Such a film, not in any obvious sense "about" colonialism, but one produced in a period when most of the world was dominated by Europe, can thus be read as an analogue of imperial expansion.[32] Similarly in recent films such as *Return of the Jedi* (1983) the conquest of outer space exists on a continuum with an imperial narrative in which the visualization of the planet provides the paradigm for the representation of Third World "underdevelopment" (deserts, jungles, and mountains). The Manichean relationship between the American hero and the new land and its natives involves exotic creatures, teddy-bear-like Ewoks whose language remains a mystery throughout the film, who worship the technologically well-equipped hero and who defend him against evil ugly creatures who have unclear motives. The American hero's physical and moral triumph legitimizes the destruction of the enemy, as does the paternal transformation of the friendly "elements" into servile objects, along with his assumed right to establish new outposts (and implicitly to hold on to old outposts, whether in Africa, Asia, or America).

The Dark Continent

The colonial films claim to initiate the Western spectator into an unknown culture. This is valid even for films set in "exotic" lands and ancient times which do *not*

Figure 5. Around the World in 80 Days: *Global ubiquity.*

Figure 6.   A Trip to the Moon (1902): Penetrating the "last frontier."

employ Western characters (for example, *Intolerance*,[33] *The Ten Commandments* (1923, 1956), *The Thief of Baghdad* (1924), and *Kismet* (1944), yet whose Oriental heroes/ heroines are played by Western stars. The spectator is subliminally invited on an ethnographic tour of a celluloid-"preserved" culture, which implicitly celebrates the chronotopic magical aptitude of cinema for panoramic spectacle and temporal voyeurism, evoking Andre Bazin's formulation of cinema as possessing a "mummy complex."[34] Often the spectator, identified with the gaze of the West (whether embodied by a Western male/female character or by a Western actor/actress masquerading as an Oriental), comes to master, in a remarkably telescoped period of time, the codes of a foreign culture shown, as Edward Said suggests, as simple, unselfconscious, and susceptible to facile apprehension. Any possibility of dialogic interaction and of a dialectical representation of the East/West relation is excluded from the outset. The films thus reproduce the colonialist mechanism by which the Orient, rendered as devoid of any active historical or narrative role, becomes the object of study and spectacle.[35]

The portrayal of a Third World region as undeveloped, in this same vein, is reinforced by a topographical reductionism, for example the topographical reductionism of the Orient to desert, and metaphorically, to dreariness. The desert, a frequent reference in the dialogues and a visual motif throughout the Orientalist films, is presented as the essential unchanging decor of the history of the Orient. While the Arabs in such films as *Lawrence of Arabia*, *Exodus* (1960), and the *Raiders of the Lost Ark* are associated with images of underdevelopment, the Westerner, as the antithesis of the Oriental desert, is associated with productive, creative pioneering, a masculine redeemer of the wilderness. The films reflect a culturally over-determined geographical-symbolic polarity; an East/West axis informs many films on the Oriental theme. As if in a reversion to deterministic climate theories such as those of Madame de Stael or Hippolyte Taine, the films present the East as the locus of irrational primitivism and uncontrollable instincts. The exposed, barren land and the blazing sands, furthermore, metaphorize the exposed, unrepressed "hot" passion and uncensored emotions of the Orient, in short, as the world of the out-of-control Id.

The Orient as a metaphor for sexuality is encapsulated by the recurrent figure of the veiled woman. The inaccessibility of the veiled woman, mirroring the mystery of the Orient itself, requires a process of Western unveiling for comprehension. Veiled women in Orientalist paintings, photographs, and films expose flesh, ironically, more than they conceal it.[36] It is this process of exposing the female Other, of literally denuding her, which comes to allegorize the Western masculinist power of possession, that she, as a metaphor for her land, becomes available for Western penetration and knowledge. This intersection of the epistemological and the sexual in colonial discourse echoes Freud's metaphor of the "dark continent." Freud speaks of female sexuality in metaphors of darkness and obscurity often drawn from the realms of archeology and exploration—the metaphor of the "dark continent," for example, deriving from a book by the Victorian explorer Stanley.[37] Seeing himself as explorer and discoverer of new worlds, Freud in *Studies on Hysteria* compared the role of the psychoanalyst to that of the archeologist "clearing away the pathogenic psychical material layer by layer" which is analogous "with the technique of excavating a buried city."[38] The analogy, made in the context of examining a woman patient, Fräulein Elisabeth Von R., calls attention to the role of the therapist in locating obscure trains of thought followed by penetration, as Freud puts it in the first person: "I would penetrate into deeper layers of her memories at these points carrying out an investigation under hypnosis or by the use of some similar technique."[39]

Speaking generally of "penetrating deeply" into the "neurosis of women" thanks to a science which can give a "deeper and more coherent" insight into femininity,[40] Freud is perhaps unaware of the political overtones of his optical metaphor. Penetration, as Toril Moi suggests, is very much on Freud's mind as he approaches femininity,[41] including, one might add, the "dark continent of female sexuality." The notion of the necessary unveiling of the unconscious requires an obscure object in order to sustain the very desire to explore, penetrate, and master. David Macey's suggestion that psychoanalysis posits femininity as being in excess of its rationalist discourse, and then complains that it cannot explain it,[42] is equally applicable to the positing of the Other in colonial discourse. Furthermore, Freud uses the language of force; for example, "we force our way into the internal strata, overcoming resistances at all times."[43] Looking at the Eastern roots of civilizations, Freud employs ancient myths and figures such as the Sphinx and Oedipus to draw parallels between the development of the civilization and that of the psyche.

(Although Freud did not speculate at any great length on Egyptian mythology, over half of his private collection of antiquities reportedly consisted of ancient Egyptian sculptures and artifacts.)[44] The psychoanalyst who heals from the suppressed past (most of Freud's studies of hysteria were conducted in relation to women) resembles the archeologist who recovers the hidden past of civilization (most of which was "found" in Third world lands). As in archeology, Freud's epistemology assumes the (white) male as the bearer of knowledge, who can penetrate woman and text, while she, as a remote region, will let herself be explored till truth is uncovered.

The interweaving of archeology and psychoanalysis touches on a nineteenth-century motif in which the voyage into the origins of the Orient becomes a voyage into the interior colonies of the "self." ("Un voyage en Orient [était] comme un grand acte de ma vie intérieure," Lamartine wrote.)[45] The origins of archeology, the search for the "roots of civilization" as a discipline are, we know, inextricably linked to imperial expansionism. In the cinema, the *Indiana Jones* series reproduces exactly this colonial vision in which Western "knowledge" of ancient civilizations "rescues" the past from oblivion. It is this masculinist rescue in *Raiders of the Lost Ark* that legitimizes denuding the Egyptians of their heritage, confining it within Western metropolitan museums—an ideology implicit as well in the Orientalist *Intolerance*, *Cleopatra*, and the *Mummy* series. (These films, not surprisingly, tend to be programmed in museums featuring Egyptological exhibitions.) [Figure 7] *Raiders of the Lost Ark*, symptomatically, assumes a disjuncture between contemporary and

Figure 7.   The Mummy (1932): *Western Knowledge rescues the ancient Egyptian past from oblivion.*

ancient Egypt, since the space between the present and the past can "only" be bridged by the scientist. The full significance of the ancient archeological objects within the Eurocentric vision of the Spielberg film is presumed to be understood only by the Western scientists, relegating the Egyptian people to the role of ignorant Arabs who happen to be sitting on a land full of historical treasures—much as they happen to "sit" on oil. Set in the mid-thirties when most of the world was still under colonial rule, the film regards the colonial presence in Egypt, furthermore, as completely natural, eliding a history of Arab nationalist revolts against foreign domination.

The American hero—often cinematically portrayed as a Cowboy—is an archeologist implicitly searching for the Eastern roots of Western civilization. He liberates the ancient Hebrew ark from illegal Egyptian possession, while also rescuing it from immoral Nazi control, subliminally reinforcing American and Jewish solidarity vis-a-vis the Nazis and their Arab assistants.[46] The geopolitical alignments here are as clear as in the inadvertent allegory of *The Ten Commandments*, where a WASPish Charlton Heston is made to incarnate Hebrew Moses struggling against the Egyptians, thus allegorizing in the context of the fifties the contemporary struggle of the West (Israel and the U.S.) against Egyptians/Arabs.[47] That at the end of *Raiders of the Lost Ark* it is the American Army which guards the "top secret" ark—with the active complicity of the ark itself—strengthens this evocation of geopolitical alliances.[48] *Raiders of the Lost Ark* significantly develops parallel linked plots in which the female protagonist, Marion, and the ark become the twin objects of the hero's search for harmony. The necklace which leads to the ark is first associated with Marion who becomes herself the object of competing nationalist male desires. She is abducted by the Nazis and their Arab assistants much as the ark is hijacked by them, followed by Dr. Jones's rescue of Marion and the ark from the Nazis. The telos of the voyage into unknown regions—whether mental or geographical—then, is that the Westerner both knows the Orient (in the epistemological and Biblical senses) and at the same time brings it knowledge, rescuing it from its own obscurantism.

Egyptology and *The Mummy*

A different perspective on these issues is suggested in the Egyptian film *The Mummy/The Night of Counting the Years* (Al Mumia, 1969).[49] Based on the actual case of the discovery of Pharaonic tombs in the Valley of the Kings in 1881, a year before the full British colonization of Egypt, the film opens with the French Egyptologist, Gaston Maspero, informing his colleagues about the black market trade in antiquities coming from the reigns of Pharaohs such as Ahmose,[50] Thutmose III,[51] and Rameses II.[52] The government's archeological commission, under Maspero, delegates an expedition, headed by a young Egyptian archeologist, to investigate the location of the tombs in Thebes in order to end the thefts. In Thebes, meanwhile, the headman of the Upper Egyptian Horobbat tribe, which had been living off extracting artifacts from the pharaonic tombs, has just died, and his brother must initiate his two nephews into the secret of the mountain. Still in grief over their father's death, the sons are repelled by the dissection of the mummy merely to get at a gold necklace depicting the sacred "Eye of Horus." The protesting brothers must choose between two betrayals, both of them grave: the vulture-like lootings of ancient kingdoms and the desecration of their mummies, or the betrayal of their father's secret with the consequence of cutting off their source of income and therefore their ability to feed hungry Horobbat mouths. Any revelation of the secret would mean ultimately destroying their family and tribe in the name of respect for "the dead" now viewed by the elders as nothing more than leathery mummies. The older brother is assassinated by the village elders when he refuses to sell the artifact on the black market, while the younger brother, Wannis, is torn between his guilt over owing his life to ancient Egyptian corpses ("How many bodies did my father violate in order to feed us?" he asks his mother) and the condemnation of his people. Wandering through the ruins of Thebes and Karnak—for him not simply a momento of an older civilization, but the very living reminder of his childhood playground—the long-take swirling camera movements reflect his ethical and even epistemological vertigo, his conflicting internalized responsibility for his Egyptian heritage vis-a-vis his immediate responsibility for present-day lives. After being reassured that the "effendi archeologists" are trying to understand Egypt's past and not plunder it, he reveals the secret knowledge to Maspero's assistant. The expedition, before the village can prevent it, empties the graves, and carries out the mummy-coffins, destined for the museum (Figure 8).

   The Mummy/The Night of Counting the Years is set in the late nineteenth-century, at the height of imperial Egyptology. By the time Britain occupied Egypt in 1882, the country was bankrupt of its archeological treasures which were exhibited in London and Paris as testimony of Western scientific progress. In the heroic, almost sanctimonious, language of the Egyptological mission, archeological reports on the 1881 discovery describe their rescue of the ancient East's powerful kings from Arab clans in a way which associates the Westerner with emperors and royal dynasties. The simplistic positing of a rupture between present and past Egypt conveniently empowers the Western claim over Egypt's past,[53] thus naturalizing the presence of the Rosetta Stone, for example, in the British Museum. Shadi Abdel Salam's film implicitly challenges the archeological master-narrative by foregrounding the voices of those on the margins of Egyptological texts. If the film opens with an archeological project and ends with its successful accomplishment, it also undermines that mission by focussing on the concrete dilemmas of living Egyptians. The non-diegetic musical motif based on Upper Egypt popular music ("Al Arian"), and the slow rhythm evocative of the regional atmosphere, furthermore, cinematically convey the cultural force of their environment.[54] The film does not end, significantly, with the narrative closure of safe placement of the artifacts in a museum, but rather with the slow vanishing of the boat carrying the Egyptologists and the mummies, all from the perspective of the devastated tribe. If *How Tasty Was My Frenchman* opens with the penetration of the Europeans seen from the perspective of the Native Americans, *The Mummy/The Night of Counting the Years* ends with the emptiness left behind by the intrusion of Europe. Reportedly, the Egyptian women of the tribe mourned when the mummies were taken, yet Shadi Adbel Salam presents, in longshot and through depsychologized editing, a unified communal silent gaze where the whistling wind becomes a voice of protest. Their gaze, far from conveying the triumphant conclusion of the archeological narrative, unveils

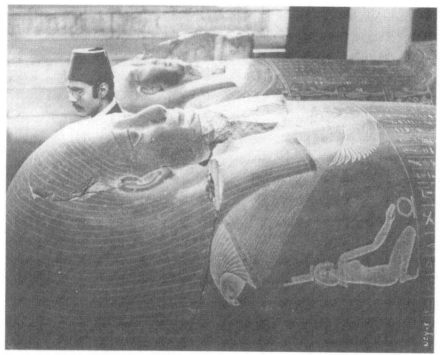

Figure 8. The Mummy/The Night of Counting the Years *(1969): Amplifying the voices on the margins of the Egyptological texts.*

the disastrous rupture in their very lives, thus subverting the self-celebratory Egyptological definitions of dispossession and theft.[55]

Archeological reports often inadvertently display metaphors which suggest capitalist values attached to their own profession. In his account of the 1881 discovery, the archeologist Howard Carter who worked on the discovery of Tut-ankh-Amen's tomb, writes: "Incredible as it may seem the secret was kept for six years, and the family, with a banking account of forty or more dead pharaohs to draw upon, grew rich."[56] Abdel Salam's *The Mummy/The Night of Counting the Years*, in contrast, emphasizes the ambivalent relationships between the tribe and the treasures, between the Egyptian people and their ancient heritage. The tribe lives on theft, yet its circumstances of hunger imply a critique of the imperial class system. The archeological redemption, in other words, must be seen in its historical and cultural context, i.e., taking the only power the tribe possessed without bringing anything in return. It would be simplistic, however, to view *The Mummy/The Night of Counting the Years* as a mere condemnation of Egyptology. The film illuminates class relations within a colonial dynamics in which the tribe, in order to survive, is obliged to deal with the "small" black market dealers, for the "effendies" from Cairo will not even pay them and arrest them. Class formations of Egyptian society, particularly within imperial context, force the small village to regard the ancient artifacts as a means of survival, a system in which the only power of the tribe is their secret. The effendies are viewed from the perspective of the tribe as strangers, cut off, in other words, from the national reality. *The Mummy/The Night of Counting the Years* in contrast with Western representations of Egypt, does not stress the grandeur of ancient Egypt at the expense of contemporary Arab lives; rather, it exposes the complex, multi-layered dimensions of Egyptian identity.

An allegory on Egyptian identity, the film offers a meditation on the destiny of a national culture. To cite Shadi Abdel Salam: "We have a national culture but it lies buried at the bottom of the memory of the people who are not always aware of its great values."[57] Speaking in an improbably literary Arabic (rather than an existing dialect), the villagers represent the Arab cultural heritage, while they are simul-taneously presented as continuous with the ancient past, emphasized, for example, through the ancient Egyptian eye make-up worn by the actress Nadia Lutfi. In a symbolic syncretic continuity of Pharaonic and Arab Egypt, the film associates the ancient "Eye of Horus," first shown in a close shot looking presumably at the brothers (directly at the spectator), with the Arab sign of "hamsa," against casting evil eye, seen on the boat on which the older brother is murdered. Similarly images of a closed gigantic hand of a monument is accompanied by a dialogue between Wannis and a stranger about "a hand holding a fate no one can read," or "what fate can you read in a stone hand?," stating that it is impossible to read fate at the hands of the monuments, i.e., a contemporary popular Middle Eastern culture of reading fate in the hand is implicitly contrasted with the immortal greatness but also the lifelessness of monuments.[58] A kind of visual dialogue of Arab Egypt with its past, furthermore, is rendered through montage, for example, when the image of the agonizing Wannis, looking up at the gigantic monument, is juxtaposed with a high-angle shot of Wannis, this time presumably from the monument's point-of-view. The presentation of Egypt's national identity as an amalgam of histories and cultures evokes the formulations, for example by the writers Taha Hussain and Tawfiq al-Hakim, of Egyptian identity as a synthesis of Pharaonic past, Arabic language, and Islamic religion. The film's opening intertitle, drawn from *The Book of the Dead*, promising that the one who shall go shall also return, and the final intertitle calling for the dead to "wake up," must also be seen within the context in which *The Mummy/The Night of Counting the Years* was produced.[59] During the post-1967 war period, after the defeat to Israel, the Gamal Abdel Nasser regime lost much of its allure, and the general mood of despair went hand in hand with a felt need for critical reassessments. In this sense, the ancient inscription of resurrection is also allegorically a call to Egypt of the late sixties for national rebirth.

B) TEXTUAL/SEXUAL STRATEGIES

The Colonial Gaze

Still playing a significant role in postcolonial geopolitics, the predominant trope of "rescue" in colonial discourse forms the crucial site of the battle over representation. Not only has the Western imaginary metaphorically rendered the colonized land as a female to be saved from her environ/mental disorder, it has also projected rather more literal narratives of rescue, specifically of Western and non-Western women—from African, Asian, Arab, or Native American men. The figure of the Arab assassin/rapist, like that of the African cannibal, helps produce the narrative and ideological role of the Western liberator as integral to the colonial rescue phantasy. This projection, whose imagistic avatars include the polygamous Arab, the libidinous Black buck, and the macho Latino, provides an indirect apologia for domination. In the case of the Orient, it carries with it religious/theological overtones of the inferiority of the polygamous Islamic world to the Christian world as encapsulated by the monogamous couple. The justification of Western expansion, then, becomes linked to issues of sexuality.

The intersection of colonial and gender discourses involves a shifting, contradictory subject positioning, whereby Western woman can simultaneously constitute "center" and "periphery," identity and alterity. A Western woman, in these narratives, exists in a relation of subordination to Western man and in a relation of domination toward "non-Western" men and women. This textual relationality homologizes the historical positioning of colonial women who have played, albeit with a difference, an oppressive role toward colonized people (both men and women), at times actively perpetuating the legacy of Empire.[60] This problematic role is anatomized in Ousmane Sembène's *Black Girl* (*La Noire de . . .*, 1966) in the relationship between the Senegalese maid and her French employer, and to some extent by Mira Hamermesh's documentary on South Africa *Maids and Madams* (1985), in contrast to the White-woman's-burden ideology in films such as *The King and I* (1956), *Out of Africa* (1985), and *Gorillas in the Mist* (1989). In many films, colonial women become the instrument of the White male vision, and are thus granted a gaze more powerful than that not only of non-Western women but also of non-Western men.

In the colonial context, given the shifting relational nature of power situations and representations, women can be granted an ephemeral "positional superiority" (Edward Said), a possibility exemplified in *The Sheik* (1921). Based on Edith Hull's novel, George Melford's *The Sheik* first introduces the spectator to the Arab world in the form of the "barbarous ritual" of the marriage market, depicted as a casino lottery ritual from which Arab men select women to "serve as chattel slaves." At the same time, the Western woman character, usually the object of the male gaze in Hollywood films, tends to be granted in the East an active (colonial) gaze, insofar as she now, temporarily within the narrative, becomes the sole delegate, as it were, of Western civilization. The "norms of the text" (Boris Uspensky) are represented by the Western male but in the moments of His absence, the white woman becomes the civilizing center of the film.[61] These racial and sexual hierarchies in the text are also clearly exemplified in Michael Powell and Emeric Pressburger (*Black Narcissus*), where most of the narrative is focalized through the British nuns and their "civilizing mission" in India. But ultimately the "norms of the text" are embodied by the British man, whose initial "prophecy" that the wild mountains of India are not suitable for and are beyond the control of the Christian missionaries is confirmed by the end of the narrative, with the virtual punishment of the nuns as catastrophes and mental chaos penetrate their order. Yet in relation to the "Natives" (both Indian men and women) the British women are privileged and form the "filter" and "center of consciousness" (Gerard Genette) of the film.

The discourse on gender within a colonial context, in sum, suggests that Western women can occupy a relatively powerful position on the surface of the htext, as the vehicles less for a sexual gaze than a colonial gaze. In these friction-producing moments between sexual and national hierarchies, particularly as encapsulated through the relationship between Third World men and First World women, national identity (associated with the white female character) is relatively privileged over sexual identity (associated with the dark male character). At the same time, the same ambivalence operates in relation to Third World men, whose punishment for inter-racial desire is simultaneously accompanied by spectatorial gratification for a male sexual gaze as ephemerally relayed by a darker man. These contradictions of national and sexual hierarchies, present in embryo in early cinema, are accentuated in the recent nostalgia-for-empire (liberal) films which foreground a female protagonist, presumably appealing to feminist codes, while reproducing colonialist narrative and cinematic power arrangements. The desexualization of the "good" African or Indian (servant) man in *Gorillas in the Mist*, *A Passage to India*, and *Out of Africa*, not unlike the desexualization of the female domestic servant as in *The Birth of a Nation* (1915) and *Gone with the Wind* (1939), is dialectically linked to the placement of the Western woman in the (White) "Pater" paradigm vis-a-vis the "natives."

Rape and the Rescue Phantasy

The chromatic sexual hierarchy in colonialist narratives, typical of Western racial conventions, has White women/men occupy the center of the narrative, with the White woman as the desired object of the male protagonists and antagonists. Marginalized within the narrative, Third World women—when not inscribed as metaphors for their virgin land as in *Bird of Paradise*—appear largely as sexually hungry subalterns.[62] In one scene in *The Sheik*, Arab women—some of them Black—fight quite literally over their Arab man. While the White woman has to be lured, made captive, and virtually raped to awaken her repressed desire, the Arab/Black/Latin women are driven by a raging libido. Here one encounters some of the complementary contradictions in colonial discourse whereby a Third World land and its inhabitants are the object of the desire for chastity articulated in the virgin metaphors, while also manifesting Victorian repression of sexuality, particularly female sexuality, through unleashing its pornographic impulse.[63]

The positing of female sexual enslavement by polygamous Third World men becomes especially ironic when we recall the subjection of African-American women slaves on Southern plantations with the daily lived polygamy of White men slaveowners.[64] Images of Black/Arab woman in "heat" versus "frigid" White woman also indirectly highlight the menacing figure of the Black/Arab rapist and therefore mythically elide the history of subordination of Third World women by First World men. The hot/frigid dichotomy, then, implies three interdependent axioms within the sexual politics of colonialist discourse: 1) the sexual interaction of Black/Arab men and White women can *only* involve rape (since White women, within this perspective, cannot possibly desire Black men); 2) the sexual interaction of White men and Black/Arab women cannot involve rape (since Black/Arab women are in perpetual heat and desire their White master); and 3) the interaction of Black/Arab men and Black/Arab women also cannot involve rape, since both are in perpetual heat. It was this racist combinatoire that generated the (largely unspoken) rationale for the castration and lynching of African-American men and the non-punishment of White men for the rape of African-American women.

It is within this logic that *The Birth of a Nation* obsessively links sexual and racial phobias. The animalistic "Black," Gus, attempts to rape the virginal Flora, much as the "mulatto" Lynch tries to force Elsie into marriage, and the "mulatta" Lydia blames an innocent White man of sexual abuse, while simultaneously manipulating the unaware politician Stoneman through sexuality. The threat of African-American political assertion is subliminally linked to Black sexual potency. It is not surprising, therefore, that the only non-threatening Black figure, the "loyal" mammy, is portrayed as completely de-sexualized. The thematization of Blacks' hyper-sexuality diacritically foils (White) masculinist acts of patriotism. It is the attempted rape of Flora that catalyzes the grand act of White "liberation" (Figure 9). The opening intertitle, which states that the very presence of the African in America "planted the first seed of disunion," and the portrayal of idealized harmony between North and South (and Masters and Slaves) before the abolition suggest that libidinal Blacks destroyed the nation. The rescue of Flora, of Elsie, and of the

Figure 9. The Birth of a Nation *(1915): The national (white) identity catalyzed by phantasies of rape and rescue.*

besieged Northerners and Southerners (who are now once again united "in common defence of their Aryan Birthright"), operates as a didactic allegory whose telos
is the Klansmen's vision of the "order of things." The closure of "mixed"-marriage
between North and South confirms national unity and establishes a certain sexual
order in which the virginal desired White woman is available only to White man.
The superimposition of the Christ figure over the celebrating family/nation provides a religious benediction on the "birth." This abstract, metaphysical Birth of the
Nation masks a more concrete notion of birth—no less relevant to the conception of
the American nation—that of children from raped Black women, just as the naming
of the mulatto as "Lynch" crudely blames the victims. Furthermore, the White man,
who historically raped Third World women, manifests latent rapist desires toward
innocent White women via a projected Black man, here literally masked in black-
face.

Even when not involving rape, the possibilities of erotic interaction in films prior
to the sixties were severely limited by apartheid-style ethnic/racial codes. The same
Hollywood that at times could project mixed love stories between Anglo-Americans
and Latins and Arabs (especially if incarnated by White American actors and
actresses such as Valentino in *The Sheik*, Dorothy Lamour in *The Road to Morocco*
(1942), or Maureen O'Hara in *They Met in Argentina* (1941) was completely inhibited
in relation to African, Asian, or Native American sexuality. This latent fear of blood-
tainting in such melodramas as *Call Her Savage* (1932) and *Pinky* (1949) necessitates
narratives where the "half breed" ("Native American" in *Call Her Savage* and "Black"
in *Pinky*) female protagonists are prevented at the closure of the films from participating in mixed-marriage, ironically despite the roles being played by "pure White"
actresses. It is therefore the generic space of melodrama that preoccupies itself with
"inter-racial" romantic interaction. The trajectory of constituting the couple in the
musical comedy, for example, could not allow for a racially "subaltern" protagonist
(Figure 10).

The Production Code of the Motion Picture Producers and Directors of America,
Inc.: 1930–1934, an even stricter version of the Hays Office codes of the 20s,
explicitly states: "Miscegenation (sex relation between the white and black races) is
forbidden."[65] The delegitimizing of the romantic union between "white" and
"black" "races" is linked to a broader exclusion of Africans, Asians, and Native
Americans from participation in social institutions. Translating the obsession with
"pure blood" into legal language, Southern miscegenation laws, as pointed out by
African-American feminists as early as the end of the last century,[66] were designed
to maintain White (male) supremacy and to prevent a possible transfer of property
to Blacks in the post-abolition era. "Race" as a biological category, as Hazel Carby
formulates it, was subordinated to race as a political category.[67] It is within this
context of an exclusionary ideology that we can understand the Production Code's
universal censorship of sexual violence and brutality where the assumption is one
of purely individual victimization, thus undermining a possible portrayal of the
racially-sexually-based violence toward African-Americans, and implicitly wiping
out the memory of the rape, castration, and lynching from the American record.[68]
The Production Code, in other words, eliminates a possible counter-narrative by
Third World people for whom sexual-violence has often been at the kernel of their
historical experience and identity.[69]

Figure 10.   Road to Morocco (1942): *The imperial path to the constitution of the couple.*

The Spectacle of Difference

An analysis of the history of First World cinema in racial and colonial terms uncovers a tendency toward national "allegory," in Jameson's sense, of texts which, even when narrating apparently private stories, manage to metaphorize the public sphere, where the micro-individual is doubled, as it were, by the macro-nation and the personal and the political, the private and the historical, are inextricably linked.[70] The national and racial hierarchies of the cinema allegorize, in other words, extra-discursive social intercourse. In the period of the Good Neighbor Policy, Hollywood attempted to enlist Latin America for hemispheric unity against the Axis. As European film markets were reducing their film consumption due to the beginning of the war, Hollywood, in hopes for South American markets and pan-American political unity, flooded the screens with films featuring "Latin American" themes. Interestingly the trope of "good neighbor" very rarely extended to winning family status through inter-racial or inter-national marriage. Marginalized within the narrative, and often limited to roles as entertainers, the Latin American characters in *The Gang's All Here* (1943), *Too Many Girls* (1940), and *Weekend in Havana* (1941) at the finale tend to be at the exact point from which they began, in contrast with the teleologically evolving status of the North American protagonists. Displaying "exoticism," the musical numbers in these films provide the spectacle of difference, functioning narratively by uniting the North American couple vis-a-vis the South Americans.

Films such as *The Gang's All Here* demonstrate a generic division of labor, whereby the solid, "serious" or romantic numbers such as "A Journey to a Star" tend to be performed by the North American protagonists Alice Faye and James Ellison, while the Latin American characters perform "unserious," "excessive" numbers involving swaying hips, exaggerated facial expressions, caricaturally sexy costumes, and "think-big" style props embodied by Carmen Miranda. Her figure in the number "The Lady with the Tutti-Frutti Hat" is dwarfed by gigantesque vegetative imagery in which the final image of her as a virtual fertility goddess links this idealized quality with the beginning of the number where goods are unloaded from the South; the North here celebrates the South as the feminine principle capable of giving birth to goods consumed by the North (Figure 11). The bananas in Miranda's number, furthermore, not only enact the agricultural reductionism of Latin America but also form phallic symbols, here raised by "voluptuous" Latinas over circular quasi-vaginal forms. (But the Latina, as the lyrics suggest, will take her hat off "only for Johnny Smith," much as the "Oriental" woman in films such as *The Road to Morocco* would only remove her veil for the Anglo-American.) This construction of Latinness (or Orientalness) as the locus of exoticism is not subsumable by hegemonic North American cultural codes. The South American characters therefore do not form part of any narrative development and their presence is "tolerable" only on the folkloric level. Character interaction, in this sense, allegorizes the larger relation between the North and South (or West and East) and reflects an ambivalence of attraction/repulsion towards those on the "margins" of the Western Empire.

The gender and colonial discursive intersection is revealed in the ways that Hollywood exploited the Orient, Africa, and Latin America as a pretext for eroticized images, especially from 1934 through the mid-fifties when the restrictive

Figure 11. The Gang's All Here *(1943): The fertility goddess consumed by Empire.*

production code forbade depicting "scenes of passion" in all but the most puerile terms, and required that the sanctity of the institution of marriage be upheld at all times. Miscegenation, nudity, sexually suggestive dances or costumes, "excessive and lustful kissing" were prohibited, while adultery, illicit sex, seduction, or rape could never be more than suggested, and then only if absolutely essential to the plot and severely punished at the end. The Western obsession with the Harem, for example, was not simply crucial for Hollywood's visualization of the Orient but also authorized the proliferation of sexual images projected onto an otherized elsewhere, much as the Orient, Africa, and Latin America played a similar role for Victorian culture.

Exoticizing and eroticizing the Third World allowed the imperial imaginary to play out its own fantasies of sexual domination. Already in the silent era, films often included eroticized dances, featuring a rather improbably melange of Spanish and Indian dances, plus a touch of belly-dancing (*The Dance of Fatima*, *The Sheik*, and *Son of the Sheik* (1926)). This filmic practice of melange recalls the frequent superimposition in Orientalist paintings of the visual traces of civilizations as diverse as Arab, Persian, Chinese, and Indian into a single feature of the exotic Orient[71]—a colonialist process that Albert Memmi terms the "mark of the plural." An Oriental setting (most of the films on the Orient, Africa, and Latin America were studio-shot) thus provided Hollywood filmmakers with a narrative license for exposing flesh without risking censorship; they could display the bare-skin of Valentino, Douglas Fair-banks, and Johnny Weissmuller as well as that of scores of women, from Myrna Loy, Maureen O'Sullivan, and Marlene Dietrich dancing with her legs painted gold to Dolores Grey moving her hips with the "realistic" excuse of other, less civilized cultures. (The code which turned Jane's two piece outfit into one piece in later films, did not affect, for the most part, the nude breasts of African women at the background of the *Tarzan* series,[72] evoking *National Geographic*'s predilection for "Native" nudity.) In the desert and the jungle, the traditional slow-paced process of courtship leading to marriage could be replaced with uninhibited fantasies of sexual domination and "freedom," and specifically with fantasies of polygamy and even rape of presumably repressed White women. The display of rape in a "natural" despotic context continues to the present, for example, in the several attempted rapes of Brooke Shields in *Sahara* (1983). The Orient, like Latin America and Africa, thus is posited as the locus of eroticism by a puritanical society, and a film industry, hemmed in by a moralistic code.

The Imaginary of the Harem

As with voyeuristic anthropological studies and moralistic travel-literature con-cerning non-normative conceptions of sexuality, Western cinema diffused the anachronistic but still Victorian obsession with sexuality through the cinematic apparatus. The outlet for Western male heroic desire is clearly seen in *Harum Scarum* (1965), a reflexive film featuring a carnival-like Orient reminiscent of Las Vegas, itself placed in the burning sands of the American desert of Nevada, and offering harem-like nightclubs. The film opens with Elvis Presley—attired in an "Oriental" head wrap and vest—arriving on horseback in the desert. Upon arrival Presley leaps off his horse to free a woman from two evil Arabs who have tied her to a stake. The triumphant rescuer later sings:

I'm gonna go where desert sun is; where the fun is; go where the harem girls dance; go where there's love and romance—out on the burning sands, in some caravan. I'll find adventure where I can. To say the least, go East, young man. You'll feel like the Sheik, so rich and grand, with dancing girls at your command. When paradise starts calling, into some tent I'm crawling. I'll make love the way I plan. Go East—and drink and feast—go East, young man (Figure 12).

Material abundance in Orientalist discourse, tied to a history of imperial enter-prises, here functions as part of the generic utopia of the musical, constituting itself, in Jamesonian terms, as a projected fulfillment of what is desired and absent within the socio-political status quo. Yet the "absence" is explicitly within the masculinist imaginative terrain. The images of harems offer an "open sesame" to an unknown, alluring, and tantalizingly forbidden world, posited as desirable to the instinctual primitive presumably inhabiting all men. In *Kismet* (1955), for example, the harem master entertains himself with a panopticon-like device which allows him to watch his many women without their knowledge. Authorizing a voyeuristic entrance into an inaccessible private space, the Harem dream reflects a masculinist utopia of sexual omnipotence.[73]

Figure 12.   Harum Scarum *(1965): Entering the inaccessible* kharim.

The topos of the harem in contemporary popular culture draws, of course, on a long history of Orientalist phantasies. Western voyagers had no conceivable means of access to harems—indeed, the Arabic etymology of the word "harem," Kharim, refers to something "forbidden." Yet Western texts delineate life in the harems with great assurance and apparent exactitude, rather like European Orientalist studio paintings, for example the famous *Turkish Bath* (1862) which was painted without Ingres ever visiting the Orient. The excursions to the Orient, and on-location paintings by painters such as Ferdinand-Victor-Eugene Delacroix, similarly, served largely to authenticate an apriori vision. Inspired by the Arab popular tradition of fantastic tales, the travellers recounted the Orient to fellow-Westerners according the paradigms furnished by European translations of *A Thousand and One Nights* (*Alf Laila wa Laila*), tales which were often translated quite loosely in order to satisfy the European taste for a passionately, violent Orient.[74] This Orient was perhaps best encapsulated in the figure of Salomé, whose Semitic origins were highlighted by the nineteenth-century Orientalist ethnographic vogue (e.g., Hugo von Habermann, Otto Friedrich).

The historical harem—which was largely an upper class phenomenon—was in fact most striking in its domesticity. Memoirs written by Egyptian and Turkish women[75] depict the complex familial life and a strong network of female communality horizontally and vertically across class lines. The isolated but relatively powerful harem women depended on working class women who were freer to move, and therefore became an important connection to the outside world.[76] Despite their subordination, harem women, as Leila Ahmed points out, often owned and ran their property, and could at times display crucial political power, thus revealing the harem as a site of contradictions.[77] Whereas Western discourse on the harem defined it simply as a male-dominated space, the accounts of the harem by Middle Eastern women testify to a system whereby a man's female relatives also shared the living space, allowing women access to other women, providing a protected space for the exchange of information and ideas safe from the eyes and the ears of men. (Contemporary Middle Eastern vestiges of this tradition are found in regular all-female gatherings, whereby women, as in the harems, carnivalize male power through jokes, stories, singing, and dancing.) In other words, the "harem," though patriarchal in nature, has been subjected to an ahistorical discourse whose Eurocentric assumptions[77] left unquestioned the sexual oppression of the West. The Middle Eastern system of communal seclusion, then, must also be compared to the Western system of domestic "solitary confinement" for upper-middle class women.[78]

European women constituted an enthusiastic audience for much of the nineteenth-century Orientalist poetry written by Beckford, Byron, and Moore, anticipating the spectatorial enthusiasm for exoticist films. As travellers, however, their discourse on the harems oscillates between Orientalist narratives and more dialogical testimonies. Western women participated in the Western colonial gaze; their writings often voyeuristically dwell on Oriental clothes, postures, and gestures, exoticizing the female "other."[79] If male narrators were intrigued by the harem as the locus of lesbian sexuality, female travellers, who as women had more access to female spaces, undermined the pornographic imagination of the harem. Interestingly, the detailed description of Turkish female bodies in Lady Mary Wortley

Montagu's letters, particularly those drawn from her visit to the *hammam* (baths), points to a subliminal erotic fascination with the female "other," a fascination masquerading, at times, as a male gaze:

I perceiv'd that the Ladys with the finest skins and most delicate shapes had the greatest share of my admiration, th'o their faces were sometimes less beautiful than those of their companions. To tell you the truth, I had the wickedness enough to wish secretly that Mr. Gervase had been there invisible. I fancy it would have very much improv'd his art to see so many fine Women naked in different postures. . .[80]

Female travellers, furthermore, were compelled to situate their own oppression vis-a-vis that of Oriental women. Lady Mary Wortley Montagu often measures the freedom endowed to English vis-a-vis Turkish women, suggesting the paradoxes of harems and veils:

'Tis very easy to see that they have more liberty than we have, no woman of what rank soever being permitted to go in the streets without two muslins, one that covers her face all but her eyes and another that hides the whole dress . . . You may guess how effectually this disguises them, that there is no distinguishing the great lady from her slave, and 'tis impossible for the most jealous husband to know his wife when he meets her, and no man dare either touch or follow a woman in the streets . . . The perpetual masquerade gives them entire liberty of following their inclinations without danger of discovery.[81]

In fact, Lady Mary Wortley Montagu implicitly suggests an awareness, on the part of Turkish women, not simply of their oppression but also of that of European women. Recounting the day she was undressed in the *hamman* by the lady of the house, who was struck at the sight of the stays, she quoted the lady's remark that "the Husbands in England were much worse than in the East; for they ty'd up their wives in boxes, of the shape of their bodies."[82]

The popular image-making of the Orient internalized, in other words, the codes of male oriented travel-narratives. The continuities between the representation of the native body and the female body, are obvious when we compare Hollywood's ethnography with Hollywood's pornography. Ironically, we find a latent inscription of harems and despots even in texts not set in the Orient. *Harem structures*, in fact, permeate Western mass-mediated culture. Busby Berkeley's musical numbers, for example, project a harem-like structure reminiscent of Hollywood's mythical Orient. Like the harem, his musical numbers involve a multitude of women who, as Lucy Fischer suggests, serve as signifiers of male power over infinitely substitutable females.[83] The mise-en-scene of both harem scenes and musical numbers is structured around the scopic privilege of the master and his limitless pleasure in an exclusive place inaccessible to other men. Berkeley's panopticon-like camera links visual pleasure with a kind of surveillance of manipulated female movement. The camera's omnipresent and mobile gaze, its magic-carpet-like air-borne prowling along confined females embodies the over-arching look of the absent/present master—i.e., of both the director/producer, and vicariously of the spectator. The production numbers tend to exclude the male presence, but allow for the fantasies of the spectator, positioning his/her gaze as that of a despot entertained by a plurality of females. Rendered virtually identical, the women in Berkeley's numbers evoke the analogy between the musical show and the harem not only as a textual construct but also as a studio practice whose patriarchal structure of casting is conceived as a kind of beauty contest (a "judgment of Paris"). Speaking of his casting methods, Berkeley himself recounted a day in which he interviewed 723 women in order to select only three: "My sixteen regular girls were sitting on the side waiting; so after I picked the three girls I put them next to my special sixteen and they matched just like pearls."[84]

The Desert Odyssey

The exoticist films allow for subliminally transexual tropes. The phantasm of the Orient gives an outlet for a carnivalesque play with national and at times gender identities. Isabelle Adaani in *Ishtar* is disguised as an Arab male-rebel and Brooke Shields as an American male racer in the Sahara desert, while Rudolph Valentino (*The Sheik* and *Son of the Sheik*), Douglas Fairbanks (*The Thief of Bagdad*), Elvis Presley (*Harum Scarum*), Peter O'Toole (*Lawrence of Arabia*), Warren Beaty and Dustin Hoffman (*Ishtar*) wear Arab disguise. Masquerading manifests a latent desire to transgress fixed national and gender identities. In *The Sheik*, the Agnes Ayres character, assisted by Arab women, wears an Arab female dress in order to penetrate the Oriental "marriage market," assuming the "inferior" position of the Arab woman in order, paradoxically, to empower herself with a gaze on Oriental despotism. The change of gender identities of female characters in more recent films such as *Sahara* and *Ishtar* allows as well for harmless transgressions of the coded "feminine" body-language. In counter narratives such as *The Battle of Algiers* (*La Battaglia di Algeri*, 1966), however, gender and national disguises take on different signification.[85] FLN Algerian women wear Western "modern" dress, dye their hair blond, and even act coquettishly with French soldiers.[86] Here it is the Third World which masquerades as the West, not as an act of self-effacing mimicry but as a way of sabotaging the colonial regime of assimilation.

Since clothing over the last few centuries, as a result of what J. C. Flugel calls "the Great Masculine Renunciation,"[87] has been limited to austere, uncolorful, and unplayful costumes, the projection to the phantastic locus of the Orient allows the imagination to go exuberantly "native." Historically, the widely-disseminated popular image in newspapers and newsreels of T. E. Lawrence in flowing Arab costume have partially inspired films such as *The Sheik* and *Son of the Sheik*, whose bi-sexual appeal can be located in the closet construction of Western man as "feminine."[88] The coded "feminine" look, therefore, is played out within the safe space of the Orient, through the "realistic" embodiment of the "Other." David Lean's Lawrence, despite his classical association with norms of heroic manliness, is also portrayed in a homoerotic light. When he is accepted by the Arab tribe he is dressed all in white, and at one point set on a horse, moving delicately, virtually captured like a bride. Drawing a sword from his sheath, the Peter O'Toole character shifts the gendered signification of the phallic symbol by using it as a mirror to look at his own newly acquired "feminine" Oriental image. More generally, the relationship between Lawrence and the Omar Sharif character gradually changes from initial male rivalry to an implied erotic attraction in which Sharif is associated with female imagery, best encapsulated in the scene where Sharif is seen in close-up with wet eyes, identifying with the tormented Lawrence (Figure 13). The inter-racial homo-

Figure 13.   Lawrence of Arabia *(1962): Inter-racial homoerotic subtext.*

erotic subtext in *Lawrence of Arabia* forms part of a long tradition of colonial narratives from novels such as *Robinson Crusoe* (Crusoe and Friday), and *Huckleberry Finn* (Huck and Jim) to filmic adaptations such as *Around the World in 80 Days* (Phileas Fogg and his dark servant Passepartout).[89] Most texts about the "Empire," from the Western genre to recent nostalgia-for-Empire films such as *Mountains of the Moon* (1989), however, are pervaded by White homoeroticism in which male explorers, deprived of women, are "forced" into physical closeness, weaving bonds of affection and desire, in the course of their plights in an unknown, hostile land.

Homoeroticism, then, can simultaneously permeate homophobic colonialist texts. Within this symptomatic dialectic we may also understand the textual (dis)placement of the heterosexual African/Arab/Latino man, as playing the Id to the Western masculinist Superego. In *The Sheik*, for example, Valentino, as long as he is known to the spectator only as Arab, acts as the Id, but when he is revealed to be the son of Europeans, he is transformed into a superego figure who nobly risks his life to rescue the English woman from "real" Arab rapists.[90] And the English woman overcomes her sexual repression only in the desert, after being sexually provoked repeatedly by the Sheik. Valentino, the "Latin lover," is here projected into another "exotic" space where he can act out sexual phantasies that would have been unthinkable in a contemporaneous American or European setting. The desert, in this sense, functions narratively as an isolating element, as sexually and morally separate imaginary territory (Figure 14). The Orientalist films tend to begin in the city—where European civilization has already tamed the East—but the real dramatic conflicts take place in the desert where women are defenseless, and White woman could easily become the captive of a romantic sheik or evil Arab. The positioning of rapeable White woman by a lustful male in an isolated desert locale gives voice to a masculinist fantasy of complete control over the Western woman, the woman "close to home," without any intervening protective code of morality. Puritanical Hollywood thus claims to censure female adventurousness, and the male tyranny of harems and rapes—but only, paradoxically, as a way of gratifying Western inter-racial sexual desires.

Figure 14.   The Sheik *(1921): The desert as the site of the sexual imaginary.*

In the more recent reworking of *The Sheik* and *Son of the Sheik*, in Menahem Golan's *Sahara*, the male rescue phantasy and the punishment of female rebellion undergird the film. In *Sahara* the central figure, Dale (Brooke Shields), feisty race car driving and only-daughter of a 20s care manufacturer, is presented as reckless, daring, and assertive for entering the male domain of the Oriental desert and for entering the "men only" race. She also literally disguises herself as a man, and adopts His profession and His mastery of the desert land through technology. Captured by desert tribesmen, she becomes a commodity fought over within the tribe and between tribes; the camera's fetishization of her body, however, is the ironic reminder of the Western projection of stars' bodies as commodity. Scenes of Brooke Shields wrestling with her captors not only suture the Western spectator to a national rescue operation but also invite the implied spectator into an orgiastic voyeurism. The desire for the Western woman and the fear of losing control over her is manifested in her punishment through several attempted rapes by Arabs. But at the end the courageous winner of the race decides "on her own" to return to the noble light-skinned sheik who had rescued her from cruel Arabs at the risk of his own life. The woman, who could have won independence, still "voluntarily" prefers the ancient ways of gender hierarchies (Figure 15).

At times, it is implied that women, while offended by Arab and Muslim rapists, actually *prefer* masterful men like Valentino.[91] Following the screening of *The Sheik*,

Figure 15.   Brooke Shields in Sahara *(1982): Gender transgressions in the Oriental desert.*

newspaper columnists were asking "Do women like masterful men?" To which Valentino replied: "Yes." "All women like a little cave-man stuff. No matter whether they are feminists, suffragettes or so-called new women, they like to have a masterful man who makes them do things he asserts."[92] Edith Hull expressed similar opinions. "There can be only one head in a house. Despite modern desire for equality of sexes I still believe that physically and morally it is better that the head should be the man."[93] Edith Hull's novel and Monic Katterjohn's adaptation, gratify, to some extent, a projected Western female desire for an "exotic" lover, for a Romantic, sensual, passionate, but non-lethal, play with the *Liebestod*, a release of the Id for the (segregated) upper-middle-class occidental woman.[94] (The author of the source novel claimed to have written the book for relaxation when her husband was in the war and she was alone in India. She decided to visit in Algeria, where she was impressed with the fine work the French government was doing.) In this sense the phantasm of the Orient can be incorporated by Western women, forming part of the broader colonial discourse on the "exotic," while simultaneously constituting an imaginary locus for suppressed sexual desires.

The rescue phantasy, when literalized through the rescue of a woman from a lascivious Arab, has to be seen not only as an allegory of saving the Orient from its libidinal, instinctual destructiveness but also as a didactic *Bildungsroman* addressed to women at home, perpetuating by contrast the myth of the sexual egalitarianism of the West. The exoticist films delegitimize Third World national identities and give voice to anti-feminist backlash, responding to the threat to institutionalized patriarchal power presented by the woman's Suffrage movements and the nascent feminist struggle. In this sense the narrative of Western women in the Third World can be read as a projected didactic allegory insinuating the dangerous nature of the "uncivilized man" and by implication lauding the freedom presumably enjoyed by Western women. In *The Sheik* and *Sahara* the Western woman directly rebels against the "civilized tradition" of marriage at the beginning of the film, calling it "captivity," only to later become literally captive of lusting Dark men. Transgressing male space (penetrating the marriage market by masquerading as an Arab woman in *The Sheik*, and participating in a male race by masquerading as a young man in *Sahara*), the female protagonist begins with a hubris vis-a-vis her Western male protectors (against the Arabians from the desert), and then goes through the "pedagogical" experience of attempted rapes. The telos, or quite literally, "homecoming" of this desert Odyssey is the disciplinary punishment of female desire for liberation and renewed spectatorial appreciation for the existing sexual, racial, and national order.

* * *

My discussion of colonial constructions of gender has aimed at analyzing the crucial role of sexual difference for the culture of Empire. Western popular culture, in this sense, has operated on the same Eurocentric discursive continuum as such disciplines as Philosophy, Egyptology, Anthropology, Historiography, and Geography. From the erotic projections of *The Sheik* to the spectacular historiography of *Lawrence of Arabia*, or from the fantastic tale of *The Mummy* (1932) to the Egyptological mission of *Raiders of the Lost Ark*, my reading has tried to suggest that despite some differences, having to do with the periods in which the films were produced, hegemonic Western representation has been locked into a series of Eurocentric articulations of power. Although a feminist reading of (post)colonial discourse must take into account the national and historical specificities of that discourse, it is equally important also to chart the broader structural analogies in the representation of diverse Third World cultures. (Post)Colonial narratives, as we have seen, serves to define the "West" through metaphors of rape, phantasies of rescue, and eroticized geographies. The popular culture of Empire has tended to rely on a structurally similar genderized discourse within different national and historical moments, a discourse challenged by resistant counter-narratives such as *How Tasty Was My Frenchman*, *Nice Coloured Girls*, and *The Mummy/The Night of Counting the Years*.

NOTES

1. Different sections of this essay were presented at several conference: Third World Film Institute, New York University (1984); The Middle East Studies Association, University of California, Los Angeles (1988); Humanities Council Faculty Seminar on Race and Gender, New York University (1988); The Society for Cinema Studies, Iowa University (1989); The Conference on "Gender and Colonialism," University of California, Berkeley (1989); The Conference on "Rewriting the (Post)Modern: (Post)Colonialism/Feminism/Late Capitalism," The University of Utah, Humanities Center (1990).
2. Here some of my discussion is indebted to Edward Said's notion of the "feminization" of the Orient, *Orientalism* (New York: Vintage, 1978). See also Francis Barker, Peter Hulme, Margaret Iversen, Diana Loxley, eds. *Europe and Its Others* Vols. 1 and 2. Colchester: University of Essex, 1985, especially Peter

Hulme "Polytropic Man: Tropes of Sexuality and Mobility in Early Colonial Discourse" (Vol. 2); Jose Rabasa, "Allegories of the Atlas" (Vol. 2). Some of my discussion here on gendered metaphors appears in Ella Shohat, "Imagining Terra Incognita: The Disciplinary Gaze of Empire," *Public Culture*, Vol. 3, No. 2.

3. Sir Walter Raleigh, "Discovery of Guiana." Cited in Susan Griffin, *Woman and Nature: The Roaring Inside Her*. (New York: Harper & Row, 1978), p. 47.

4. St. John de Crèvecoeur, *Letters from an American Farmer*, 1782. Cited in Henry Nash Smith, *Virgin Land: The American West as Symbol and Myth* (Cambridge, Massachusetts: Harvard University Press, 1950), p. 121.

5. See Henry Nash Smith, *Virgin Land: The American West as Symbol and Myth*. For 19th century North American expansionist ideology, see Richard Slotkin, *The Fatal Environment: The Myth of the Frontier in the Age of Industrialization, 1800–1890*. (Middletown, Connecticut: Wesleyan University Press, 1985).

6. For an examination of the representation of the American frontiers and gender issues see Annette Kolodny, *The Lay of the Land: Metaphors as Experience and History in American Life and Letters* (Chapel Hill: The University of North Carolina Press, 1975); and *The Land Before Her: Fantasy and Experience of the American Frontiers, 1630–1860* (Chapel Hill: The University of North Carolina Press, 1984).

7. R. W. B. Lewis, *The American Adam: Innocence, Tragedy, and Tradition in the Nineteenth Century*. (Chicago: The University of Chicago Press, 1959.) Hans Blumenberg, interestingly, points out in relation to Francis Bacon that the resituation of Paradise, as the goal of history, was supposed to promise magical facility. The knowledge of nature for him is connected to his definition of the Paradisiac condition as mastery by means of the word. (*The Legitimacy of the Modern Age*. Translated by Robert Wallace. Cambridge, Massachusetts: MIT Press, 1983).

8. Jan Van der Straet's representation of America has been cited by several scholars: Michel de Certeau 'Avant propos' in *L'Ecriture de l'histoire*. Paris: Gallimard, 1975; Olivier Richon, "Representation, the Despot and the Harem: Some Questions Around an Academic Orientalist Painting by Lecomte-du-Nouy" (1885) in *Europe and Its Others* (Vol. 1).

9. The gendering of colonial encounters between a "feminine" nature and "masculine" scientist draws on a pre-existing discourse which has genderized the encounter between "Man and Nature" in the West itself. For a full discussion see, for example, Susan Griffin, *Woman and Nature: The Roaring Inside Her*.

10. Michael de Certeau, 'Avant propos' in *L'Ecriture de l'histoire*.

11. The film was distributed in the U. S. as *How Tasty Was My Little Frenchman*.

12. For a close analysis of *How Tasty was My Frenchman* see Richard Peña, "How Tasty Was My Little Frenchman," in Randal Johnson and Robert Stam, *Brazilian Cinema*. East Brunswick, New Jersey: Associated University Presses, 1982 (Re-printed by University of Texas Press, 1985).

13. The report concerns another tribe, the Tupiniquim who were massacred by their "allies," the Portuguese, confirming the Native American stance, mediated in the film through the Tupinamba tribe, that despite tactical alliances, the Europeans, whether French or Portuguese, have similar desires in relation to the Native American Land.

14. The film which was shot in Parati (Brazil) has the actors and actresses mimic Native American attitudes towards nudity by living nude throughout the duration of the shooting. This production method is, of course, different from the industrial approach to shooting scenes of nudity. *How Tasty Was My Frenchman* can also be seen as part of a counterculture of the late sixties, and its general interest in non-Western societies as alternative possibilities.

15. *How Tasty Was My Frenchman* does not criticize patriarchal structures within Native American societies.

16. Although Cleopatra was addressed as Egypt in the *Antony and Cleopatra* play, Shakespeare here and in *The Tempest* offers a complex dialectics between the West and "its Others."

17. Colonialist representations have their roots in what Martin Bernal calls the "Aryan model," a model which projects a presumably clear and monolithic historical trajectory leading from classical Greece (constructed as "pure," "western," and "democratic") to Imperial Rome and then to the metropolitan capitals of Europe and the United States. (See *Black Athena: The Afroasiatic Roots of Classical Civilization. Volume I, The Fabrication of Ancient Greece 1785–1985*. New Brunswick: Rutgers University Press, 1987.) "History" is made to seem synonymous with a linear notion of European "progress." This Eurocentric view is premised on crucial exclusions of internal and external "others": the African and Semitic cultures that strongly inflected the culture of classical Greece; the Islamic and Arabic-

Sephardi culture which played an invaluable cultural role during the so-called "dark" and "middle" ages; and the diverse indigenous peoples, whose land and natural resources were violently appropriated and whose cultures were constructed as "savage" and "irrational."

18. Egyptology's mania for a mere ancient Egypt, for example, is ironic in an Arab context where Egypt is often perceived as *the* model of an Arab country.

19. This is true even for those films produced after the great wave of national liberation movements in the Third World.

20. Tracey Moffatt's *Nice Coloured Girls* explores the relocations established between White settlers and Aboriginal women over the last two hundred years, juxtaposing the "first encounter" with present-day urban encounters. Conveying the perspective of Aboriginal women, the film situates their oppression within a historical context in which voices and images from the past play a crucial role.

21. Female voyagers occupy very rarely the center of the narrative (*The King and I, Black Narcissus*). In contrast to scientist heroes, they tend to occupy the "feminine" actantial slot: educators and nurses.

22. The passive/active division is, of course, based on stereotypically sexist imagery.

23. See for example Suleiman Mousa, *T. E. Lawrence: An Arab View.* Translated by Albert Butros. New York: Oxford University Press, 1966.

24. See Francis Bacon, *Advancement of Learning* and *Novum Organum*. New York: The Colonial Press, 1899.

25. Francis Bacon, *Advancement of Learning* and *Novum Organum*. In *Advancement of Learning*, p. 135.

26. Francis Bacon, *Novum Organum* in *The Works of Francis Bacon.* James Spedding, Robert Ellis and Douglas Heath, eds. London: Longmans & Co., 1870, p. 82.

27. Hans Blumenberg, *The Legitimacy of the Modern Age*, p. 389.

28. For an illuminating reading of Haggard's *King Solomon's Mines* see Anne McClintock, "Maidens, Maps, and Mines: The Reinvention of Patriarchy in Colonial South Africa." *The South Atlantic Quarterly*, Vol. 87, No. 1 (Winter 1988).

29. Television has incorporated this penchant for spinning globe logos especially in News programs, displaying its authority over the world.

30. *Around the World in 80 Days* feminizes national maps by placing images of "native" women on the backs of maps of specific countries. The balloon used by the protagonist is referred to as "she" and called "La Coquette."

31. The feminine designation of "the moon" in French, "La Lune," is reproduced by the "feminine" iconography of the moon.

32. Georges Méliès' filmography includes a relatively great number of films related to colonial explorations and Orientalist phantasies such as *Le Fakir-Mystère Indien* (1896), *Vente d'Esclaves au Harem* (1897), *Cleopatre* (1899), *La Vengeance de Bouddah* (1901), *Les Aventures de Robinson Crusoe* (1902), *Le Palais des Milles et Une Nuits* (1905). Interestingly, Méliès' early fascination with spectacles dates back to his visits to the Egyptian Hall shows, directed by Maskelyne and Cooke and devoted to fantastic spectacles.

33. I am here referring especially to the Babylon section.

34. Bazin's Malraux-inspired statement in the opening of "The Ontology of the Photographic Image" suggests that "at the origin of painting and sculpture there lies a mummy complex." (*What Is Cinema*, translated by Hugh Gray, Berkeley: University of California Press, 1967, p. 9). The ritual of cinema, in this sense, is not unlike the Egyptian religious rituals which provided "a defence [sic] against the passage of time," thus satisfying "a basic psychological need in man, for death is but the victory of time." In this interesting analogy Bazin, it seems to me, offers an existentialist interpretation of the mummy, which, at the same time, undermines Egyptian religion itself; since the ancient Egyptians above all axiomatically assumed the reality of life after death—toward which the mummy was no more than a means.

35. In this essay, I refer to some of the various subgenres of the Hollywood Orientalist film of which I have identified seven: 1) Stories concerning contemporary Westerners in the Orient (*The Sheik* (1921), *The Road to Morocco* (1942), *Casablanca* (1942), *The Man Who Knew Too Much* (1956), *Raiders of the Lost Ark* (1981), *Sahara* (1983), *Ishtar* (1987)); 2) Films concerning "Orientals" in the first world (*Black Sunday* (1977), *Back to the Future* (1985)); 3) Films based on ancient history such as the diverse versions of *Cleopatra*; 4) Films based on contemporary history (*Exodus* (1960), (*Lawrence of Arabia* (1962)); 5) Films based on the Bible (*Judith of Bethulia* (1913), *Samson and Delilah* (1949), *The Ten Commandments* (1956)); 6) Films based on *The Arabian Nights* (*The Thief of Baghdad* (1924), *Oriental Dream* (1944), *Kismet* (1955)); 7) Films in which ancient Egypt and its mythologized enigmas serve as pretext for contemporary

horror-mystery and romance (the *Mummy* series). I view these films partially in the light of Edward Said's indispensable contribution to anti-colonial discourse, i.e., his genealogical critique of Orientalism as the discursive formation by which European culture was able to manage—and even produce—the Orient during the post-Enlightenment period.

36. Mallek Alloula examines this issue in French postcards of Algeria. See *The Colonial Harem*. Translated by Myrna Godzich and Wlad Godzich. Minneapolis: University of Minnesota Press, 1986.

37. Freud associates Africa and femininity in *The Interpretation of Dreams* when he speaks of Haggard's *She* as "a strange book, but full of hidden meaning . . . the eternal feminine . . . *She* describes an adventurous road that had scarcely even been trodden before, leading into an undiscovered region. . . ." *The Standard Edition of the Complete Psychological Works of Sigmund Freud*, ed. James Strachey. London: The Hogarth Press, 1953–74, SE IV–V, pp. 453–4.

38. Joseph Breuer and Sigmund Freud, *Studies on Hysteria*. Translated by James Strachey in collaboration with Anna Freud. New York: Basic Books, 1957, p. 139.

39. Breuer and Freud, *Studies on Hysteria*, p. 193.

40. Sigmund Freud, "On Transformations of Instinct as Exemplified in Anal Erotism," in *The Standard Edition of the Complete Psychological Works of Sigmund Freud*, SE XVII, pp. 129, 135.

41. Toril Moi, "Representation of Patriarchy: Sexuality and Epistemology in Freud's Dora," in Charles Brenheimer and Claire Kahane, eds. *In Dora's Case: Freud, Hysteria, Feminism*. London: Virago, 1985, p. 198.

42. David Macey, *Lacan in Contexts*. London, New York: Verso, 1988, pp. 178–180.

43. Breuer and Freud, *Studies on Hysteria*, p. 292.

44. Stephan Salisbury, "In Dr. Freud's Collection, Objects of Desire," *The New York Times*, September 3, 1989.

45. "My voyage to the Orient was like a grand act of my interior life."

46. Linking Jews to the history, politics and culture of the West must be seen as continuous with Zionist discourse which has elided the largely Third World Arab history and culture of Middle Eastern Sephardic Jews. For a full discussion of the problematics generated by Zionist discourse, see Ella Shohat, "Sephardim in Israel: Zionism from the Standpoint of Its Jewish Victims," *Social Text* 19/20 (Fall 1988). This debate was partially continued in *Critical Inquiry* Vol 15, No 3 (Spring 1989) in the section "An Exchange on Edward Said and Difference." See especially, Edward Said, "Response," pp. 634–646.

47. *The Ten Commandments*, partially shot on location in Egypt, was banned by the Egyptian government.

48. On another level we might discern a hidden Jewish substratum undergirding the film. In the ancient past Egypt dispossessed the Hebrews of their ark and in the present (the thirties) it is the Nazis; but in a time tunnel Harrison Ford is sent to fight the Nazis in the name of a Jewish shrine (the word "Jewish" is of course never mentioned in the film) and in the course of events the rescuer is rescued by the rescuee. A phantasy of liberation from a history of victimization is played out by Steven Spielberg, using Biblical myths of wonders worked against ancient Egyptians this time redeployed against the Nazis—miracles absent during the Holocaust. The Hebrew ark itself performs miracles and dissolves the Nazis, saving Dr. Jones and his girlfriend Marion from the Germans who, unlike the Americans, do not respect the divine law of never looking at the Holy of Holies. The Jewish religious prohibition of looking at God's image and the prohibition of graven images (with the consequent cultural de-emphasis on visual arts) is triumphant over the Christian predilection for religious visualization. The film, in the typical paradox of cinematic voyeurism, punishes the hubris of the "Christian" who looks at divine beauty while at the same time nourishing the spectator's visual pleasure.

49. *Al Mumia* (*The Mummy*) was exhibited in the U. S. under the title *The Night of Counting the Years*.

50. Ahmose freed Egypt from the Hyksos invaders and ushered in the "New Empire" period of ancient Egyptian history.

51. Thutmose III was Egypt's greatest warrior pharaoh who conquered Palestine and Syria.

52. Rameses II is the reputed Pharaoh of the Exodus.

53. Howard Carter and A. C. Mace's narrative of their predecessor's 1881 discovery, for example, links the Egyptologists' rescue of mummies to the ancient Egyptian priests' protection of their Kings: "There, huddled together in a shallow, ill-cut grave, lay the most powerful monarchs of the ancient East, kings whose names were familiar to the whole world, whom no one in his wildest moments had ever dreamed of seeing. There they had remained, where the priests in secrecy had hurriedly brought

them that dark night three thousand years ago; and on their coffins and mummies, neatly docketed, were the records of their journeyings from one hiding place to another. Some had been wrapped, and two or three in the course of their many wanderings had been moved to other coffins. In forty-eight hours—we don't do things quite so hastily nowadays—the tomb was cleared; the kings were embarked upon the museum barge." (Shirley Glubok, ed., *Discovering Tut-ankh-Amen's Tomb*. (Abridged and adapted from Howard Carter and A. C. Mace, *The Tomb of Tut-ankh-Amen*) New York: Macmillan Publishing, 1968, p. 15.)

54. In a relatively recent interview following the screening of *The Mummy* on Egyptian television, Shadi Abdel Salam was slightly criticized for relying on a Western musician when Egypt has its own musicians. Abdel Salam insisted that the Italian musician was chosen for his technical knowledge, and that his role was basically to arrange a pre-existing popular Egyptian music. Khassan Aawara, "*Al Mumia*," *Al Anba*, October 30, 1983. (Arabic)

55. In addition to Edward Said's pioneering critical writings on Orientalist discourse and specifically on Egypt, see also Timothy Mitchel, *Colonising Egypt*. Cambridge: Cambridge University Press, 1988.

56. Shirley Glubok, p. 15.

57. Guy Hennebelle, "Chadi Abdel Salam Prix Georges Sadoul 1970: "La momie" est une reflexion sur le destin d'une culture nationale." *Les Lettres Francaises*, No. 1366, December 30, 1977, p. 17.

58. "They were the mightiest Pharaohs. What became of them?"—a meditation in the film reminiscent in some ways of Shelly's "Ozymandias."

59. See *The Book of the Dead*, ed. E. A. Wallis Budge. London: Arkana, 1989.

60. See for example Cynthia Enloe, *Bananas Beaches and Bases: Making Feminist Sense of International Politics*. (Berkeley: University of California Press, 1989), pp. 19–41.

61. See Boris Uspensky, *A Poetics of Composition*. Berkeley: University of California Press, 1973.

62. For a critical discussion of the representation of Black female sexuality in the cinema see Jane Gaines, "White Privilege and Looking Relations—Race and Gender in Feminist Film Theory," *Screen* Vol. 29, No. 4 (Autumn 1988). On Black spectatorship and reception of dominant films see for example Jacqueline Bobo, "*The Color Purple*: Black Women as Cultural Readers" in Diedre Pridram, ed. *Female Spectators: Looking at Films and Television* (New York: Verso, 1988); Manthia Diawara, "Black Spectatorship: Problems of Identification and Resistance" in *Screen* Vol. 29, No 4 (Autumn 1988).

63. The mystery in the *Mummy* films which often involves a kind of Liebestod or haunting heterosexual attraction—for example *The Mummy* (1932), *The Mummy's Curse* (1944), *The Mummy's Hand* (1940)—can be seen in this sense as allegorizing the mysteries of sexuality itself.

64. In her striking autobiography, Harriet Jacobs, for example, recounts the history of her family, focussing especially on the degradation of slavery and the sexual oppression she suffered as a slave woman. Her daily struggle against racial/sexual abuse is well illustrated in the cases of her master, who was determined to turn her into his concubine, his jealous wife, who added her own versions of harassments, and the future congressman, who, after fathering her children, did not keep his promise to set them free. *Incidents in the Life of a Slave Girl Written by Herself*, Fagan Yellin, ed. Cambridge, Massachusetts: Harvard University Press, 1987.

65. Citations from The Production Code of the Motion Picture Producers and Directors of America, Inc.—1930–1934 are taken from Garth Jowett, *Film: The Democratic Art* (Boston: Little, Brown and Company, 1976).

66. Here I am especially thinking of Anna Julia Cooper and Ida B. Wells.

67. Hazel V. Carby, "Lynching, Empire, and Sexuality." *Critical Inquiry* Vol. 12, number 1 (Autumn 1985).

68. For discussion of rape and racial violence see for example Jacquelyn Dowd Hall, " 'The Mind that Burns in Each Body': Women, Rape, and Racial Violence" in Ann Snitow, Christine Stansell and Sharon Thompson, eds. *Powers of Desire* (New York: Monthly Review Press, 1983).

69. Haile Gerima's *Bush Mama* anatomizes contemporary American power structure in which rape performed by a white policeman is subjectivized through the helpless young Black woman.

70. Fredric Jameson, "Third World Literature in the Era of Multinational Capitalism." *Social Text* 15 (Fall 1986). Although Jameson speaks of allegory in a Third World context, I found the category germane for the First World, increasingly characterized by "othernesses" and "differences" within itself.

71. For example, Ferdinand-Victor-Eugene Delacoix, as Lawrence Michalak points out, borrowed Indian clothing from a set designer for his models, threw in some "Assyrian" motifs from travel books and Persian miniatures, and invented the rest of the Maghreb from his imagination. ("Popular French

Perspectives on the Maghreb: Orientalist Painting of the Late 19th and Early 20th Centuries," in *Connaissances du Maghreb: Sciences Sociales et Colonisation*, Jean-Claude Vatin, ed. Paris: Editions du Centre National de la Recherche Scientifique, 1984).

72. Images of nude breasts of African women in the *Tarzan* series relied on travelogues. Trinh T. Minh-ha in *Reassemblage* (1982) attempts to question the focus on breasts in ethnological cinema. For her broader critique of anthropology see *Woman, Native, Other* (Bloomington: Indiana University Press, 1989), pp. 47–76.

73. Fellini's *8½*, meanwhile, self-mockingly exposes this pornographic imagination of the King Solomon-style harem as merely amplifying the protagonist's actual lived polygamy.

74. For the Orientalist ideology undergirding the translations of *A Thousand and One Nights* to European languages see Rana Kabbani, *Europe's Myths of Orient* (Bloomington: Indiana University Press, 1986).

75. See for example Huda Shaarawi, *Harem Years: The Memoirs of an Egyptian Feminist (1879–1924)*. Translated by Margot Badran. New York: The Feminist Press at The City University of New York, 1987.

76. See Lois Beck and Nikki Keddie, eds. *Women in the Muslim World*. Cambridge, Massachusetts: Harvard University Press, 1978; Mervat Hatem, "The Politics of Sexuality and Gender in Segregated Patriarchal Systems: The Case of Eighteenth- and Nineteenth-Century Egypt." *Feminist Studies* 12, No. 2 (Summer 1986).

77. For a critique of Eurocentric representation of the Harem see Leila Ahmed "Western Ethnocentrism and Perceptions of the Harem," *Feminist Studies* 8, No. 3 (Fall 1982).

78. The artistic representation of the solitary confinement of upper-middle class Western women within the household is fascinatingly researched and analyzed by Bram Dijkstra, *Idols of Perversity*. New York: Oxford University Press, 1986.

79. Protofeminist Western women such as Hubertine Auclert, Françoise Correze, Mathea Gaudry, and Germaine Tillion, as Marnia Lazreg suggests, reproduced Orientalist discourse in their writings. For a critique of Western feminism and colonial discourse see for example Marnia Lazreg "Feminism and Difference: The Perils of Writing as a Woman on Women in Algeria," *Feminist Studies* 14:3 (Fall 1988); Chandra Talpade Mohanty, "Under Western Eyes: Feminist Scholarship and Colonial Discourses," *Boundary* 2:12 (Spring/Fall 1984); Gayatri Chakravorty Spivak, "French Feminism in an International Frame," *Yale French Studies* 62 (1981); *In Other Worlds: Essays in Cultural Politics*, Chapter 3 "Entering the Third World" (New York and London: Methuen, 1987).

80. Robert Halsband, ed., *The Complete Letters of Lady Mary Wortley Montagu*, Vol. I (London: Oxford University Press, 1965), p. 314.

81. Robert Halsband, ed., *The Selected Letters of Lady Mary Wortley Montagu*, New York: St. Martin's Press, 1970), pp. 96–97.

82. Robert Halsband, ed., *The Complete Letters of Lady Mary Wortley Montagu*, Vol. I, pp. 314–315.

83. For an analysis of the "mechanical reproduction" of women in Busby Berkely's films, see Lucy Fischer, "The Image of Woman As Image: The Optical Politics of *Dames*," in Patricia Erens, ed. *Sexual Stratagems: The World of Women in Film*. New York: Horizon Press, 1979.

84. Quoted in Lucy Fischer, "The Image of Woman As Image: The Optical Politics of *Dames*," p. 44.

85. For a detailed analysis of *The Battle of Algiers*, see Robert Stam, "Three Women, Three Bombs: *The Battle of Algiers* Notes and Analysis" *Film Study Extract*, MacMillan Press, 1975. See also Barbara Harlow's introduction to Malek Alloula, *The Colonial Harem*, pp. ix–xxii.

86. In *Battle of Algiers* FLN Algerian men at one point wear Arab female dress—a disguise whose ultimate goal is to assert Algerian national identity. This ephemeral change of gender identities within anti-colonial texts requires a more elaborate analysis of the Third World masculine rescue operation of Third World women from the violation of First World men. Such feminist criticism directed at the works of Frantz Fanon and Malek Alloula within the Algerian/French context has been addressed, in the Black/White North American context, at Malcolm X and the Black Panthers.

87. See J. C. Flugel, *The Psychology of Clothes* (London: Hogarth Press, 1930). For an extended discussion of Flugel writing on fashion see Kaja Silverman "The Fragments of a Fashionable Discourse," in *Studies in Entertainment: Critical Approaches to Mass Culture*, ed. Tania Modleski (Bloomington: India University Press, 1986); Also Silverman, *The Acoustic Mirror: The Female Voice in Psychoanalysis and Cinema* (Bloomington: Indiana University Press, 1988), pp. 24–27.

88. The American journalist Lowell Thomas was instrumental in the popularization of T. E. Lawrence in

the West; his show, which consisted of lecture and footage he shot from the Middle East front, was, after a short time, moved to Madison Square Garden. See John E. Mack *A Prince of Our Disorder: The Life of T. E. Lawrence*. Boston: Little Brown and Company, 1976.

89. Leslie Fiedler argues that homoerotic friendship between White men and Black or indigenous men is at the core of the classical American novel. See *Love and Death in the American Novel* (New York: Criterion Books, 1960).

90. Interestingly Leslie Fiedler's *The Inadvertent Epic* comments on another white woman novelist, Margaret Mitchell, whose *Gone With the Wind* is structured according to scenarios of inter-ethnic rapes.

91. For an analysis of Valentino and female spectatorship, see Miriam Hansen, "Pleasure, Ambivalence, Identification: Valentino and Female Spectatorship." *Cinema Journal* 25, No. 4 (Summer, 1986).

92. *Movie Weekly*, November 19, 1921.

93. *Movie Weekly*, November 19, 1921.

94. Denis de Rougemont partially traces the liebestod motif to Arabic poetry. See *Love in the Western World*, Translated by Montgomery Belgion. New York: Harper & Row Publishers, 1974.

Exile Discourse and Televisual Fetishization

Hamid Naficy

EXILE AS LIMINALITY

It is now nearly two years since I have become a refugee in this place, spending every few nights in a friend's house. I feel uprooted. Nothing seems real. Paris buildings all seem like theatrical set pieces. I imagine I am living inside a postal card. I fear two things: one is sleeping the other is waking (Sa'edi, 1986:4).

So wrote Gholam Hosain Sa'edi, a celebrated Iranian writer and a psychiatrist who died in 1985 in exile in Paris, France. It is fitting to begin with pain and paralysis because it is with them that exile begins: pain because of loss and separation, paralysis because of disorientation and epistemic confusion. So, let's continue with pain and paralysis by quoting a passage from Mahshid Amirshahi's introduction to her recent novel written in exile:

Sometimes, it seems to me that time passes like a meteor; sometimes, I think it has stopped in its track like a heavy rock. Sometimes, events seem connected like a chain; sometimes, they seem discreet like beads in a rosary. Sometimes, I do not venture outside for days; some-times, I do not return home for nights. Sometimes, all states seem figurative; sometimes, all things appear real. Sometimes, I sulk at the world; sometimes, I fight it. Sometimes, I cannot tolerate myself; sometimes, I cannot stand other people. Sometimes, I feel lonely in the midst of others; sometimes, while alone I imagine a crowd. Sometimes, I want to forget everything; sometimes, I don't want anything to pass without having committed it to memory. Some-times, anger overcomes me; sometimes, shame. Sometimes, fear blocks my breathing; sometimes, tears. Sometimes, I am a spectator; sometimes, an actor. Sometimes, resigned; sometimes, rebellious. Sometimes, I say to myself I should live in order to see; sometimes, I want to die and not to know (1987: introduction, no page number).

This compound sense of pain and paralysis is not due solely to the displacing conditions one finds in exile but also often it is related to the dire circumstances one has left behind. Tragedy at home, which often drives people out of their countries, looms large, even larger, in exile. All of these and more fuse to create in exile an uncanny, agonistic, liminal state; that is, a threshold state in which the liminars or the exiles live on the threshold between two cultures. Often they are stripped of their former status, rank, property, and family links and separated from language and the various ideological apparatuses of home culture. Thus freed from these traditional constraints, they are "deterritorialized" (Deleuze and Guattari, 1986).

HAMID NAFICY's *works have appeared in such journals as* Literature-Film, Jump Cut, Quarterly Review of Film Studies, Third World Affairs, Journal of Film and Video, Emergences, *and* Public Culture. *His book on culture in exile is forthcoming from the University of Minnesota Press. He currently teaches at UCLA Department of Film & TV.*

Salman Rushdie, in his "exile novel," *The Satanic Verses*, describes the fall to earth of Gibreel Farishta and Saladin Chamcha from their exploding jumbo jet in terms which evoke the sense of deterritorialization employed here:

[M]ingling with the remnants of the plane, equally fragmented, equally absurd, there floated the debris of the soul, broken memories, sloughed-off selves, severed mother-tongues, lost loves, the forgotten meaning of hollow, booming *words, land, belonging, home.* (emphases are in the original, 1988:4).

Iranian poet Esma'il Kho'i, who now lives in England, too, in the following passages written in English, graphically sums up the internal dynamics of the type of deterritorialization spawned by the liminal state of inbetweenness:

The refugee is, and will remain HOMELESS in this sense. For him or her, everything is, and is to remain, unsettled. This is his/her predicament. The time is ALWAYS the time being, and HOME is dreamland in the far far away. Un-wanting to be in the host society and unable to go back home. Un-welcome here, and un-wanted there—except, of course, for imprisonment and/or torturing and/or shooting. An outsider here, an outcast there. Physically here, mentally there. Not a split personality, but a split person. The refugee is, and is to remain, the typical example of what I call "People In Between" (emphases are in the original, 1987:13).

However, liminality not only causes paralysis and deterritorialization, but also it positions the exiles to play and to reterritorialize themselves, i.e., build themselves anew.

Cultures are not monolithic nor univocal and no discussion about the manner in which exiles deal with their experience is complete without taking into consideration their contradictory impulses and the polysemy of their cultural productions. Thus, the feeling of deep celibacy expressed in the above excerpts, which chiefly characterizes the discourse of the elite in exile, is offset by a reverse sense of intense celebration which infuses the popular culture of the exiles. For example, in the Iranian popular culture in Los Angeles, one is exposed to many instances of liminal ecstasy, in the elaborate weddings, funerals, concerts, and various religious and national holiday celebrations; in frequent political demonstrations, popular poetry reading nights; and in the profusion of nightclubs and discos. Of course, Iranian television programs produced in Los Angeles, as a mass communication medium, both reflect and shape the exile experience in the two modalities of celibacy and celebration.

This discourse on high and popular cultures in exile is useful because it illuminates, by way of contrast, something about the multivalent way in which cultures process the conditions of exile. In that sense, even the characterization of the elite as celibate and the popular as celebrant is problematic, since both cultures at times partake of both attitudes. Further, neither of the two cultures is entirely coherent as each contains within itself contradictory impulses. In fact the dialogic and conflictual interaction between these two cultures is perhaps one of the best locations from which one could study the dynamics of cultural discourse in exile (Naficy, 1991b).

For some, liminality is a finite phase which terminates when the exiles are incorporated into the host culture. But incorporation or assimilation is neither total nor irreversible. In fact, for most, liminality is a continuous state, a "slipzone" of denial, ambivalence, inbetweenness, doubling, splitting, fetishization, hybridization, and syncretism. Located in the slipzone, where home and host cultures overlap and slide over and under and past each other, the liminar exiles are inbetween the structural force fields of both social systems, and as a result they are able to question, subvert, modify, or even adopt attributes of either or both cultural systems. It is this distance from and ambivalence towards the authority of both cultures that makes the boundaries of exilic "positionality"—the separation of self from other, younger generation from older generation, colonizer from colonized, third world from first world—different from both the Hegelian master/slave paradigm and the phenomenological projection of Otherness. In exile, one is "positioned" to question the "common senses" of both home and host cultures and to reconfigure them in ways that potentially either threaten or enrich both. As Victor Turner has noted, "it is the analysis of culture into factors and their free recombination in any and every possible pattern, however weird, that is most characteristic of liminality [. . .]" (1974:255). Any cultural space, such as the liminality created by exile, which structurally encourages analysis and reconfiguration of deep values, is capable of breeding radicalism, conservatism, or in general extremism of all kinds.

The exilic ambivalence stems from holding two essentially incompatible positions or attitudes simultaneously, one involving the disavowal and the other the recognition of difference—racial, ethnic, historical, and knowledge and power differences that exist between host and home cultures. The exiles know they are different but simultaneously they deny it; they know they are separated from home but simultaneously they disavow it. If these twin but conflicting processes are not operative, then, unproblematical assimilation into the host society or domination by the host culture is likely. But, that is not usually the case. Indeed, disavowal and recognition are both present and create an ambivalent slippery space where assimilation and resistance to assimilation can coexist. Disavowal of difference encourages assimilation and recognition of difference results in resistance through "ethnic resilience." Resistance, or resilience, however, need not entail oppositional acts of a political nature, nor involve negation of the content of another culture. Rather, as Homi Bhabha states, resistance can be

[T]he effect of an ambivalence produced within the rules of recognition of dominating discourses as they articulate the signs of cultural difference and reimplicate them within the deferential relations of colonial power—hierarchy, normalization, marginalization, and so forth. Domination is achieved through a process of disavowal that denies the *différance* of colonialist power—the chaos of its intervention as *Entstellung*, its dislocatory presence [. . .] (1986:172).

Ambivalence itself, this dislocatory presence, is complex. It involves two chief processes, fetishism and hybridity, both of which are based on partial repression and splitting of the subject. In this essay, I will concern myself with fetishism and since I want to use exile-produced television as a site for reading the polysemy and the dynamics of the slipzone of liminality, particularly fetishism, it is necessary to become familiar first with the discourse of such TV programs. On an average, every week in Los Angeles, TV programs are broadcast in some 14 different languages. As a case study, I will use TV programs produced by Iranians in Los Angeles.

IRANIAN TELEVISION IN EXILE

No current reliable statistics about the demography and the number of Iranians living in the United States or in Los Angeles exists as yet. However, widely circulated press estimates (which are highly suspect) give the figure of between 200,000 to 480,000 in Los Angeles alone, making it the largest Iranian community outside Iran (Mofid, 1987:19; Beckland, 1987:27; *Javanan* 10/21/1988:30; *Kayhan-e Hava'i* 8/30/89:2).[1] Despite the paucity and the unreliability of demographic data, it is clear that Iranians living in the U.S. are not homogeneous: they differ widely in religion, social status, ethnicity, language, gender, political persuasion, education, their timing and reasons for departure, and finally their legal status. While acknowledging their heterogeneity, however, I will apply to Iranians living in the U.S. the term "exile" because during the liminal period (in which they presently live), the idea of return is a dominant feature of their popular culture and discourses.[2]

The explosive growth of this population (the bulk of the emigres entered this country after the anti-Shah revolution of 1978),[3] its high concentration in one locality (Southern California), and its heavy use of TV (as one of the first televisual exile groups) are motivating factors for this study. In addition, this particular group is still undergoing exilic changes, since it has not yet emerged from liminality. For these reasons, the situation of Iranians in Los Angeles offers an opportunity to examine the tensions and processes of exilic discourse as they evolve.

Although relative newcomers, Iranians have been some of the most active users of television among the many ethnic minorities in this country. In fact, with the exception of Hispanic programming, Persian language television broadcasts top all other *locally produced* "ethnic" programs in the Los Angeles area. Even though Chinese and Korean language programs exceed in volume, they cannot be considered exile-produced since by far the greatest majority of them are preproduced and imported from the respective home countries.

PROGRAM PRODUCTION: The first Iranian TV program produced in exile, *Iranian*, began in March 1981 as a 30 minute weekly show, but soon expanded to one hour (Figure 1). Since that initial effort, some 28 *regularly scheduled* programs have been aired, with the current number standing at 15 shows totaling 17 hours per week (Table 1). All of them are produced in Los Angeles.

From a political point of view, all the current and past TV shows have been and are secular and highly partisan, opposing the Islamic government in Iran. In fact, they are predominantly royalist. This political partisanship reflects a) the exile community in Southern California which generally favors the return of some type of monarchy to Iran; b) the religious belief and the political disposition of producers themselves, many of whom belong to minorities persecuted in Iran (Jews, Baha'is, Armenians); c) the anti-"terrorist" mind-set of successive U.S. administrations (and mainline media), which leads TV stations to deny broadcasting access to unfriendly governments such as the one in Iran;[5] and d) TV producers' general lack of formal training in TV production and in procedures of "objective" journalism despite the fact that almost all of them have had what we might call "show business" backgrounds (Naficy, 1990).

Many of these TV programs are syndicated, that is, they are "bicycled" to other cities in the U.S. (e.g., Washington D.C., New York, San Francisco, San Diego, Sacramento, Houston) for regular rebroadcast by local stations.

AUDIENCES—There is a great deal of uncertainty about the size and the demographic profile of audiences watching the so-called "ethnic television" programs.

Figure 1. The ad for Iranian, the first TV program in exile, announcing its inaugural broadcast on 3/15/1981.

TABLE 1. Regularly scheduled Iranian TV programs
originating in Los Angeles, 1981–August 1989[4]

Program title	Length	Began	Current status	Frequency
Iranian A.M.	60	1981	Continues	Weekly
Jam-e Jam	60	1981	Continues	Weekly
Sima-ye Ashna	30	1982	Continues	Daily
Melli	60	1982	Ceased	Weekly
Mikhak-e Noqreh'i	60	1983	Ceased	Weekly
Mehr-e Iran	60	1983	Ceased	Weekly
Jonbesh-e Melli	60	1983	Continues	Weekly
Parsian	60	1984	Ceased	Weekly
Sima-ye Azadi	60	1986	Ceased	Weekly
Iranian Music TV	60	1986	Ceased	Weekly
Jom'-eh	60	1986	Ceased	Weekly
Mellat	60	1986	Ceased	Weekly
Iran	30	1987	Continued	Daily
Pars	60	1987	Continues	Weekly
Melli-e Pars	60	1987	Ceased	Weekly
Midnight Show	60	1987	Continues	Weekly
Cheshmak	30	1987	Ceasaed	Weekly
Negah	30	1988	Ceased	Weekly
Jong-e Bamdadi	30	1988	Continues	Daily
Omid-e Iran	30	1988	ceased	Daily
Jahan Nama	30	1988	Continues	Weekly
Arya in L.A.	30	1988	Continues	Weekly
Didar	60	1988	Ceased	Weekly
Sobh-e Ruz-e Jom'eh	30	1988	Continues	Weekly
Iranian, P.M.	30	1989	Continues	Weekly
Tamasha	30	1989	Continues	Weekly
Iran va Jahan	30	1989	Continues	Weekly
Ma TV	60	1989	Continues	Weekly

This is because with the exception of Hispanic audiences, none of the rating services, such as the Nielsen or the Arbitron, compile regular statistics on the viewing habits and preferences of ethnic viewers. However, one source that gives us a clue is the research conducted by individual stations themselves who cater to exile TV programs. According to the latest figures compiled by KSCI-TV, the 1987 Iranian viewing audience in Los Angeles was approximately 70,000 weekly households and 240,000 weekly viewers.[6] The producer of one program, *Jonbesh-e Melli*, claims that viewers of his program exceed two million world-wide (Ketab Corp, 1989:362) and producers of two other programs, *Jam-e Jam* and *Iranian*, contend that copies of their shows are seen in Canada, Western Europe, Persian Gulf countries and Iran itself.[7] The viewership world wide is even harder to substantiate but these claims indicate the ambition and the self-importance with which producers view their own work.

PROGRAMS—During the liminal phase of exile, much experimentation with program form and format took place. However, between 1981 and 1987 the discourse of exile TV remained relatively stable and homogeneous. An "exile genre" of TV programming emerged, the dominant feature of which is pastiche and the maga-zine format, typically consisting of political newsreports from Iran, the U.S., and the world; local Los Angeles news consisting chiefly of reports about Iranian entertainers; highly partisan news commentary; a brief comedy sketch, usually mocking the Islamic government or some aspects of life in exile; musical numbers featuring singers singing and dancing; and sometimes a brief section of a serial imported from Iran. Of course, there is experimentation with segments within the format (for example, adding a children's section), but the basic magazine form is generally unaltered until the late 1980s (Figure 2).

Cementing the various sections are numerous commercials for Iranian products and services, chief among them the following: physicians, lawyers, insurance companies, real estate brokers, beauty products, cars and automotive services, household furniture, nightclubs, restaurants, and fresh vegetables and fruits.

The discourse of these liminal shows, invariably, is nourished by home—Iranian nationalism, racial difference, cultural authenticity, secularism, and monarchy as borne out by the titles of the shows and their logos, a topic to which I will return later. At this point, little attention is paid to the process of adaptation or to the American social institutions or politics. News about Iran dominates and the news-casts present a strictly Iranian point of view, effacing the fact of exile and giving the impression of living and watching news in Iran.[8] In addition, these programs heavily feature Iranian classical and popular music and songs, which are often repackaged old show numbers recorded in Iran prior to the revolution. Thus, both ideas and products of home dominate.

Further, the discourse of these early exile shows is infused by Iran in the manner in which the notion of authority is deployed in them. Until late 1988, when *Didar* appeared, all programs were produced and organized by a male patriarch whose vision, connections, financial resources, and personality entirely dominated the discourse as well as the screen itself (since most producers also appeared as on-camera talent). Patriarchal authority is circulated also in the heavily news-oriented shows which repeatedly run film clips of leading officials of the Islamic government and their political opponents in exile, almost all of whom are men. Even when women host a show or read the news, they slip into the dominant (male) style: their facial expressions are serious and earnest, their discourse is highly political and uncompromising, and their language is very literary and formal. The vernacular and the private is suppressed in the interest of the formal and the public.

The uniformity of patriarchal authority extends to the production of programs, for which, with few exceptions, little division of labor or sharing of authority is evident.[9] This applies to audiences as well. The notion of viewers as differentially situated groups of spectators capable of being addressed separately emerges only gradually. Viewers are seen generally as a homogeneous mass of people uprooted from home and without roots in exile. Thus, programs and commercials are not specialized; they address the entire family.

ADVERTISING-DRIVEN SCHEDULE—There has been considerable fluctuation in the fate of exile TV programs through the years. Nearly as many as are being currently aired (15) have expired (13). Nonetheless, overall, the number of new shows has risen, particularly in the last four years. Table 1 shows the following rate of growth: two new programs in 1981, two in 1982, three in 1983, one in 1984, none in 1985, four in 1986, five in 1987, seven in 1988, and four in the first six months of 1989.

Figure 2.   Ad for daily live news show, Jong-e Bamdadi. *(Courtesy Ketab Corp.)*

To accommodate the increased fare and to position the audiences to receive advertisers' messages, an advertising-driven schedule has gradually developed supported by a proliferating Iranian business community. Table 2 shows the broadcast schedule of all current Iranian programs in Los Angeles as well as the type of programming under which they predominantly can be classified. With the exception of *Iran*, which is cablecast, all others are broadcast over the air by KSCI-TV, Channel 18. Programs are in the Persian language, six of them are one hour and nine are 30 minutes in length.

The political economy of this schedule is such that now TV programmers can target their audiences and deliver them to advertisers more frequently at more propitious prime time hours, which by KSCI's account includes the regular prime time hours, from 7:30 P.M. to 11 P.M., as well as late night hours and the weekend.[10]

The possibility of using more than one station to air exile programs increases the ability of producers to engage both in counter-programming and in reducing the cost of air time by playing one station against the other. More importantly, access to more than one station can encourage political and ideological diversity. This is borne out by what happened to *Sima-ye Azadi*, produced by the Mojahedin, the opposition group working to overthrow the Islamic regime. The program was taken off the air by KSCI-TV because it supported the ideology and the politics of the Mojahedin, which the Reagan administration and the Congress had labeled as terrorist.[11] But, soon, the program resumed broadcasting on another channel, KDOC-TV, Channel 56, continuing its advocacy of the group. Whatever its shortcomings, this program provided an alternative view to that espoused by almost all the other programs, since it was neither royalist nor in favor of the Islamic government in Iran (Figure 3).

The financial dimensions of the political economy of such an advertising-driven schedule are also far reaching. With the exception of *Sima-ye Azadi*, which was entirely underwritten by the Mojahedin and was therefore free from commercials for consumer products, all other programs are run on a commercial basis, whereby clusters of ads frequently interrupt the flow of TV texts. In fact, the amount of time devoted to commercials on Iranian TV increased so dramatically that by mid 1987 it reached an alltime peak of 40 minutes per one hour of programming. After much criticism from viewers and haggling, the station and the programmakers agreed on a limit of 20 minutes per hour of commercials, which seems to be holding so far.[12]

Businesses place commercial announcements for their products within the TV programs and pay between $3 to $6 for each second of the commercial, depending on the popularity of the program and the number of times and the length of period during which the ad is aired. Thus, a thirty second commercial can cost a business between $90 and $180.[13] My calculations show that Iranian producers earn close to $4 million annually through the sale of airtime for ads. The cost of renting air time from the broadcasting station, too, varies depending on the time of the day and the day of the week. For example, in 1987–88 KSCI-TV charged program producers the following rates per half hour of air-time for broadcasting their programs during week days: early morning hours, $1,400; primetime evening hours, $3,600; and late night hours, $2,000. A half-hour of air time on Sunday afternoons, a standard time slot for flagship Iranian programs, cost around $2,000.[14] Again, my calculations show that Iranian producers pay nearly $2 million annually to TV stations to air

TABLE II. Broadcast schedule of Iranian programs in Los Angeles, KSCI channel 18 and cable TV channels, week of July 31–August 6, 1989

Time	Monday	Tuesday	Wednesday	Thursday	Friday	Saturday	Sunday
07:30	Sima-ye Ashna [Feature stories]	Sima-ye Ashna	Sima-ye Ashna	Sima-ye Ashna	Sima-ye Ashna	—	—
08:00	Jong-e Bamdadi [News and Commentary]	Jong-e Bamdadi	Jong-e Bamdadi	Jong-e Bamdadi	Jong-e Bamdadi	—	—
08:30	—	—	—	—	Sobh-e Jom'eh [Variety]	—	—
11:00	—	—	—	—	—	—	Iranian A.M. [News/Comments]
12:00	—	—	—	—	—	—	Jonbesh-e Melli [News/Comments]
13:00	—	—	—	—	—	—	Jam-e Jam 1 [Variety/News]
14:00	—	—	—	—	—	Iran	Iran
21:00	Iran [Variety and Entertainment]	Iran	Iran	—	Iran	—	—
21:30	—	—	—	—	—	—	—
22:30	Tamasha [Variety]	—	—	—	—	—	—
23:00	Jam-e Jam 2 [Variety/Comedy]	—	—	—	—	—	Iranian P.M. [Variety]
23:30	—	—	—	—	—	—	Iran va Jahan [News/Commentary]
24:00	Arya in L.A. [Variety]	—	—	—	Pars [Variety]	—	Midnight Show [Talkshow]
00:30	—	—	—	—	Ma TV [Talkshow]	—	—
01:00	—	—	—	—	—	—	—

Figure 3.   Simay-e Azadi *logo: Dove of freedom.*

their programs. These combined figures show that Iranian TV in exile has become a veritable "ethnic economy" which, in the words of program producers, single-handedly is responsible for making Iranian community in Los Angeles become what it is today: highly visible and economically viable. According to them, without TV programs (and the advertising-driven broadcast schedule), both Iranian businesses and communities in Southern California would have failed to flourish. While such a contention seems plausible, more sociological studies are needed to establish its incontrovertibility. The broadcast schedule has aided exile TV to become a viable ethnic economy since it has expanded from an exclusively weekend time slot containing a 30 minute program in 1981 to a schedule that in 1989 distributes 17 hours of programming across all days and nights of the week.

The increase in the number of programs and the development of an advertising-driven schedule have resulted in increasing diversity in a number of areas: the authoritarian univocal discourse of the early liminal shows have weakened; the male discourse is being challenged by women who produce and host their own shows (e.g., *Didar* and *Ma TV*); the notion of audiences as homogeneous has given way to one that is differentiated by program type and the schedule; the rigid magazine format is fast evolving, with many shows emulating programs aired by American TV networks;[15] local serial production has increased and diversified to include comedies as well as soap operas about exile;[16] and, finally, the limited bicycling of copies of TV programs for rebroadcast at other cities has expanded to include a syndication system as well as a type of brokered broadcast network (Figure 4).

FETISHISM AND LIMINALITY

Fetishism and the repeated and wide circulation of fetishes are essential in the life of today's exiles who live in the age of electronic reproduction of images and simulation. As a cultural force, the electronic reproduction and commodification of fetishes would have been impossible in the pre-multinational, consumer capital era. Fetishization functions multiplexively, even contradictorily: during the liminal phase of exile, it aids in the formation and consolidation of ethnic identity, while at the same time, the electronically mediated circulation and commodification of

Figure 4.   *Ad and logo for* Didar, *the first exile program produced by a woman.*

fetishes helps to imbricate the exiles into the dominant host ideological and socio-economic systems. In this essay I will focus on its role in promoting ethnic solidarity.[17] As I have shown elsewhere (Naficy 1990), the sense of the self and of the everyday experiences and relationships of people who live in different civilizations are profoundly different from one another because they have a different experiential and affective sense of the self and of relationships as well as vastly different internalized world views. However, there are also certain features which are shared. For the sake of analysis in this essay, I am assuming that psychic life is to a large extent universal, and I will use Western theories cross-culturally without intending to Westernize thy psyche or the unconscious.

In psychoanalysis, fetishism is defined as a form of perversion that results from the threat of castration posed by the absence of the penis in the mother. Two contradictory attitudes arise in the male child. One is a recognition of the lack. The second is a disavowal of the lack through fetishization of the difference, resulting in the splitting of the ego (Freud, 1969:58–61). The fetish blocks the view of the absence but, paradoxically and inevitably, in its own existence it points to the absence, it becomes an index of the absence. As Freud has said, the fetish as a substitute memorializes the absence: "The horror of castration sets up a sort of permanent memorial to itself by creating this substitute" (1961b:154). The child thus alternates between belief and disbelief and this is precisely a major source of the ambivalence in fetishism. A Fetish masks the absence but not hermetically or permanently.

In Freud's discourse, both males and females undergo castration complex but very differently: the male experiences it as castration anxiety (fear of losing the penis) which is resolved when the Oedipus complex is brought to an end, while the female experiences it as penis envy (envy of not having a penis) which is resolved when the Oedipus complex is inaugurated (Freud, 1969:47–51). The castration scenario as a threat of loss, therefore, is a crucial moment in the formation of male sexuality. In Lacanian psychoanalysis, on the other hand, male and female both undergo castration equally when they leave the Imaginary to enter into the Symbolic realm, particularly language. According to Lacan, consciousness, or the formation of the subject, is possible only in language (1977:149), but this produces an eternal split between the subject and its representation in language, which is distinct from the organism or the subject itself. Castration for Lacan has nothing to do with presence or absence of a real penis; rather, it has to do with its symbolic value (i.e., the phallus), or with the recognition of both a biologic and a symbolic lack in the field of the Other. Fear of both biologic and symbolic castration engenders both fetishism and voyeurism. And it is the symbolic castration that is of interest in exilic discourse.[18] Even though males and females both pass through the castration phase, according to Lacan, castration is experienced somewhat differently by each gender: for the male the castrated mother constitutes a threat (of losing the penis) and for the female a nostalgia (for something she does not have). Desire, thus, is wedded to a threat or to a nostalgia (Gallop, 1985:145–6) and it is disavowed in the fetish. As will become evident in the course of this essay, Lacan's terms "threat" and "nostalgia" are more useful in the context of exile discourse than those of Freud's "threat" and "envy."

No discussion of fetishism is complete, of course, without an examination of what Marx has to say about the subject. However, his discourse on "commodity fetishism," formulated in volume one of *Capital* (1967:72), will not be deployed here. Suffice it to say that despite their differing formulations and the disparate spheres of human activity for which they developed their concept of fetishism, both Marx and Freud invoked the religious conceptions of fetishism prevalent in the eighteenth century studies of anthropology of religion which posited that human beings, who invent fetishes and invest them with powers and spirits, ultimately submit themselves to the powers of their own inventions by forgetting their manufactured inception—as if the source of power was some transcendental entity beyond human community.

Any fetish as a substitute object embodies a three-way power relationship among unequal elements: (1) the person who is fetishizing (2) the person or item being fetishized, and (3) the fetish object itself.[19] Seen in this way, the discourse on fetish, fetishism, and stereotyping (a form of fetishism) becomes productive not only in the discussion of personal relationships but, more importantly for this paper, in the context of cultural difference and cross-cultural power relationships. As Foucault has shown, knowledge and power are reciprocally intertwined (Foucault, 1979, 1980); similarly, fetishization and stereotyping are related to knowledge and power. Bhabha has shown that in the context of colonial discourse, a stereotype can act as a fetish which entails power because it arrests in time and space a certain configuration of knowledge about the fetish object, the colonized. The recognition of racial and sexual difference between the colonizer and the colonized is disavowed by the fixation on an object, i.e., a stereotype, that masks the difference and restores an original presence. because a stereotype is based on the recognition and disavowal of difference, it gives access as much to mastery and pleasure as to anxiety and defense. Now, for it to be productive in terms of power and knowledge, the stereotype must serve to simplify. Such simplification is not false representation, but an "arrested, fixated form of representation" (Bhabha, 1983:27). At the same time, the fetish or stereotype must remain immobile and immutable, refusing to acknowledge history and change. This frozen piece of knowledge about the other, or as Edward Said has called it this "typical encapsulation" (1979:58), then can be cycled and recycled both to marginalize and control the other and to "guarantee," in the words of Walter Lippman, our own "self-respect" (1922:103).

Freud, Metz, Bhabha, Lacan, and Mulvey and many other feminists seem to focus chiefly on fetishism based on disavowal of *lack* (castration), while Gaylyn Studlar, using Deleuze's works, has attempted to theorize fetishism based on disavowal of *separation* from the object of desire, the mother. The former turns the pain of the lack into sadistic pleasure by mastering the woman and controlling her fetishes, while the pleasure in the latter stems from identification with the woman, submission to her, and ultimately symbiosis with her. According to Studlar, "Masochistic disavowal transcends castration fear. Rather than relegating the woman to a position of lack, it exalts her to an idealized wholeness imitated in the son's fetishistic wish to restore identification and oneness with her [. . .]" (1988:43).

A critique of Freud's theory of fetishism based on its male-centeredness has already been voiced. In evaluating Bhabha's formulation, too, it must be noted here that he largely *desexualizes* the fetish which is based on lack; however, by *racializing* it, Bhabha makes fetishism-as-stereotyping useful in postcolonial and exilic discourses. In the same vein, masochistic fetishism can be taken not merely in its erotogenic and gendered configurations, as Studlar takes it, but in its moral dimension as well. In "moral masochism," the subject "as a result of an unconscious sense of guilt, seeks out the position of victim without any sexual pleasure being directly involved" (Laplanche and Pontalis, 1974:244). In exile, dual fetishism based on disavowal of both the lack and the separation is operative, as a result of which the exiled subject vacillates between the binary pairs of active/passive, controlling/ submissive, stability/instability.

FILM AND TELEVISION AS FETISHES

Christian Metz in an article in *October* provides a useful discourse on fetishism, photography, and film which I will use here as a point of departure. He posits that film, unlike a photograph, cannot be considered a fetish chiefly because it is narrativized, temporally organized, and collective in its reception. Further, film imposes its own reading time on its audience and cannot be held in hand, in pocket, or placed on the mantle. In addition, film's relationship with the dead moments that it captures is such that it seems to revive them. Finally, the off-screen world in film is substantially present even if it is off screen, through reframing, actor's movements, actor's voice, and sound effects. A photograph, on the other hand, possesses many of the attributes of a fetish. It is not usually narrativized nor is it temporally organized as it fixes a scene in time and space. It can be used privately, can be held in hand, and viewed and reviewed at will. A photograph often has a real referent, parts of which it cuts away, freezes, and preserves as a fetish. In terms of its relationship with death, a photograph maintains the memory of the dead as dead; lacking movement, it does not revive those moments. Finally, the off-screen world of a photograph remains forever off screen, inaccessible to viewer. For all these reasons Metz states that "film is more capable of playing on fetishism, photography more capable of itself becoming a fetish" (1985:90).

Television, on the other hand, has a status and a use that allows it to both play on fetishism and become itself a fetish. This is because of attributes that TV, and especially video, shares with both film and photography. Chief among them are the following:

1. The conditions of the reception of TV like that of a photograph are usually private; reception occurs in one's home and often by solitary individuals (at least in the U.S.). This parallels the usual way of looking at a photograph. Moreover, the viewer has the capability of recording a program and replaying it at will, from any point, and in any mode and speed desired—all of which help to denarrativize the images and allow the viewer to determine the viewing activity. The pervasiveness and versatility of TV sets and VCRs, the ease with which they can be operated, and their now pocket-size portability, render both the hardware and the software (videocassettes and videodisks) into potential fetishes which, like photographs, can be transported to any location and held in hand as well as in memory.

2. The conditions of the transmission of TV images are markedly different from film. Various strategies of repetition, such as the repeated airing of programs and series, tend to lower the narrative line of programs by over-familiarization. In

addition, the electronic reproduction and manipulation of images by freezing single frames, fragmenting a single image, or repeating frame fragments takes those images out of their contexts and gives them an abstract status, making them capable of becoming fetishes. Displaying these fragments in varying speeds at heightened narrative moments not only could denarrativize those moments but also render them open to iconic, indexical, and symbolic uses. In Peircian semiotics, a photograph is chiefly an index of what it pictures; however, the iconic and the symbolic effects foregrounded by image manipulation techniques enhance the fetishistic aspects of TV.

These uses of televisual fetishes will be explored in the remainder of this essay, first as producers of stability and then as maskers of instability.

FETISHIZATION AND STABILITY

A chief precondition for turning a photograph or a film (and for that matter TV) into a fetish, which Metz seems to ignore both in the *October* article and in his *Imaginary Signifier*, is the trauma (of castration) that must be experienced before the fetishization process is set into motion. I do not agree with the assertion that there is "no comparable sense in which the film image can be said to traumatize the viewer" (Singer, 1988:8). There is trauma and it is most clearly evident in crosscultural cinematic contacts and in women's representation on the screen. The figure of the colonized on the screen constitutes for the colonizer a threat (as well as pleasure), likewise the image of the colonizer for the colonized. As far as women's representation on the screen is concerned, as early as Laura Mulvey's essay on the visual pleasure, feminists have theorized that the image of women represents a threat to male audiences. In both the colonial and the patriarchal representations, the threat is disavowed through fetishization and exoticization.

In exile, separation from home and the motherland is a form of symbolic castration, of severing of deeply held ties, which constitutes a major source of trauma and pain, especially during the liminal period. During this time, the exiles have an "affective fixation" (to invoke Freud), to the traumatic experience of separation, which causes them to repeat and relive that experience as though they were "not finished with the traumatic situation, as though they were still faced by it as an immediate task which has not been dealt with" (1977:275–6). The shock of the new culture, too, further enhances the pain. This is, I believe, the general condition of liminality, shared by new emigres, but each culture brings its own specificity to the situation.

In the case of Iranian exiles three factors deepened the trauma of separation and the pain of the absence of home. The first is the 1978–79 revolution which drove the majority of them out of the country and constituted for some of them a great *personal loss*—of property, status, power, and link with family members.

The second factor (which is true also for Vietnamese, Kampuchians, Laotians, Salvadorans, Nicaraguans, and Palestinians, to cite just a few recent cases), is the ravages of a war on the home front.[20] For example, the long and deadly war with Iraq, which began shortly after the revolution in September 1980 and lasted until ceasefire was declared in August 1988, constituted for many exiles a profound *national loss*—of human, natural, and economic resources; of honor; and of world prestige, particularly for those in exile who experienced the effects of the war second hand as mere observers or first hand through loss of property and of loved ones. The destruction and loss caused by the war, the inability to affect its course from a distance, and the guilt of living in safety and in relative opulence in the West, all compounded the inherent trauma of exilic dislocation, causing dysphoria (Good *et al.*, 1985).

The third factor was the act (and its repercussions), of taking 50 American hostage in the American embassy in Tehran in November 1979 and holding them until January 1981. This indefensible act, which turned the newly formed Islamic government into an international pariah, aroused widespread chauvinistic sentiments in the U.S., fanned by two Presidents, Carter and Reagan, and by a generally deferential media (Dorman and Farhang, 1987). The media and politicians labeled the hostage-takers, and by implication all Iranians, variously as "students, militants, terrorists, kidnappers, criminals, and barbarians" (Naficy, 1984:xx). Mediawork, the combined operation of the signifying institutions, commidified these messages further: T-shirts bore slogans such as "Nuke Iran." Demonstrators carried banners which said "Camel Jockeys, Go Home." Pop records such as "They can Take Their Oil and Shove It" became national hits on radio. Jokes about Iran and Iranians cropped up regularly on *Saturday Night Live, Johnny Carson's Tonight Show*, radio talkshows, in comedy clubs, improvisational theaters, and Las Vegas Acts (Naficy, 1989a:232–33). The exiles came under considerable financial and legal pressures as well: President Carter canceled the visas of all Iranian students, forcing them to reregister. Those found in violation were deported. The severing of all diplomatic and economic relations between the two countries made the transfer of funds and legal documents, travel, and communication an ordeal. Many Iranians in the U.S. were taunted and beaten up in counterdemonstrations, refused service, denied apartments, and jailed (one for stealing a single grape from a store). Both the "news" and their own personal experiences deeply embarrassed and humiliated the exiles. There was also a sense of outrage at being subjected to shame for actions committed by the clerics who the majority of the exiles disliked.

Aesthetics of Fetishization Based on Loss

While the first two factors made separation from home and loss of homeland painful, the latter made life in exile and loss of face and prestige in a foreign land unbearable.

HOME AND PAST AS FETISH—It is the recognition of the aforementioned multiple losses which televisual fetishization of home as an unchanging stereotype disavows, masks, and ultimately turns into pleasure. Exile TV produces fetishized stereotypes by fixating on Iran prior to its tripartite "loss" to the Islamic Republic, to the war, and to exile. Fixation on pre-war Iran is a psychological form of repressing the trauma and shielding the self from its effects in exile. Fixation on pre-Islamic iconography, which is the dominant mode in exile, is a form of ideological repression of the current Islamic state. Put another way, the psychic process involved in the transplantation of an emigre can be analogized to the entry of the child from the Imaginary (homeland) into the Symbolic (exile), which reduces the function of the mother, in the words of Mulvey, to "a memory, which oscillates between memory of maternal plenitude and memory of a lack" (1975:14). Thus, through identification with the fixated images of the past, the splitting of the subject in exile (Where do I belong? Where do I stand?) is thwarted as he/she returns to the narcissism of the Imaginary, united with the "mother"land. In this way, during the liminal stage, the exile remains psychologically whole, and home remains partially repressed as a fetish. Through controlling "there" and "then" the exile can control "here" and "now."[21]

Intense focalization on and overinvestment in the fetish demands that the fetish and its synecdoche remain pure, unsullied, unambiguous, irreproachable, and authentic. When the fetish involves a nation and its history, however, such views can lead to a shortsighted form of nationalism and to racially prejudiced stances, both of which are evident and implied, respectively, in the discourse of Iranian exile media which insist on distinct authenticity, historical antiquity, and racial difference. In this manner, the media, especially TV, produce in exile a cultural artifact, an imaginary nation, or as formulated by Benedict Anderson, an "imagined community," whose characteristics are that it is (a) imagined, (b) inherently limited, (c) secularly sovereign, and (d) viewed as a community (1983:14–16).[22]

IRAN AS FETISH—In the discourse of Iranian exile TV, which is primarily royalist, nothing is more fetishized than "Iran" itself, a homeland that is undergoing rapid fundamental change under the Islamic Republic, but whose televisual simulacrum (i.e., imagined nature) in exile, at least during the war with Iraq, remains generally stable and seemingly eternal (i.e., limited). In terms of power relations, this "original," "authentic" (but fast disappearing) Iran (i.e., community) memorialized through fetishization is usually projected as a secular, non-Islamic (i.e., sovereign) community (as its fetishes continually refer either to the Pahlavi era prior to the Islamic revolution of 1978–79 or to the far distant pre-Islamic past of the 7th century). It seems that the more the exile community is incorporated into mainstream American culture, albeit "marginalized," the more exile TV clings to a fetishized televisual construct of homeland and of the past that fails to take into account the reality of changes taking place in Iran. As the original present-day Iran is found wanting or is receding, this myth of a secular pre-Islamic Iran continues to act through televisual surfaces like a series of Lacanian mirrors within which exile members must find themselves. Through suture and interpellation, Iranian exiles not only find themselves located in that social imaginary but also negotiate a position as televisual subjects. Simulacrum thus ends up replacing the lack.

FETISHISTIC ICONOGRAPHY—The iconography of this imagined community on TV consists of the following: pre-revolutionary Iranian flag flying high, waving with a gentle breeze against a blue cloudless Iran-like sky (Figure 5). Often, this nostalgic visual is accompanied by patriotic songs, such as the one aired on *Iran* program (3/7/1988), with the following refrain: "people always people, Iran always Iran." Program logos, important identification devices, are likewise used by a majority of TV programs in such a way as to highlight their link to the fetishized past by borrowing either from ancient pre-Islamic Persian motifs (e.g., *Jam-e Jam*,

Figure 5. *Electronically processed prerevolutionary Iranian flag behind "bars." (Source:* Jonbesh *TV.)*

Omid programs) or from Pahlavi era motifs (e.g., *Iranian*, *Jonbesh-e Melli* programs). Further, clips from Albert Lamorisse's highly visual film on Iran, *The Lovers' Wind* (1969), are either used in opening and closing titles of TV programs (e.g., *Jam-e Jam*, *Iranian*) or within program texts and music videos themselves when a reference is made to Iran. In fact, this single film, produced under the Pahlavi government, which shows the Iranian landscape and people filmed from a roving helicopter, has become so closely identified by exile TV programs with the "authentic" but "lost" or "vanishing" (hence imagined) Iran that it can be said to be occupying all three definitions of the sign in the Peircian semiotic system. Pictures of other pre-Islamic monuments (Persepolis, for example) are also continually circulated within the music videos recorded in exile and shown on exile TV. Almost entirely absent are any images of the magnificent Islamic buildings and monuments, an absence which helps to secularize such national imaginings in exile.

Titles of shows, too, testify to the desire among producers to posit in exile some sort of Iranian authenticity, antiquity, and nationalism. Terms such as Iran, national, the nation, Pars, Aryan—which are repeated in show titles in various iterations and combinations—reverberate these themes: *Iranian, The Bowl of Jamshid, Iran's Love, National, National Movement, Persians, The Nation, Iran, Pars, Hope of Iran, Arya in L.A.* Through this sort of iconography and titling, exile TV constructs Iran in the past tense. By so doing, not only does it serve to contain the threat of the homeland slipping away but also it recoups the "loss" of that homeland from those it considers to be usurpers and highjackers of Iranian discourse, i.e., Islamic "hardliners." Such an ahistorical frozen fetish can now be held in memory and captured, recaptured, and reworked on TV without pain (Figures 6–9).

Figure 6.   Iran Television *logo: map of Iran and prerevolution Shahyad monument.*

Program titles also point to the way exile TV symbolically constructs life in exile itself. Titles abound which connote friendliness (*Familiar Face, Visit*), togetherness (*Our TV*), and human interaction (*Wink, Gaze, Silver Carnation, Visit*).[23] A number of conclusions can be drawn here. Reflecting the role of TV during liminality of exile, these titles emphasize an imaginary but cohesive community in exile. Here, TV is producing an "electronic communitas" in exile. The majority of the shows in this category are recent and focus more on life in exile than on life in the home country. Finally, both the titles and the shows themselves construct life in exile in the present tense, life in the process of being lived, life full of action and interaction.

Figure 7.   Jam-e Jam *TV logo: Bowl of Jamshid, a golden prehistoric bowl. (Courtesy of Ketab Corp.)*

Figure 8.   Arya in L.A. *TV logo: mixture of Aryan and pre-Islamic, Zoroastrian motifs. (Courtesy Ketab Corp.)*

AESTHETICS OF FETISHIZATION BASED ON SEPARATION

Exile TV, of course, does not ignore the current Islamic social order. But when it does deal with Iran under the Islamic Republic, it unleashes the same mummification process as applied to pre-Islamic Iran with one major difference. That is, as much as the fetishization of Iranian past is celebratory, the fetishization of its present Islamic conditions is celibate. Like Iranian intellectuals and writers abroad, the dominant mode of discourse adopted by Iranian TV in exile is one of tragedy (White, 1973) in which masochistic pleasure is produced by overemphasis on disparagement, denunciation, disfigurement, destruction, and death. The relationship of TV as fetish to this tragic, masochistic mode is four fold. TV (1) constructs a representation of present Islamic Iran as a ruined land in the throes of death, (2) eulogizes the death of the present by mourning it, (3) memorializes the past by commemorating and celebrating it, and (4) produces pleasure by identifying with the tortured and dying country. As Studlar has noted, in masochism, "pleasure does not involve mastery of the female but submission to her body and her gaze. This pleasure applies to the infant, the masochist, and the film spectator" (Studlar,

تلویــزیون ایــرانیان
ساعت۱۱بامداد هریکشنبه
از کانال۱۸لوس آنجلس و کانال۴۸ساندیاکو
(818) 760-4070

Figure 9. Iranian *TV logo: Colors of Iranian flag surround the lion, the sun, and the sword—emblems of prerevolutionary flag.*

1988:29–30). Likewise, the spectators of this tragic construction of Iran draw pleasure by overemphasis on and by identification with that construction.

HOME AS INDIGENT—The masochistic aesthetics of exile TV befits the liminal exile state as TV programs heavily draw upon the "symbolic vocabulary of poverty and indigence," a feature which characterizes all liminal states (Turner, 1974:245). TV programs accomplish this by foregrounding the poverty and the hardship that has beset Iran since the revolution, disregarding all else. The symbolic value of the poor is enormous and many renowned thinkers and politicians have used this symbolism. Note the power of Rousseau's Noble Savage, Marx's Proletariat, Gandhi's Untouchables (*Harijans*), or Khomeini's Dispossessed (*Mostaz'afan*) in mobilizing these various discourses as well as activist political movements. In the same manner, the predominantly royalist and chauvinist exile TV uses the symbolically constructed image of Iran as indigent to mobilize the exiles against what it presents as the cause of that indigence, i.e., the Islamic government.

As part of this discourse, Iran is portrayed to be, especially before the ceasefire with Iraq, a total ruin and a vast cemetery, with the result that any reference to it seems to necessitate a unidimensional verbal or visual evocation of destruction and waste. A case in point is *Omid* TV's program aired on 3/7/1988, during which the host painted a harrowing verbal picture of Tehran as a ruin under the first wave of Iraqi bombs:

Tehran is without water, without electricity, without doors or windows, and without gas in the cold of winter. But, for years our people have gotten used to such things. Now, Iran is being transformed into a city empty of women, empty of men, empty of children, empty of laughter, empty of sweet little girls. A city which has no night, no dawn, no drop of tears, no songs. A city which is only a cry. What shame is greater than a city which is only a cry!

This depiction, and many other similar ones during the war period which foreground the destruction, are accurate enough; however, they overlook the resistances, the resilience, and other types of responses by Iranians in the face of this senseless and criminal war. The point of view is external not internal; it is one emanating from a position of exile.

The univocal tragic discourse serves to evoke a sense of utter helplessness and passivity, characteristic of masochism. Even when resistance is shown, it is injected with tragedy and helplessness. For example, in the same program we see the footage of a demonstration staged by Iranians in Los Angeles against the so-called "war of the cities." We see participants marching and making rousing and impassioned speeches. Then, we see some of them breaking into tears, weeping publicly for what has befallen Iran. At this point, over the visuals we hear an extradiegetic song added to the soundtrack whose refrain is, "lonely homeland, indigent homeland." Clearly, this song represents the filmmaker's own commentary about the futility of action which undermines the activism of demonstrators.

Sometimes, such visual or verbal invocations of home as a ruin are inappropriate and irrelevant, but they serve to deepen the sense of loss and passivity. Again, the same program ran a segment of film, *Ruyeshi Digar* (*Another Growth*), which emphasized the destruction of the city of Khorramshahr by Iraqis some seven years *earlier*, long before bombing of cities became an Iraqi practice. This is tantamount to ahistoricization of the documentary evidences, which unanchors them from their particularity and allows them to be used interchangeably with unrelated material; images from a particular situation can be used in another situation at another time. It is here that the power of the stereotype to simplify and therefore to control the other is revealed. If Islamic Iran is designated as a signified for "ruin," then any picture of ruins taken at any time might do as a signifier of the current Iran.

RETURN—For many, grief over loss is unresolvable, thus leading to depression (Good *et al.*, 1985:391). For others, disavowal of the loss and the separation from home is augmented in exile by another impulse, that of return; of reunion with the object of fetish, the (m)otherland; of regression into the prelapsarian narcissism of childhood. This is a characteristic that sets exiles apart from all other displaced people such as emigrés, expatriates, refugees, and immigrants. Indeed, "exile is a dream of glorious return" (Rushdie, 1988:205), a dream that must remain unrealized. Music videos frequently employ the theme of the return. In one video, the singer Sattar sings about departing from home but leaving his heart with his family who remain behind. As he sings in exile about this sense of loss, a family group photo, taken in Iran apparently in his absence, appears behind him. At this point, Sattar's singing image, which had dominated the foreground, gradually grows smaller until it fits in a spot inside the group photo in the background. The foreground fuses with the background. The singer has found his rightful place in the family photo thereby symbolically united with them. If reunion is not possible physically, it at least can be staged metaphorically. Thus, the ever-threatening loss is averted and the lack is filled-in metaphorically, and the pain is presumably assuaged. Looking through photo albums, reading and writing letters, and conversing on the phone are recurring "return" images in music videos.

THE BODY IN CRISIS—The iconography of the masochistic mode of fetishization surfaces also in what Michel Foucault has called the "political economy of the body," whereby the body is made to be "both a productive and a subjected body" (1979:25–26). The bodies depicted on TV are made productive economically and ideologically to the extent that they are shown to be subjected to the pervasive disciplinary technologies of the Islamic regime. Further, bodies are made productive iconographically by continually showing them maimed, tortured, and destroyed. Political activists who have managed to leave Iran appear on TV to show either the scars left on their bodies or entire limbs removed from their bodies by torture. For example, Mojahedin supporters who have been tortured in the prisons of the Islamic Republic and who have succeeded in leaving Iran, have appeared a number of times on *Simay-e Azadi* program to show their scars and tell of their plight. Accounts of various kinds of assassinations, hangings, stoning, and raping of women are also repeated by eye-witnesses or through second hand reports in other TV programs. Here, the tortured body, the exposed flesh, becomes a text (Kroker and Cook, 1986:25), indeed a "minor literature" in the sense employed by Deleuze and Guattari, on which visions of power and resistance, of difference and transgression, are inscribed.

A music video entitled *Sorud-e Hambastegi* (*Song of Unity*), widely shown on various TV shows in January 1988 (e.g., *Negah TV* on 1/31/88) condenses the themes of indigence and of the body in crisis. Appropriately, it is a syncretic bit of cultural production in that it borrows an American vehicle for the expression of a specifically Iranian concern. The vehicle is the conception of the work as a music video which, following its popular American model, *We Are the World*, shows a group of well-known exiled Iranian entertainers standing in front of a giant Iranian flag (minus its recently added Islamic emblem) and singing a choral song whose haunting, oft repeated, refrain is: "O' spring breeze, tell me about friends, tell me about friends who are hanging from the gallows." The scene of singing in the studio is constantly interrupted by a parade of electronically processed images of death and destruction in Islamic Iran: people hanging from gallows in public, fighting during the revolution, Iranian flag waving against a blue sky, ruins of the ancient palace of Persepolis, the setting sun, Iranian landscape and countryside, a flag-draped coffin, map of Iran, cemeteries, women mourners crying and showing pictures of their lost sons, scenes of execution by firing squad, and bodies of executed generals (Figures 10–11).

By fetishizing and continually *repeating* these tortured images, exile TV invites identification and pleasure in the return to loss, and, thereby feeds into the masochistic economy of desire. Thus, the divided, fragmented self in exile is made whole again through symbiosis. But this production of unity out of the fragmentation and the chaos of exile is achieved also by creating models of beauty to be emulated, a process Jean Baudrillard has called "a perfectionist vertigo" (1981:94), in which exile TV participates with a vengeance. In this process, inner beauty is supplanted by valorization of exterior beauty. Body beautiful veils the essential split subjectivity of the exiles and negates the symbolic castration engendered by separation from home. Restoring wholeness, Baudrillard tells us, is no longer achieved "by endowing the individual with a soul or a mind, but a body properly all his own (1981:96). The fragmented, disappearing body in exile is restored to its relative former unity "properly all its own" through fashion, makeup, makeover, body building, and reconstructive surgery—all of which are repeatedly urged in TV

Figure 10.   Pop stars singing in the studio from Sorud-e Hambastegi *video. The song's refrain: O' spring breeze, tell me about friends, tell me about friends who are hanging from the gallows.*

Figure 11.   Electronically processed image of dead bodies hanging from the gallows, from Sorud-e Hambastegi *video.*

commercials and in interviews with surgeons. The latter, the most invasive of all the techniques to the body in exile, is curiously reminiscent of the torture which has racked the body in Iran. Both plastic surgery and torture reconstruct the body. The difference, of course, is that the former is embedded not in a discourse of tragedy, indigence and crisis but rather in a discourse of perfection achieved through "art" and "aesthetics." This aestheticized discourse is best seen in advertisements for Iranian plastic surgeons. A large cover photo in the weekly magazine *Rayegan* (12/9/1988), for example, hyperbolically identifies the plastic surgeon Dr. Asurian as the "Michelangelo of the Twenty First Century" and the ad copy inside calls him an "artist," whose aim is to make his patients "more complete" by "recreating" their faces. Likewise, an ad for a Dr. Hosain Najafi in another weekly magazine, *Javanan* (9/22/1989:18), carries the following breathless copy in English:

Alter your ego. Reward yourself with a beautiful new you. Get the ultimate artistic results, achievable only by a gifted surgeon with the aesthetic sense and imaging skills of a true artist (Figure 12).

The Iranian self is theorized to be different from the American-Western self in that it is not completely individuated, but is a "communal" self that involves one's significant other(s) as well. This means that these others are part of the subjective experience of the self (Moradi *et al.*, 1989:16). Significant for Moradi's study, however, is his finding which indicates that acculturation in exile has increased individuation and as,a result has intensified narcissism among Iranians living in the U.S. Perhaps the seeming obsession with the body beautiful can be attributed partially to this newly "learned" narcissism, which can serve to veil the fractured exilic self.

Figure 12.   Ad for Dr. Najafi, the plastic surgeon.

FETISHIZATION AND INSTABILITY

As critic George Steiner has aptly stated, "It is not the literal past that rules us . . . It is images of the past. . . . The image we carry of a lost coherence, of a center that held, has authority greater than historical truth" (1971:3,8). Iranian exile TV has produced such a coherent image by fetishizing and stereotyping Iran either in an ahistorical, secular, past tense or in a tragic, tortured present tense. But in exile the historical truth, the fact of living in exile, intrudes in that coherent and authoritative image of the past. As long as the trauma that produces exile persists (the "hostages crisis," separation from home, and the war with Iraq), so do the relative coherence and unity of the fetishes of home and of the past. However, with the end of the hostage crisis and particularly with the ceasefire, two major sources of trauma were removed and, with that, the inherent ambiguities and instabilities which accompany both fetishization and exile began to surface more fully.

Fetishization operates synecdochically, whereby parts (fetishes) stand for the whole. To be sure, this focalization on fragments eases the pain of loss and masks the trauma of separation from home, but it also impoverishes life in exile because it closes one off through fixation in the same moment that liminality opens one up to new possibilities. In the words of Ernest Becker, the fetish is a segment of the world which "has to bear the full load of life meaning" (1969:14). But this supercharged overinvestment in the fetish cannot possibly fulfill forever the promise of satisfaction with which it is burdened. Fetishes (fragments) of Iran cannot replace the whole of Iran, or "bear the full load" of Iran. Fetishization assuages the pain of loss and masks the separation, but it cannot remove the lack or the distance.

In addition, the televisual fetish like any other type of fetish is unstable because it is paradoxically an index of that which it is masking. It thus memorializes and reminds one of the lack—which constantly threatens, and in some instances succeeds and ruptures through to the surface. Further, by incessantly circulating these representations of home, TV programs not only acknowledge the continued existence of home, but also paradoxically and masochistically elevate what they consider to be inferior and marginal, i.e., Islamic Iran, to assume a higher, central position within the exile discourse. In exile, home colonizes the mind.

This then becomes productive for TV producers, as it helps them purchase goodwill and legitimacy in the eyes of their audiences as supporters of the dispossessed and the tortured, with whom the exiles identify. This is so because fixation in the mode of tragedy is both an expression and an instrument of communitas, whereby exiles not only get to sympathize with those living in that ruined land, but also through moral masochism, they are able to assuage the guilt they feel for abandoning that land in time of trouble—all of which tends to validate their continued stay in exile.

On the other hand, as a form of partial repression or splitting, fetishization constitutes the first step in repressing and forgetting the homeland, of pushing the center to the periphery—something that the exiles in the liminal period at least are loathe to do. Thus, the exiles are caught in a situation where they alternate between belief and disbelief, avowal and disavowal, lack and plenitude, identification and repression, stability and instability. The ambiguities, the fragmentation, and the syncretic hybridities that exile TV displays structurally, iconographically, narratologically, and stylistically are marks of this sort of tension—topics I cannot discuss in this essay.

It is fitting in the end to reinvoke Turner and ask, what role has TV played in "the analysis of cultures into factors and their free recombination"? The answer would be that Iranian TV in exile in the nine years of its existence has reflected and shaped the lives of its audiences by helping them to renegotiate their relationship with themselves and with their home and host cultures.

In fact, TV has proved instrumental in the twin exilic processes of liminality and assimilation. In the liminal phase, the subject of this essay, which followed the arrival of emigrés into the U.S., Iranian TV created a hermetically sealed discourse in Persian language using the relative uniformity and homogeneity of emigrés politics, program matter, generic conventions, targeting of audiences, formatting, deployment of authority figures, adoption of an official style, and finally, circulation of ideas and products from home. In the liminal, inbetween state of exile in which clearcut social and symbolic structures are missing, television created an electronic communitas, an imagined community, by casting a symbolic and ideological net around its spectators, in which it continually captured fetishized representations of home. This symbolic, electronic enclosure is in effect a private Iranian oasis in exile that bestows a degree of cohesiveness and stability on the exile community and buttresses it against the trauma of loss, the panic of loneliness, and the fear of the future. In a sense, we are witnessing the symbolic circling of wagons by Iranians living in exile.

The sensory overload, generated by the fragmented discourse of pastiche and bricolage characteristic of the magazine genre of exile TV also becomes a form of closing the self off from the threatening outside. It is tantamount to whistling in the dark when alone or carrying a boom box.

In all these ways, exile TV has been able to achieve one of the chief cultural and ideological functions of modern media, identified by Stuart Hall as

The selective construction of *social knowledge*, of social imagery, through which we perceive the "worlds," the "lived realities" of others, and imaginarily reconstruct their lives and ours into some intelligible "world-of-the-whole," some "lived reality" (1977:341–2).

However, this achievement is neither complete nor impenetrable. This is because exile TV is an instance of what Jacques Derrida has called double reading and writing, exemplified by his own "Tympan," among others, in which neither of the two adjacent texts on the page obtains primacy, as each resonates against and with the other, thereby helping to deconstruct one another (1982). Likewise, in exile TV, programs (text) and interstitial ads (supertext) taken together produce scenes of double writing and reading. These texts inscribe cultural, racial, ethnic, historical, and linguistic differences and tensions which can be read when one pays attention to their interpermeability. When read thusly, they reveal tensions. Split subjects produce split texts: during liminality of exile, program matter is largely encoded by home while the ads are encoded by host cultural values. The result is that the cohesiveness of the private symbolic enclave created by televisual texts is threatened constantly by the implosion of the dominant host values by means of both the commercials which interrupt the texts and by the commodification practices of exile TV.

In psychoanalysis and cultural studies it has become customary of late to speak about the relative porousness of the human psyche and of culture, through whose cracks the subconscious seeps into consciousness and the marginalized erupts into the dominant discourse. Here, however, I am talking about a reverse process, namely, the implosion of the dominant host values into the marginalized exiles and into their subconscious. The result is a liminal process of becoming, which is never final nor complete nor univocal (at least for the first generation immigrants), because it involves the constitution of a new subjectivity in exile, one that is based on fetishization, double incorporation, ambivalence, hybridity, and syncretism—involving articulation of the home with the host cultural values and practices. In this process, as we have seen, TV plays a significant and signifying role.

This liminal process of subject formation, however, exceeds the life span of the first generation, as the euphoria and the pain associated with it can become a source of memory—not merely memory of home where the idiom is one of loss but one that looks back to the future. And when this attitude of "backward look forward" is passed on, it can become a source of validation. In this, too, TV can play a significant and signifying role through its archival function.

NOTES

1. In the only comprehensive analysis of existing statistics on Iranians in the U.S., Mehdi Bozorgmehr and Georges Sabagh estimate the number of Iranians in the whole of U.S. and in Los Angeles not to exceed 341,000 and 74,000 respectively (Bozorgmehr and Sabagh, 1988:16). For a reliable and a more definitive count one must await the results of the 1990 U.S. census.
2. Iranian exiles characterize their own status variously: immigrant (*mohajer*), political refugee (*panahandeh-ye siasi*), exiled (*tab'idi*), refugee (*panahandeh*), stranger (*gharib*), homeless (*avareh, dar beh dar*), fugitive (*farari*), and student (*mohassel, daneshij*). Fugitive is a term that the Islamic government generally applies to many of the exiles in order to foreground the perception that they have deserted their homeland. This term also covers young draft dodgers, who escaped the country in droves during the eight-year war with Iraq.
3. For an analysis of Iranians who emigrated before and after the revolution see Sabagh and Bozorgmehr, 1987.
4. All programs in this table, with the exception of *Sima-ye Azadi* which was aired on KDOC-TV (channel 56) and *Iran TV* which is cablecast, are currently being aired by KSCI-TV (channel 18) in Los Angeles.
5. While, in sharp contrast, TV programs produced by government-controlled South Korean television are aired regularly by KSCI-TV in Los Angeles and elsewhere.
6. Figures supplied by KSCI-TV.
7. Author's interviews with Manuchehr Bibian and Ali Limonadi producers respectively of *Jam-e Jam* and *Iranian* shows.
8. This is particularly true in cases where news anchors in exile are the same people who anchored news in Iran prior to the revolution.
9. One might be able to argue that exile TV along with avant-garde videos and music videos are the only types of TV which come close to being an "auteur" form of TV.
10. Saturdays and Sundays are not considered prime time for regular American television, but are considered so for exile television because of the supposed extended family structure of the new exiles and their habit of collective viewing of TV on those days. Author's interview with Rosemary Fincher, KSCI-TV Station Manager, February 16, 1988.
11. Mojahedin is the abbreviated name for *Sazman-e Mojahedin-e Khalg-e Iran* (the Organization of Fighters for Iranian People), an Iranian guerrilla organization which engaged in armed struggle against the Shah in the 1970s and, after a period of cooperation with the nascent Islamic government,

turned to armed struggle against it in 1981. The headquarters of the organization at present is Baghdad, Iraq, from where a number of incursions against the Iranian forces have been made. The organization produces and airs a regularly scheduled TV show in Iraq, *Sima-ye Mogavemat*, which is beamed to Western Iran. *Simay-e Azadi*, aired in Los Angeles, borrowed heavily from the mother program in Iraq.

12. KSCI-TV has attempted to ensure compliance by assigning a native Iranian to monitor the ratio of commercials to program matter. This monitor also reports ont he contents of programs in order to prevent the airing of libelous, obscene, and politically inappropriate materials. Interview with Karen A. Garces, Client Services Manager of KSCI-TV, 2/16/1988, Los Angeles.

13. These ad rates are based on my interviews with brokers for commercials and with program producers.

14. This information is taken from KSCI-TV's "Airtime Rate Schedule" effective 5/1/1987.

15. For example, *Midnight Show* seems to pattern itself after ABC's *Nightline*, *Ma TV* after syndicated talkshow *Oprah Winfrey Show*, *Arya in L.A.* after KABC-TV's tourist magazine show *Eye on L.A.*, *Jong-e Bamdadi*, after *CBS Morning*, and *Simay-e Ashna* after ABC's *Good Morning America*.

16. Serials are shown on various Iranian programs in brief installments of five to ten minutes duration, lasting several months.

17. The contradictory function of fetishization in promoting also the commodification and assimilation of exiles into the host's cultural values are discussed in my dissertation (Naficy, 1990).

18. Fetishism in Lacan's work, therefore, should be thought of as a general process of formation of sexuality of *both* sexes, a conception that differs drastically from that of both Freud's and Laura Mulvey's.

19. Television as a fetish *does* involve such an unequal power and knowledge relationship. The panoptic regime of television, comprising the advertising driven schedule, rating and audience measurement systems, programming and counterprogramming strategies, and the ceaseless flow of programs which does not depend on the presence or control of viewers, all contribute to establishing essentially unequal power relations between the TV set and the viewer.

20. Freud himself refers to war as a recent source of traumatic neurosis (1977:274).

21. For an elaboration on the dynamics of "here" and "there," in crosscultural discourses, see Geertz, 1988 and Naficy, 1989b.

22. Such imagined communities can be found in many parts of the world. For example, two films, *Ori* (1989) and *Quilombo* (1984) document and recreate the rise and fall and the continued imaginary existence of *Quilombo de Palmares* in Brazil.

23. Here are the titles of all the Iranian programs in the original Persian and their English translation: *Iranian*, *Jam-e Jam* (*The Bowl of Jamshid*, a mythical Iranian king), *Simay-e Ashna* (*Familiar Face*), *Melli* (*National*), *Mikhak-e Nogreh'i* (*Silver Carnation*), *Mehr-e Iran* (*Iran's Love*), *Jonbesh-e Melli* (*National Movement*), *Parsian* (*Persians*), *Sima-ye Azadi* (*Vision of Freedom*), *Iranian Music TV*, *Jom'-eh* (*Friday*, Iranian weekend), *Mellat* (*The People*), *Iran*, *Pars* (*Pars*, an ancient province, the seat of one of Iran's oldest monarchies), *Melli-e Pars* (*National Pars*), *Midnight Show*, *Cheshmak* (*Wink*), *Negah* (*Gaze*), *John-e Bamdadi* (*Morning Anthology*), *Omid-e Iran* (*Hope of Iran*), *Jahan Nama* (*The World Show*), *Arya in L.A.* (*Aryan in L.A.*), *Didar* (*Visit*), *Sobh-e Ruz-e Jom'-eh* (*Friday Morning*), *Tamasha* (*Spectacle*), *Iran va Jahan* (*Iran and the World*), *Ma TV* (*Our TV*).

WORKS CITED

Amirshahi, Mahshid
   1987   *Dar Hazar* [*At Home*]. London: OrientScript.
Anderson, Benedict
   1983   *Imagined Communities: Reflections on the Origin and Spread of Nationalism*. London: Verson.
Baudrillard, Jean
   1981   *For a Critique of the Political economy of the Sign*. Charles Levin, trans. St. Louis: Telos Press.
Becker, Ernest
   1969   *Angel in Armor: a Post-Freudian Perspective on the Nature of Man*. New York: George Brazillier.

Beckland, Laurie
  1987 "Iranian Who Set Himself Afire Interred," *Los Angeles Times* (October 11). P. 27.
Bhabha, Homi K.
  1983 "The Other Question . . . The Stereotype and Colonial Discourse," *Screen* (November–December). Pp. 18–36.
  1986 "Signs Taken for Wonders: Questions of Ambivalence and Authority Under a Tree Outside Delhi, May 1817," in *'Race,' Writing, and Difference.* Henry Louis Gates, Jr., ed. Chicago: University of Chicago Press. Pp. 163–184.
Baudrillard, Jean
  1981 *For a Critique of the Political Economy of the Sign.* Charles Levin, trans. St. Louis, MO: Telos Press.
Bozorgmehr, Mehdi, and Georges Sabagh
  1988 "High Status Immigrants: a Statistical Study of Iranians in the United States," *Iranian Studies* Vol. 21, Nos. 3–4. Pp. 5–35.
Deleuze, Gilles, and Felix Guattari
  1985 *Kafka: Toward a Minor Literature.* Dana Polan, trans. Minneapolis: University of Minnesota Press.
Derrida, Jacques
  1982 "Tympan," in *Margins of Philosophy.* Alan Bass, trans. Chicago: University of Chicago Press.
Dorman, William A., and Mansur Farhang
  1987 *The U.S. Press and Iran: Foreign Policy and the Journalism of Deference.* Berkeley: University of California Press.
Foucault, Michel
  1979 Discipline and Punish: The Birth of the Prison. Alan Sheridan, trans. New York: Vantage.
  1980 *Power/Knowledge: Selected Interview & Other Writings 1972–1977.* Colin Gordon, ed. Leo Marshall, John Mephan, and Kate Soper, trans. New York: Pantheon.
Freud, Sigmund
  1961a *Beyond the Pleasure Principle.* London. Standard Edition vol. 18.
  1961b "Fetishism," in *The Standard Edition of the Complete Psychological Works of Sigmund Freud.* Vol. 21. London: Hogarth Press. Pp. 152–157.
  1969 *An Outline of Psycho-Analysis.* James Strachy, trans. & ed. c. 1949. New York: W. W. Norton.
  1977 *Introductory Lectures on Psychoanalysis.* James Starchy, trans. & ed. Standard Edition. New York: Norton and Co.
Gallop, Jane
  1985 *Reading Lacan.* Ithaca: Cornell University Press.
Geertz, Clifford
  1988 *Works and Lives: the Anthropologist as Author.* Stanford: Stanford University Press.
Good, Byron J., Mary-Jo DelVecchio, and Robert Moradi
  1985 "The Interpretation of Iranian Depressive Illness and Dysphoric Affect," in *Culture and Depression: Studies in the Anthropology and Cross-Cultural Psychiatry of Affect and Disorder.* Arthur Kleinman and Byron Good, eds. Los Angeles: University of California Press. Pp. 369–428.
Hall, Stuart
  1977 "Culture, the Media and the 'Ideological Effect,'" in *Mass Communication and Society.* James Curran, Michael Gurevitch and Janet Wollacott, eds. London: The Open University Press.
Ketab Corp.
  1989 *The Iranian Directory Yellow Pages.* Ketab Corp.: Los Angeles.
Kho'i, Esma'il
  1987 "People in Between," in *Children from Refugee Communities: A Question of Identity: Uprooting, Integration or Dual Culture?* Oakwood, Derby (UK): Refugee Action (July). Pp. 5–13.
Kroker, Arthur, and David Cook
  1986 *The Postmodern Scene: Excremental Culture and Hyper-Aesthetics.* New York: St. Martin's Press.
Lacan, Jacques
  1977 *Ecrits: A Selection.* Alan Sheridan, trans. New York: Norton.
Laplanche, J., and J.-B. Pontalis
  1977 *The Language of Psychoanalysis.* Donald Nicholson-Smith, trans. New York: Norton and Co.
Lippman, Walter
  c1922 "Stereotype," in *Voices of the People: Readings in Public Opinions and Propaganda.* Second edition,

Reo M. Christenson and Robert O. McWilliams, eds. New York: McGraw-Hill. 1967. Pp. 95–103.

Marx, Karl
  1967   *Capital: A Critique of Political Economy.* Vol. 1. Samuel Moore and Edward Aveling, trans. New York: International Publishers.

Metz, Christian
  1977   *The Imaginary Signifier: Psychoanalysis and the Cinema.* Celia Britton, Annwyl Williams, Ben Brewster and Alfred Guzzetti, trans. Bloomington: Indiana University Press.
  1985   "Photography and Fetish," *October* 34 (Fall). Pp. 80–90.

Mofid, Ardavan
  1987   "Dar A'ineh-ye Ghorbat," [in the Mirror of Exile] *Iran News* (October 20). Pp. 15, 19, 56.

Moradi, Gilbert, Larry Peters, Marylie Karlovac, and David Meltzer
  1989   "A Cross-Cultural Study of Narcissism Among Iranians in Iran, Iranians in the U.S., and Americans." Unpublished manuscript.

Mulvey, Laura
  c1975   "Visual Pleasure and Narrative Cinema," in *Visual and Other Pleasure.* Bloomington: Indiana University Press. 1989. Pp. 14–26.

Naficy, Hamid
  1984   *Iran Media Index.* Westport, CT: Greenwood Press.
  1989a   "Mediawork's Representation of the Other: the Case of Iran," in *Questions of Third Cinema.* Jim Pines and Paul Willemen, eds. London: BFI. Pp. 227–239.
  1989b   "Autobiography, Film Spectatorship, and Cultural Negotiation," *Emergences* 1 (Fall). Pp. 29–54.
  1990   *Exile Discourse and Television: A Study of Syncretic Cultures: Iranian Television in Los Angeles.* Unpublished Ph.D. dissertation, UCLA.
  Forthcoming 1991a   "From Liminality to Incorporation," in *Iranian Exiles and Emigres.* Asghar Fathi, ed. Costa Mesa, CA: Mazda Publishers.
  Forthcoming 1991b   "Popular Culture in Exile: Iranians in Los Angeles," in *Irangeles: Iranian Life and Culture in Los Angeles.* Jonathan Friedlander and Ron Kelley, eds. Berkeley: UC Press.

Rushdie, Salman
  1988   *The Satanic Verses.* New York: Viking.

Sabagh, Georges, and Mehdi Bozorgmehr
  1987   "Are the Characteristics of Exiles Different from Immigrants?" The case of Iranians in Los Angeles," *Sociology and Social Research* 71:2 (January 2). Pp. 77–84.

Sa'edi, Gholam Hosain
  1986   "Sharh-e Ahval" [Biography], in *Alefba* [Paris] 7 (Fall 1986). Pp. 3–6.

Said, Edward
  1979   *Orientalism.* New York: Vintage Books.

Singer, Ben
  1988   "Film, Photography, and Fetish: an Analysis of Christian Metz," *Cinema Journal* 27:4 (Summer). Pp. 4–22.

Steiner, George
  1971   *In Bluebeard's Castle: Some Notes Towards the Redefinition of Culture.* New Haven: Yale University Press.

Studlar, Gaylyn
  1988   *In the Realm of Pleasure: Von Sternberg, Dietrich, and the Masochistic Aesthetics.* Urbana: University of Illinois Press.

Turner, Victor
  1974   *Dramas, Fields, and Metaphors: Symbolic Action in Human Society.* Ithaca: Cornell University Press.

White, Hayden
  1973   *Metahistory: the Historical Imagination in Nineteenth-Century Europe.* Baltimore: The Johns Hopkins University Press.

Williams, Linda
  1989   "Fetishism and the Visual Pleasure of Hard Core: Marx, Freud, and the 'Money Shot'," *Quarterly Review of Film and Video* 11:2. Pp. 23–42.

Recodings: Possibilities and Limitations in Commercial Television Representations of African American Culture

Herman Gray

. . . There is great drama in our lives, in our past, in our culture and in our Africanisms. I'd like to see more of that portrayed. . . .

Rosalind Cash (actress who appeared on Frank's Place)

Actress Rosalind Cash has identified one of the persistent and dominant assumptions in commercial television's representation of African American culture.[1] American commercial television programs about blacks position viewers to experience African American culture from the vantage point of the white middle class experience, which is assimilationist (Gans 1979) or pluralist—blacks simply function, in outlook, character, and setting as copies of whites (Gray 1990). In a society such as the United States which remains characterized by social inequality and racism, such representations of black life and culture function, ideologically, to sharpen the "normativeness" of the white middle class experience.

Frank's Place, a novel but short lived commercial television treatment of black life in America, breaks significantly with this pattern. *Frank's Place* achieves this departure precisely because African American culture and black American subjectivity are central to the series' content, aesthetic organization, setting, narrative, characters, and assumptions (Childs 1984).

In *Frank's Place* we see an attempt to rewrite and reposition African American culture and black subjectivities. By rewriting and repositioning I refer to the strategy of appropriating (or re-appropriating) existing formal, organizational, and aesthetic elements in the commercial culture in general and television in particular and refashioning them into different representations. These different representations often serve as alternatives to (and occasionally critique) the dominant forms of existing culture (Foster 1985, Williams 1977).

Television representations of blacks in *Frank's Place* activated African American sensibilities that were historically experienced on television, through absence, silence, and invisibility. Since the televisual reality is dominated by "normative" representations of white middle class subjectivities and sensibilities, blacks and other communities of color have had to create and fill in the televisual spaces where

HERMAN GRAY *is the author of* Producing Jazz *(Temple University Press) and is at work on a book about the representation of blacks in contemporary commercial TV. He teaches in the Departments of Sociology and Anthropology at Northeastern University in Boston.*

African American representations might otherwise fit. For various sectors of the black American community *Frank's Place* worked through affirmation rather than silence. And it is not just the fact that the show featured blacks at the level of character and setting. The show achieved this affirmative stance through its complex treatments of social class, gender, region, and theme—all of which were rooted in an African American point of view.

In commercial television culture where assumptions and representations of African Americans continue to operate largely within the limits of assimilation and pluralism (Gray 1990), I regard *Frank's Place* as a moment of displacement, an attempt to push the limits of existing television discourses about blacks. The representations on *Frank's Place* are expressions of the most recent struggles over the representations of race in general and African American culture in particular. (These struggles are expressed in other arenas of contemporary television, most notably cable—where music television, Black Entertainment Network, and sports continue to be the areas that are the most open and available for the expression and articulation of a Black American cultural sensibility.)

THE SOCIAL PRODUCTION OF *FRANK'S PLACE*

Frank's Place aired on CBS during the fall 1987 television season with a 14.9 rating and a 25 share. The series was produced by co-executive producers Hugh Wilson and Tim Reid for Viacom Studios.[2] Reid and Wilson developed a friendship and working relationship on *WKRP Cincinnati*, which Wilson produced and in which Reid starred. The results of that collaboration and friendship led to the development of *Frank's Place*.

The concept for the show was developed by Wilson, Reid, and by former CBS Television Head of Entertainment Kim LeMasters. Because of its drop in the ratings the previous season CBS needed a show for its new season. The network was therefore willing to take a chance with an innovative show such as *Frank's Place*. Moreover, network executives were familiar with Wilson's record as a producer/writer/director and with Reid's work in the successful series *WKRP Cincinnati*, and *Simon and Simon*. Indeed, Reid and Wilson were able to extract a hands off deal in most areas in the development and production of the series. This unusual control over the show afforded Wilson and Reid the opportunity to develop the show with minimal interference from network executives. It was an important element in the innovative (and risky) character of the show. One other manifestation of this kind of control was that both Wilson and Reid were committed to (and hired) a multiracial crew.

The central premise of the show was this: Frank Parrish, a Professor of Renaissance History from Boston, inherited his father's restaurant (The Chez Louisianne) in New Orleans. Parrish knows little about New Orleans and even less about managing a restaurant. Over the course of the series we, along with Parrish, learn the nuances of managing a restaurant and about aspects of a local black community in New Orleans. The primary characters in the show included the staff at the restaurant—Miss Marie, an elderly black woman; Big Arthur, the chef and his white assistant, Shorty; Anna, a middle aged black waitress; Tiger, the elderly black bartender and his assistant, Cool; the regular cast also included members of the local community—a local entrepreneur (a black female funeral home director and her daughter Hannah—played by Daphne Maxwell Reid); The Reverend Deal, a colorful local minister; and Bubba, a white lawyer.

Once the concept for the show was set Wilson and Reid took several trips to New Orleans to get a feel for the ambience and the texture of life in that city. On these trips both Reid and Wilson visited with members of the local black community. They were especially interested in getting an interior sense of New Orleans from members of the black business community. Wilson likened their activities on these trips to the field work of oral historians.

After setting the story concept, Wilson established a certain look for the show which he then let dictate the writing, editing, and dramatic approach. As producer/writer/director Wilson wanted to get as much of New Orleans on the television screen as he possibly could. This required that Wilson, a former film director, get away from the existing conventions of television direction, camera work, and lighting (Barker 1985).[3] As a result Wilson developed a more self consciously cinematic look for the show, shooting with film instead of video tape, treating the main camera ('B') as the major narrative voice rather than using three cameras to achieve this as is usually done in filming for television, using a faster and crisper editing technique, eschewing the use of sweeteners and a laugh track, and using original music on the show (Barker 1985). (To achieve the look that they wanted Wilson was especially meticulous about lighting the show. He hired an award winning film cinematographer—William A. Fraker—to shoot the pilot, and then had the lighting for the subsequent episodes approximate the look of the pilot. This look provided one of the consistent and defining qualities for the series.)

The production schedule was even dictated by the look and feel that Wilson and Reid were trying to achieve. Thus, as Wilson described it

We had to start shooting at seven o'clock in the morning. By then the lights were on. We just shot it film style. We'd rehearse it, shoot it and shoot it out of order so they (the network) couldn't send anybody over. There was no run through to see and so consequently we were left totally free.[4]

This strategy, in addition to creating the look of the show, was also a way of maintaining control over production of the project.

To achieve the look and feel of the show that Wilson wanted was an expensive proposition (by television standards for half hour situation comedies). *Frank's Place* cost $650,000 an episode to produce.[5] According to Wilson, they began the series at a deficit since CBS paid Viacom $425,000 to produce the show. In retrospect Wilson believes that part of the commercial failure of the show, at least in terms of network support and their unwillingness to ride out the early storm of low ratings, was due to the cost involved in producing the show. At some point in the season, CBS decided that the costs and the risks of the show were too high and they decided "to cut their losses."[6]

Wilson's and his production team's commitment to creating a different kind of show was evident not just in the aesthetic look and texture of the show's content, but also in the social relations of its production. The crew was multiracial and composed of men and women. More importantly, the entire production team served as an important barometer for monitoring the pulse of the show. The most immediate place (and impact) for the collaborative style that defined the show (especially with respect to the representations of black cultural sensibilities), occurred among the writers, the crew, and the actors. (On this point Tim Reid's relationship with Wilson, the crew, and the actors was crucial.) Wilson assembled a team of four writers, two of whom he had previously worked with on other projects and two of whom he had not. For a short period there was one female on the team (she did not work out), and a black writer who wrote regularly for the show.

Wilson described the writing for the show as truly collaborative, save the fact that as the chief writer he exercised final authority to shape a story:

We would discuss these stories in a group. And we would talk and talk. And sometimes we would talk about a story for days and then decide to abandon it. But then if we had something we liked whoever the writer was who had that assignment would then write an outline and we would all read the outline. And then talk that to death. Then the writer would write a draft and sometimes a second draft. Then he would give it to me and I would write the third draft. That's why the shows sort of have a singularity of viewpoint. Because they all, with the exception of one show, would come through my final filter.[7]

They did occasionally take scripts from outside the writing staff, but even these had to go through this process of refinement and collaboration by Wilson and his team.[8] With respect to the representations of African American culture, I believe that this collaborative process (at all stages of production) is an important way to insure a variety of viewpoints, sensibilities, and visions.

Finally, two important personal and biographical points about Wilson's and Reid's roles ought to be emphasized as they specifically concern cultural sensibilities that appeared on *Frank's Place*. Wilson is a Southerner who identifies himself primarily as a writer. Since Wilson grew up, was educated, and worked in the South (where he also participated in the Civil Rights Movement), he remained sensitive to Southern race relations as well as the sensibilities that defined African American culture there. Secondly, working with Tim Reid and other black members of the crew, Wilson not only trusted their inputs and their sensibilities (seeking them out), but he seems to have been able to effectively use his own position as a Southern white male to monitor the show's representations of black Southern life and culture. This willingness to collaborate on these matters is important, especially in the production and presentations of black life in commercial television.

Critically, *Frank's Place* received rave reviews. It was hailed by television critics and various segments of the public as innovative and refreshing television. Because of the absence of a laugh track, the absence of traditional resolutions at the end of each episode, and its blending of comedy and drama the show was referred to by many critics and industry observers as a dramedy.[9] Unfortunately, the show failed to receive sufficient ratings throughout its run and was eventually canceled by CBS.[10] The final episode aired October 1, 1988 with a 5.6 rating and a 10 share. In January 1990, The Black Entertainment Network (BET) began broadcasting all twenty-two existing episodes of *Frank's Place*.

THE LOCATION OF *FRANK'S PLACE* IN TELEVISION DISCOURSES ABOUT RACE

I think blacks are looked upon in this country in a very peculiar way . . . I don't think we are taken seriously as a group that has something to say in film or theater . . . I think musically we're more apt to be accepted musically and in comedy. . . .

Rosalind Cash

Socially and aesthetically the distinctive character of *Frank's Place* derives from a variety of historical, generic, and aesthetic elements: situation comedy, the workplace family, American racial memory, shows about region and location, and the tradition of black situation comedy. To understand the lineage of black representations that made a series like *Frank's Place* possible (and with which it remained in dialogue), I want to situate the show in relationship to series that preceded it as well as to other contemporary black oriented series.[11]

Frank's Place and the aesthetic and cultural representations which it expressed were possible because *The Cosby Show* effectively cleared the contemporary commercial and aesthetic television landscape (Downing 1988, Gray 1990). Also included in the lineage of shows about blacks that eventually helped make *Frank's Place* possible are programs from the late seventies and early eighties including *The Jeffersons*, *Benson*, *Webster*, and *Different Strokes*. In these shows upward social mobility and middle class affluence replaced urban poverty as both setting and theme (Gray 1989, 1986).

Television programs about black life such as *Good Times*, *Florence*, *Baby I'm Back*, *That's My Mama*, and *Sanford and Son*, which were set in lower class poverty and which appeared in the nineteen seventies, were themselves a response to the social protest and petitions by blacks against American society in general and the media in particular for the absence of black images in the media (MacDonald 1983, Winston 1982). Black programs in the nineteen seventies were a response to network attempts to soften (i.e., whiten) black stars like Bill Cosby (*I Spy*), Diahann Carroll (*Julia*), Nat King Cole (*The Nat King Cole Show*), and Greg Morris (*Mission Impossible*) who appeared on television in the fifties and sixties (MacDonald 1983). These programs and the representations of blacks that they presented anticipated a set of discourses that I have elsewhere called assimilationist (Gray 1990). In contrast to pluralist and recoded discourses, assimilationist discourses present blacks as invisible and for all practical purposes just like whites.[12] Finally these more acceptable representations developed in response to stereotypes of blacks which appeared in the earliest days of television in shows such as *Amos and Andy* and *Beulah* (MacDonald 1983, Montgomery 1989, Winston 1982).

Reading the *Bill Cosby Show* (and subsequently *Frank's Place*), against these early programs and the discourses in which they were embedded helps account for its middle class focus and more importantly for its consistent reappropriation of the stable black middle class family.[13] That the *Cosby* show features a black family is, ideologically at least, significant evidence of American racial equality and pluralism. African American culture, whether expressed as language, music, or style of life, provides props along the narrative path of social mobility—small nonthreatening indicators of difference that confirm the possibility of a benign pluralism (or postmodernism) rooted in the ideology of middle class equality (Miller 1988). In cultural and social terms the show is just black enough not to offend and middle class enough to comfort.

Many of the qualities of *The Cosby Show* are also found on other contemporary black oriented programs such as 227, *Family Matters*, and *AMEN*, which offer comfortable nonthreatening renderings of black life. These shows seldom explore the centrality of African American culture as guides for action or clues for what happens to people of African American descent in modern American society.

By contrast, in *Frank's Place*, African American culture is central to the lives of the characters and the structure of the show. As I show in the next section, it is the cultural and historical ground from which the show operated. In this respect the show was different from the others that form part of its lineage, including *The Cosby Show*. At the same time, *Frank's Place* can only be read against these shows, their familiarity, advances, and silences (Gates 1989).

In addition to the history of black television shows, *Frank's Place* also drew on and remained in dialogue with the lineage of shows about place.[14] The culture and location of New Orleans was central to the show's identity. In *Frank's Place*, food, language, setting, dress, and music are collectively used to establish the centrality of black New Orleans to the theme and feel of the show.

Frank's Place also owed much of its formal character to a previous generation of television programs about the workplace and to those that used comedy and drama innovatively in the half-hour format (Taylor 1989). Norman Lear's *Soap* and *Mary Hartman, Mary Hartman* are often cited as the forerunners in the innovative use of comedy and drama in the comedic format as well as in the use of endings that lack resolution (Barker 1985, Feuer 1986, Newcomb and Alley 1983). The workplace family on *Frank's Place* was also very similar to those found on *Mary Tyler Moore*, *M*A*S*H*, *Barney Miller*, and *Cheers* (Feur 1987, Taylor 1989).

Frank's Place then, forms part of a continuing strategy of adjustment, displacement, and reappropriation of television representations of black life. It momentarily transformed and occasionally challenged rather than reproduced the conventional representations of black Americans in commercial network television.

RECODING AFRICAN AMERICAN CULTURE IN *FRANK'S PLACE*

In my neighborhood I saw people who I respected: the shopkeeper, the butcher, the cobbler . . . the man who used to come through and sharpen knives . . . I never saw that on the screen.

Rosalind Cash

Before examining the central role of African American culture in *Frank's Place*, I want to clarify my view of culture and its specific application to the African American experience. What I intend is some specification of the way that mass mediated commercial culture in general and television in particular expresses the impulses, tones, and consciousness of contemporary black lives in American society (i.e., those qualities described by Rosalind Cash in the epigraph which begins this section)—especially as these are lived and practiced in everyday life.

I am interested in the way that the practices and sensibilities of people in marginalized and subordinated positions vis-à-vis the dominant culture are expressed, especially in the realm of mass mediated popular culture. The aim is to identify the specific ways that these sensibilities get articulated, mediated, and appropriated in contemporary mass produced and distributed popular culture.

What are the elements of African American cultural sensibilities present in *Frank's Place*? First, compared to existing television programs about blacks, the series was distinguished by its explicit recognition and presentation of the habits, practices, manners, nuances, and outlooks of black Americans located in New Orleans. In subtle matters of language, dress, sense of place, the relationship to time, pace, body movements (especially nonverbal expressions), the show expressed a distinct sensibility or "structure of feeling" (Williams 1977).

Consider one episode's rendering of the following scene:

A group of white male New York corporate executives enter The Chez for a late night dinner meeting. They are dressed in business suits that signal their social class and professional status. They present themselves in the formal manner and demeanor of urban businessmen—formal, reserved, controlled. In a relaxed but deliberate manner a young black waiter slowly approaches the table. In the process of taking their order, he strikes up a conversation. "Yall from New York City?" he asks. "Yes," one of them replies. The waiter continues, "Thought so. My brother lives up there but he don't like it much." "How come?" asks one of the businessmen. "Because some dude knocked out his eye, that's how come," answers the waiter before continuing to disclose more details of the incident, its location, and so on to his surprised patrons.

This exchange is significant because it points up the contrast in language, pace, detail, and relationship to public talk between these white Northern businessmen and this Southern black man. Reading this scene from a white middle class view one might regard the waiter's behavior as slovenly, even rude. As a black American born and raised in the South, I see his behavior in contrast to the public formality and reserve of the white professional businessmen as black and Southern. The young man does not think about his warrant to offer or solicit private information from these complete strangers. Rather, as public talk it is an assumed part of the folkways of the community where he lives. The businessmen are in The Chez and in New Orleans which is the young black man's turf. It is they, not him, who are made uncomfortable by the exchange.

As I've noted, in the content and structure of the program, setting, approach to production, organization of the cast, themes addressed (voodoo, jazz, basketball recruitment, homelessness) lie the elements and expressions of a distinctive African American orientation. Formally, viewers are positioned through the setting, the script, camera placement, editing, and coding to understand the show from the point of view of black New Orleans' residents. We *must* negotiate the world of *Frank's Place* through the experiences of black subjects. In this sense the show is not simply didactic nor does it merely offer a voyeuristic tour of black experiences which disempowers or exoticizes black subjects.

Since the program explicitly operated from an African American subject position, the multiracial cast (and viewing audience), remains grounded in assumptions that structure an African American reality. To make sense of and appreciate the show, viewers (especially whites and others outside of this specific cultural milieu), cannot simply operate outside of the "structure of feeling" that defined the show.

The white members of the cast, Shorty, (the cook), and Bubba, (the lawyer), participate as full members of this community. In language, habits, and assumptions, they actively participate in the cultural definitions and sensibilities that ordered the world of *Frank's Place*.[15]

The show's setting also expressed elements of an African American sensibility. The historical and social significance of New Orleans in the American past (slavery and the origins of black American music), was represented and repeatedly reinforced through the musical and visual montage that opened the show. This montage works almost viscerally to establish New Orleans as a concrete place of cultural location in America and African Americans as a significant cultural community.[16] The tightly edited sepia-toned stills of New Orleans' life include scenes of Mississippi Riverboats, the Mississippi River, Louis Armstrong, The Preservation Jazz Orchestra, The French Quarter, and Congo Square. These scenes move rapidly across the screen to strains of Louis Armstrong's classic recording "Do You Know What it Means to Miss New Orleans." The combined effect is to aurally and visually place the viewer into the experience of black New Orleans. In constructing this representation, the producers foreground African American New Orleans, thereby situating its location and identity within an African American sensibility. This is not just anywhere USA populated by anonymous folk, but black New Orleans with its own particular history and story.

Food was also central to the program's identity. The cuisine featured was Creole (rather than the French Canadian derived cajun which enjoyed a period of trendy culinary popularity in the mid-1980s). The centrality of food to the show and its location within African American culture is revealed in a telling scene from an episode (described below) on African musicians and jazz. Upon their arrival at the Chez, a group of touring African musicians are treated to dinner. After dinner the troupe is given a tour of the kitchen and introduced to the staff. Immediate rapport and cultural commonality is established between the musicians and the staff of the Chez through their discussions (and lessons) about foods, especially those which they have in common. In the dialogue between the two groups the symbolic connections (and distinctions) between Africans and African Americans is established.

Also central to explicitly establishing the show's preferred cultural point of view were nuances about the people and socio-economic characteristics of the community. Indeed, I think it is significant that the restaurant is a small black business located in a black working class community (rather than the French Quarter), frequented mainly by blacks. The complex class character of the program was explored in an early episode when Frank asked Tiger (the bartender) about the absence of local restaurant patrons during the middle of the week. In response to Frank's inquiry Tiger notes, "These are all working people in our neighborhood; they don't go out to dinner on week nights. White folks are afraid to come down here after dark." A simple and clear observation rendered from the viewpoint of a working member of a community who knows his customers and his neighbors.

By highlighting aspects of working class life in New Orleans, the show moved a considerable distance from other programs that remain contained by "normative" middle class cultural sensibilities. With its serious, ironic, and humorous exploration of issues such as drugs, sports, voodoo, middle class status, and homelessness, the show tilted toward a more noble and serious representation of black working class experience. The aspirations, pressures, joys, and troubles of waiters, cooks, and regular folk were represented with integrity in this show rather than the derision, exaggeration, and marginalization that is too often the case in other television representations of blacks and working class people. Finally, while set in a working class context, the show moved between various class positions and experiences even as it addressed tensions between these different classes.[17]

What distinguished the use of cuisine, language, and music in *Frank's Place* from other programs with similar themes was the use of these elements as expressions of an African American "structure of feeling." These elements were the subjects of various episodes and more significantly they consistently provided the context and setting for action. In at least one episode each, both food and music were dominant themes. Formally music was used, as it has been conventionally in television, to begin and end each episode as well as to suggest emotion, cue action, and segue from scene to scene. The show's particular use of black popular musical forms such as blues, jazz, and rhythm and blues reproduced the central relationship between the role of music and African American culture. Music was a constant in the show—it was always there, whether formally as a background device, on the jukebox as entertainment in the club, or as the subject of an episode.

What is more, *Frank's Place* (with the exception of *The Bill Cosby Show*) was one of the few places on commercial network television which actively used blues and jazz performed by original artists in settings like those found in black communities. Reid's and Wilson's commitment to present the original music by Louis Armstrong, Lightnin Hopkins, Jimmy Reed, Slim Gallard, Slam Stewart, B. B. King, Muddy Waters, and Dizzy Gillespie represents a rare moment of commercial network television's treatment of African American music as a cultural resource and the African American musician as a cultural hero.

Aside from these formal uses, black music was also the major motif of at least one episode. Written by novelist and screen writer Samm-Art Williams, this episode brought members of an African music and dance troupe to the Chez Restaurant. During their New Orleans visit, one of the troupe's members (Adele), a master African musician and devout jazz lover, discovers that Dizzy Gillespie is scheduled to perform in town. As the narrative develops it is revealed that Adele is so enamored of jazz that he plans to defect to the United Stated in order to play professionally.

Viewed against marginalization and trivialization of things African by the dominant commercial media, this was an unusual moment in American commercial network television's representations of blacks. As a black American, I find this representation especially significant because the narrative adopted a "pan African" recognition of music, culture, food, and customs.[18] (The representation of Adele's desire to play American jazz with Dizzy Gillespie is also significant from the viewpoint of African American cultural history, since Gillespie was the first American jazz musician to incorporate African and Afro-Caribbean influences into his music (Gillespie 1979).[19]

At the level of narrative content *Frank's Place* explored an extraordinary range of themes—homelessness, greed and exploitation, basketball recruitment, voodoo, music, and personal relationships. The program's critical appeal and aesthetic

innovation owed much to this rich thematic range. Aside from the explicit representations of African American culture, the jazz episode stands out for its attempt
at cross cultural understanding and the location of living African American cultural practices (food, music, dance) at the center of the narrative.

An episode about the recruitment of a black high school All American basketball
player (Calvin) addressed issues—sports, education, male culture—"relevant" to
significant segments within black communities. The show examined the aspirations and complicated connections between Calvin and a white middle aged
recruiter named Chick. The episode explored the stakes, excesses, confusion,
exploitation, and competition involved in recruiting black high school athletes. By
using humor and irony to focus on the exploitation and absurdity in the athletic
recruitment game, the episode called attention to the need for community resources to help Calvin (and countless others like him) through this process—the
politics of recruiting, the balance between academics and public relations, excessive
hype and reliable information, and the destinies of young black athletes.

The narrative, organized as a montage, followed Calvin's initial recruitment
through the announcement of his selection of a college. The visual montage (risky
for the genre of situation comedy) was presented from the vantage points of the
various people (and interests) involved in the recruitment process—the athlete
(Calvin), the adviser (Frank), the coach, the recruiter (Chick), and the mother. By
moving from one perspective to another, we learn the motives of the various people
involved. From the angle of these different interests we come to appreciate the
enormous pressures, frustrations, and risks of exploitation that young black athletes like Calvin face.[20]

This episode was unusually explicit about the racial exploitation and arrogance
which accompanies the circus atmosphere of college athletic recruitment. In this
exchange between two elderly black women, Calvin's mother and Miss Marie (one
of the major characters in the show), notice the sense of personal and cultural
violation these women feel at the hands of insensitive white male recruiters.

Calvin's mother: "Some (recruiters) just write, but others, they call my house all hours of the
day and night. They drive by my house."

Miss Marie: "And they even come by the church."

Calvin's mother: "Yea! All these white men dropping money in the collection plate so I
can see."

This exchange reveals the clash of culture and the different assumptions that order
each world. Viewers are forced to choose sides, and those who identify and
sympathize with these women quickly become suspicious of the recruiters and
impatient with the process. Emotionally the suspicion, impatience, and identification with the plight of these elderly women is an articulation of the episode's
critique of the recruitment process, especially the precarious terms on which the
decisions about the futures of black youngsters rest.

A number of other qualities from this episode suggest its operation and location
within a black American cultural sensibility. As Calvin's adviser, Frank, the middle
class university professor, represents many of the concerns of a black parent about
sending a young adult to college—ratio of students to faculty, ratio of blacks to

whites, school population, the background of the students, the graduation rates for black athletes. Significantly, Frank also mentioned "the small all black college" as an option for Calvin. Although much of this seems lost on Calvin, it was not lost on black viewers especially those for whom historically black colleges remain a major route for the education of young blacks.[21]

When taken together these explicit articulations of concerns relevant to black Americans reveal elements of African American experiences which are usually silent and absent in American commercial network television. It is not enough that such concerns are explicitly mentioned however; it is in the specific selection, organization, and use of these elements that their legitimacy and resonance operates.

FRANK'S PLACE AND THE LIMITS OF TELEVISION REPRESENTATION OF AFRICAN AMERICAN CULTURE

While *Frank's Place*'s rewriting of African American representations in commercial network television offer alternatives to dominant representations, there are even limits to this most hopeful set of representations. After all, the series operated within the slippery and contested terrain of commercial television. Therefore even this welcome corrective does not constitute a complete break (Foster 1985, Taylor 1988). As *Frank's Place* pressed the limits of dramatic and comedic television representations of black Americans, it illustrates the hegemonic strategies of containment operating in the commercial television system. Thus while it challenged conventional aesthetic and generic boundaries and offered new ways to represent aspects of black life in America, *Frank's Place* failed to find resonance in the high stakes world of commercial popularity.

In addition to its muted commercial appeal, the show's critical insights were often contained and limited. For example, in its incisive critique of high school basketball recruitment, it is not clear where the critique was directed—the college recruitment system, urban public school education which produces students like Calvin, parents, individual recruiters, individual coaches, or students. (In an episode on homelessness, a sympathetic and insightful portrait of a homeless person is drawn, but the question of homelessness as a complex social problem remains essentially Frank's moral problem.)

Within this structure of containment the character of Frank is important. It was usually Frank who expressed critical insight and moral outrage. He expressed these responses in a variety of ways: by looking away in disgust at the offending character's (Reverend Deal's) indiscretions; by sanctioning Cool for his errant drug dealings; by judging Bubba's need to mislead his family (about his and Frank's homosexual relationship) to get out of a difficult situation. Frank, the sophisticated but naive college professor, represents the critique and strategies for change. (Consistent with the conventions of character development in commercial television, Frank was not infallible; he too suffered loss, disappointment, and bad judgment (Fiske 1987.)

Significantly the show was also contained by the social and cultural limitations of an American social order where racism, social inequality, and deep suspicions of cultural differences remain. *Frank's Place* required its audience to engage directly the issue of cultural difference. The show also demanded the necessary competence, patience, and engagement to produce pleasure and maintain interests. The narrative structure, thematic approach, and cinematic look of the show disturbed the normal television experience. In a sense the show required too much work; it asked too much of an audience for whom African American culture remained a fuzzy and distant experience. Its potential audience simply had to work too hard to make sense of the African American life and culture represented in the show (and never mind that they also had to work to find the show in the network's programming schedule.)

The show's commercial failure resecured the center of the genre of situation comedy, rather than inviting explorations of the margins. It reinforced the limited terms within which the general American television audience can explore the interiors of black social and cultural life. *Frank's Place* daring but short life is perhaps the exception that proves the rule in commercial television as it concerns blacks: representations of African Americans will remain an active part of American commercial television offerings to the extent that we remain contained, nonthreatening, and familiar.

NOTES

1. Thanks to the following colleagues and friends for critical readings, discussions, and support in the preparation of this paper: Clyde Taylor, Tommy Lott, George Lipsitz, Rosa Linda Fregoso, Teshome Gabriel, Hamid Naficy, Valerie Smith, Jimmie Reeves, Richard Campbell, Horace Newcomb, and The Center for African American Studies at UCLA.
2. Most of the information in this section was taken from a day long seminar and discussion with *Frank's Place* co-executive producer Hugh Wilson. The seminar was held in New Orleans, Louisiana in November 1988. Many of the details of the production of the show are more fully reported and developed in Richard Campbell's and Jimmie L. Reeves's "Television Authors: The Case of Hugh Wilson" (unpublished paper 1989).
3. Wilson's most well known and commercially successful film was *Police Academy I.*
4. Seminar discussion with Wilson, November 1988.
5. Even this figure seems modest compared to the reported $1 million dollars per episode cost of *The Cosby Show*. See Lippman 1990.
6. In the course of its twelve month run CBS moved the show to six different time slots and four different nights.
7. Seminar discussion with Wilson, November 1988.
8. It is not surprising that Wilson used this approach since he honed his writing and directing skills at MTM studios, where this approach was widely used.
9. Some observers in the television industry attribute the show's commercial failure to its blurring of these genres and its failure to develop a clear identity.
10. The cancellation of *Frank's Place* prompted widespread protests and letter writing campaigns from organizations such as the National Urban League and the NAACP.
11. Discussions with Tommy Lott and Clyde Taylor helped shape many of the ideas in this section.
12. See Gray, "Watching Television, Reading Race" (unpublished manuscript 1989).
13. The recently acclaimed *Arsenio Hall Show* is similar in this respect. The chatty and occasionally gossipy format is really about the class and mobility aspirations of a new generation of young blacks and whites.
14. Other notable programs about place include *Dallas* (Texas), *The Bob Newhart Show* (Vermont), *The Andy Griffin Show* (North Carolina), *Designing Women* (Atlanta), *Spencer For Hire* and *St. Elsewhere* (Boston).
15. This universe of African American cultural sensibilities is rare in commercial television; one other site where such representation occurs is music television, namely music video.

16. My observations on this point are indebted to Rosalinda Fregoso who offers a similar analysis about the use of music to establish cultural location and significance in Chicano film. For her analysis of the role of music in Chicano film see: Rosalinda Fregoso (1990) "Hybridity in Chicano Cinema" paper presented at the International Association for the Study of Popular Music. New Orleans (May).

17. One episode explored color caste and class conflicts within the Southern black experience. In this particular episode, Frank was faced with the difficult choice of choosing between two black male fraternal organizations which were distinguished, in this case, by class background and skin color. A similar theme was, of course, at the center of Spike Lee's *School Daze*.

18. The presentation of music was also significant because of the space in the program given both to traditional African music and dance and to American jazz. Musicians and dancers performed in traditional African costumes. A further affirmation of the close relationship between Africans and African Americans was expressed by Hannah's mother, who during the performance by the African troupe, explained to Tiger (and the audience) the origins of various costumes and the symbolism of the instruments.

19. In the nineteen fifties Gillespie hired the Cuban drummer Chano Pozo to play in his band.

20. For example, as a family acquaintance and adviser, Frank is interested in securing the best academic environment for Calvin; Calvin's mother, who is both proud and tired, wants Calvin to make the right decision and for the circus act to end; Calvin's high school coach wants a university coaching position; Chick, the university recruiter wants a successful basketball program and to compete in the final four NCAA basketball tournament; Calvin wants "to wear #17, to play on national television, to start [his] freshman year, and a twelve million dollar NBA contract." In contrast to these collective pressures and interests, Calvin's aspirations seem simple albeit poorly prioritized. Against the background of his eighth grade reading ability and weak high school preparation his goals seem out of reach.

21. *The Bill Cosby Show* must also be credited with introducing references to historically black colleges into the plots and narrative of situation comedy. For a while Denise attended Hillman, a fictitious black college. Filmaker Spike Lee's influence on this issue should not be lost since his successful musical *School Daze* was also set in a Southern Black college.

REFERENCES

Barker, David
    1985   "Television Production Techniques as Communication." In *Critical Studies in Mass Communication*. 2:234–246.

Childs, John Brown
    1984   "Afro-American Intellectuals and the People's Culture." *Theory and Society*. 13: Pp.

Downing, John H.
    1988   "'The Cosby Show' and American Racial Discourse." In Geneva Smitherman-Donaldson and Teun A. Van Dijk. 46–74. *Discourse and Discrimination*. Detroit: Wayne State University Press.

Fiske, John
    1987   *Television Culture*. London: Methuen.

Feur, Jane
    1987   "The MTM Style." In Horace Newcomb, ed. 52–84. *Television: The Critical View*. (4th Edition) New York: Oxford University Press.
    1986   "Narrative Form in American Network Television." In Colin MacCabe, ed. *High Theory/Low Culture: Analyzing Popular Television and Film*. New York: St. Martin's.

Foster, Hal
    1985   *Recodings: Art, Spectacle, and Cultural Politics*. Port Townsend, Washington: Bay Press.

Gans, Herbert
    1979   *Deciding What's News: A Study of the CBS Evening News, NBC Nightly News, Newsweek and Time*. New York: Pantheon.

Garfinkel, Perry
    1988   "*Frank's Place*: The Restaurant as Life Stage." *New York Times* (February 17): C1.

Gates, Henry Louis
    1989   "TV's Black World Turns—But Stays Unreal." *New York Times* (November 12): Arts and Leisure Section, 1.
Gillespie, Dizzy
    1979   *To Be Or Not To Bop*. New York: Doubleday.
Gitlin, Todd
    1986   *Watching Television*. New York: Pantheon.
Gray, Herman
    1990   "Watching TV: Reading Race." Presented at the Annual Convention of the American Sociological Association. Washington D.C. (August).
    1989   "Television, Black Americans and the American Dream." *Critical Studies in Mass Communication*. 6, 4: 376–387.
    1986   "Television and the New Black Man: Black Male Images in Prime-time Situation Comedy." *Media Culture and Society*. 8: 223–242.
Hall, Stuart
    1981   "Notes on Deconstructing the Popular." Pp. 227–240 in Raphael Samuel, ed. *People's History and Socialist Theory*. London: Routledge and Kegan Paul.
Lippman, John
    1990   "Cosby Makers Ask NBC for a $1 Million Bonus." *Los Angeles Times*. (March 22): A1.
MacDonald, J. Fred
    1983   *Blacks and White TV*. Chicago: Nelson-Hall.
McClaurin-Allen, Irma
    1987   "Working: the Black Actress in the Twentieth Century; Interview with Rosalind Cash." *Contributions in Black Studies: A Journal of African and Afro-American Studies*. 8: 67–77.
Miller, Mark Crispin
    1988   "Cosby Knows Best." In his *Boxed In: The Culture of TV*. Evanston, ILL: Northwestern University Press.
Montgomery, Katheryn
    1989   *Target Prime Time*. London: Oxford.
Newcomb, Horace, and Robert S. Alley
    1983   *The Producer's Medium*. New York: Oxford.
Newcomb, Horace
    1984   "On the Dialogic Aspects of Mass Communication." *Critical Studies in Mass Communication*. 1: 34–50.
Taylor, Clyde
    1988   "We Don't Need Another Hero: Anti-thesis on Aesthetics." Pp. 80–85 in Mbye B. Cham and Claire Andrade-Watkins, eds. *Critical Perspectives on Independent Black Cinema*. Cambridge, Massachusetts: MIT University Press.
Taylor, Ella
    1989   *Prime Time Television Families*. Berkeley: University of California Press.
Reeves, Jimmie L.
    1988   "Rewriting Newhart: A Dialogic Analysis." *Wide Angle*. 10,1: 76–91.
Williams, Raymond
    1977   *Marxism and Literature*. New York: Oxford University Press.
Wilson, Hugh
    1988   "Observations on Making of *Frank's Place*." Seminar on *Frank's Place*. Speech Communications Association. New Orleans (November).
Winston, Michael
    1982   "Racial Consciousness and the Evolution of Mass Communication in the United States." *Daedalus*. 111: 171–182.

Catalan Cinema: Historical Experience and Cinematic Practice

Marvin D'Lugo

SOMETHING LIKE A NATIONAL CINEMA

Jaime Camino's 1986 documentary drama, *Dragón Rapide*, is a striking example of the little understood development of Catalan film that has emerged in recent years to challenge the more generally accepted conception of a unified Spanish national cinema.[1] In addition to attempting to recuperate the long-suppressed sense of a regional cultural identity for Catalonia, Camino's film also questions the cultural constructions of nationhood that have stabilized the idea of a homogeneous Spanish nation at the expense of its distinctive regional cultures.

On the surface, the film looks like yet another historical reconstruction of aspects of the Civil War period, not unlike the spate of such films that, for more than a decade now, Spanish filmmakers have been churning out as a form of national catharsis through which to expose for their countrymen many of the interdicted images and perspectives on the war that the iron hand of Francoist censorship had long prohibited. In chronicling the plotting by right-wing politicians and army officers in the summer of 1936 to overthrow the Spanish Republican government, however, Camino appears less interested in historical vindications than in finding a way to mobilize his audience's involvement in their own interrogation of political and cultural history. He finds that strategy by first presenting the narrative of the plan to transport the young General Franco from the Canary Islands to the Spanish mainland in a private airplane, the Dragón Rapide of the film's title, to head the insurrection, and then punctuating that narrative with a series of five brief scenes that have nothing to do with the military and political intrigues but are important indicators of the film's underlying political allegiance. The noted Catalan cellist, Pablo Casals, appears in each segment, first preparing and then rehearsing an orchestra and chorus in Barcelona's Palace of Music for a performance of Beethoven's Ninth Symphony.

What draws our attention to this micro-narrative embedded into the larger plot is not only its apparent lack of connection with the main action, but also the fact that during these scenes Casals addresses his performers in the Catalan language. In the last sequence, the fateful eighteenth of July, he speaks to the orchestra and chorus for one final time to announce that the concert for which they have rehearsed

MARVIN D'LUGO, *teaches Spanish and Latin American cinemas at Clark University. His articles have appeared in QRFS, Wide-Angle, and Literature-Film Quarterly. His book on the cinema of Carlos Saura was recently published by Princeton University Press.*

Figure 1.   Dragón Rapide *juxtaposes the narrative of the army's conspiracy against the Republic with images that suggest Catalan cultural achievement.*

has been cancelled because the army has risen up against the Republic. In a gesture of hope and "fraternity," Casals asks the group to play and sing Beethoven's "Ode to Joy." The singing fades as the final image of the film shows the airplane landing in Tetuán delivering Franco to lead the invasion of the peninsula.

As some critics have argued, Camino's presumed *Catalanidad*, his "Catalanism," leads him to insert this eccentric and irrelevant chain of scenes into his historical drama. Yet, far from being irrelevant, the Casals scenes which culminate in the "Ode to Joy" sum up in narrative terms an underlying enunciative strategy that seeks to identify and develop a unique form of Catalan spectatorship. Juxtaposing the tradition of Catalan cultural achievement in arts and letters as embodied by Casals with the venality and ruthlessness of the Castilian-speaking military officers and politicians, *Dragón Rapide* invites its audience to reflect upon the historical events that imposed the Francoist hegemony on the Spanish nation while marginalizing and suppressing all other forms of popular cultural expression.

Camino is not alone in his effort to move his audience to a meditation/inquiry about the nature of the cultural identity that has been constructed for it by the dominant ideology of the Francoist state. *Dragón Rapide* connects in a logical way with a body of films by other Catalan directors, films which since the early 1960s have insistently challenged not only the dominant Spanish film productions coming out of Madrid, but, as well, the very notion of Spanishness to which such cultural production subscribes. These films do not easily fit into our conventional notions of autonomous national cinema, nor do they adhere to the folkloric prescriptions of regional, ethnographic film. Rather, they reflect the larger historical problematic of a number of marginal cinemas, that is, the filmic production of "subnational" cultural or ethnic groups whose self-realization as cultures threatens the coherence and possibly even the integrity of the political units within which they exist. In this respect, the experience of Catalan cinema can prove highly instructive to the understanding of the cultural dynamic of any emerging national cinema, as it does to the more immediate question that cinematic Catalanism raises about the nature of Spanish film itself.

Raymond Carr and Juan Pablo Fusi have argued that "the Catalan view of Spanish history was [that] Spain was a plural society of different peoples artificially hammered into the straitjacket of unity by Castilians."[2] Like Catalonia itself, Catalan cinema challenges the assumption of Spain as a unified cultural unit by mobilizing a variety of discourses of regional identity in opposition to that cultural otherness. Though not a national cinema in the conventional sense that one speaks of Italian or German cinemas, for instance, the multiple expressions of Catalanism in film nonetheless suggest to us something like a national cinema. While lacking a formal state apparatus through which to authenticate its "nationhood," Catalan cinema is marked by a pattern of conceptualizations—shared cultural-historical traditions and textual coherencies across a significant body of different filmic texts over time—that in other contexts would lead us to consider it as a national cinema.[3] The pivot of these "coherencies" lies in the deployment of certain issues of history into a chain of discursive practices that inscribe the historical trace of Catalan identity into the enunciative structure of a variety of films. Such strategies are understandable as a response to the sustained practices of the Franco regime to eradicate all overt signs of regional cultural identity from public life and gradually to erase even their memory. For that reason the conceptualization of history and the intertextual construction of a Catalan historical referent will play a pivotal role in the development and evolution of modern Catalan cinema.

CATALANISM AND CINEMA

At its root, the problematic status of Catalan cinema derives from the disjunction between Catalonia as a historically-rooted cultural community and the imposed constructions of political authority of the Spanish state that over centuries have sought to subsume all regional differences under the rubric of Castilianized, Spanish culture. "Catalanism" is the term that has traditionally been applied to any one of the variety of political and cultural positions that focus on the notion of Catalonia as a community separate and unique from the Castilian culture that dominates most of the rest of Spain. Situated on Spain's eastern Mediterranean shores, Catalonia historically comprised the provinces surrounding the city of Barcelona and the adjacent province of Valencia, as well as the Balearic islands. Throughout its history, however, this region claimed to be more than simply a geographic entity. It boasted a distinct language dating back to the ninth century and a strong literary heritage that, in the medieval period at least, rivaled that of Castilian literature. Catalonia had been politically associated with the Castilian monarchy of the central plateau since 1469. What remnants of political autonomy it enjoyed ended in 1715 when it was officially incorporated into the monarchy of Philip V. Nevertheless, there is ample evidence in eighteenth and nineteenth century writings to suggest that Catalans continued to think of themselves as a nation apart, bolstered as they were by their linguistic and cultural differences, and by their closer identification with the rest of Europe, an identification nurtured by the region's coastal location and Barcelona's strength as a mercantile center.

The mid-nineteenth century *Renaixença* or renaissance of Catalan literature brought a rebirth of nationalist spirit as it awakened interest in earlier Catalan culture as a source of distinctive regional identity.[4] Though understandably restricted to a cultural elite, the *Renaixença*'s emphasis on the rich heritage of Catalan letters was to contribute to the more generalized view in later decades of a profound Catalan difference from the rest of Spain. By the end of the century, Catalan economic development had contributed to the transformation of Barcelona into a city quite unlike any other in the Iberian peninsula. Rich in imaginative architecture and proud of its prosperous cosmopolitan air, the city and the region invited invidious comparisons with the decidedly more provincial Madrid. This Catalanist spirit was not restricted to the empowered classes alone. The ideal of a politically independent state, freed from the domination of Castilian Spain, inspired at least two popular uprisings against the Spanish monarchy, in 1909 and 1917, both of which were quickly suppressed by the central government.

Catalan demands for some form of home rule were a constant of Spanish parliamentary politics during the first decades of the twentieth century, but not until 1931, with the fall of the monarchy and the formation of the Second Republic, did the regional aspirations of self-governance become a realistic political possibility. Under a series of agreements with the Republican government, Catalonia was given semi-autonomous legal status, with the right to its own parliament, administration, law courts, budget, and the development of its own culture.[5] The Republican legitimization of Catalan autonomy gave hope to the Basques who, like their Catalan neighbors, also claimed historical, linguistic and political justification for their own political self-determination within the new republicanism, thus lending credence to the view of the Spanish Right that the new Republic was aimed at dismantling Spain province by province.[6] The passage of the statute of Catalan autonomy in the Republican parliament was said to have pushed Franco definitively toward his alignment with various military conspirators against the Republic.[7]

Catalonia's allegiance to the Republican government during the Civil War was unswerving, for survival of the Republic clearly meant hope for the continuation of a semi-independent Catalan state. As the war dragged on and the fortunes of the Republic waned, Catalonia became progressively more autonomous, experiencing what amounted to a degree of political nationhood during the final months of the war. With the Republican defeat, and as a bitterly ironic twist to their nationalist aspirations, Catalans were treated by the triumphant Francoist armies as a defeated enemy nation. Francoist policies in the immediate post-war period suggested that the goal of the fascist victors was the intentional extinction of Catalan culture. The Catalan language was banned in public, and a new law prohibited the use of any language but Spanish in films shown in Spain.

The massive blockage of all public display of Catalan culture persisted well into the 1960s, and only under the gradual redirection of the Franco dictatorship did the possibility of some sort of cultural and cinematic revival of the Catalan difference take form. The period of 1963–1969 was the era of the first major liberalization of the censorship system in Spain. Under the direction of Manuel Fraga Iribarne, as Minister of Information and Tourism, and his director of the ministry's film division, José María García Escudero, the country experienced a relaxation of the rigid patterns of permissible representation in film. This liberalization coincided with the first open manifestations of cultural nationalism in the region since the war's end. In this context, and against the historical backdrop of the Catalan struggle for some form of cultural self-definition and self-realization, we see the emergence of a new generation of filmmakers. The maintenance of the official film censorship apparatus, however, assured that there would be no overtly pro-Catalanist films for many years to come. Yet, as the decade progressed, it gradually became obvious that the recent history of political autonomy and the ferocious suppression of Catalan cultural identity were the important historical intertexts out of which these young filmmakers were shaping their own sense of cinematic Catalanism.

Perhaps the most problematic aspect of this early group of Catalanist films is the apparent lack of any overt signs of common textual or political referents that might constitute a coherent and unified body of filmic works. Not merely films made in Catalonia, nor films that espouse the usual themes of patriotic Catalanist culture, these were works that mobilized the concept of Catalan identity in a variety of ways in order to rewrite and ideally to displace the Francoist ideal of a Castilianized Spanishness. The conceptual gesture most common to the young Catalanist filmmakers was their subtle exploitation of the old Manicheanism that pitted Europeanized and culturally developed Catalonia against provincial and backward Castile. Though their strategies vary, their common stance was to conceive of their own cultural activity as filmmakers against the specter of Spanish national cinema as defined by the body of filmic and political practices as well as the cultural ideology that historically has sought to suppress and marginalize the Catalan difference.

Yet as much as these were works born of cultural opposition, it is often difficult to read into them the kind of political message that is most often associated with traditional Catalanist rhetoric. For instance, the conceptual opposition between Catalonia and Francoist Spain that inspires a number of these films reveals a gradual slippage of the idea of the Catalan "difference," not towards the identification of Catalonia with the political and artistic avant-garde of Europe, as Catalan nationalists had long argued, but precisely as the creative frontier or "supplement" of liberated culture and modernity capable of revitalizing the rest of Spain. In the sense that it emerges in Catalan films of the last decade and a half before Franco's death, Catalanism focuses on the image of Catalonia as a creative margin within a larger national consciousness extending beyond the limits of its geographically defined region.

Consistent with that conceptual tendency we find these films taking their common inspiration from a notion of Catalonia in general and Barcelona in particular as the bastion of pluralistic Spain and the haven of tolerance. Though not overtly historical, such a characterization carries with it the power of allusion, specifically the evocation of a Utopian Catalonia as the defender of the values of toleration and pluralism commonly associated with the political philosophy of the Republican government. Out of this conceptual move comes the earliest serious efforts by filmmakers to problematize cultural history around a series of interrogations of contemporary Catalanism in ways that, perhaps surprisingly for many Spaniards, transcend mere regionalism and are linked with the larger question of a Spanish national identity.

TEXTUALIZING DIFFERENCE

During the early 1960s, and under the aura of the regime's liberalization of its censorship norms, we find the first films made in Catalonia which focus on Catalan cultural images, although most of these are embedded in secondary plot elements or merely provide local color. Following the inspiration of the *Nova Cançó* movement, Jaime Camino's first film, *Los felices sesenta* (1964: *The Happy Sixties*), is the first, for example, to use a song interpreted in Catalan (by the popular folk singer, Raimón), in its credit sequence. Of more substantive import are three films, Josep María Forn's *La piel quemada* (1964: *Burnt Skin*), Camino's *España, otra vez* (1968: *Spain, Again*), and Vicent Aranda's *Fata Morgana* (1966: *Mirage*), which represent serious efforts to rechannel into aesthetic structures the idea of Catalonia's cultural and political identity.

Burnt Skin is perhaps the first film in Francoist Spain to center explicitly on a wholly Catalan theme. The government's promotion of economic expansion on the Catalan Costa Brava, in large measure through the development of tourism, had led to the large-scale migration of workers from Andalusia to the coastal areas of northeastern Spain. The film traces one fateful day in the life of José, a migrant worker. By the use of radical juxtaposition of simultaneous actions, we follow José's last day of bachelorhood before his wife's arrival, and Ana's travel from her stark Andalusian village to the train station, then the long trip to Barcelona, and finally, to the coastal town where José will meet her. These juxtapositions are, in turn, punctuated by a series of silent flashbacks of José's memories of the economic hardships that led him to go to Catalonia, temporarily breaking up his family.

Forn's script underscores the popular notions still held in many quarters, of Catalonia as a frontier for Spaniards who have been economically and socially marginalized by the regime's failed economic policies, and also of Catalonia as a "melting pot." The individual's struggle, therefore, appears to transcend the horizons of purely proletarian narrative and borders on the mythic narrative of foundation. Tellingly, Forn joins the theme of economic hardship with the question of cultural and national identity by introducing at certain points reference to the new settlers' linguistic difference. The treatment of old-guard Catalans who refuse to speak Castilian to José, for instance, are made to seem like the Francoists of earlier decades who mocked the language and customs of their fellow Spaniards.[8] If there are those who taunt José, however, there are also more generous, giving Catalans who treat him with warmth and camaraderie.

Juxtaposed against José's experiences are moments showing Ana and her children on their pilgrimage to Catalonia that evoke the iconography of the war years, particularly the images of whole families fleeing to safety beyond the reach of the Francoist armies. While only a single verbal reference to the war is made (by an old man Ana meets on the train who tells her about how it was when he first arrived in Barcelona), the indelible memory of the war and of the Catalonian haven clearly informs the film's narrational structure. The emphasis in *Burnt Skin* is clearly contemporary, but the elements of Forn's script cast the film's action into the figuration of recognizable national history.

In Jaime Camino's *Spain Again* we find a suggestively similar structuration of the suppressed historical image of Catalan identity. Jointly scripted by Camino, Spanish film historian Román Gubern, and Alvah Bessie, the Hollywood screenwriter who was also a participant in the Abraham Lincoln Brigade during the Civil War, *Spain, Again* focuses on the recuperation of blocked personal and historical memory. The plot is deceptively simple. Thirty years after the departure of the International Brigades from Spain, David Foster (Mark Stevens), an American physician, returns to Barcelona accompanied by his wife. His journey triggers a series of memories of the war and bittersweet reflections on the figure of the Spanish army nurse, Maria, with whom he had a passionate affair. Foster's days in Barcelona are filled with the pursuit of people from his past. He encounters Maria's daughter, and the two visit the site of the terrible battle of the Ebro River. Confronting the impossibility of retrieving his past and recognizing his own precarious mental state in which he confuses his former lover with her daughter, Foster, a frustrated and broken old man, leaves Barcelona with his wife.

By the 1960s, the memory of the savage Civil War as the origin of Francoist power had become something of an embarrassment to a regime still seeking acceptance by the western democracies. For that reason, Camino's film stands as a significant landmark, not only as it recuperates the Catalan experience of nationhood, but also as it rekindles memories of the shameful origins of the contemporary regime through David Foster's personal remembrances of Barcelona and the noble defense of the Republic. To be sure, the narrative of *Spain, Again* was shaped around explicit pressures of the censors:[9] The hero had to be a foreigner, not a Spaniard; the plot had to foreground contemporary actions, "carefully avoiding anything that might implicitly or explicitly suppose a reference or interpretation of our war that does not have an absolutely 'integrating' character."[10] Despite the coercive effect of the censors during the scripting of *Spain, Again*, the film retains much of its force as a simulation of and powerful inducement to the audience's recuperation of its own remembrance of the almost mythic unity of independent Catalonia fighting for its survival.

What is most striking here is the narrativization of Barcelona as the center of the Republic's final resistance to the Nationalist forces, cleverly eliding in this manner the evocation of independent Catalonia with the cause of the Republic. In effect, this move transforms Barcelona into a quasi-sacred space, the noble metropolis defending the Republic. This subtle metonymy is developed through the film's enunciative strategy of inserting rapid flashback images of war scenes as Foster visits specific sites in the city. These flaskbacks are, of course, read as the protagonist's recall of his past experience of these places. But since his previous experience of Barcelona was during the war, inevitably we read the metaphoric substitutions of the city for the nation. In this way Barcelona becomes the embodiment not only of

Catalonia, but of a more elevated ideal of Republican Spain itself: the solidarity of classes engaged in the defense of democracy fighting the good fight. Ironically, the film's title, *Spain, Again* comes to mean something akin to *Finnegan's Wake*, Barcelona having specifically become the reconstituted historical ideal of enlightened Spanishness.

Tellingly, both *Burnt Skin* and *Spain, Again* rely heavily on a fragmenting discursive structure through which to articulate their thematics of cultural integration. Implicitly, Forn and Camino's conceptualization of Catalonia is of a historically-bound structured absence. The process of each film, a folding back upon and expanding of the notion of Spanishness so narrowly defined by Francoism, suggests a complementarity between the Castilian Spain and its otherness in the generous and noble character of Catalan solidarity.

In the films of the so-called "Barcelona School" of the mid-1960s we find perhaps the most radical approach to the question of cultural identity to surface in that decade. The Barcelona School was a group of young filmmakers, most of them from upper middle-class backgrounds, who organized a cooperative of film productions which, as they theorized, would repudiate nearly everything dominant Spanish cinema stood for. Their rejection of the realist penchant of the Castilian-language opposition cinema—which included the established filmmakers such as Juan Antonio Bardem and Luis Berlanga, as well as the recently promoted "New Spanish cinema" of Carlos Saura, Mario Camus and Basilio Martín Patino—was a way of rejecting the provincialism of the Spain that those films reflected. Instead, the cooperative embraced a more cosmopolitan Europeanism whose modernity was evident as much in the settings and characters they depicted as in the thematic foci, inspired by the recent works of Antonioni, Godard, and Resnais. One particular feature of the modernity the group embraced was the emulation of a glossy, fashion magazine style and chic television advertising techniques. Even in terms of production, the group repudiated the Castilian style of filmmaking by arguing that experience, rather than academic training of the sort the National Film School (*Escuela Oficial de Cine*) provided, was what counted in filmmaking. To that end they established their own production cooperative, with directors collaborating on both the technical and directorial aspects of each other's films.

At its core, these "positions" voiced by members of the Barcelona School represented a critique of everything dominant Spanish cinema stood for. The essence of that critique was the ideological cleavage between cosmopolitan, universalist culture in Barcelona, strongly identified with the intellectual and artistic currents of the rest of Europe, and the Francoist Castilianism of Spanish culture and film which was, in their eyes, provincial and anachronistic.[11]

Visually, the films of the Barcelona School did not even look Spanish. When they were not modernist, constructed landscapes, their settings were shot precisely in those areas of Barcelona that would give a futuristic feel to the films. As one sympathetic Catalan film historian would later write, this was "an aristocratic, left-thinking intelligentsia, but their films were all variations on personal myths and disconnected from anything even a liberal Catalan audience might identify with."[12] Had they at least been spoken in Catalan, which was by the late 1960s a legal option, these films might have been more easily identifiable as a repudiation of Madrid. But, in fact, the Barcelona School seemed disengaged from its potential audiences by virtue of its strong commitment to a reconceptualization of the visual aesthetics of cinema.

Of the various filmmakers associated with the Barcelona School,[13] the only one to achieve wide attention after the dissolution of the group in 1968 was Vicente Aranda. Of Aranda's work in the sixties, perhaps the most significant film was his *Fata morgana* (1966: *Mirage*), actually made prior to the formation of the Barcelona School, but often cited as the perfect embodiment of the group's aesthetic. Aranda recalls that when writing *Mirage*, he and fellow filmmaker, Gonzalo Suárez, sacrificed "conventional coherence" for the cinematic and phenomenological possibilities of each action. This was, he claims, a move to distract the censors' attention from the covert political implications of the film by use of the stock genres of detective and science fiction films.[14]

Mirage recounts the story of Gim (Teresa Gimpera), a highly successful and famous fashion model, who receives a mysterious message informing her that she will be assassinated. The warning arrives on the very day that the city is being abandoned by its population, impelled by some inexplicable fear. Gim chooses to remain but is agitated by continual anxiety caused by the death threat. She comes into contact with three mysterious figures: a professor, who has made the prophecy of Gim's assassination in a lecture on the nature of victims; J. J., a secret agent charged with finding Gim and saving her; and Miriam, the assassin who is in search of her victims. J. J. never finds Gim, but Miriam does assassinate J. J. The model finally manages to escape from the city accompanied by a group of youths. As this brief plot suggests, in *Mirage* Aranda seeks to define an aesthetic texture to his film devoid of the topicality of provincial, Francoized Spain. By its very narrative and cultural insufficiency, the plot of *Mirage* becomes an aesthetic enigma, problematizing for its audience the question of its own identity. The flaunting of a structured absence (What city is this? What is the fear that grips the populace?) initiates a hermeneutic chain, the decipherment of which should motivate the spectator to read the entire film as the allegory of suppressed Catalan identity.

Such questions lead us back into the social and historical geography of Francoist Spain and are textualized within the narrative space, as personal and collective identity are continually put under a mark of interrogation. Combining a blockage of concrete national, geographical, or even historical specificity with suggestive dialogue, the film dramatizes the persecution and annihilation of the urbane, cultured identity seen but never verbally identified as Catalan. That historical-political intertext is suggested in the professor's lecture on the theory of the victim in which he tells his audience that "only a desired fatality can truncate an existence and that fatality is the daughter of fear, fear the authentic whip, the true epidemic, so contagious that all of the city, all of the country change into its victim."[15]

The twin questions of identity and identification are at the source of the film's various enigmas. J. J.'s efforts to find Gim and help her, Miriam's parallel effort to find Gim and kill her, even the professor's claim that some individuals were born to be victims are all part of a register of the struggle to identify and thereby "fix" the identity of the other. *Mirage* begins with Gim's disavowal of the group by her insistence on remaining in the city when everyone else leaves; it ends as she departs in the company of the youths. Discursively, the film follows a similar shifting trajectory, for it begins with a refusal to root itself in a specific cultural milieu, but then gradually situates its axis of meaning within the narrow specificity of a political allegory of the cultural subjugation of Catalonia by the forces of Francoism.

Mirage is an undeniably complex work, and, given its flaunting of popular detective and science fiction genres, it stands as a rare example of cryptic narrative in the constrained cinematic production of Spain in the 1960s. Yet, finally, it is not as unfathomable as Spanish critics have made it out to be. Like Saura's *La caza* (1965: *The Hunt*), it employs a political intertext to expose suppressed historical memories. But whereas Saura elected to posit the explicit historical referent of the Civil War, Aranda and Suarez follow the implicit model of Kafka's *The Trial*, actively involving their audience in the questioning of suppressed cultural identity by staging the past as a suppressed *mise-en-scène* in which the spectator's active interrogation of the symbolic blockage of that past leads to a form of historical reflexivity.

RECUPERATIONS

The decade following Franco's death in November, 1975, saw the dismantlement of the repressive apparatus of state censorship and the establishment in Barcelona of a regional government administration that, in accordance with the new federal constitution of 1978, sought to normalize the existence of Catalan culture by, among other measures, developing film as a form of expression of regional cultural identity. The volume of production of Catalan cinema in this period is prodigious and includes, among other notable achievements, the production, beginning in 1977, of *Noticiari de Barcelona*, the first Catalan-spoken movie newsreels in nearly four decades. Yet in many ways this new freedom of expression and the government incentives to develop previously interdicted Catalan themes only seemed to dilute the force and even the appeal of the enterprise, for once the obstacles to expression were removed, very few filmmakers took seriously the interrogation of the concept of Catalanism.

The rise and fall of the flamboyant ideal of Catalan national cinema can be traced through the fortunes of two films by Antoni Ribas, each of which celebrates the Catalan nationalistic spirit and the solidarity of Catalans in freeing themselves from the political and cultural yoke of Castilian hegemony. The much heralded *La ciutat cremada* (1976: *The Burnt City*) follows the fortunes of a liberal Barcelona family from the disastrous defeat of Spain by the United States in 1898, through the 1909 Barcelona uprising called "The Tragic Week," in which anarchists, anti-clerics and communists attempted to topple the monarchy of Alfonso XII. Ribas's fresco of workers, the middle-class, and the ruling oligarchy of Catalonia is a stunning epic film of a scale rarely seen in Spanish cinema. Though the film's message is that the various social groups who joined in the 1909 uprising lacked a firm sense of political consciousness, the three-hour work itself becomes the occasion in which the contemporary audience is invited to identify with the historical antecedents of a modern Catalan spirit of autonomy.

Eight years later, the apparent death knell of that nationalist fervor is sounded in *Victoria!*, Ribas's three-part, eight-hour panorama of three critical days in Barcelona's history in 1917 when workers and military officers staged another failed uprising against the government. The ambitious scale of *Victoria!*, which boasts more than five-hundred speaking parts but little narrative or historical coherence, suggested to many that the idea of a Catalan cinema had simply run its course. In fact, the problem of this and other well-publicized Catalanist films lay not so much in the general impossibility of a legitimate cinema of historical and political consciousness, but rather appeared to be the very narrowness of conception of film projects which seemed only to reinforce the impression of an intensively parochial regionalism that was to prove too esoteric even for Catalan audiences. *The Burnt City* was generally well-received outside of Catalonia, in part, because it appealed to the sense of historical vindication which many Spaniards felt and could identify with. *Victoria!*, on the other hand, seemed in scale and focus to be beyond the grasp or interest of any but the most die-hard Catalan nationalists.

The epic scale of Ribas's films tend to overshadow the more modest notion of Catalan cinema which continues to emerge during these years.[16] Of the more than one-hundred productions that the Catalan regional government, the *Generalitat*, has claimed as Catalan films since 1979, two sub-genres emerge which rigorously stabilize a notion of Catalan identity in light of the thinking of the films of the Sixties. The first is an apparent continuation of the theme of historical recuperation, but unlike Ribas's films, these works sustain their focus on the thematics of the Civil War as the single historical epoch which transcends parochial local themes. Perhaps playing on the general view of Barcelona throughout Spain as a place of liberal and liberated culture, the second sub-genre narrativizes that liberation thematics, particularly in terms of sexual liberation, a theme that connects with the Civil War ethos of Barcelona. A closer examination of representative examples of these genres suggests that they are more than a random grouping of films, but actually cohere with the historical poetics of Catalan cultural identity established in earlier films.

Films by Catalan directors dealing with the theme of the Civil War abound in the years after Franco's death. Camino's *Las largas vacaciones del '36* (1975: *The Long Vacation of '36*), Francesco Bertriu's *La Plaça del Diamant* (1982: *Diamond Square*) and *Requiem por un campesino español* (1983: *Requiem for a Spanish Farmer*), Gonzalo Heralde's *Raza, el espíritu de Franco* (1977: *Raza: The Spirit of Franco*), Forn's *Companys: Proceso a Cataluña* (1979: *Companys: Catalonia On Trial*), and José Luis Madrid's *Memorias del General Escobar* (1984: *The Memoirs of General Escobar*) are only some of the dozen or so films which attempt historical reconstructions of events of the Civil War with a specific anchoring in the Catalan experience. In truth, however, a large number of these seem inspired by a notion of historical vindication for the Francoist excesses rather than by an effort to sustain the vision of contemporary Catalan identity forged in the noble and generous vision of the past.

By far, the most significant of these works of meaningful recuperation and, to many critics, the most significant Spanish film dealing with the Civil War is Jaime Camino's third treatment of the Civil War theme, *La vieja memoria* (1977: *The Old Memory*). *The Old Memory* is a documentary film consisting of a series of interviews with eighteen people who played prominent roles on either side of the fighting, people such as Enrique Lister, the communist commander of the Republican "People's" Army in Barcelona, Dolores Ibarruri, better known as *La Pasionaria*, and the anarchist, José María Gil Robles, the leader of the right-wing deputies in the pre-civil War Republican parliament. While asking each informant to recall specific events during the war, Camino employs a technique of testimonial engagement, including in each interview shots of the other interviewees reacting to the speaker's descriptions, often shaking their heads in disagreement or derision at a given interpretation. The cross-cutting technique produces a continuous chain of *faux raccords* as it appears that these individuals are "sitting around the table" in conversation when, in fact, they are merely being filmed viewing and reacting to other filmed interviews. Interviews are, in turn, interspersed with documentary footage of the events described by the witness-participants.

The ostensible objective of the film is to understand the complex weight of history and the distortions and suppressions of memory on Spaniards. Memory is not history, as Camino insisted to interviewers, but a subjective recall. The stunning visual richness of the documentary-cross-cut interviews vividly drives home that point. Román Gubern contends that the device of *faux raccords* highlights the theme of distorted and manipulated history of the Civil War by members of both sides, but, in the process, the technique also poses a critique of the assumed neutrality of the archive, for the pairing of archival and interview images works continuously to place in question the nature and the source of the events which the participants appear to remember with such vividness.[17]

Out of this questioning of the archive, Camino is able to deftly pose another, less conspicuous project. While carefully balancing the political leanings of his interviewees between Republican loyalists and Nationalists, the key periods of the war he chooses to focus on in the interviews give decided prominence to Catalonia in

Figure 2.   The Old Memory, *documentary footage of war-torn Barcelona.*

general and Barcelona in particular. The failure of the July, 1936 miliary coup in Barcelona is stressed, for instance, and its importance is underscored by the assertion that it gave inspiration for the later Defense of Madrid against German air attack. Barcelona is characterized as the site of the people's war (Figure 2), as opposed to the government's war in the central plateau. Instead of ending with the often shown images of the fascist victory, Camino stresses the theme of defeat, destruction, and exile: Spaniards crossing the frontier into France as the sound track plays the strains of the "Internationale." Those final images evoke the subsequent "other" identity of Catalonia: marginalization and the suppression of identity during the bitter post-war years.

A reflection on the frailty of historical memory which is being lost by Spaniards, *The Old Memory* is also a subtle reinsertion/recuperation of the idea of Barcelona as the popular cultural embodiment of the very ideals which metonymically have been identified with the whole of Republican Spain. Importantly, and quite unlike the vast majority of films of historical recuperation, it actively engages its audience in the dialectical process of both remembering and challenging the sources of their recollections. Camino is thus able to make the viewing process the occasion for the spectator to embrace the possibility of an historical revision of contemporary Catalan identity through a cathartic engagement with the past.

A similar, though less intricate process occurs within a more conventional narrative framework in Vicente Aranda's *La muchacha de las bragas de oro* (1979: *The Girl in*

Figure 3. The Old Memory *engages its audience in the dialectical process of both remembering and challenging the sources of their recollection.*

the Golden Panties), in which a prudish ex-falangist, Luis Forest, writes his memoirs with the aid of his niece, Mariana, and constructs a totally distorted and self-serving image of his personal life as well as the fascist cause which led him to prominence as a writer during the post-war period. Inspired by the interior mono-logues of the Juan Marsé novel upon which it is based, Aranda's film intercuts excerpts from Forest's past which serve as corrections to his often distorted per-sonal version of his memories. As in *The Old Memory*, what is distinctive here is the way in which the larger Spanish scenario of recuperation and correction of the memory of the past is enacted in a seemingly irrelevant *mise-en-scène*. Forest lives at Sitges on the Costa Brava, not far from Barcelona, and the sensual environment combined with his sexually liberated niece's presence become the catalysts for his gradual recognition of the self-deceptions which have shaped his memoirs as well as his life.

Less emphatically than in Camino's film, *La muchacha de las bragas de oro* nonethe-less reiterates the idea of Catalonia, particularly Barcelona, as the signifier of an integrated, balanced notion of Spanish identity that was the essence of pre-Franco Spain and has reasserted itself in the post-Franco period. The ironic twist of the film's ending, Forest's discovery that Mariana, with whom he has slept, is not his niece at all, but really his daughter, symbolically states the inextricable bond between the two ideas of identity in Spain: the prudish, hypocritical, Francoist ideal of chaste Spain, and the liberated, youthful, honest Catalan way of being that is so closely identified with Mariana and that emblemizes not only the life-style but the spirit of Barcelona.

Consistent with that theme, which is clearly an outgrowth of the Civil War ideal of Barcelona as the tolerant, generous city of the Republic, we find an increasing number of films that depict the hedonist, libertine, but finally liberating ambience of Barcelona. Though seemingly unconnected with the earlier noted political and historical treatments of the city, these films share a common feature in their depiction of Barcelona as the refuge for individuals who have been marginalized within intolerant, orthodox, Francoist Spain. While the theme of "Black Barcelona," the ideal licentious setting for Spanish *film noir*, has been around for a number of decades, the treatment of the city as a haven for socially marginal characters is a pointedly less exploitative thematic. We can see this, for instance, in Aranda's 1976 film, *Cambio de sexo* (*A Change of Sex*), which chronicles in almost documentary fashion the torment of a young man who undergoes a sex change operation. The backdrop to the film's action is once again the tolerant Barcelona which accepts difference without the oppressive persecution that historically is identified with the rest of Spain.[18]

Of the various films which have developed this theme in the decade since Franco's death, perhaps none has so potently expressed the message of that sexual/political liberation as Ventura Pons's *Ocaña; retrato intermitente* (1978: *Ocaña: A Partial Portrait*). This is a unique film, even within the rich range of Spanish documentary. Pons interviews the Andalusian transvestite painter, José Pérez Ocaña, about his life, about his art, and about Spain. Born in 1947, Ocaña's life is a tale of marginality within the straitjacket of Catholic social mores. Tormented in Andalusia for his homosexuality, the gifted artist found no respite in either Seville or Madrid. Finally fleeing to Barcelona, he discovered freedom and a comradeship that helped him to flourish as an artist.

The film is structured as a series of interviews between Pons and Ocaña in which the artist details his childhood in Andalusia, his interest in painting, and his search for a community in which he will not be an outsider. These interview sequences are punctuated by scenes in which Ocaña is viewed parading in drag along the Ramblas, Barcelona's downtown boulevard, or in nearby plazas. Gradually, it becomes evident that the real protagonist of the film is Barcelona, the haven for Spaniards marginalized by the conformist spirit that has dominated so much of the rest of Spain.

One Catalan film critic called *Ocaña* "the first authentic portrait of post-Franco Spain,"[19] and, although its focus is not in any conventional sense political, the specter of Francoist politics remains the continual intertext of the film. There is, for instance, an extended sequence of newsreel footage showing Ocaña participating in a political rally on behalf of gay liberation. Indeed, Ocaña's spiritual itinerary from Andalusia through Castile, and finally to Catalonia, coupled with this portrait of Barcelona as the city of an enlightened sexual liberation seems a logical extension of those earlier visions of Barcelona as the Mecca of the politically and socially repressed other Spain.

Ocaña and *Dragón Rapide* seem from every point of view as unrelated as any two films could be. Yet, unquestionably, both works are rooted in a common conceptual project centered on the historical intertext of a liberating Catalan cultural identity that transcends the narrow regionalism of which Catalanism is often accused. By means of their persistent address to their audience through an often intricate system of historical allusion, Catalan filmmakers have insistently constructed a concept of their cultural heritage that opposes the narrowness of the old Francoist mythology and displaces it with a notion of Catalonia as the spiritual complement to that other Spain. The conception of Catalan identity inscribed in this body of filmic texts is, as we have seen, a persistent impulse that seeks not only to demarginalize the Catalan cultural community within Spain, but perhaps more importantly, to challenge the traditional Castilian monolithic view of a single and unitary definition of Spanish culture itself. As such films insistently demonstrate, Catalan cinema does not attempt to draw barriers, but instead, to address all Spaniards in ways that both history and geography have conspired through the years to frustrate.

NOTES

1. The research for this essay was conducted in Spain during the 1986–87 academic year under the auspices of a grant from the U.S.-Spanish Joint Committee for Cultural and Education Exchange.

2. Raymond Carr and Juan Pablo Fusi, *Spain: Dictatorship to Democracy*, Second Edition (London: Allen and Unwin, 1981), p. 11.

3. In making the case for the consideration of Catalanist film as approximating the category of a national cinema, I am indebted to Philip Rosen's reading of the methodological implications of the concept of national cinema as it is used in the classical works on the subject by Siegfried Kracauer and Noel Burch. Rosen identifies three areas of conceptualization as central to the rigorous formulation of a national cinema:

   (1) not just a conceptualization of textuality, but one which describes how a large number of superficially differentiated texts can be associated in a regularized, relatively limited intertextuality in order to form a coherency, a "national cinema"; (2) a conceptualization of a nation as a kind of

minimally coherent entity which it makes sense to analyze in relation with (1); (3) some conception of what is traditionally called "history" or "historiography."

See Philip Rosen, "History, Textuality, Nation: Kracauer, Burch, and Some Problems in the study of National Cinemas," *Iris* 2, no. 2 (1984):70–71.

4. Benjamín Otra, Francesc Mercadè, Francesc Hernández, *La ideología nacional catalana* (Barcelona: Editorial Anagrama, 1981), pp. 19–20.

5. Pierre Vilar, *Spain: A Brief History* (Oxford: Pergamon Press, 1967), p. 93.

6. Ibid.

7. Juan Pablo Fusi, *Franco: autoritarismo y poder personal* (Madrid: Ediciones El País, 1985), p. 31.

8. There is a curious underplaying of the Catalan language as a critical mark of cultural identity in films of this period. While language is used at times to evoke some feature of Catalan culture, it is never seen as *the* exclusive mark of identity. In a country in which, for nearly fifty years, all foreign-language films were regularly dubbed into Castilian, and where, even today, audiences still prefer Castilian-dubbed to subtitled films, language has ceased to be a stabile signifier of cultural identity.

9. Román Gubern, *1936–1939: La guerra de España en la pantalla* (Madrid: Ministerio de Cultura, 1986), pp. 163–164.

10. Ibid.

11. The frequent identification of Catalan cinema with European rather than Spanish artistic movements should not be read as a mark of a colonized film culture, but instead as a sign of a powerful strategy of resistance against Castilian culture.

12. Domenèc Font, *Del Azul al verde: el cine español durante el franquismo* (Barcelona: Editorial Avance, 1976), p. 270.

13. Critics often dispute exactly who were the actual members of the group. Of those most frequently cited, Jacinto Esteva, Gonzalo Suárez, and Carlos Durán were, according to Juan Antonio Martínez-Bretón, the "nucleus" of the group. During the two-year life of the School (1967–68), various others became closely identified with that core. These included: Vicente Aranda, José María Nunes, Jorge Grau, Pedro Portabello, and Joaquín Jorda. See Juan Antonio Martínez-Bretón, *La denominada Escuela de Barcelona* (Madrid: Universidad Complutense, Facultad de Ciencias de Información, 1984), pp. 609–610.

14. John Hopewell, *Out of the Past: Spanish Cinema After Franco* (London: BFI Books, 1986), p. 69.

15. Hopewell, p. 70.

16. Ribas's historical treatment of Catalan themes is matched by the immensely successful contemporary visions of Catalan life-styles in the films of Francesc Bellmunt. Bellmunt became recognized as a popular voice of Catalan youth with his two folk-rock documentaries, *La Nova Cançó* (*The New Song*) and *Canet Rock*, both made in 1976. He later turned to an equally popular series of "Catalan comedies," mostly set in Barcelona and detailing the lives and mores of youthful protagonists. These include *La orgía* (1978: *The Orgy*), *Salut i Força al Canut* (1979: *Long Live The Happy Couple*), and *La radio folla* (1985: *Radio Screws!*). What most sets these films apart as Catalan, however, are external elements: the use of the Catalan language and their Barcelona setting. When exhibited outside of Catalonia in their Castilian-language version, these films are barely recognizable as products of a Catalan national cinema.

17. Gubern, op. cit., p. 179.

18. The identification of Barcelona with deviant sexuality reaches its most explicit expression in José Luis Bigas Luna's films of the late Seventies, particularly *Bilbao* (1977) and *Caniche* (1978: *It's a Dog's Life*). Spanish critics have lately viewed these films as the expression of the "de-Francoization" of Spanish cinema. Though this may indeed be the case, there is little in these films that explicitly connects them to the issues of historicized cultural politics.

19. Terenci Moix, "De la Diosa Ocaña a Sebastián, el Mártir," *El País Semanal*, June 25, 1978, p. 13.

Making a Nation in Sembene's *Ceddo*

Philip Rosen

"It would be a dangerous step backwards, to revert to our traditions . . ."

"That's not what I'm saying, *Joom Galle*," she interrupted. "We must achieve a synthesis . . . Yes, a synthesis . . . A new type of society.

There followed a brief silence.

Kad was observing them. This elderly couple amazed him. He was full of admiration for them.

"You've a most interesting theme there, Kad. You must work it out well," said the old man, his masculine vanity slightly wounded by his wife's forceful points."

from Sembene Ousmane, *The Last of the Empire*

For the Third World filmmaker, it is not a question of coming to overwhelm the people, because technical prowess is very easy, and after all, cinema, when you know it, is a very simple thing. It is a question of allowing the people to summon up their own history, to identify themselves with it. People must listen to what is in the film, and they must talk about it.

Ousmane Sembene[1]

Nations are made, not born. Or rather, to exist they must be made and remade, figured and refigured, constantly defining and perpetuating themselves. Classic distinctions in political and social theory differentiate nation and state. Nations are cultural, discursive fields. They are imaginary, ideal collective unities which, especially since the nineteenth-century era of nationalism, aspire to define the state. The state is an institutional site constructed as overt repository and manager of legitimated power. Nation is on the side of culture, ideological formations, civil society; state is on the side of political institutions, repressive apparatuses, political society.

Conceiving of cinema in relation to the nation is familiar enough. In the West, the notion of a national cinema has a range of uses, from delineating institutionalized sub-fields for scholars and teachers, to providing an advertising rationale for such organizations as the American Film Institute. In third world countries where cinema retains a mass appeal, however, the question of national cinemas partakes of the ambiguities of postcolonial national identities and cultural practices. Intellectuals and artists do not have the luxury of opting out of this issue, which so obviously exceeds merely methodological debates. Especially strong examples are provided by sub-Saharan Africa, where postcolonial states were often defined as a result of colonial histories and political configurations, with less relation to cultural

PHILIP ROSEN *is Associate Professor of Modern Culture and Media Studies at Brown University.*

and linguistic groupings and indigenous histories than other colonized areas such as southeast Asia.

Historiography can thus become a primary concern, for the very concept of a nation presupposes a past, and both nation and state are concepts emphasized in the effective heritage of modern historical representation as it developed in the nineteenth century West. Rooted in very different cultural contexts as well as ideological and political purposes, crucial discussions and figurations of African culture and identity are intricately tied up with reconsidering the hegemonic categories of Western historiography. The broad implication is that even a consideration of Western historiography (including, more modestly, film history) would do well to take into account perspectives from regions such as sub-Saharan Africa. The problem of constructing postcolonial cinemas and making films specific to African experiences and needs provides one of the best nodal points for exploring resulting issues. What follows approaches these issues through *Ceddo* (1976), a film that deliberately sets out to reconfigure a key moment in West African history, realized by a leading narrative artist from that region, Ousmane Sembene.

Sembene's Senegal has experienced many of the ambivalences and difficulties involved in the making of postcolonial nations and states. For example, at least six indigenous languages are used within state borders. Yet the area gained independence as Senegal, formally speaking a centralized nation-state on the colonizer's model. Sembene's film *Xala* (1974) finds it ironically appropriate that the language of official business remains French. Economics as well as the structure of international power relations have made this kind of dialectic of colonialism and liberation a central fact in the existence of such states. Hence the gravity of issues of identity and self-definition for those working in culture and ideology, as inevitable sites of contradiction, ambiguity, and struggle. Sembene's career as a self-educated, distinguished West African novelist who turned to cinema as a medium that addresses a mass African audience has consistently centered on issues deriving from the heritage of colonialism and liberation, on African identity, and consequently on history. Since 1968 all his films have employed Senegalese dialects and languages, usually Wolof (the most widely used). In *Ceddo* (1976) the issue of the nation and its representation is located as a problem of history and *its* representation. Only in the constructions of its histories will a nation be defined. All of this also applies to the question of making a national cinema. For, after all, one of the founding facts of African film history is that cinema is a machine which, like the French language, was imported from the West.

1

Two aspects of *Ceddo* can serve as useful starting points. First, the clarity of the film's visual style is inseparable from the directness of its editing. This is to assert that the shot-to-shot succession of camera positions and mises-en-scène generally provide immediate access to the most pertinent narrative events, but of course this is not an exhaustive description of their functioning. For example, it would be possible to analyze a rather consistent, though not exclusive, horizontal organization of movement, both within the frame and of the frame (pans). Along with the exterior location shooting and choices of shot scales and camera positions, this helps emphasize both the flatness of the ground and the spaciousness of mise-en-scene. All of these contribute to the strong sense of rural, elemental background environment that is a constant element of the film.

Similarly, it would not be correct simply to say *Ceddo* diminishes the effects of cutting in its concern for narrative clarity. Aside from certain strategically surprising jumps in time and space discussed below, the film's visual organization of conversational scenes (but not only these) most often depends on a spatially analytical impulse, in which cuts into scenic space provide immediate visual delineation of speakers and interlocutors.[2] This clear access to the central narrative agents of a scene can be alternated with cutaways to peripheral spaces, as in shots of listeners not participating in central conversations, that can also serve as coverage for changes in camera position with respect to the main action.

Sometimes it seems possible to describe this with reference to mainstream practices. Indeed, principles of scene construction recognizable as virtually classical are established in the very first dialogue sequence, between Princess Dior and her Ceddo kidnapper. Their brief, angry exchange is presented in a shot/reverse shot construction, setting up an axis of action and adhering to the 180-degree rule. In a classical kind of nicety, all shots keep Dior's head in frame, but not her kidnapper's, to underline her position as the ultimately privileged political object and narrative agent (Figs. 1–2). Although this description will shortly be modified, so far it seems that the dialectic of colonialism and liberation holds for Sembene's film, for at least in this scene cinema is being used in Western ways by this African filmmaker.

A second starting point for analyzing *Ceddo* is its emphasis on collectivities. As a Senegalese filmmaker dealing with Senegalese history and nationhood in a film whose general issues are familiar in many African states, Sembene is concerned in the first instance to address spectators as members of collectives (whether African or specific Senegalese nationalities.) But relatedly, as a historical film *Ceddo* embodies an attitude toward history and its representation. For Sembene, history is to be comprehended as the interplay of collective groups and forces. The film, set in an unidentified Wolof Kingdom at some indefinite time perhaps in the eighteenth or early nineteenth century, abstracts itself from absolute chronological precision in order to function as a microcosm of the pre-twentieth century political and cultural forces and contradictions which were the crucible of the modern Senegalese nation. Four of the most important are:

Black African power vs. foreign power and influence. The decision-making power of the King and his aristocracy are at stake in the game being played by the European slave trader, the European Catholic priest, and the Arab imam. Most of the common people are Ceddo. They resist the imported influences in a traditional way, which is to kidnap a hostage—Princess Dior—against their demands to the King to restore their rights to be heard and their traditional freedom of choice.[3] The imam's goal is achieved late in the film, when he takes the position of King and puts his own disciples in positions of aristocratic power.

Religious divisions within the foreigners and within the Wolof. At the beginning of the film, the Muslim import has already defeated the Christian import among the

Figure 1

Figure 2.

Wolof aristocracy led by the family of the King; however, the bulk of the population is Ceddo, and the most explicit narrative issue is whether or not the entire nation will accede to Islam. In the precolonial period, the word *ceddo* designated crown slaves of special distinction whose support might be necessary to the power of the King, but it has since taken on a range of meanings. Sembene himself emphasizes that the term, which is used in several Senegalese languages, signifies those who cling to the old ways and resist the onslaught of the foreign, especially Islam. In the film, the Ceddo are the common people, who remain true to the traditional fetish religion against the increasingly successful converting zeal of the Muslims. The recession of the traditional religion upsets the self-determining balance of indigenous African political structures, leading to a loss of institutional continuity. This is exemplified by the shift from traditional, ritualistically circumscribed uses of violence to settle disputes by individual combat to the more pragmatic, anything-goes uses of violence ordered by the imam and justified by militant Islam. Sembene's representation of Islam as a historically foreign force and the imam as a short, distinctively lighter-skinned Arab who uses tactics reminiscent of the trickster figure of African narrative should be read in terms of Senegal's being the most overwhelmingly Muslim state in Black Africa. It may have contributed to the film's being banned there.[4]

Political divisions within the Wolof. The Ceddo, having lost their old political rights and under pressure to convert, formally announce their opposition to the court and the consequent hostage-taking by planting the traditional challenge stick (the *samp*), which gives them the opportunity to articulate their grievances. Later, treasonous nobles among the Islamic Wolof desert the king. Furthermore, the anti-Islamic forces, divided by caste distinctions, cannot unite: Princess Dior holds the Ceddo in contempt as slaves until the final scenes; the fearsome warrior Saxewar is anti-Muslim but never even imagines allying with the lower-caste Ceddo; and after recanting Islam to maintain his own right of succession to the throne, Prince Madior does not seek to join the Ceddo but instead becomes a commenting character marginal to the determining actions. Such divisions are conditions for the shift away from traditional social and cultural forms.

Matrilineal succession vs. patrilineal succession. Not just the nature of power, but how it is transferred is a site where religious and political issues conjoin. This conjoining implicitly demonstrates that, as Sembene has put it, African religion is not mere animism but "a creed which has its foundations, its laws, and its theory." Patrilineal succession is foreign, imported to the court through Islam and inextricable from its own vision of power. When the King accepts it, he undermines the basis of his authority, which is Senegalese in origin and matrilineal in its rationale. In this sense, this change stands for the social, political, and cultural subordination of women in the colonization of Africa. But, as we will see, the film's interrogation of the symbolic and political significance of women exceeds this narrow equation. The narrative importance of the conflict between these two modes is part of a network of other elements having to do with women, ranging from the carved female figure at the head of the *samp* to the fact that the story concludes when Princess Dior shoots the imam in the genitals. Sembene has suggested that, considering the position of women in Islam, for a female to kill the imam is "more than sacrilege." He also once

said that the only reason the film was banned in Senegal was the symbolic significance of the princess.[5]

The clear narrative representation of such a dynamic historical complex (not
exhausted by these four levels) is itself an achievement worthy of notice. However,
let us proceed here by considering a possible contradiction in Sembene's use of
analytic editing in a film that represents history as an interplay of collective groups
and forces. This issue can be understood within the history of narrative film style,
so a brief digression is required.

Western cinema has its own historiographic practices, which most often depend
on focalizing narrative and hence historical knowledge through the experiences
and knowledge of privileged individualized characters. This is the case even when
a film emphasizes supra-individual determinations, and not only in routine mainstream productions. For example, *The End of St. Petersburg* (Pudovkin, 1927) conceives of history from a class perspective, but its famous finale emotively solicits
empathy with the new comprehension of a single working class woman walking
through the Winter Palace and grounds that now belong to the people. At another
extreme, the narrative of *The Leopard* (Visconti, 1962) proceeds with an emphasis on
Prince Salina's exceptional perceptions and consciousness, so that a scene in which
he expresses his reflections on why Sicily, by its very nature, necessarily resists
modernization is privileged as historical explanation. Throughout film history,
there is a wide range of such strategies for aligning narrative authority with
individual characters. In a historical film, whether routed through emotive empathy or analytic discourse or varying combinations of the two, the drama of attaining
historiographic comprehension is then commonly anchored for the spectator in such
individualized authority. This authority, this identification (if that is the best term),
becomes associated in different ways with a plane of secure knowledge of history—
its outcomes, its causes, historical explanation.

This ties even such distinctive historical films to the mainstream development of
analytic editing. Textually, the film-historical innovation and standardization of
analytic editing in the transition from preclassical to classical cinema instituted a
double move inwards: enlarged shot scale signified movement into a scene, naturalized as physical closeness to objects of the mise-en-scene for such purposes as
better viewpoint and hence more reliable or interesting information. But also, such
spatial closeness can undergo a second transformation, or rather it has a central
special case: "closeness" to characters is translated into access to psychological and
moral interiority of individualized characters. The counter-example of Eisenstein
indicates that analytic editing need not necessarily be tied to a concern with interior
character depth or even individualized character goals. But the narrative priorities
of mainstream cinema have massively instituted the link between scene analysis
and individual interiority; the facial closeup becomes the signifier of motivation
and/or psychology, and speech becomes allied with the face as a locus from which
interior truth can come. One of the common techniques of this tendency most
discussed among Western scholars is the shot/reverse shot dialogue sequence. But
this binary spatial alternation, so useful in pinning editorial analysis of a scene to
character face and voice, is not determining in itself; rather, it is exemplary as one
standardized pattern within a larger project that makes decoding of an interiorized

character goal, soul, psychology and/or knowledge the task of reading the scene. The impact of this general impulse is indicated by the fact that even the example from *The End of St. Petersburg* depends on eyeline matching, and the one from *The Leopard* depends on a more complex combination of narrative presence, eyeline matching, and authoritative speech throughout the film.[6]

Ceddo is particularly interesting in this regard. Sembene presents its complex mix of collective historical forces using analytical editing, yet resists the institutionalized models of narrative authority and the ideologies of individualism with which this practice is historically allied. We can undoubtedly assume the filmmaker's acquaintance with such generally instituted practices. But beyond biography (the imported films he is likely to have seen in Senegal, the facts that when a young man he was a worker in France and that he studied filmmaking in the Soviet Union), as a leading and self-consciously African filmmaker, Sembene confronts such historically instituted stylistic options from a novel and distinctive position. By the time he took up filmmaking, several of his novels had already situated Sembene as an *auteur*, but of a particular type: the anti-colonialist African intellectual, familiar with certain Western techniques of knowledge and/or culture, who experienced the transition to independence. Thus, the place of his work within a comparative history of cinema could only be established on the basis of his African context, within which he is also inventing something distinctive, but from his understanding of African traditions, needs, and modes of apprehension.

More specifically, we can begin examining certain unobtrusive complexities in the editing of *Ceddo* by considering them in relation to the stylized speech of individual characters, who appear as functions of historical groups and supra-individual forces. As noted above, a standard shot/reverse shot construction is employed in the first dialogue sequence of the film, thus seeming to invite the viewer to a film employing standard spatial articulations. Yet, it is not quite correct to call this a *dia*logue, for there is a third present, whose name is Fara (see Fig. 1). Though for long periods Fara does not speak, the princess and the kidnapper usually address one another through Fara as intermediary, with locutions such as "Fara, tell her that. . . ." This form of address is clearly courtly and ceremonial. Mbye Baboucar Cham has carefully explained it as adhering to the Wolof communicative concept of *jottali*, or formally passing on an utterance.[7] The pervasiveness of *jottali* in *Ceddo* is one of the major instances of several traditional Senegalese social and cultural practices which the film employs or to which it makes reference. But of special interest in this early dialogue is that its utilization runs counter to the potential intimacy of the situation and the power of conventional shot/reverse shot editing to reinforce the impression of a binary relation between two interiorized individuals, for it opposes the dual space of the shot/reverse shot to the presence of a third.

Jottali is a central aspect of the very lengthy scene which follows, a meeting of the Wolof nation called by the King to investigate and decide on responses to the kidnapping of the princess. In it, the complex of forces and contradictions outlined above are laid out by spokespersons for the various groups and viewpoints, and its construction is worthy of extended analysis. Narratively, the scene proceeds as a series of debates, seemingly taking shape as a series of binary confrontations: the Ceddo elder Diogomay against the King, Prince Biram against Diogomay, Diogomay against the imam, the warrior Saxewar against Prince Madior, Madior against Biram, and so forth. This binarism of character divisions reveals a fragmentation of national interests and forces, but by the end of the scene there has emerged a unifying logic which does not, however, drive the divided representative characters to unify: the growing power of Islam and the consequently far-reaching changes occurring in indigenous culture and politics. At the level of narration, there are also factors that can be said to counter the binarism in the presentation of these conflicts. The most striking of these is, again, a third participating in the successive debates that make up the public discussion, a court noble Jaraaf. In fact, throughout the scene, he is the most constant visual and verbal presence. Jaraaf is a more active intermediary than Fara, introducing speakers, often commenting on their words and even taking sides—all with rhetorical flourish and verbal imagery.

Jaraaf's verbal flamboyance and the fact that Fara has a *xalam* (a stringed musical instrument) makes the cultural reference for this third evident: the noted West African figure of the *griot*. The griot can be public storyteller, rhetorician, musician, hired praise-singer, poet. Despite an often lower-caste aura, griots traditionally function at all social levels, including noble families, and today can even work for politicians and their parties. The griot is possessor of verbal and narrative expertise, a repository of the power of the word and of social memory. Sembene has often compared himself to the griot, and indicated his desire to use the Western machine, cinema, in this traditional sociocultural function.[8]

A number of commentators emphasize that the strong presence of the griot in *Ceddo* is an overt reference to the centrality of African oral tradition, which has been one of the most important sources of the specificity of postcolonial African film in general. Oral culture is often considered to be a most significant determinant of many aspects of Sembene's filmmaking, from character typology to narrative structure and the pictorial organization of space and especially time. Indeed, in *Ceddo* speech is generally ceremonial and/or declamatory, and proverbs are skillfully used to punctuate already conventionalized conversations. In addition, acting and gesture are stylized and some objects are overtly symbolic, all of which underlines the fact of the diegetically immediate performance of word and sign. These and other procedures are evidence of the film's self-conscious connection with oral tradition. The imam's first official act after the victory of Islam is linguistic: in an elaborate public ceremony, he inaugurates the Ceddo into what he had previously called "the beautiful language of the Koran" by renaming each one individually after figures in the Islamic Holy Books. When Islam is victorious, then, one aspect of its triumph is the advent of the authority of the book—the imam always carries and claims authority from the Koran—over performed speech.[9]

I would add that the presence of the griot can also be read as overdetermining a historiographic project. If the griot, as representative of African cultural tradition, is an intermediary witness to as well as conveyor of dialogue, then the appearance of the griot marks the interest of the collective in all individual speech and the definition of the individual through the collective. With respect to establishing agencies of narrative authority, the apparently standard shot/reverse shot sequence of the first dialogue scene does not isolate individuals as such because the presence of the third—*a recognizable socio-cultural function*—is manifest. The practice of *jottali* announces the emphasis of the film as a whole. Even in scenes without griots, all conversations are to and for a group, sometimes implicitly and usually explicitly. In short, even during the most binary spatial articulations, there is no discussion between a pure *two* in the film. From another perspective, this necessarily requires a theatricalization of action and speech, for there is always an audience beyond the immediate speech situation. This theater has two publics: the diegetic audience within the film, which is the Wolof nation defining itself through all the speech it witnesses, and the film-going public which, if African, is constructed as a collective in some way continuous with the first—through national traditions, histories, and politics.

The breakup of individualized intimacy and interiority, signalled in the first dialogue by the presence of a third, is related to the film's analytic editing. This can be described in some ways as deviating from standard Western analytic *découpage* but, from a different perspective, it manifests Sembene's solution to the problem of clearly articulating spaces while maintaining the collectivization of discourses, associated by the film with African tradition. The most complex and significant scene in this respect is the general convocation of the nation already mentioned, which exemplifies some of the stylistic means by which the film sustains the presence of the collective. The succession of binary conflicts takes place in a spacious, somewhat circular enclosure delimited by the placement around a large open area of the various national factions—King and court, imam and disciples, the European slave trader and priest, and, most numerous yet directly across and thus most distant from the court, the Ceddo (Fig. 3). Those who speak through Jaraaf to the King or who argue with each other step into the enclosure, which thus becomes a kind of arena or stage for national politics. The entire nation attends to the arguments.[10]

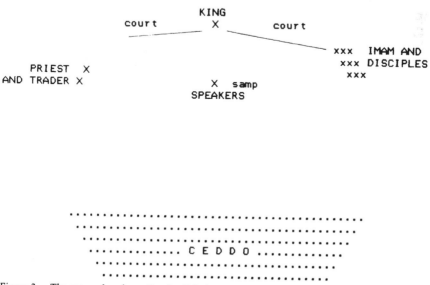

Figure 3.   *The geography of a national political arena.*

The editing of this scene intermittently incorporates various cutaways from the binary conflicts, including brief closeups of Ceddo and especially non-Ceddo individuals. The most significant of these might be described as reverse shots away from the arguing speakers to the King listening; these closeups spatially isolate the King as a decisive aristocratic presence who remains silent unless announcing a question or a decisive order. (Their slight strangeness is heightened by the fact that they are a bit "off-line" according to a 180-degree logic, but despite the early dialogue between Dior and her kidnapper, the 180-degree rule is not a consistent factor in this film.) These shots of the King thus establish something like a "reverse field" superior to whatever discourses are in play in the center of the enclosure. But when the binary conflicts occur in the center of the enclosure, there are no shot/ reverse shots between the debaters who share center stage with Jaraaf anyway. Rather, whatever sense of dual spatial alternation exists is between the inside of the enclosure and certain positions on its border.

Throughout the scene, then, what might count as reverse shots are of the rim of the enclosure. If at first these are cuts to the King and court, as the growing power of Islam is revealed by the progression of disputes, debates become addressed to the imam, and some of the reverse shots are established between the participants in the center of the enclosure and a different point on the rim, the Islamic group. The difference is that the imam, unlike the King, engages in spoken debate with opponents inside the circle and, unlike the King, is not spatially isolated with big facial closeups. But it turns out that it is the imam's declaration that the Koran mandates patrilineal inheritance which determines the King's ruling. The cutaway shots to Ceddo or Europeans on the rim never function as "reverse fields," either through verbal address or eyelines towards them from the enclosure. Shots of the Europeans especially possess a certain ambiguity; mute, they seem powerless in this highly verbalized world. But the patient, every-ready presence of the slave-trader turns out to be a significant plot element. In sum, the spatial construction of the scene emphasizes the play of power among addressers, addressees, and by-standing witnesses to the verbal and symbolic actions inside the enclosure. But they reflect relations of diegetic authority, strengths and weaknesses, the shifting constructions that result also mark the area of the reverse shot and audiences as a place of potential national power or exploitation.

Thus, as an exercise in avoiding reverse shot constructions within the enclosure, the scene reserves the potential power of reverse fields for a diegetic audience.[11] A review of some of the spatial articulations in successive segments of this scene illustrates the theatricalizing strategy, already emphasized by the stylized language and acting, that the editorial analysis of scenic space augments. For example the debate between Saxewar and Madior is theatricalized through the camera's being positioned in the reverse field of the court, which motivates the debaters' occasionally playing directly to the camera (Fig. 4). Then, when the next and key debate between Biram and Madior introduces the linkages between political power, religion, and matrilineal succession, the two discussants and the griot Jaraaf are blocked triangularly in the center of the circle. The 180-degree rule becomes irrelevant as the film cuts to all sides of the triangle, generally centering frontally whichever of the three is speaking, to theatricalize the scene further (Figs. 5–7). This motivates the succeeding debate witnessed by the nation, between Madior and the imam. Spatially, this discussion is presented in part by setups which do reverse fields, though not in the repetitive binary alternation from one side of an axis of action so familiar from mainstream Western cinema, not without interruption from a cutaway, and with variation in the shot scale of Madior. In another binary setup, Madior appeals to the King, who breaks his silence to decide in favor of the imam. Next, when Saxewar and the imam exchange threats, there is a brief alternation of setups which does look very much like a standard shot/reverse shot, since camera placement remains on one side of an axis of action; however, this mechanism is by now just one option among many for filming such confrontations.

The import of this stylistic analysis might be claims for a denormalization of historically dominant Western editing patterns. Given the international experience and sophistication of Sembene (typical of postcolonial African writers and film-makers) such an approach might seem reasonable. But the denormalization re-vealed here is not just defamiliarizing in a simplistically formalistic sense, nor is it "deconstructive" à la Godard, whereby a dominant aspect of reading the film would at some point be an explicit awareness of stylistic self-reflection and critique as such. What deserves special emphasis about *Ceddo* is how functional Sembene's strategies are in narrative and historiographic terms. The editing of this scene, for example, causes no problems in the viewer's spatial orientation or access to story events. Rather, it operates in concert with a narrative and historical logic that does not induce concern with the interiority of individual narrative agents but insists on their collectivization. This collectivization is established by a theatricalization of discourse that is associated with strong markers of African tradition and that in-sists on the importance of address to the nation as African.

Figure 4.

Figure 5.

Figure 6

Figure 7.

2

In the film as a whole such limits on individualized interiorization have their most important payoff for historiographic positionality precisely at moments when the film seems, finally, to cue us most unavoidably to read the image as the subjectivity of individual characters. At one point, when the European priest sees Prince Madior observing his church, the priest approaches Madior, looks up apparently to the heavens, and in a heavily marked false eyeline match, we dissolve to a shot straight up at the interior of a cathedral dome painted in a Christian iconography of angelic ascent in which all the figures are Blacks. Along with the music (part of a choral mass sung in African harmonies and to African percussion and rhythm), this announces the extended sequence that follows. It is an outdoor, twentieth-century African Christian communion service, presented in part by means of some seeming cinema-verité footage. In addition to many extras, all major characters of the film—Muslims and traditionalists—participate as Christians, with Prince Madior presiding as a bishop and the priest appearing as an honored corpse. We then return to the village and the shot of the priest which opened the communion sequence.

Conventional codes of editing and punctuation at the beginning and end of this sequence signify we are seeing the priest's subjectivity. That is, the sequence appears to objectify his motivation and goals, the future of Africa for which he works, a Christian Senegal—in short, the priest's dream in the sense of the dream of his life. Yet, the sequence cannot be exhausted by this reading, simply because of the reality-effects. Reinforced by the documentary style, the twentieth-century detail—the clothing, the music—is too correct; how could the priest know how people would dress and sing in the twentieth century? We are seeing a version of the priest's "dream" that exceeds his knowledge and therefore psychological motivation in his interiority. Thus, the surprise of this sequence is not only formal, inasmuch as there had been no warning of or preparation for a break in the film's straightforward narrative succession of story events, but is also a kind of historically shocking *false flashforward*, directed at a spectator who knows that modern Senegal is overwhelmingly Muslim and therefore recognizes the falsity of a scene depicting the contemporary triumph of Christianity. This is a variant of Senegalese history which did not happen, a historical option lost.

The priest's pseudo-dream of something which did not happen anticipates another, that of Princess Dior. As her Ceddo kidnapper is killed, we dissolve from a closeup of Dior to shots of her offering water to the kidnapper returning to a village home, in a traditional regional gesture of respect and love. Again, an interiorized reading is incomplete. This seemingly internalized vision represents Dior's subjectivity, her changed attitude toward the Ceddo, but the earlier false flashforward suggests a simultaneous reading: Here is another eventuality not occurring, mutual respect between Wolof social strata that have been divided by caste, something that could have been a basis for staving off Islam in the name of indigenous tradition.

This reading bears directly on the historiographic wish-fulfillment of the finale, another historical falsity which is, however, *not* marked as dream or individual subjectivity but whose status is instead left ambivalent. The princess, as Wolof nobility and bearer of matrilineal succession, and as holder of a name similar to that of a famous nineteenth-century Senegalese anti-colonial leader (Lat-Dior), kills the imam while the Ceddo place their bodies in front of Muslim rifles. This enacts a peculiar sort of retrospective utopianism. In the microcosmic terms of the film, the traditional fetish religion defeats Islam. Yet, Senegal is today overwhelmingly Islamic and the film ends uneasily, in a freeze frame centered on Dior looking at the camera in a mise-en-scene filled with Muslim disciples (Fig. 8). *Ceddo's* narrative resolution is achieved with another historical option defeated in Senegalese history—an actualized political and military alliance of the old nobility and the Ceddo to preserve indigenous ways.[12]

In fact, the inappropriate reality–effect of the priest's "dream" is only the most startling example of something which informs the film as a whole, namely strategies that invite spectators towards a consciously present-oriented consideration of options and consequences even as they observe this enactment of the past. These can be overt references (for example, the new Muslim names given all the Ceddo by the imam—including Ousmane—are common in Senegal today) or subtle deviations from the normal expectations for historical cinema. Perhaps the most praised example is the film's music. Title and nondiegetic background music are made up of African-oriented modern jazz by Manu Dibango. But aspects of this twentieth-century mode are directly based on "authentic music created by a griot more than a hundred years ago;"[13] this is indicated early in the film when the nondiegetic music takes up a theme being played diegetically by Fara, the griot for the Ceddo. What is most forceful here is not a pure authenticity of period music from the Senegambian region used as movie music, for the jazz style reshapes even

Figure 8.

such themes mined from the past into a late twentieth-century mode. This alone is a signal of historiography in the process of being written for current purposes. But more subtly, it is also as if the nondiegetic music of the film acts as a reminder of a historical sequence within music itself, from traditional Africa to modern jazz. The link in this musical history is the African-American gospel song "I'll Make It Home Some Day," used as nondiegetic music correlated with narratively digressive sequences of slaves bought by the White slave trader. This song typifies a music originating neither in the area nor at the historical moment being depicted, but rather developed by these slaves and their descendents when they reach the New World. Within music history, this gospel song mediates between indigenous African music and Dibango's jazz. But within the film's narration of national history, it manifests awareness of another historical consequence to the decisions being made in the narrative: the African diaspora.

Such tactics promote a certain fluidity of historical temporality in apprehending *Ceddo*, for they join the collective positionality of the film to an active historiographic one. If the film's representation of history is premised on the significance of collective forces, ultimately history can only be understood as a set of options in the play of those forces as they lead to differing futures including the present. *Historical* comprehension occurs in consideration of futures which did not occur as opposed to those which did. Historiographically, the result is to loosen the inevitability of "this happened" or "this happened because," the third-person past and causal theses so familiar from classical narrative and historical representation. This has repercussions at the level of historical knowledge defined as explanation, for even as the film microcosmically explains how things happened, it does this by confronting the spectator with what did not happen, what choices were and were not made.

The culmination of this operation is a certain open-endedness reinforced by the uneasiness of the film's final shot, the freeze frame that isolates Dior from her new Ceddo allies as she stares at the camera. That Dior's action is not explained verbally leaves questions open, but it might be argued that this simply continues to pull the film away from individualized motivations, thus encouraging spectators to place her action within the overall sociopolitical framework of events. But this scene, which has a forcefully climactic impact, actually leaves much unsettled. First, the militant Muslim faction remains strong, so peaceful coexistence between religions demanded by the Ceddo is by no means secure (and, again, this is reinforced by the fact that Senegal is today predominantly Muslim.) Second, the prerogatives of the White slave trader have never been questioned. Third, with both King and imam dead, the political problem has not been solved. Or rather, the solution poses its own questions.

Whatever modicum of satisfying resolution is provided has to do with bridging the gulf that has separated the aristocratic anti-Islamic forces from the Ceddo. Yet, the very tradition being defended cannot encompass that resolution, for it makes Dior the leader of the traditionalist forces. In that case, as a female descendant, she would represent a break with traditional practice by which the maternal nephew should inherit the throne. It is important to emphasize that there is no preparation for the idea that Dior should govern, which is to some degree promoted by the finale. Even discussions among the Ceddo never include women; in fact, Dior is the only woman who speaks in the entire film. Yet, male leaders—shrewd Madior, strong Saxewar, and admirable Diogomay—are all unable to conceive of the necessary conditions for a firm resistance on the part of tradition.

As is typical in Sembene's written and cinematic corpus, ultimate success for indigenous African self-interest and resistance encounters a crucial non-traditional imperative: rethinking the sociocultural place of African women. Yet, if the logic of the strong action concluding the narrative is Dior's assumption of national leadership, contradictions around that solution remain outstanding. Therefore, while the story comes to a definite conclusion, the narrative world is not harmonized by the completed knowledge usual in a formally totalized narrative nor, consequently, a completed historical sequence. This returns us to the present-oriented play on audience knowledge exploited by the film. For the solution offered by the film has not been historically effective. (Some of Sembene's films, especially *Mandabi* (1968) and *Xala*, include satiric probes of the dynamics of polygamy in the context of a modernizing, contemporary Senegal.) In this sense, the narrative solution in *Ceddo* represents another lost historical option and challenge to the audience.

3

From another perspective, all of this indicates that *Ceddo* is not only a distinctive formulation of representative moments in a national history, but an experiment in modes of constructing historicity. While certain aspects of *Ceddo* such as the use of indigenous language, the foregrounding of certain regional cultural practices, the status of Islam, and so forth, are more or less anchored in Senegalese history, Sembene himself insists that the film is intended to stimulate a historical conscious-ness in all African ethnic groups.[14] In that case, the film's specific references to cultural and historical aspects of the Senegambian region outrun that specificity in order to suggest a set of relatively common issues that structure many African histories. At this level, for instance, even the decision to make the film in the Wolof language is a strategy of exemplification; instead of an exclusively Senegalese purport, it serves to emphasize the ubiquitous sub-Saharan fact of localized lan-guages. This is all to suggest that a decisive context for the film is the most generalized problematics of African history.

Pervasive constructions of African history explicitly or implicitly invoke a famil-iar but fundamental opposition between tradition and modernity. V. Y. Mudimbe has summarized some of the epistemic determinations, connotations, and conse-quences of this fundamental paradigm. It is linked to a number of others, such as agrarian, customary communities vs. urbanized, industrial societies; subsistence economies vs. highly productive economies; and oral cultures vs. written/print cultures. Historically, such paradigms are embedded in an imperialist object-subject, other-self dialectic with wide epistemological and ideological resonance. For example, one of the central discursive strains in definitions of Africa is classical anthropology, whose development coincided with the colonial division of the continent and which, like colonialist ideologies, defines itself by positing its object as other to "civilization." This problematic is a trap that catches concepts of African identity and nation in the opposition between two static, monolithic, mutually exclusive terms. When it infiltrates historiography, the only movement possible to validate is along a uni-directional path *out from* traditional forms of culture and social organization *towards* modern, written cultures, an inescapable journey *from* the tribal nation *to* the centralized nation-state.[15]

Nevertheless, the heritage of the tradition-modernity paradigm can sometimes seem ambivalent. While it continues to sustain regressive significations of Africa as Other, it has also supported influential attempts to formulate a distinctive African identity and development. One famous and controversial example is the theory of Negritude. The term was originally introduced by a group of Francophone Black poets and intellectuals. A leading figure in its theorization was Léopold Senghor, philosopher, poet, and founding president of Senegal who was still in office when *Ceddo* was made and banned. Among other things, his version of the theory identifies contributions to human culture and consciousness lacking in White experience but essential to Black experience. Not only the characteristics attributed to a specifically Black subjectivity but the essentialism of the concept have led to important debates, polemics, and discussions.[16] Already by 1952 Frantz Fanon, another Black intellectual familiar with current French thought, asserted that "what is often called the black soul is a white man's artifact." He set out the terms of the problem by maintaining the search for position yet calling the project of an ontol-ogy of Negritude into question:

In the *Weltanschauung* of a colonized people there is an impurity, a flaw that outlaws any ontological explanation. Someone may object that this is the case with every individual, but such an objection merely conceals a basic problem. Ontology—once it is finally admitted as leaving existence by the wayside—does not permit us to understand the being of the black man. For not only must the black man be black; he must be black in relation to the white man. Some critics will take it on themselves to remind us that this proposition has a converse. I say that this is false. The black man has no ontological resistance in the eyes of the white man. Overnight the Negro has been given two frames of reference within which he has had to place himself. His metaphysics or, less pretentiously, his customs and the sources on which they were based, were wiped out because they were in conflict with a civilization that he did not know and that imposed itself on him.[17]

Mudimbe's recent overview of knowledges of Africa exemplifies a current conception of this problem. Familiar with Foucaultian and poststructuralist thought, he argues that conceptions of African identity should be based less on delimiting a primordial African object of study or an essential African Being than on establishing an intermediary, ambiguous epistemological attitude which nevertheless recognizes the links between power and claims of knowledge. Yet the issue of identity remains politically and ideologically unavoidable. For Mudimbe, even an "ideology of otherness" (i.e., Negritude) can provide an important historical counter to the primitivist anthropological heritage, as a "historical legend" providing a network of metaphors and concepts acceptable to African intellectuals and artists. Yet it is also subject to the kinds of critique mounted by those such as Fanon. Mudimbe suggests that one good definition of underdevelopment is marginality, conceived as a state of affairs between the two extremes of the paradigmatic opposition of traditional and modern. However, if African identities must be found here, the question consequently posed is whether the instabilities of this discursive position can be turned to advantage.[18]

The forms in which historical accounts are usually presented presume identities—clearly identifiable historical agents, whether conceived individually or collectively. Making African constructions of identity both necessary and ambiguous thus has historiographic implications. This is first because if African identities necessarily reflect intermediary positions between the extremes of the various tradition-modernity oppositions, this means that they still assume that basic opposition and hence the Western historiographic paradigm. On the other hand, they would ultimately question the dialectic of self and other that grounds the oppositions in Western discourse. Although concerned with theoretical constructions of Africa, Mudimbe's formulation is reminiscent of Fanon's opposition to ontology in that it leads to a placement of African identities as always in transition, in time, in history. Thus, while the strategic bind around identity and nation has long been a prominent burden of Black African intellectuals and artists, it can also drive them politically and practically to the most searching confrontation with the ideologies of self that, from African perspectives, ground the massive historiographic reification by which the Western episteme has defined and positioned their practices and nations.[19]

As a construction of historicity by one of the most renowned Black African artists of the generation that experienced the transition to postcolonial status, *Ceddo* can be situated in this problematic. In *Ceddo* history appears as perpetual transition, as always in process, and consequently so are nation and identity. History comprehended as an ongoing play of collective forces presenting options for different histories and different futures is in opposition to history as the blocked or progressive path so persistently implanted—especially with respect to Africa—in Western philosophy, anthropology, and ideology. The active positionality of the film as described above certainly does not spring from a rejection of narrative as a historiographic form, but it is intricated with limitations on the uni-directionality and inevitability of a closed narrative enchainment associated not just with Western commercial cinema, but with Western historiographic knowledge.[20]

Economically and culturally crucial as the opposition between the traditional and the modern is both for Africa's history and its recent politics, it has been a privileged concern of African cinema in general and *Ceddo* in particular. But Sembene counters the reification of these two extremes which anchors the paradigm's power as ideology. It is sometimes noted that *Ceddo* functions in part as an archeology, representing and foregrounding precolonial political practices as well as social functions such as *jottali* and the griot. However, while Sembene's counter-history is unthinkable without the recovery of repressed or denigrated African practices and events, it also refigures the tradition-modernity opposition that has been the basis for conceptions of Africa since the modern West defined the study of history in its own self-image.

More specifically, the film's historicity accepts the opposition of the old and the new, the indigenous and the foreign, but neither is static or monolithic. For example, not only are non-indigenous forces split into European/Christian and Arab/Muslim factions, but also the weakness of the Europeans, who never speak, pushes the anticolonialism struggle back in time. Although Senegal ultimately obtained independence as a state from France, the setting and subject matter of *Ceddo* make the non-European force of Islam an invader. To set the film at a transitional historical moment during which, microcosmically, a non-European foreign force is about to decimate indigenous African culture and politics may have special resonance in the context of Senegalese history. However, it also emphasizes the permanent presence of transition, invasion, and conflict in African history. The encounter with the new and foreign is not a historically novel moment with the onslaught of European colonialism, but rather a complex historical constant. The radically critical implications of this perspective should not be underestimated, for it can lead even to problematizing the origins of non-European values most dear to some Africans, such as the status of Islamic clerics in Senegal. The militant imam with unquestioning disciples in *Ceddo* must call up some echoes of the Sufi brotherhoods that have been so important in West Africa and Senegal and some of which can even claim a heritage of resisting French colonialism.

Furthermore, what the film defines as indigenous tradition is also split into factions and is by no means unambiguous. We have already seen the paradoxical inability of tradition to triumph without radical revision with respect to its placement of women. In addition, consider the film's most striking sign of tradition, the griot. The magnificently dressed Jaraaf is a court schemer, and ultimately a traitor not only to African tradition but to the King who honors him with his position. On the other hand, Fara, with his poor clothes and musical instrument, is allied with the people's travails. Thus, the presence of the griot in itself does not signify a primordial authenticity that is automatically beneficial. While the film's sympathies are clearly with the Ceddo, the indigenous tradition they defend is not uniformly and necessarily a virtuous lost world. The agencies of tradition are just as subject to the play of collective interests and power as other agencies in the film. Indeed, insufficiencies within tradition are indicated by the fact that Sembene, who sometimes discusses his own cinema as an attempt to construct a modern equivalent of the griot, refuses the socially integrative, harmonious resolutions of traditional African storytelling and in *Ceddo* and other works instead provides endings with socially critical implications.[21]

Finally, consider the film's emphasis on the one major division within the Wolof not explicitly and articulately explained in this highly verbalized film: slavery. Slavery pervades all corners of the social world of *Ceddo*, and some of its historical consequences are emphasized by the African-American gospel song from another future, a future that—as opposed to the priest's dream or the possibility implied in the film's ending—the audience knows did indeed occur. In *Ceddo*, slavery has two determining contexts, one foreign and one indigenous. First, based on a non-African market for slaves, the White trader promotes a nascent European exchange economy but one whose medium is Black bodies, which are used as currency to buy his goods ranging from wine to rifles. Yet if the worst of slavery is represented as the delivery of slaves to the White, there is an insidious vulnerability to these methods of exchange among even the most admirable of the Black figures.

For the second context of slavery is its complete naturalization within Wolof society. Its presence never provokes formal discussion as does, say, the choice between matrilineal and patrilineal inheritance. Yet it is what fragments the forces defending tradition, making them tactically vulnerable. An outraged Dior notes in the first conversation with her captor that the Ceddo are slaves, and her final act of killing the imam is possible only after she acquires new respect for these crown slaves and thus overcomes the caste division that separates her from them. But this climax—which, as we have seen, partakes of a historical vision that did not happen—is the only moment in the film when such a social transformation becomes conceivable. Contempt or simple disregard for slaves is also enacted by the other traditionalist aristocrats, Madior and Saxewar. Even the majority of the Ceddo, finally driven to plan a fruitless rebellion, can only imagine obtaining guns by reluctantly trading their own children to the White slaver. A film knowingly influenced by oral cultural traditions, *Ceddo* forcefully verbalizes many of the problems and options confronting its narrative agents; even the political option of having a woman ruler is discussed in order to be dismissed by courtiers. However, Black over Black slavery and the trade of Black slaves to the White is a central element of the social world whose validity remains unquestioned and unnoted by any character. This is a condemnation of a massive failure of traditional Africa to take care of its own. Here is a historical aspect of tradition that *needed* contradiction and change.[22]

4

As an abstract historiographic structure, the relation between tradition and modernity can be conceived as an unchanging antinomy, in which case modernity becomes absolutely unavailable to traditional cultures ("primitive mentalities") and they become absolutely other to modernity. Alternatively, this relation can be conceived as a quasi-historical one, insofar as a mythic super-narrative of progressive or regressive passage, gradual or not, from one state of being to another is envisaged. This alternative is not *radically* historical because the two antipodes of the process retain atemporal identities; as beginning and end points of a temporal process, they are themselves static, outside of time, and therefore define the limits of historicity itself. This suggests a third possibility, wherein not only their relationship, but the two poles themselves are conceived as temporal entities, subject to constant internal contradiction and change. In this case, the relationship between tradition and modernity is conceived as radically historical, for a deessentialization of the extremes moves the entire configuration of anthropological historicity into time.

As a conclusion, then, we can propose that *Ceddo* bases itself on a radical historicity. While its narrative plays out a version of the confrontation between tradition and modernity, neither is an unfractured whole. The most striking aspect of this operation is the fluid complexity and sometimes the resultingly critical edge of the film's construction of tradition. Not even the indigenous assumes a seamlessly positive value to be defended and restored in its integrity. This marks the categorical depurification embodied in the film's historiography.[23]

It is also possible to ascribe a radical historicity to other levels of the film as discussed above. One kind of definition of an indigenous, or national, cinema seeks textual distinctiveness; hence, the interest of such components of *Ceddo* as its particular patterns of analytic editing. These patterns work first of all in ways specific to this text, for instance in connection with its mobilization of a culturally-rooted stylization of speech that aids in collectivizing the issues being narrativized. Yet, this does not mean it is simply irrelevant to compare them to modes of editorial scene analysis familiar from a more internationalized perspective on the history of film style. As a methodological point, to establish distinctiveness requires a comparative outlook. But also in question is how one regards film history. As a moment in a textual commentary, to treat *Ceddo* in an international, film-historical context extends the basic impulse of the film's own historiography as depurification. Even textual distinctiveness is situated as a site of transition and transformation, of contradictory as well as collective determinants, as radically historical.

This also applies to my descriptions of the film's aspirations for its spectator. As a "historical film," *Ceddo* includes something of a restorationist impulse. It constitutes the physical and social world of a carefully delineated past, with images and sounds of striking regional settings and reconstructed details and actions. On the other hand, the spectator is invited to reflect on contradictions and historical options, not only by the overtly stated dramatic rationales of characters but also by a series of occurrences that, judged from knowledge available in the spectator's own time, might variously be false, possible, or actual. Thus, there are shifting, differential levels in narrative security possible in the contradiction between a truth of depicted archeological detail and the conveying of narrative events and actions; and there always remain ambivalences and limitations on any historical understanding solely on the basis of diegetic occurrences, for narrative authority as a site of absolute historical knowledge never quite finds an adequate delegate—such as a Prince Salina—within the diegesis. Comprehension as understanding a play of

collective forces presenting options for differing futures privileges historical knowledge, but as a confrontation with alternatives instead of as an integral and closed
past. Ultimately, then, the spectator is also conceived as a historical agent, an agent
asked to reflect on options for comprehending the history of Africa from his or her
own historicized temporality.

But does not a radical historicity call any identity into question? If all terms in the
opposition between tradition and modernity—and by extension, the indigenous
and the foreign—are in perpetual transition, it might seem that *Ceddo* exceeds any
simple placement as African cinema conceived as purely imitative of, or as purely
other to Western cinema. This is a way of situating *Ceddo* in the framework of
tradition vs. modernity, in order to propose that the film collapses this founding
opposition. However, such a purely deconstructive description loses the historical
and political basis of the film's radical historicity, the sense that it is answering to
problems of special import in Africa. The dialectic of colonialism and liberation,
and the tradition-modernity opposition with its related paradigms such as indigenous vs. foreign, are part and parcel of the very conditions of existence for a film
such as *Ceddo*, conditions that come from a historical and political specificity.

Sembene is an artist who militantly bases his films in the signs and structures of
African cultural tradition, so that, for example, his proclivity for partially indeterminate character motivation and partially open endings to promote discussion and
reflection by the audience can be said to derive from the African dilemma tale; on
the other hand, he can discuss Brechtian components in his work.[24] His emphasis
on collectivity is associated with African cultural experience; but he also has a
background in labor organizing and Marxism. *Ceddo* is a self-consciously African
project drawing on African narrative traditions and Senegalese historical experience to tell its story; yet, these are mobilized and conveyed in a historical film made
in the unprecedented political and ideological milieu of the postcolonial African
nation-state—and cinema, the epistemological privilege of critical historiography,
and the centralized nation-state (nationalism) were all Western developments during the colonialist period.

Nevertheless, there can be little doubt that *Ceddo* remains positional. If, based on
such oppositions and contradictions, one described *Ceddo* as synthetic, this "synthesis" is not an ideal, balanced supercession of contradictories. Rather, the film is a
reflection of, and sometimes less overtly, a reflection on its own status at a certain
moment in African and film history. It is thus not just its subject matter that makes
Ceddo a specifically Black African work. The reconceptualization of historical comprehension and address it embodies answers to questions crucial in the context of
sub-Saharan Africa, where the confluence of transition and identity are unavoidable issues. The radical historicity of *Ceddo* is rooted in and inseparable from the
drive to construct a self-consciously postcolonial national cinema in Senegal, in the
sense of a cinema rising from the specifics of African cultures, politics, and
histories.

If nations as such are entities that must be culturally and discursively made and
remade in order to exist, *Ceddo* exemplifies some of the ways in which the foundations of nationhood are at issue in African cultural practices and thought. This
article has repeatedly suggested that such discourses have wider implications for
perspectives on conceptualizations of nation and historiography.[25] But it is the

film's African concerns that ultimately lead to a historicization of the terms of identity and nation, for identity and nation are special and intertwined problems in Africa in the first place. It is only because *Ceddo* deals with nation by making diverse African histories imaginable that it contributes to conceiving of different cinemas, and therefore can also contribute to making diverse film histories imaginable.

ACKNOWLEDGMENT

This article is based on material from a forthcoming book, *Past Present: Cinema, Theory, Historicity*. I am grateful to Teshome Gabriel, Neil Lazarus, and Hamid Naficy for their comments on earlier drafts.

NOTES

1. Sembene Ousmane, *The Last of the Empire*, trans. Adrian Adams (London: Heineman, 1983), 135. Boureddine Ghali, "An Interview with Sembene Ousmane," *Cinéma 76*, no. 208 (April, 1976), translated in John D. Downing, ed., *Film and Politics in the Third World*, (New York: 1987), 46.
2. This approach differs in emphasis from that of the most authoritative commentators on Sembene's films. Françoise Pfaff *The Cinema of Ousmane Sembene, a Pioneer of African Film* (Westport CT: Greenwood, 1984), 51–52, notes his interest in juxtaposing contrasting spaces but claims that Sembene's historical, rural films employ longer takes than do his contemporary, urban films. Yet, even if the takes are longer in *Ceddo* than, say *Mandabi* or *Xala*, this usually does not affect spatial articulations to the extreme of leading to sequence shots or extended scenes composed only of a couple of shots. While there are occasional examples of such constructions in *Ceddo* (especially the long take in which the court nobles decide to betray the King), for the most part scenes are edited according to a spatially analytical impulse. (*Emitai*, on the other hand, seems better to match her description.) Manthia Diawara goes further in his important article "Popular Culture and Oral Traditions in African Film," *Film Quarterly* 41, 3 (Spring, 1988), describing the court scene in *Ceddo* whose analytical aspects are discussed below as composed of deep focus long takes as opposed to "the fast editing style of European films" (p. 11).

    These writers, with Sembene himself, explain that editing and other rhythms in Sembene's films generally tend to seem slower than those of many Western aesthetics and practices because they originate in Black African traditions of narrative and temporality. This seems very likely, but it also seems problematic to use the long take as the representative device. The long take is well known elsewhere, and was an established option even in Hollywood at the time that it was codified most influentially into French cinema aesthetics by Bazin's celebrations of such directors as Renoir and Welles. (One wonders if this shouldn't be a significant consideration for interrogations of oppositional components of films from Francophone Africa.) Perhaps the term *long take*, especially given its influential heritage from Bazin, is not sufficiently exact, or too limited a formulation, to describe the specificity of Sembene's distinctive practices with respect to temporal rhythms, for these have to do not just with absolute shot length but relations of narrative, image, and sound.
3. In an interview which provides some of the most sophisticated formulations for dealing with this film, Sembene argues that the actions of the kidnapper must be read as those of a collective rather than a rebellious individual, in part because hostage taking as a tactic in disputes is known in several cultural traditions of the region. Françoise Pfaff, "Entretien avec Ousmane Sembène," *Positif*, no. 235 (October, 1980): 56.
4. For Sembene on the term *ceddo*, see Pfaff, "Entretien avec Ousmane Sembène," pp. 55–56. Elsewhere, Sembene seems to stress some of the precolonial grandeur of the Ceddo: "it is . . . a manner of being with rules and regulations. The Ceddo is a lively mind or spirit, rich in the double meaning of words and knows the forbidden meanings. The Ceddo is innocent of sin and transgression. The Ceddo is jealous of his/her absolute liberty," *Nations Nouvelles*, 1976: 28, quoted in Teshome H.

Gabriel, *Third Cinema in the Third World: The Aesthetics of Liberation* (Ann Arbor MI: UMI Research Press, 1982), 87. On pp. 86–87, Gabriel stresses Ceddo as anti-Islamic "outsider." For additional perspectives, see also the entry under *cedo* (the officially legitimated spelling rejected by Sembene) in Lucie Gallistel Colvin, *Historical Dictionary of Senegal* (Metuchen NJ: Scarecrow, 1981); on *tieddo* Cheikh Anta Diop, *Precolonial Black Africa* (Trenton NJ: Africa World Press, 1987), 46–47; and for a commentary on the *tyeddo*, anti-colonialist conflicts, and Muslim-pagan struggles in the nineteenth century, Donal B. Cruise O'Brien, *Saints and Politicians: Essays in the Organization of a Senegalese Peasant Society* (London: Cambridge University Press, 1975), 26ff. On the theme of the ceddo as applied to the anti-colonial struggles in recent Senegalese literature, see Dorothy S. Blair, *Senegalese Literature: A Critical History* (Boston: Twayne, 1984), 27–30.

The suggestion that the imam has attributes of the trickster is made in Mbye Baboucar Cham, "Ousmane Sembene and the Aesthetics of African Oral Traditions," *Africana Journal* 13, nos. 1–4 (1982): 32–33. Cham points out that in oral traditions the trickster is a protagonist, but Sembene's protagonists are often victimized by tricksters. It is important that Sembene does not just reproduce an indigenous cultural configuration but uses and reshapes it, in this case by inversion of values. One recent summary of the strength of Muslim institutions and power in Senegal and their political relations to the state and national identifications is Mar Fall, "La question islamique au Sénégal: Le regain récent de l'islam; la religion contre l'État?" *Présence Africain* no. 142 (1987): 24–35. The sociocultural potency of Islam is exemplified for Fall by the fact that a leader of the communist Parti Africain de l'Indépendence opens his meetings with a Muslim formula; Fall, p. 28, n. 16.

5. Pfaff, "Entretien avec Ousmane Sembène," p. 56. Interview with Sembene in *Seven Days*, March 10, 1978: 27, quoted in Pfaff, *The Cinema of Ousmane Sembene*, 174.

6. For claims about the formal ("deconstructive?") play possible on such goals already in the 1920s and 1930s, see Noël Burch on Lang's early career, culminating with an account of *M* as a structure organized around the unveiling of the murderer. At first his face is obscured and, we might add, he has no speech, but the film progresses through increasing revelations culminating in a full frontal closeup and correspondingly full speech, which combine to reveal and explain his anguished interiority. Burch, "Fritz Lang: The German Period" in Richard Roud, ed. *Cinema: A Critical Dictionary*, vol. 2 (Norwich: Secker and Warburg, 1980), 593–99.

7. Cham, 35ff

8. A brief introductory definition and a gloss on the contemporary functions of the *griot* is in Sheldon Gellar, *Senegal: An African Nation Between Islam and the West* (Boulder CO: Westview Press, 1982), 96–97. Cham, 25–26, summarizes ambivalences in the social status of griots (or *gewels*), and also social distinctions among types of storytellers. On Sembene as griot, see Pfaff, Chapter 2.

9. Diawara, "Popular Culture and Oral Traditions in African Film;" Cham, *passim*. Cf. Pfaff, Chapters 2, 3, and another article by Manthia Diawara, "Oral Literature and African Film: Narratology in *Wend Kuuni*," *Présence Africaine*, no. 142 (1987): 36–49. The transition from oral to written authority is emphasized in Serge Daney, "*Ceddo*," *Cahiers du cinéma*, no. 304 (October, 1979): 51–53.

10. One wonders whether this national arena, suggesting at least a partial ring of onlookers around the debaters/performers, does not also bear some relation to the figure of the griot. The word *gewel* (meaning the formally functioning griot) is said to derive from *geew* (circle), from the practice of forming a circle around the praise-singer/musician. See the glossary in Sembene Ousmane, *The Last of the Empire*.

11. The confrontation between the Ceddo spokesperson Diogomay and Prince Biram is edited mostly with 180-degree cuts along an axis bisecting the enclosure at a right angle to the court. The alternation includes cuts from frontal medium shots of the speakers to medium long shots from behind Diogomay with King and court in extreme background. In the name of precision, someone might want to treat this as being close to a reverse shot construction within the enclosure. But, at least in contemporary Western shot/reverse shot editing, 180-degree reversals are unusual. This pattern, incidentally, has a number of functions, ranging from covering Biram's entrance into the enclosure to placing the camera, for the only time in the entire scene, in a position close to that of the Ceddo people.

12. See Pfaff, *The Cinema of Ousmane Sembene*, 176 on Dior's gesture. Pfaff notes the reference to Lat-Dior, 175.

13. Sembene in Pfaff, "Entretien avec Ousmane Sembène," 57.

14. Pfaff, "Entretien avec Ousmane Sembène," 55.

15. See in general V. Y. Mudimbe, *The Invention of Africa: Gnosis, Philosophy and the Order of Knowledge* (Bloomington: Indiana University Press, 1988), *passim*. On the paradigmatic opposition between the traditional and the modern, see e.g., 3–5, 16–18.

16. For a brief response to such critiques, see Léopold Sédar Senghor, *On African Socialism*, trans. Mercer Cook (New York: Praeger, 1964), 72–75. In this 1960 lecture, Senghor continues to associate African knowledge with closeness as opposed to distance, touch as opposed to sight, and feeling and intuition as opposed to analytic reason. Senghor finds a vindication for valuing this kind of knowing in the critiques of classic modes of Western rationalism by French phenomenologists and existentialists, concluding his defense with an appeal for an integration of the two modes of knowledge. (Cf. 140, where he appeals in another lecture to Teilhard de Chardin to justify his theory of Negritude.) Senghor attributes to the "young people" who criticize him a "complex" for believing that such Negro-African modes of reasoning are inferior to European modes.

17. Frantz Fanon, *Black Skin, White Masks*, trans. Charles Lam Markmann (New York: Grove Press, 1967), 14, 109–110. In general, see the essay "The Fact of Blackness," from which the latter passage is excerpted.

18. Mudimbe, 5. Cf. Mudimbe's discussion of Fanon and Senghor on pp. 92–94. Given that he utilizes contemporary Western theory from Lévi-Strauss through Foucault, Mudimbe is more sympathetic to Senghor than one might expect, partly in reaction against critiques of the latter and partly in alliance with a view of historical constructions as myths. On "historical legend," see 191–94.

19. For a recent overview of issues concerning cultural identity and transition that makes some parallel arguments in connection with cinema and the Black diaspora, see Stuart Hall, "Cultural Identity and Cinematic Representation," *Framework*, no. 36 (1989): 68–81. Cf. Teshome H. Gabriel, "Thoughts on Nomadic Aesthetics and the Black Experience of Independent Cinema: Traces of a Journey," in *Blackframes: Critical Perspectives on Black Independent Cinema*, ed. Mbye B. Cham and Claire Andrade-Watkins (Cambridge, MA: MIT University Press, 1988), especially the section entitled "Axis and not Poles,"; 72–73.

    While historical and experiential differences must be kept in mind, it might be productive to compare the binds around identity and essentialism encountered in decades of such Black theoretical discourses and controversies with those found in feminist theory.

20. The most influential recent critiques within Western thought of the dominant narrative forms of its own modes of historical knowledge—rooted in the nineteenth-century diffusion of modern critical historiography—are undoubtedly those of Hayden White. See, for example, the first three essays reprinted in Hayden White, *The Content of the Form: Narative Discourse and Historical Representation* (Baltimore: The Johns Hopkins University Press, 1987): "The Value of Narrativity in the Representation of Reality," "The Question of Narrative in Contemporary Historical Theory," and "The Politics of Historical Interpretation: Discipline and De-Sublimination."

21. On different kinds of *griots* marking the ambivalences of tradition, see Diawara, "Popular Culture and Oral Traditions in African Film," *passim* and esp. 9–12 on Sembene. See also Diawara, "Oral Literature and the African Film: Narratology in *Wend Kuuni*." The point about resolutions in Sembene is taken from a discussion of delimitations on narrative linearity in his work in Cham, 27–28.

22. Slavery was a centuries-old practice in the Senegambian region when the French gradually outlawed it between 1848 and 1905. By the nineteenth century and stimulated at first by the Atlantic slave trade (already banned by France in 1815), the export of people captured in raids on neighboring kingdoms was a leading economic factor in the politics of the area. However, it should be noted that in this region, slavery was a more complex system than in New World plantations. There were distinctions between menial and aristocratic slaves, such as the Ceddo, and slaves had certain rights, such as holding property—including their own slaves. Hence in the film the Ceddo seek to reclaim certain older privileges, abrogated by the new power of Islam, that might make their status as slaves seem equivocal to Western audiences. See Colvin, entries under "slave" and "slave trade;" and O'Brien, 25–30. For the most optimistic perspective on precolonial slavery in this area, see Diop, 1–5.

    A commentary on *Ceddo* emphasizing slavery as well as other themes stressed here such as the representation of history and the theatricalization of discourse is Th. Mpoyi-Buatu, "Sembene Ousmane's *Ceddo* and Med Hondo's *West Indies*," in Downing, especially 55–63.

23. This is to reject the kind of reading of the film exemplified by statements such as "Sembène Ousmane dismisses Islam and Catholicism, all forms of conversion being a reduction of the African soul to

something other than itself." Jean-Luc Pouillaude "L'emblème: sur *Ceddo*," *Positif*, no. 235 (Oct. 1980): 53 (my translation). Clearly the film values African history and practices. But the idea of an African "soul," essence, or coherent and noncontradictory identity that preexists encounters with forces exterior to itself, and that can and should be preserved without change and outside history, is exactly what, in my reading, the film surpasses.

24. Pfaff, *The Cinema of Ousmane Sembene*: 37; Margaret Tarratt, "The Money Order," *Films and Filming*: 20, 4 (1974), quoted in Pfaff, 139.

25. Cf. Mudimbe, 196, during a concluding discussion of African identity, the perpetuality of transition, and history: "acculturation is not only an African disease but the very character of all histories. In the sequences, mutations and transformations that we can read, all histories deploy in effect a dispersion of the violence of the Same, which from the solid grounding in the present invents, restores or endows meaning to the Other in a past or in geographically remote synchronic cultures."

Doubleness and Idiosyncrasy in Cross-Cultural Analysis

Scott Nygren

The rule according to which every concept necessarily receives two similar marks—a repetition without identity—one mark inside and the other outside the deconstructed system, should give rise to a double reading and a double writing.

Jacques Derrida[1]

This paper will consider Japanese film at the juncture of Western critical methodology and cultural difference. At this juncture, contemporary methodology enables a critical reading of an alternative cultural context, while cultural difference conversely functions to help read the limits and character of critical methodology itself. My interest here is in Japan as a specific case of non-Western cultural production where cross-reading becomes an issue, and neither a cultural tradition in its own terms nor critical methodology per se suffices as a controlling discourse.

With few exceptions, recent discussion of national cinemas has tended to move away from these central methodological problems, back toward more basic, traditional issues of industry analysis, historical accuracy, and auteurist stylization.[2] In part, this is an understandable and even welcome development, given the important films produced in national cinemas from China and Vietnam to India and Africa over the last decade and exhibited in the West. Yet this access to new materials should not obscure or petrify the theoretical argumentation on which comprehension of these materials must be based. To proceed, one must address the theoretical complexity that arises from the intersection of critical methodology and specific international/historic contexts.[3]

The argument in this paper will be that a certain doubleness is unavoidable in the production and interpretation of film in cross-cultural contexts, and that idiosyncratic figures in texts can provide significant sites to unravel such doubleness. By doubleness, I mean to borrow here from Derrida's concept of a double reading and a double writing, in which two texts are set against each other without being resolved into a dialectical opposition. Instead, the two texts function to deconstruct the other's unconscious premises, as in Derrida's *Glas* where juxtaposed essays on Genet and Hegel work to open each text to the conflict and exchange of determining tropes.[4]

In such instances the romantic figure of the doppleganger, or formation of difference as an oppositional otherness, decays into what Jean-François Lyotard calls a *différend*, or term which continues to shift meaning according to context.

SCOTT NYGREN *is an Associate Professor in the Department of English at the University of Florida. He has published in such journals as* Wide Angle, The Journal of Film and Video, Afterimage *and* Iris.

As distinguished from a litigation, a differend [*différend*] would be a case of conflict, between (at least) two parties, that cannot be equitably resolved for lack of a rule of judgment applicable to both arguments.[5]

The doppleganger is a figure that lies at the basis of Orientalist exoticism. Doubleness, as Derrida uses the term, functions to reposition difference from a dialectical or oppositional otherness within a closed system to a plural process of conflict and exchange where the ideological determinants of a system themselves come into question.[6] Although the two irreconcilable texts of *Glas* both derive from Western discursive formations, this model implicitly extends to cross-cultural circumstances where conditions of irreconcilability and undecidability are the norm. In this paper, Kurosawa's *Ikiru* will be discussed as an example of this process of repositioning, in part because it is one of the most familiar and justifiably famous Japanese films known in the West.

Once recognized, the doubleness inhabiting texts cannot be "gone beyond" in the sense of reestablishing a new syncretic universal transparency of meaning, but idiosyncratic sites can be explored which foreground the displacements of meaning engendered by double contexts. Such sites include texts normally marginalized from serious discourse, such as the autobiographical travelogue novels considered here, and can inform readings of contemporary films. Ishii's *Crazy Family* will be considered in these terms.

To address current problems in cross-cultural analysis, one might begin by considering methodological approaches that generate productive work in the field. By juxtaposing developments in several different areas of critical analysis that either partially overlap or are usually considered separately, it becomes possible to problematize assumptions implicit within different discursive formations. The argument here is that this process of juxtaposition cannot be fully conceived as dialectical (in the sense of a strict binary) and instead seems to invite supplementary connotations of discrepancy, *méconnaissance*, and destabilization.

In this fashion, one could somewhat arbitrarily identify two or three relatively stable areas of activity that function to orient (to use a deliberately loaded term) current work. First, applying the techniques of literary and textual analysis to the domain of cultural studies is now long established but still remarkable, as for example in Roland Barthes's *Empire of Signs*.[7] Second (or as a variation on or partial split within the first), the reorientation of political and ideological analysis toward the domain of cultural forms remains pivotal, as in Edward Said's *Orientalism*.[8] Last, the necessary empirical detail of a specific cultural practice is being transformed by a younger generation of historians. Original materials once available only in native languages are now being translated or studied by new historians who are frequently bilingual (often native to Japan and writing in English), such as Hiroshi Komatsu, Kyoko Hirano, Peter High, Keiko MacDonald, Larry Greenberg, and others.[9]

The problems that these recent developments suggest can be posed by imagining an intertextual dialogue of multiple voices. Voices can be imagined as being generated by the positions from which individual texts are written without restricting the discourse to these texts alone. The pursuit, application, and cross-referencing of these positions by other writers become part of the voices as well. This approach as a technique of contemporary criticism has been pursued elsewhere by such writers as Jane Gallop in *The Daughter's Seduction*,[10] and is part of a critical era oriented by such operations as the split writing of Jacques Derrida's *Glas* and the multiple voices or equivocity of James Joyce's *Finnegan's Wake*.

A first voicing, or intersection, of this material, might be Tony Rayns's critique of Barthes in his introduction to the new generation of Japanese filmmakers that has emerged since 1980, which parallels Scott L. Malcomson's critique of Barthes (and Noël Burch) in *Screen*.[11] Their texts pose the critique of what I am calling here an ideological analysis against the literary or textual methodology of Barthes. Rayns and Malcomson argue Said's position, that the West inevitably perceives the Orient as a projection of its own other, thereby inevitably casting it in the form of exotic opposition. Orientalism, as an enthusiasm in the West, developed in the 17th and 18th centuries through the collecting of objects such as ceramics and furniture newly possible through developing trade routes to the East. In its original context, the Orient seems to have included everything east of Vienna, so that Egypt, Arabia, India, and the Far East were all equally and interchangeably intriguing. Moorish disguises in opera (for example, Mozart's Turkish ambassadors in *Così Fan Tutte*), mock Egyptian furniture styles that followed Napoleon's conquest of Egypt, and ceramic collections from China coexist with fake Oriental landscapes done in oils such as can be found in the Queen's chamber at Fountainebleau.[12] Rayns, without recalling the historical details, argues that this position is still maintained by Barthes's presentation of Japan in terms of an absolute difference from the West. Rayns then advocates an alternative position: that Japan, now completely industrialized and a major participant in an international information economy, has more in common with the West than it does in contrast. He goes on to clarify that this does not mean he wishes to deny all cultural specificity to Japan, but rather that any such specificity must be rethought in the context of an international economy where sameness outweighs and recontexts such difference.

Barthes, of course, has already anticipated such a critique in his original formulation of *Empire of Signs*, when he argues that he is articulating an imaginary place which he will call Japan and which has no necessary connection with any real place of the same name. To Malcomson this is a clever but inadequate ploy that does not undo the damage: romantic implications emerge precisely from positioning Japan in the place of the Imaginary. (Along these lines, see Victor Burgin's rereading of *Camera Lucida*, where he argues that Barthes's later writings "betray" the "positions" taken in his earlier texts.[13]) But there is more to be said.

Barthes's position might be better described as parallel to that of Godard and Miéville's film *Içi et ailleurs* (1974), where a certain doubleness operates. On the one hand, Godard and Miéville's images of Palestine are motivated by rhetorical tropes of political commitment and social conscience, and yet precisely because of this commitment those images are driven within the film to a point of self-imposed limitation. The filmmakers acknowledge the impossibility of any adequate image of Palestine being produced by a non-Palestine, i.e., by a European, a Westerner.[14] Sol Worth pursued similar conclusions in his collaboration with Ted Adair to give cameras to the Navaho. Their goal was to facilitate film documentation of a non-

Western society that might be less biased by Western cultural assumptions than films by outside anthropologists.[15] Worth and Adair's project, of course, overlooked both the ideological assumptions built into the camera as apparatus and the eighty years of extensive Western cultural collaboration to develop cinematic codes to articulate such documents.

On the other hand, Miéville and Godard redirect our attention to the location of the Imaginary in the West, as mass produced and consumed within the totalized information economy represented by television. Consequently, in *Içi et ailleurs*, we cut back and forth continuously from images of the Palestinian conflict to images of a French working-class family watching television. The doubleness or dilemma might be formulated something like this: Westerners cannot *not* think of the struggles of non-Western societies; to simply not think would be fundamentally irresponsible. However, any such thinking unavoidably engages the operations of the Western Imaginary and must be addressed directly as such. Barthes's text does this, or perhaps implies this, by its playful thinking through of Japan in terms of desire and the Imaginary. However, if we are to recognize and build on this problematic, we must do more than simply allow the differential construction of Japan in *Empire of Signs* to remain a closed text, which would indeed open its formulations to a romanticized recuperation. We must instead continually rewrite *Empire of Signs* as a text open at every point to further exchange and make explicit in this work of writing the dilemma or doubleness implicit within Barthes. The doubleness here implies Lacan's distinction between other and Other (*objet petit a* or *autre* vs. *Autre* or *grand Autre*), or between the object of desire and the operations of the unconscious which Lacan identifies with language and the letter.[16] Barthes's inscription of Japan is open to both a recuperation within Orientalist fantasy and a repositioning of the exotic other into the framework of language and writing that constructs relationships between self and other.

A second voicing of the material, within an intertextual configuration of contemporary cross-cultural methodologies, might be the historian's critique of Noël Burch's book, *To the Distant Observer*.[17] This would position an empirical analysis against textual and ideological methodologies. Burch more than anyone has taken seriously the differential conceptualization of Japanese formal signification and inherent ideology proposed by Barthes. Briefly, Burch first argues that the formal elements of traditional Japanese aesthetics, as reinterpreted by Barthes in terms of decentered space and textuality, were adapted to film during the 1930s, long before the popularity of Japanese film in the West during the 1950s after *Rashomon* won at Venice. More significantly, he then argues that the resulting formal practices articulate the ideological values of a nonhumanist society, a parallel oriented by Althusser's rereading of Marx in terms of ideological representations. Burch unfortunately blurs together "prebourgeois" presentational practices, Brechtian modernnsm, and proletarian mass culture, as if the three were interchangeable through their opposition to the capitalist hegemony of the West.

In one sense, this sliding over of Japanese traditional aesthetics such as *wabi, sabi,* and negative space into the deconstructive domain of decentering, and of the consensus society of Japanese patriarchy into Althusserian Marxism, is open to the same critiques as that of Barthes by Rayns and Malcomson. It sees the East in terms of the West and imagines somehow that the East is always already there before us where our latest theoretical methodologies allow us to arrive. This tendency of Western argumentation is complicit with certain contemporary arguments in Japan, for example, that Japan has always already been postmodern and feminist, positions that represent too complex a *méconnaissance* to go into fully here, but which function in Japan to support a neoreactionary closure of Japan to Western influence and ideological change.[18]

One symptom of this sliding over process, the unconscious transference from East to West and vice versa, is the problem of totalitarian politics that Burch himself acknowledges is unresolved within his text,[19] namely the militarist dictatorship that contextually surrounded and supported development of a Japanese national style and that corresponds with disturbing precision to the unresolved issue of Stalinism in Althusser's own texts. This occurs despite Burch's lack of naivety about his project, which he carefully situates at the outset, not like Barthes in terms of the Imaginary, but by quoting Merleau-Ponty's assessment of the interest in reexamining non-Western societies:

The point is not to seek truth or salvation in the pre-scientific or the philosophically pre-conscious, nor to transfer whole segments of mythology into philosophy; in dealing with these variants of mankind who are so different from us, our aim should be to gain further insight into the theoretical and practical problems which confront our own institutions, to gain new awareness of the plane of existence in which they originated and which the long record of their achievements has made us forget. The "puerility" of the East has something to teach us, if only the narrowness of our adult ideas.[20]

Ironically, a book that seems to otherwise have little in common with Burch (i.e., does not share Burch's post-essentialist and rigorous textual analysis), that is, Joan Mellen's *The Waves at Genji's Door*,[21] has this in common with *To the Distant Observer*: that it seeks in the East a cultural correlative to Western ideological developments, in Mellen's case, feminism. Mellen sees in Japanese film, such as Mizoguchi's *Life of Oharu* (*Saikaku Ichidai Onna*, 1952), far more powerful treatments of the situation of contemporary women than she finds in commercial films in the West.

However, in this second, historicist, voicing of the material, I am thinking of a different kind of critique, namely that Burch gets his facts wrong. Like Barthes himself, Burch is not a specialist in Japanese studies. Barthes and Burch both visited Japan briefly (according to this critique) and based sweeping interpretations of cultural dynamics largely on the novelty value of first impressions. As a result, Burch sometimes describes both films and historical contexts in imaginary terms at variance with other research. For example, his description of *Souls on the Road* may misconceive its story, and his assertions about the role of modernist movements in Japan are open to question.[22] This kind of problem, that of inadequate understanding of Japanese films and contexts by Western observers, will continue to be corrected by the new generation of historians, and by the reinvention of Japanese film history through careful serious examination of the original materials by native speakers.

However, Orientalist and historicist critiques of Burch's text do not exhaust its arguments. Despite all of the problems with Burch's work, it remains the only book in English to seriously raise theoretical questions that derive from post-structuralist issues.[23] Again, as with *Empire of Signs*, an active rewriting is necessary that treats

To the Distant Observer as a text open at all points to further discourse, as a text that raises many serious questions without mobilizing all the resources necessary to fully answer, thereby generating unresolved intertextual momentum.

Yet if historians can critique Burch, the opposite is also true: Burch's text stands as an implicit open critique to all those historians who would pursue historical artifacts as self-defining objects already positioned within the hierarchical organization of linear time and centralized space dictated by humanist ideology. This hierarchy centers the West as ultimate frame of reference and value in order to organize the material, and it is this hierarchization that so frequently goes in the West by the name "history." Linear organization of the material can function as a logocentric projection of time based on the alphabet's prioritization of diachronic grammar over the synchronic display of visual representation, a division masked by the repression of the polychronic configurations potential in writing. Space becomes centralized insofar as Western Europe and the humanist values of Western civilization are represented as the center to which all history and all other cultures, including Japanese, can be claimed to aspire by predefinition. Nothing of course could be less true, and the rewriting of history toward a more complex and adequate intertextual simulacrum of cross-cultural dynamics will require the contemporary methodological issues and questions raised by Barthes and Burch as well as the ideological and empirical methods of Said, Mellen, and the new historians.

Herein lies a third voicing of this array of intertextual forces: an ideological critique of the writing of history. This voicing places ideological and textual analysis against the supposedly neutral methods of historical empiricism. Textual/ ideological questions are thereby seen as unavoidable because these problems are present in the language through which one writes. An already ideologized dialectic is embedded in the terms East/West (implicit in the categories of Orient or Far East), as if these already formed a magical polarity rather than a juxtaposition of different social and cultural constructs. Not only East/West, but other ideological polarities, such as man/wife and representation/object, saturate the English language. In writing, one might continue to use such terms, knowing they are incorrect, to produce a problematic intelligibility without constant neologisms. Similarly, terms such as "Gothic," "Cubist," and "Structural Film" continue to be current in art and film history, despite their known misrepresentations. In such writing, one expects acquaintanceship with the critique of these terms integral to their continued usage, much as we continue to say "the sun rises." (The derivation of "Orient" is from the Latin *oriens*, rising, rising sun, east, from *oriri*, to rise.) One knows differently, but the history of a knowledge system is preserved as a trace in the circulation of an established and familiar discursive figure.

At this point, doubleness becomes clearer as a methodological component of current cross-cultural work. It is not enough to simply open a discourse among these different texts, since discursive analysis already too easily implies the dialectical processes of the Western imagination. In placing different critical projects next to one another, such as Third World ideological critiques of the Western Orientalist imaginary, and Western post-structural interpretations of Eastern cultural dynamics, one cannot simply assume a potential new whole made of oppositional components. Necessary schisms remain an integral part of the process of analysis which can never be recuperated into a single, unproblematic, and unified whole. The point here is that there is not and cannot ever be a transcendent or idealist solution to the active interplay of separate cultural languages, knowledge systems, or representations. Any attempt at ultimate synthesis would be yet another imaginary position. If we as Westerners can only conceive of the Orient by speaking or writing through the Other of Western ideology, then it is also true that the West appears to the East in terms of its own Other.

Japan's view of the West through its Other is as valid, as problematic, and as unavoidable as the West's conception of Japan through its own Other. This does not reject a dialectical analysis where it indeed operates, frequently within rather than between cultures and most often and clearly in Western logocentric culture, but acknowledges an alternative and simultaneous cross-cultural operation. Doubleness here articulates a juxtaposition of difference that cannot be fully resolved into a dialectical opposition of same or other. Any adequate representation of cross-cultural dynamics will necessarily involve a split writing (to adapt a Lacanian term for the formalization of this practice) that recognizes the doubling of ideology and Otherness between such different cultural contexts as "East" and "West." Split writing as a practice works to foreground these disjunctions, in order to destabilize what Julianne Burton calls the myth of "a unitary, autonomous, ideologically transparent cultural practice," a fantasy that often undermines cross-cultural analysis.[24] The term also suggests both the methods of textual analysis and the operations of desire that animate a text, and invites a split reading to interact with double positioning in texts. Split reading/writing is unavoidable insofar as the textual dynamics of ideology and desire need to be problematized by the recognition of a double process in a cross-cultural context.

Kurosawa's *Ikiru* remains a classic text that demonstrates this process. This single text sustains an irreconcilable conflict between the so-called feudal pejorative view of Western individualism and the Western humanist discounting of traditional Japanese consensus society. The double positioning within the film is repressed only if one accepts unconditionally the diachronic progression of the film as valorization of truth, and the centrality of character development as conclusive. The text of the film undermines such conclusions by its numerous flashbacks and multiple points of view, but such features are often overlooked by Western critics in their search for a unified meaning.

As *Ikiru* is well known, let me recall only a few significant features of the film. In brief, after the central character Watanabe learns he has cancer, he goes through an extended crisis that ultimately results in his taking individual action against the bureaucracy to build a city park. The operative node of this conflict in the film can be understood as resting between *giri,* or the traditional Japanese concept of obligations, and "rights," a Western concept of individual human rights for which the traditional Japanese language has no word, and which in the West implies individual initiative, action, and accomplishment. Within the framework of *giri,* obligations to larger social groups "naturally" precede those of smaller social units. As a result, obligation to the Emperor was paramount, since the Emperor represented in his body or person the entirety of Japanese culture. After the Emperor, any position of social authority follows along the same principle, so that feudal lord or corporate/*zaibutsu* director become interchangeable, and the patriarch within the family is owed duty as the person responsible for that social group. Personal "rights," while not forbidden (as are personal pleasures in the traditional Western ethical mapping of the body), are simply last in priority. In other words, pleasure, including sexual pleasure (presumably restricted by patriarchy to exclusively male control), is forbidden not in itself, but only if it conflicts with a higher obligation. The feudal structure finds its organization through a bodily representative: the physical body of the Father signified through the phallus is transferred to the physical body of the Emperor as phallus of the nation,[25] and sexual pleasure is also determined by the imaginary "possession" of the phallus.

In *Ikiru*, Watanabe at first represents a broad and social *méconnaissance* of the significance of human rights, namely that individualist human rights can only be conceived as a reversal or otherness of tradition, an opposition to the established system of priorities. If human rights are now paramount, rather than obligation to the Emperor, then personal selfishness must be the rule. As a result, Watanabe begins his search for meaning through the Western inspired or modified establishments dedicated to personal indulgence, from cheap bars to dance halls and strip joints. After this period of self-indulgence, Watanabe becomes fascinated with the younger generation, which however only conceives of autonomy as survival and self-interest in a new world based on the violation of social norms. Watanabe's final stage of development is the transference of the concept of autonomy from its imaginary site in the younger generation to his own cancerous body. The body of tradition, terminally ill and no longer able to sustain power over the cultural domain of representations, is transformed or rewritten into the body or person of individual rights, the person who can make choices and initiate action. As is well known, the second half of the film is then a complex series of flashbacks intercutting between Watanabe's actions and their effects, consequences, and decipherment among his personal group of co-workers and immediate family.

It is important, when thinking of this film, not to allow the humanist ideology that clearly makes Watanabe the center and ideal of post-Occupation Japan to erase the doubleness implicit in the film: the Japanese critique of Western selfishness is coexistent and co-valid with the American critique of Japanese consensus society as authoritarian, paralyzed, and incapable of individual action. Occupation Japan and its aftermath remain interesting as a boundary area between feudal and modern (i.e., humanist) constructs, and can be read both ways, backwards and forwards in historical sequence, as a continuing critique of each by the other.

If we maintain this doubleness and read out from the film, this reading functions as a valuable critique of recent developments in our own society. Note that the entire feudal system operates through the body, and that corporations are similarly linked to the body in English through the cognate terms of "corporate" and "corporeal." The desire for a body or personal representative of collective social processes has been signified by the election of political figures from FDR to Reagan who are best known through their media images, and by a resanctification during the 1980s of the corporation as the ideal organization of the economy. The persons of corporate directors (Perot, Iococca, et al.) are then cast into heroic form by the media (a process inevitably dismissed as a "production device"). Similarly, sexual pleasure has been newly included as an acceptable "right" within the system of consumer society, primarily allocated through the phallocentric domain of male-oriented pornography and pornographically influenced fashion and narrative design. The hierarchization of sexual power articulated through pornography coincides with the renewal of so-called family values in the sense that the latter aspires to reestablish traditional patriarchy through the defeat of the ERA and other militantly antifeminist measures. All of these developments bypass what function as traditional values in the West: the humanist principles of democratic/rationalist argumentation, individual enterprise (what used to be known by the term "industry" with a small "i"), and romantic sexuality in the sense of individual choice.

In short, the West, it appears, is trying to recast itself in terms of an Empire, a process Umberto Eco refers to as neofeudalism in *Travels in Hyper Reality*.[26] As Eco points out, since we no longer live under feudal conditions, any such attempt to recast contemporary society as a feudal domain exists solely in the domain of the Imaginary, in the tacit analog of corporate centralism to a land-based warrior aristocracy (hence the frequent pop fantasy motif of juxtaposed swords and computers). In the West, this imaginary construct has become dominant through its appearance in the mass media. One of the unresolved questions of cross-cultural analysis is why the West should so wish to recast itself.

If doubleness is a useful term, then it refers not only to the unavoidability of the process by which each society observes difference by means of its own Other, but to the simultaneity of a double process. If this is a dialectic, then it is at least a double one, of two societies coexisting in their attempt to conceive of each other. Better, the interplay of cultures cannot so much be conceived as enclosed within a logocentric dialectic as open to undecidable conflict and exchange between two relatively autonomous intertextual arrays. Several consequences follow. First, of course, this situation demands an increasing sophistication in the analysis of otherness as a means by which difference has been inscribed (a related example here would be to consider King Vidor's 1952 film *Japanese War Bride* to sketch the limits of this approach). At the same time, the interplay of a double process of otherness and unconscious ideology demands recognition as such in terms of a split reading or writing to foreground the determining tropes at stake in the exchange. This strategy becomes an essential component of any attempt to formulate difference without resorting to an imaginary unifying discourse.

In this context, it is sometimes the most familiar things that most reward rereading. For example, it is perhaps the contemporary neofeudal impulses of the West that make Kurosawa's earlier film *No Regrets for Our Youth* continue to be interesting to Western feminists. In this film a humanist resistance to feudal power is the ideological means of telling the story of the thirties, of pre-Occupation Japan. Rather than seeing the Japanese *méconnaissance* of Western "rights," we see here instead the alienation, significant gestures, and limits of Japanese humanism under the unrestricted hegemony of militarist imperialism. The continuing appeal of this film in the West undoubtedly draws on a reading of the female lead character insofar as she suggests the position of women on the left in the United States after the defeat of the ERA under the Reagan administration. Here a split writing is generated by the juxtaposition of Western "reading formations" with the discursive formations of feudalism and humanism within the film.

Because doubleness as an approach foregrounds the necessary distorting process of the Imaginary or Other as a means by which difference can be conceived, what

Lacan calls *méconnaissance* becomes significant as a symptomatic text of where real difference lies. ("Lies" is precisely the right word here, with its double meaning in English of "falsifies" and "is situated," the condition of articulating difference through *méconnaissance*.) Lacan argues that psychoanalytic symptoms are not simply mistakes or inappropriate behavior but marks of a misconstrual of subject/object relationships, and that such misconstructions (*méconnaissance*) are unavoidably bound up with knowledge (*connaissance*).[27] A symptomatic reading looks for traces of such misconstrued relationships in the text as symptomatic of gaps or breaks in discourse. In this sense, what could be dismissed as individual and ephemeral idiosyncracy is sometimes the site where the most interesting and suggestive articulations of difference can be observed. I'm thinking now of those incidents or narratives, frequently anecdotal in form, that are too often dismissed as entertaining interludes in an analysis, but which might better be taken somewhat more seriously. For example, Seward writes of a mysterious sign in Occupation Japan that read "Dirty Water Punishment Place," which he only later realized was an attempt at literal translation of the Japanese for "Sewage Treatment Plant."[28] If we laugh when we read this anecdote, is not our laughter in part a symptom of the incompatibility of languages and the inability to directly translate from one to the other, and the inevitable shift or *différance* that emerges at these boundary sites? Here, the idiosyncratic translation, specific to this historical conjuncture, undermines the Occupation army's wish for a transparency of language and translation and foregrounds the shift of meaning that inevitably occurs in the move from one symbolic domain to another.

Another and more telling example can be found in John David Morley's *Pictures from the Water Trade*, a travel book about Japan that receives its title from an updated translation of *ukiyo-e*, the Japanese name for Edo era woodblock prints. Usually translated as "images of the floating world," i.e., representations of the pleasure quarters, the *ukiyo-e* have long functioned as a center of Western fascination with Japan. The premise of the book is that the contemporary "water trade," or leisure world of small neighborhood bars, perpetuates the intimacy and emotional "wetness" of an older Japan. Morley's is both a trivial and an interesting book, for many of the same reasons as Joan Mellen's novel about Japan, *Natural Tendencies*, an often unread parallel to her text on feminism and Japanese film.[29] In both Morley and Mellen's books, which cannot in any sense be taken seriously as academic research or cross-cultural analysis, we read the same story: that of a Westerner frustrated by a cross-cultural love affair in Japan. The type of this romance goes back to Lafcadio Hearn, who like the Portuguese writer Wenceslau de Moraes first traveled to Japan as a Western writer, married a Japanese native as a living representation of the exotic other, and then suffered disappointment and increasing isolation.[30]

Morley and Mellen's books are simultaneously naive and oddly touching precisely because they report on a lived-through *méconnaissance*, the attempt to sincerely enact in its fullest and most complete form (i.e., in its plentitude) the positioning of cultural difference through its psychoanalytic dimension, through the figuration of the symbolic Other as a sexual other. That cultural difference can somehow be engaged or resolved by a romance is based on unquestioned humanist assumptions about an imaginary universal emotional response. What is especially interesting about each of these texts is not just the failure of these romantic attempts, but the traumatic and disruptive effects of this failure on the protagonist. One is reminded of the psychiatric clinics in Japan designed to treat Westerners who are supposedly suffering neurotic consequences from an attempt to remain in Japan and live as a Japanese.[31] Not only do the romances fail through the un-acknowledged confusion of otherness and difference, but the failure functions in such a way as to destabilize the protagonist's attempt to maintain authority and centrality in his or her text. The unconscious of the text is unintentionally evoked, and that unconscious is in a sense represented through madness. The text itself opens into the domain of the symbolic Other, not the sexual otherness of romance reminiscent of the mirror stage.

These intimate, even embarrassingly personal texts, should not simply be dis-missed as what in fact they also are: idiosyncratic and narrow travelogues, isolated within their own specificity. Their specificity provides precisely the material neces-sary for an analysis that addresses rather than evades the interplay of desire and ideology between cultures. A symptomatic and deconstructive reading much more strongly highlights the (unavoidable) processes of *méconnaissance* involved with cross-cultural exchange, much more viscerally, effectively, and through the body than its cognitive formulations through academic analysis alone. This situation recalls Derrida's concept of literature, relatively aware of its own tropes, in contrast to logocentric philosophy, which struggles to repress its determining metaphors. It is not literature here, but paratexts, documents surrounding the "serious" work of cross-cultural study and adjacent to it, that come into question.[32]

Similarly, to pursue a doubleness for the moment, a symptomatic reading of Kurosawa's *Something Like an Autobiography*[33] functions in much the same way: although by no means embarrassing or naive as are the cited Western texts, and in some ways self-conscious about its own procedures, Kurosawa's text unavoidably evokes the same kinds of discrepancies between intentional language and the unconscious of the text. In *Something Like an Autobiography*, we read a text not entirely dissimilar, however, unintentionally, to *Roland Barthes* by Roland Barthes: the representation of a single life by someone who does not exactly believe that a single life exists separable from the Other. We are reading an equivocal work of authorship by someone who does not believe in the authority of an author. Inter-estingly, we can see the same process at work in Eisenstein's autobiography as described by Jacques Aumont in *Montage Eisenstein*,[34] namely that all of what the Western reader would anticipate as important details are left out: no information on childhood traumas, interiorized memories, or subjectifying moments that draw us into character depth and recast the role of individual in history as a dramatic subject in Aristotelian terms. Instead, in Kurosawa (as in Eisenstein and Barthes) we read a sustained contemplation of shifting rhetorical tropes configured in relation to shifting historical circumstances and group process.

Again, idiosyncratic material, apparently superficial and limited to the circum-stances of a single case history, provides key material: this time, for understanding the cross-cultural role of the subject. The role of the subject does not remain constant, as imagined by a universal humanism, but shifts its formation in relation to culture and history. The kind of analysis pursued by Foucault, to locate the subject in the context of different discursive formations,[35] can be pursued cross-culturally by the examination of paratexts that surround and inform theoretical and artistic practices. The operation of desire within the text to formulate determining tropes can thus be clarified, not only in the work of internationally exhibited filmmakers like Kurosawa but in the work of cross-cultural film analysis. The work of Richie, Barthes, Burch, Mellen, and others on Japan is informed in part by the desire to constitute alternate signifying practices to those dominant in Western discourse, a desire usually masked by the stylistic illusion of a history that categorically precedes its analysis. The figuration of desire within analysis does not invalidate their work of interpretation, since desire and determining tropes are unavoidable in any text. Rather, their activity when recognized can help locate the parameters of discursive activity thereby constituted and clarify intertextual transactions among them and with Japan. Although the relation of Mellen's novel to her critical work on film is the sole example suggested here, an analysis of the writing of Japanese film history in terms of its discursive formations and determining tropes has yet to be written.

Idiosyncracy is not a value for its own sake, but is foregrounded here insofar as it functions as the *punctum*, to use Barthes's term from *Camera Lucida*, within the cross-cultural scene. Barthes distinguishes the *punctum* as that element of photography that destabilizes desire:

A Latin word exists to designate this wound, this prick, this mark made by a pointed instrument: the word suits me all the better in that it also refers to the notion of punctuation, and because the photographs I am speaking of are in effect punctuated, sometimes even speckled with these sensitive points; precisely, these marks, these wounds are so many points. . . . *punctum* is also: sting, speck, cut, little hole—and also a cast of the dice. A photographer's *punctum* is that accident which pricks me (but also bruises me, is poignant to me).[36]

The idiosyncratic is the illuminating or captivating detail where desire comes into play, where psychoanalytic configurations inform the text, and the unconscious of the text emerges. Culture ceases to appear as a one-dimensional system of binary oppositions, and approaches instead a libidinal economy, as Lyotard calls it,[37] a cross-cultural project informed by doubleness and idiosyncracy that articulates cultural dynamics as decentered, multiple, and indeterminate. Power, desire, and knowledge are inextricably interwoven in the intertextual fabric that constitutes social process. The result of such a project may risk subordination within the tropes of an unreflexive postmodern or poststructural analysis, but we should be wary of any moves in cross-cultural work, especially those projecting themselves as "new," which do not go so far even as this. The risk instead would be a lapse back to empiricist, logocentric, or humanist assumptions already irretrievably problematized by contemporary critical methodology.

To summarize, any cross-cultural project must be compound and reversible: no universal system or *grand récit* (to use Lyotard's term)[38] exists that transcends cultural difference, but no cultural specificity thereby escapes critical evaluation. Cross-cultural reading is always at least double, and articulates both cultural situations, that of the reader and that of the read, unavoidably and simultaneously. No absolute truth-value can ever inhere in any reading or metareading, but cultural difference can at times be most clear at idiosyncratic junctures that undermine and multiply the imaginary transcendence of unitary approaches.

As a last example, Sogo Ishii's black comedy, *The Crazy Family* (*Gyakufunsha Kazoku*, 1984), provokes an articulation of cross-cultural conflict and a figuration of difference by parodying the Japanese integration of Western values. Ishii's film reconstructs an Ozu-like family intimacy within a new American-style suburban house (called a two-by-four, after the familiar precut lumber used in its construction). This idiosyncratic combination of figures generates a Nietzschean explosion of incompatible trajectories. Open warfare breaks out among the three generations, the house is destroyed, and the family relocates to an empty space under a throughway overpass.

The disjunction of Western and traditional Japanese values in this film can be read as open to an exchange of tropes at multiple sites. When the father hysterically attacks his narcissistically Westernized son in a desperate attempt to enforce patriarchal family unity, he uses a gigantic power drill, displacing a trope of contemporary Western horror films (e.g., the oversized phallic technology attacks in *Texas Chainsaw Massacre* or *Body Double*, themselves highly self-conscious parodies) into Japanese middle-class domestic drama (or *shomin-geki*). The family itself is transposed both from Ozu's films and from such contemporary reworkings of the family as Morita's *The Family Game*, a film that Ishi and his cowriter Yoshinori Kobayashi dismissed as "timid,"[39] into a Westernized two-by-four undermined by termites. This decentralized displacement of tropes, in contrast to the categorical opposition of Western and Japanese formal systems characteristic of 1950s Japanese films, could be described as a mark of the film's postmodern condition. It also generates much of the comedy through inappropriate or absurd dislocation.

The dislocations are idiosyncratic, in the sense of being necessarily specific to this film, since no familiar arrangement of tropes would break apart the illusionary stability of repeating formulas. Each dislocation pivots on an intertextual *punctum*, where desire's investment in meaning is repositioned into a new context. Such idiosyncratic incidents can better articulate positional difference within a libidinal economy than a systematic accounting of cultural differences, insofar as a destabilization of fixed meaning thereby enters into the account being given. New meaning shuttles back and forth between at least two contexts, so that fertile *différends* spring idiosyncratically from a double writing. Doubleness and idiosyncrasy are linked processes which derive from the cross-cultural situation, but which also transform it into a site of new signifying practices.

NOTES

1. Jacques Derrida, *Dissemination*, trans. Barbara Johnson from *Dissemination* (Paris: Éditions du Seuil, 1972), (Chicago: University of Chicago Press, 1981), p. 4.

2. See, for example, Allan Casebier, "Turning Back the Clock in Japanese Cinema Studies: Kurosawa, Keiko McDonald, and Tadao Sato," *Quarterly Review of Film Studies* (Spring 1985): 166–69.
   Exceptions include the "Other Cinemas, Other Criticisms" issue of *Screen* 26, nos. 3–4 (May-August 1985), dedicated to problems of cross-cultural analysis.

3. See Julianne Burton, "Marginal Cinemas and Mainstream Critical Theory," *Screen* 26, nos 3–4, (May-August 1985): 2–21. Burton articulates both the problems with and the need for theorizing Third World cinema.

4. Derrida, *Glas: Que reste-t-il du savoir absolu?* (Paris: Éditions Denoël/Gonthier, 1981).

5. Jean-François Lyotard, *The Differend: Phrases in Dispute*, trans. Georges Van Den Abbeele from *Le Differend* (Paris: Les Éditions de Minuit, 1983), (Minneapolis: University of Minnesota Press, 1988), p. xi.

6. See also Homi K. Bhabha, "Of Mimicry and Man: The Ambivalence of Colonial Discourse," *October* no. 28 (Spring 1984): 125–33; "The Other Question—the Stereotype and Colonial Discourse" *Screen* 24, no. 6 (November-December 1983): 18–36; and "Sly Civility," *October* no. 34 (Fall 1985): 71–80. Bhabha argues that a "double articulation" ("Of Mimicry and Man," p. 126) is characteristic of colonial discourse, through which the miming of Western forms in a non-Western context simultaneously implies their disavowal. Bhabha's work is not unrelated to the concept of doubleness explored here, although Japan was never colonized and its relation to Western discourse is therefore different.

7. Roland Barthes, *Empire of Signs*, trans. Richard Howard from *L'Empire des signes* (Genéve: Editions d'Art Albert Skira S.A., 1970), (New York: Hill and Wang, 1982).

8. Edward W. Said, *Orientalism* (New York: Vintage, 1979).

9. Hiroshi Komatsu and Charles Musser, "Added Attraction: Benshi Search," *Wide Angle* vol. 9, no. 2, pp. 72–90. Kyoko Hirano, *Japanese Cinema and the American Occupation: 1945–1952* (Ann Arbor: University Microfilms, 1989). Peter High, *The Imperial Screen: A Social History of Japanese Film, 1897–1945*, unpublished ms. Larry Greenberg is currently translating Tadao Sato's forthcoming comprehensive history of Japanese film. Casebier, who cites McDonald and Sato as "turning back the clock" on theoretical developments, simultaneously acknowledges their invaluable contributions to problems of historical detail and accuracy.

10. Jane Gallop, *The Daughter's Seduction: Feminism and Psychoanalysis* (Ithaca: Cornell University Press, 1982). Gallop constructs imaginary theoretical encounters among such writers as Juliet Mitchell and Lacan, Michéle Montrelay, Ernest Jones, Luce Irigaray, Stephen Heath, the Marquis de Sade and Eugénie Lemoine-Luccioni.

11. Tony Rayns, "Nails that Stick Out: A New Independent Cinema in Japan," *Sight and Sound* 55, no. 2 (Spring 1986): 98–104; Scott L. Malcomson, "The Pure Land Beyond the Seas: Barthes, Burch and the Uses of Japan," *Screen* 26, nos. 3–4 (May-August 1985): 23–33.

12. Although the broad outlines of Orientalism and Japonisme are well known and summarized in encyclopedia entries, and Said has written the classic critique of the phenomenon, much of its specific history remains to be written. See, for example, Suzanne Esmein, "Une bibliothèque japonaise en France au milieu du XIXᵉ siècle: celle de Léon de Rosny," *Nouvelles de l'estampe* No. 85 (March 1986): 4–15.

13. Victor Burgin, *The End of Art Theory: Criticism and Postmodernity* (Houndsmills, Basington, Hampshire: MacMillan, 1986).

14. See Colin MacCabe, *Godard: Images, Sounds, Politics* (London: MacMillan, 1980).

15. Sol Worth and Adair, *Through Navaho Eyes: An Exploration in Film Communication and Anthropology* (Bloomington: Indiana University Press, 1972).

16. Jacques Lacan, *The Four Fundamental Concepts of Psycho-Analysis*, trans. Alan Sheridan from *Le Seminaire de Jacques Lacan, Livre XI, 'Les quatre concepts fondamentaux de la psychanalyse'*, ed. Jacques-Alain Miller (Paris: Éditions du Seuil, 1973), (New York: Norton, 1981).

17. Noël Burch, *To the Distant Observer: Form and Meaning in the Japanese Cinema* (Berkeley: University of California Press, 1979).

18. See Robert Crusz, "Black Cinemas, Film Theory and Dependent Knowledge," *Screen* 26, nos. 3–4 (May-August 1985): 152–56; and Stuart Hall, "Culture, the Media and the 'Ideological Effect,'" in *Mass Communication and Society* (London: Open University Press, 1977). Crusz and Hall warn against Western theoretical colonization of non-Western texts.

19. Burch, *To the Distant Observer*, p. 269.

20. Ibid, p. 9.

21. Joan Mellen, *The Waves at Genji's Door: Japan Through Its Cinema* (New York: Pantheon, 1976).

22. Burch, *To the Distant Observer*, pp. 100–07. Although I am not fluent in Japanese, according to my translator at the Tokyo Museum of Art the characters Burch identifies as "an aging country squire, his devil-may-care daughter and . . . the farmer's younger son" are a concierge, a housekeeper and a servant. See also James Peterson, "A War of Utter Rebellion: Kinugasa's *Page of Madness* and the Japanese Avant-Garde of the 1920's," *Journal of Film and Video*, forthcoming.

23. As part of his critique, Malcomson acknowledges Burch as "the only large-scale critical work on the

Japanese cinema to attempt to incorporate the theoretical innovations of the last twenty years, particularly those of French origin"; "The Pure Land," p. 23.

24. Burton, "Marginal Cinemas," p. 6.

25. Jack Seward, *Japanese in Action* (New York: Weatherhill, 1983), p. 72.

26. Umberto Eco, *Travels in Hyper Reality: Essays*, trans. William Weaver from the Italian (San Diego: Harcourt Brace Jovanovich, 1986).

27. Lacan, *The Four Fundamental Concepts*, p. 281.

28. Seward, *Japanese in Action*, p. 72.

29. John David Morley, *Pictures from the Water Trade: Adventures of a Westerner in Japan* (London: A. Deutsch, 1985); and Joan Mellen, *Natural Tendencies* (New York: Dial Press, 1981).

30. See Armando Martins Janeira, "Two Western Writers Who Lived Within Eastern Civilization," in *Japanese and Western Culture: A Comparative Study* (Rutland, Vermont: Charles E. Tuttle, 1970).

31. Robert Whymant, "Adapting to Life in Japan Has Costs for Westerners," *International Herald Tribune* (May 26, 1986), p. 5.

32. See Gregory L. Ulmer, *Applied Grammatology: Post(e)-Pedagogy from Jacques Derrida to Joseph Beuys* (Baltimore: Johns Hopkins University Press, 1985). Ulmer summarizes Derrida's thinking on literature and philosophy from his preference of Joyce over Husserl in his earliest book to his later practice of experimental writing in his own texts (e.g., pp. x–xi). Derrida addresses paratexts in *The Truth in Painting*, trans. Geoff Bennington and Ian McLeod from *La Verité peinture* (Paris: Flammarion, 1978), (Chicago: University of Chicago Press, 1987).

33. Akira Kurosawa, *Something Like an Autobiography*, trans. Audie E. Bock from *Gama no abura*, (New York: Vintage, 1983).

34. Jacques Aumont, *Montage Eisenstein*, trans. Lee Hildreth, Constance Penley, and Andrew Ross from *Montage Eisenstein* (Paris: Éditions Albatros, 1979), (Bloomington: Indiana University Press, 1987), pp. 1–5.

35. See, for example, Michel Foucault, *Discipline and Punish: The Birth of the Prison*, trans. Alan Sheridan from *Surveiller et punir: naissance de la prison* (Paris: Éditions Gallimard, 1975), (New York: Vintage, 1978).

36. Roland Barthes, *Camera Lucida: Reflections on Photography*, trans. Richard Howard from *La Chambre claire* (Éditions du Seuil, Paris, 1980), (New York: Hill and Wang, 1980), pp. 26–27.

37. Jean-François Lyotard, *Economie Libidinale* (Paris: Les Éditions de Minuit, 1974).

38. Lyotard, *The Postmodern Condition: A Report on Knowledge*, trans. by Geoff Bennington and Brian Massumi of *La Condition postmoderne: rapport sur le savoir* (Paris: Les Éditions de Minuit, 1979), (Minneapolis: University of Minnesota Press, 1984).

39. "*Gyakufunsha Kazoku (The Crazy Family)*." *Monthly Film Bulletin* 53, no. 625, (February 1986).

All-Owning Spectatorship

Trinh T. Minh-ha

. . . Of late, a friend's mother died. One day the family chanced to eat steamed sorghum, which was of a reddish color. A local pedant felt that while in mourning it was inappropriate to have a meal with the main course in so gay a color, so he took up this point with them, pointing out that red was always indicative of happy events, such as weddings. The friend replied: "Well, I suppose all those people eating white rice every day are doing so because they are in mourning!"[1]

Through classical Chinese humor, a position of indirection is assumed; a reaction to social conditions is woven in the fabric of an anecdote; a laughter momentarily releases demonstration from its demonstrative attribute. Some call it a "directorial trick," highly valued among feature-story makers. Others mumble "clumsy dramatic devices," "poor exposition," "muddy connectives," "lack of clear thought." Public opinion prefers immediate communication, for quantified exchange dominates in a world of reification. To have knowledge, more and more knowledge, often takes precedence over knowing. The creed constantly reads: if one has nothing, one is nothing.

A mother died. What holds the reader? What motivates the story and generates the action? A reddish color; a family's attempt; a local pedant; a "steamed" meal; people's white rice . . . in mourning. Red is the color of life. Its hue is that of blood, of the ruby, of the rose. And when the world sees red, white could become the international color of mourning. Conventionally a bridal color in many Western societies, white is indeed the funeral color in numerous African and Asian cultures. Passionate reds and pinks also populate the joyful decor of weddings, but they cut across the borderlines of both Western and Eastern cultural traditions. Even the bride is clad in red in some parts of the Eastern World. Whoever has taken a stroll in Chinatown on Chinese New Year's days, cannot have missed the sight of doorways vividly adorned with red scrolls and of streets thickly coated with the red refuse of firecrackers. Children are accordingly greeted with red envelopes, with lucky money inside, and words of Luck, Prosperity, and Happiness on the outside. The return of spring is celebrated as a renewal of life, growth, and emancipation—supposedly for women for example, who after days of intense preparation, can enjoy five days of idleness when, in order to preserve good luck, they are spared the drudgery of cooking, washing, and sweeping (activities which, at such time,

TRINH T. MINH-HA, *is a filmmaker, writer, and composer. Her works include the films* Reassemblage *(1982),* Naked Spaces—Living is Round *(1985), and* Surname Viet Given Name Nam *(1989); and the books* En minuscules *(Le Meridien Editeur, Paris, 1987) and* Woman, Native, Other *(Indiana University Press, 1989). She presently teaches as Associate Professor of Cinema at San Francisco State University.*

metaphorically mean throwing away the happy fortune). At once an unlimited and profoundly subjective color, red can physio- or psycho-logically close in as well as open up. It points to both a person's boundless inner voyage, and the indeterminate outer burning of the worlds of war. Through centuries, it remains the badge of revolution.

Here is where the earth becomes blue like an orange.[2] To say red, to show red, is already to open up vistas of disagreement. Not only because red conveys different meanings in different contexts, but also because red comes in many hues, saturations and brightnesses, and no two reds are alike. In addition to the varying symbols implied, there is the unavoidable plurality of language. And, since no history can exhaust the meaning of red, such plurality is not a mere matter of relativist approach to the evershifting mores of the individual moment and of cultural diversification; it is inherent to the process of producing meaning; it is a way of life. The symbol of red lies not simply in the image, but in the radical plurality of meanings. Taking literalness for naturalness seems, indeed, to be as normal as claiming the sun is white and not red. Thus, should the need for banal concrete examples arise, one could say, in one's daily existence, never has one experienced society as objective and fully constituted in its order; rather, only as incessantly recomposed of diverging forces wherein the war of interpretations reigns.

Seeing red is a matter of reading. And reading is properly symbolic. In a guide listing the elements of screenwriting, a voice of authority dutifully calls attention to cultural differences and the many ensuing contradictory behaviors of characters in relation to an event; but it further warns: "If ten viewers can walk away from a film with ten different interpretations, maybe the film was about nothing specific. Perhaps, they were looking at the proverbial emperor's new clothes. The marks of the artsy-craftsy film are withholding basic exposition and leaving the viewer confused. The illusion of profundity is not the same as being profound."[3] True, in a world where the will to say prevails (a "good" work is invariably believed to be a work "that *has* something to say"), the skill at excluding gaps and cracks which reveal language in its nakedness—its very void—can always be measured, and the criteria for good and bad will always exert its power. The emperor's new clothes are only invoked because the emperor is an emperor. But what if profundity neither makes sense nor constitutes a non-sense? Where, for example, does profundity stand in: "A, black; E, white; I, red"?[4]

More likely to persist in bordering on both profundity and absurdity, the work of saying in unsaying, or of unsaying in saying again what is already said and unsaid, seems always uneasily and provocatively fragile. Playing between "absurdities," anecdotes, and decisive analysis, or between non-sense and critical languages, it often runs the risk of being mistaken immediately for the-sky-is-blue-the-grass-is-green type of work, and can be both condemned and praised within that very reading. It is easy to commit an outrage on those (men) who fulminate against what they call "those school*boyish* evidences" (referring here to statements in a film uttered by women's voices), when the work succeeds to lure them into a spectacle that shows neither spectacular beings nor sensational actions; offers neither a personal nor a professional point of view; provides no encased knowledge to the acquisitive mind; and has no single story to tell nor any central message to spread, except the unconcealed one(s) about the spectators themselves as related to each specific context.

The inability to think symbolically or to apprehend language in its very symbolic nature is commonly validated as an attribute of "realistic," clear, and accomplished thinking. The cards are readily shifted so as to turn a limit, if not an impoverishment of dominant thinking into a virtue, a legitimate stance in mass communication, therefore a tool for political demagogy to appeal to widely naturalized prejudices. Since clarity is always ideological, and reality always adaptive, such a demand for clear communication often proves to be nothing else but an intolerance for any language other than the one approved by the dominant ideology. At times obscured and other times blatant, this inability and unwillingness to deal with the unfamiliar, or with a language different from one's own, is, in fact, a trait that intimately belongs to the man of coercive power. It is a reputable form of colonial discrimination, one in which difference can only be admitted once it is appropriated, that is, when it operates within the Master's sphere of having. Activities that aim at producing a different hearing and a renewed viewing are undifferentiated from obscurantism and hastily dismissed as sheer incompetency or deficiency. They are often accused of being incoherent, inarticulate, amateurish ("it looks like my *mother's* first film," says a young to-be-professional male), or, when the initiating source of these activities happens to be both female and "articulate," of "intellectualism"—the unvarying target of attack of those for whom thinking (which involves reflection and reexamination) and moreover thinking differently within differences, remains a male ability and, justifiably, an unwarranted threat.

Figure 1. Reassemblage.

As the proverbial line goes. He only hears (sees) what He wants to hear (see), and certainly, there are none so deaf (blind) as those who don't want to hear (see).

"All the prejudice against intellectuals originates from the narrow-mindedness of small producers," wrote the *Beijing Review* not long ago, to rectify the "Left" mistakes perpetuated from the time of the Cultural Revolution.[5] The moment she opens her mouth, she is immediately asked to show her identification number and to tell the (reluctant) listener in whose name she is speaking. ("Is this a semiological approach?" "Who taught you?" Whose work do you like?" "What I find badly missing in your talk are the models! Where do we go without models?" "If it is a deliberate attempt at breaking *the rules*, then I certainly applaud you, but I doubt it is consciously done, and if it is *just a subjective approach*, then I don't see where it leads us . . .") If she relies on names, she finds herself walking in line both with "the penis-envy" women, and "the colored-skin-white-mask" oppressed who blindly praise their oppressor's deeds. If she distrusts names and names no master, she will, whether she likes it or not, be given one or several depending on the donor's whims ("The film reminds me of Kubelka's *Unsere Afrikareise* and of Chris Marker's *Sans Soleil*"; "How different are these films from Godard's?"); otherwise, she is bound to face fiery charges of circulating "schoolboyish evidences." This type of charge repeats itself endlessly in varying faces. Knowledge is no knowledge until it bears the seal of the Master's approval ("She doesn't really know what she does"). Without the Name, the produce is valueless in a society of acquisition. (Thus, after having, for example, taken over the floor during the entire length of a film debate session, where angry reactions were continuously thrown out at a woman film-maker, a number of men approached her individually afterwards to intimate: "All that is very *cute* . . . and I *commend* you for your effort, but you can't *have* an answer for every question!")

She is both inarticulate and too articulate. *Although one can speak of intellectuals, one cannot speak of non-intellectuals, because [they] do not exist. There is no human activity from which every form of intellectual participation can be excluded* (Antonio Gramsci).[6] Standardization and sameness in variations is the unacknowledged agenda of media suppliers and consumers who, under the banner of "accessibility," work at levelling out differences to defend their property, whether this property takes the form of mercantile monopoly or of political tenure. While the craving for *accession* to power seems to underlie every intolerance for alternatives that may expose the totalizing character of their discourses (whether rightist or leftist), the goal is to render power sufficiently invisible so as to control more efficaciously the widest number down to the smallest details of existence. ("Self-help" and "Do-it-yourself" systems are an example.) The literal mind has to dominate if accessibility were to be equated with efficacity. Literal and linear readings are thus not simply favored; they are championed and validated as the only ones "accessible" to the wide number, in all media work, whether documentary or narrative. (Even Francis Coppola who is "the best of what *We have* in America" is blamed for emphasizing the visuals at the cost of a good story line.) Mass production, as Gandhi defined it, is production by the fewest possible number. The needs (for orderly literal thinking) created by the few and voiced back in chorus by the many are normalized to the extent that not only consumers come to internalize the suppliers' exploitative rationale, but the latter more often than not become the victims of their own practices. "The greatest error I've committed in my career is to have once made a film for people who think," says a respected Hollywood director (not to name any name); "it featured in all the festivals, but never made it at the box office. . . . Don't forget that people in the media are all very smart and creative, but the audience is invariably simple-minded."

With such a rationale, the hackneyed question of elitism arises again, albeit reversed and slightly displaced: who appears more elitist here? The institutional producer who caters to the needs of the "masses" while down- and de-grading their mentality in the interest of mercantilism (the Master's sphere of having)? Or the "independent" producer who disturbs while soliciting the audience participation in rethinking the conditions of this "society of the spectacle," and therefore neither pleases the large number nor expects to make it at the box office? The biased question should probably remain without answer after all, for in a situation where the suppliers are victims of their own supplies, no clear-cut division operates between makers and consumers. Only the *humanism of the commodity* reigns, and the vicious circle continuously reactivated provides no response to inquiries such as: "Is it the media which induce fascination in the masses, or is it the masses which divert the media into spectacle?"[7] The media's message may condemn war, violence, and bloodshed, for example, but its language fundamentally operates as a form of fascination with war; and war scenes persist in dominating the spectacle. (The only way to represent war, or to speak about it in the language of commodified humanism, is to show war scenes; any form of indirection and of non-literalness in approaching the subject of war is immediately viewed as a form of absence of war). Thus, under the regime of commodities, even the distinction between institutionalized and independent (or mainstream and alternative) producers becomes problematic; and, within the realm of independent filmmaking there are nuances to bring out, there are varied ramifications, and there are crucial differences.

If Hollywood films are consistently condemned for their capitalist enterprise and "apolitical" commitment to film as an industry; the "political" films (or "issue films" as Hollywood members call them) are looked down upon by mainstream feature producers as representative of the unimaginative mediocres' domain: "Don't apply the criteria of today's politics in feature films; otherwise they will all look like PBS products, which are boring as hell!" Whether political, educational, or cultural (if one can momentarily accept these conventional categories), rational linear-literal communication has been the vehicle of quantified exchange. The imperative to produce meaning according to established rationales presents itself repeatedly in the form of moralizing information: every film made should inform the masses, raise their cultural level, and give objective, scientific foundation to all explanations on society. *The revolutionary viewpoint of a movement which thinks it can dominate current history by means of scientific knowledge remains bourgeois* (Guy Debord).[8] Here, almost never is there any question of challenging rational communication with its normalized filmic codes and prevailing objectivist, deterministic-scientific discourse; only a relentless unfolding of pros and cons, and of "facts" delivered with a *sense of urgency*, which present themselves as liberal but imperative; neutral and value-free; objective or universal.

Yesterday's anti-colonialists are trying to humanize today's generalized colonialism. They become its watchdogs in the cleverest way: by barking at all the after-effects of past inhumanity (Raoul Vaneigem).[9]

Figure 2. Naked Spaces.

Red is the color of life. Nearly all cultures attribute a greater potency to red, but red can never be assigned a unitary character. Giving the physiological impression of "advancing" toward the viewer rather than receding, it is analyzed as having "a great wealth of modulations because it can be widely varied between cold and warm, dull and clear, light and dark, without destroying its character of redness. From demonic, sinister red-orange on black to sweet angelic pink, red can express all intermediate degrees between the infernal and the sublime."[10] Thus, whether red radiates luminous warmth or not depends on its contextual placement in relation to other colors. On white it looks dark, while on black it glows; with yellow, it can be intensified to fiery strength. In the costuming and make-up of Vietnamese opera, red symbolizes anger; black, boldness; and white, treachery. In classical Chinese symbolics, red characterizes Summer and the south; black, Winter and the north, while green, the color of virtue and goodness represents Spring and the east; and white, the color of war and penalty, stands for Fall and the west. The color of life and of revolution may thus remain a transnational sign of warmth and anger, but whether or not it is associated with war, violence and bloodshed—as it is unfailingly in the modern concept of revolution—depends largely on one's praxis of revolution. To think that red is red, no matter whether the red is that of blood or that of a rose, is to forget that there is no red without non-red elements, and no single essential red among reds.

If, in the opening Chinese anecdote, red humoristically incurs the risk of being fixed as a sign "always indicative of happy events" by "a local pedant," in Dogon (Mali) cosmology, red is (with black and white), one of the three fundamental colors whose complex symbolism exceeds all linear interpretations and remains inexhaustible. A sign opening constantly onto other signs, it is read in practice with all its signifying subtlety and density. The Dogon myth of the red sorghum tells us, for example, that its grains grew at the time when the pond had become impure, its water having served to wash the corpse of the ancestor Dyongou Serou—the first human dead, also called the "great mask." The impurity of death had tainted the pond, and the color red of the sorghum is a manifestation of this contamination. Red is also the glare of the sun. The latter is associated with putrefaction and death (it rots Dyongou Serou's corpse), although it remains absolutely necessary to agriculture and plants; in other words, to the growth of life.[11] The sun, being essentially feminine in Dogon mythology, the ambivalent character of the notion of femininity is here asserted as in many other instances of the culture's symbolics.

Red as the Sun is both beneficial and maleficial. Women, who are the bearers and givers of life, are also the cyclical producers of "impurity." Dogon societies abound with rituals in which the "bad blood"—menstruation, the blood shed at childbirth, the dark blood that clots—is distinguished from the bright healthy blood that flows in the body. The latter which is evoked when a wife is pregnant ("your body's blood is good"), is also identified with men's semen; it is said to represent the successful fecund sexual act, while the former results from a failure of the couple to reproduce. Yet the bright red flowers of the Kapok tree are associated with menstruation and death, and it is with its wood that masks are carved. Women are raised to fear "the mask with a red eye," for the masks are the men's domain and he who is angry is said to have "the red eye," while he whose anger gets violent has "the red heart." However, men are also referred to as "having their periods" when their blood runs during circumcision time or when they carve the masks and tint the fibers red. Their words are then "impure" and women are strictly forbidden to come near while they carry out these tasks. Paradoxically, to decorate the masks and to tint the fibers amount to nursing the sick; for, the white wood and fibers do not look healthy— just like the sick people—and to paint and tint them with vivid colors is to "heal" them.[12]

The reading of red as impurity and death would prove very appropriate the eating of red sorghum during mourning time in the Chinese anecdote. Should the friend of the dead mother remember this, he or she would have more than one witty answer to reply to the pedant. And depending on the context, this friend could also decide whether or not it is at all necessary to resort to another color for comparison . . . ("Remember" is here adequate, for even without knowledge of Dogon cosmology, the relation commonly drawn between red and blood evokes meanings that cut across cultural borderlines.) Rich in significations and symbols, red defies any literal elucidation. Not only do its values vary between one culture and another, but they also proliferate within each culture itself. The complexities are further multiplied when reading takes into consideration the question of gender. "Impurity" is the interval in which the impure subject is feared and alienated for her or his potential to pollute other clean(sed) and clear(ed) subjects. It is also the state in which gender division exerts its power. (Just as women are excluded from the tinting process of the masks, no Dogon man can witness a woman giving birth, nor can he come near her when she has her period. For, like many women from other parts of the world, Dogon women temporarily separate themselves from the community during menstruation, living in confinement—or rather, in differentness— in a dwelling built for that very purpose.)

Many of us working at bringing about change in our lives and in others' in contexts of oppression have looked upon red as a passionate sign of life and have relied on its decisive healing attributes. But as history goes, every time the sign of life is brandished, the sign of death also appears, the latter at times more compelling than the former. This does not mean that red can no longer stand for life, but that everywhere red is affirmed, it im-purifies itself, it necessarily renounces its idealized unitary character, and the war of meanings never ceases between reds and non-reds and among reds themselves. The reading of "bad blood" and "good blood" continues to engender savage controversies, for what is at stake in every battle of ideologies are territories and possessions. While in conservative milieus, the heat and anger surrounding the debates generate from the emblem of red itself ("What can you expect but hostilities? You are waving a red flag in front of the bull!"); in (pseudo-)progressist milieus they are more likely to have to do with sanctified territories and reified power. The dogmatic mind proceeds with ready-made formulas which it pounds hard into any ear it can catch. It validates itself through its own network of law-makers and recruited followers, and constantly seeks to institute itself as an ideological authority. Always ready to oppose obvious forms of power but fundamentally uncritical towards its own, it also works at eliminating all differences other than those pre-formulated; and when it speaks, it prescribes. It preaches revolution in the form of commands, in the steeped-in-convention language of linear rationality and clarity. At length, it never fails to speak *for* the masses, *on behalf of* the working class, or *in the name of* "the American people."

Nazism and facism were only possible insofar as there could exist within the masses a relatively large section which took on the responsibility for a number of state functions of repression, control, policing, etc. This, I believe, is a crucial characteristic of Nazism; that is, its deep penetration inside the masses and the fact that a part of the power was actually delegated to a specific fringe of the masses . . . You have to bear in mind the way power was delegated, distributed within the very heart of the population. . . . It wasn't simply the intensified central power of the military (Michel Foucault).[13]

Power is at once repulsive *and* intoxicating. Oppositional practices which thrive on binary thinking have always worked at preserving the old dichotomy of oppressor and oppressed, even though it has become more and more difficult today to establish a safe line between the government and the people, or the institution and the individual. When it is a question of desire and power, there are no possible short-cuts in dealing with the system of rationality that imprisons both the body politic and the people, and regulates their relationship. There are, in other words, no "innocent people," no subjects untouched in the play of power. Although repression cannot simply be denied, its always-duplicative-never-original sources cannot be merely pointed at from a safe articulatory position either. As it has been noted, in the society of the spectacle (where the idea of opposition and the representation of oppression are themselves commodified), "the commodity contemplates itself in a world it has created."[14]

A woman viewer:—By having the women re-enact the interviews, you have defeated your own purpose in the film!
The woman filmmaker:—What is my purpose? What do you think it is?
The viewer, irritated:—To show women's power, of course!

Every spectator mediates a text to his or her own reality. To repeat such a banality in this context is to remember that although everyone *knows* this, everytime an interpretation of a work implicitly presents itself as a mere (obvious or objective) decoding of the producer's message, there is an explicit reiteration of the fetishistic language of the spectacle, in other words, a blind denial of the mediating subjectivity of the spectator as reading subject and meaning maker-contributor. The same applies to producers who consider their works to be transparent descriptions or immediate experiences of Reality "as it is" ("This is *the* reality of the poor people"; "the reality of the nine-to-five working class is that they have no time to think about 'issues' in their lives"). Literal translations are particularly fond of "evident truths," and the more they take themselves for granted, the more readily they mouth truisms and view themselves as *the* ones and the only *right* ones. The self-permitting voice of authority is common in interpretation, yet every decoding implies choice and is interpellated by ideology, whether spoken or not. Reading as a creative responsibility is crucial to every attempt at thwarting "the humanism of commodity." Although important in any enterprise, it is pivotal in works that break off the habit of the Spectacle by asking questions aloud, by addressing the reality of representations and entering explicitly into dialogue with the viewer/reader. Each work has its own sets of constraints, its own limits and its own rules, and although "anything could be said" in relation to it, this "anything" should be rooted in the specific reality of the work itself. The interpreters' conventional role is disrupted since their function is not to tell "what the work is all about," but to complete and "co-produce" it by addressing their own language and representational subjectivity:

> The Text is a little like a score of this new kind: it solicits from the reader a practical collaboration. . . . The reduction of reading to consumption is obviously responsible for the "boredom" many feel in the presence of the modern ("unreadable") text, the avant-garde film or painting: to be bored means one cannot produce the text, play it, release it, *make it go*" (Roland Barthes). [15]

Ironically enough, both the all-too-familiar (PBS conventions according to Hollywood standards) and the un-familiar have been qualified as boring. In one case, the question is that of instituting representational habits and of providing alibis of ownership, while in the other, that of disturbing and dispossessing them of their evident attributes. Yet what links these two "boring" modes of production is precisely this lack: that of the Spectacular, the very power to appeal. In the first instance such lack usually derives from a normalized deficiency: the (involuntary, hence lesser) spectacle never admits to itself it is a spectacle; in the second instance, it results from an ambiguous rupture: the spectacle(-on-trial) fractures its own unicity by holding a mirror to itself as spectacle. Being the site where all the fragments are diversely collected, the viewer/reader remains, in this situation of rupture, intimately involved in the dialogue with the work. The latter's legibility and unity lies therefore as much in its origin as in its destination, which in this case cannot be righteously predetermined—otherwise Commodity and its vicious circle will triumphantly reappear on the scene. With such emphasis laid on the spectator's creative role and critical resistance to consumption, it is amazing (although not the least surprising) to hear the unfamiliar or different/autonomous work morally condemned in the name of a humanism which hypocritically demands respect for the viewers/readers, claiming, sure enough, to speak on their behalf and advocate their rights.

Among the many realms of occupied territories, one of particular relevance to the problems of reading here is the concept of the "political." Although much has already been said and done concerning the "apolitical" character of the narrow "political," it is still interesting to observe the endlessly varying ways the boundaries of "the political" are being obsessively guarded and reassigned to the exclusive realm of politics-by-politicians. Thus, despite the effectiveness and persistence of the women's movement in deconstructing the opposition between nature (female) and culture (male) or between the private (personal) and the public (political), despite the growing visibility of numerous Third-Worldist activities in decommodifying ethnicity, displacing thereby all divisions of Self and Other or of margin and center based on geographical arbitrations and racial essences, despite all these attacks on pre-defined territories, a "political" work continues unvaryingly for many to be one which opposes (hence remains particularly dependent upon) institutions and personalities from the body politic, and mechanically "barks at all the after-effects of past inhumanity"—in other words, which counteracts safely within the limits of pre-formulated, codified forms of resistance.

Particularly intriguing here are the kinds of questions and expectations repeatedly voiced whenever films made on and by members of the Third World are concerned. Generally speaking, there is an excessive tendency to focus on eco-

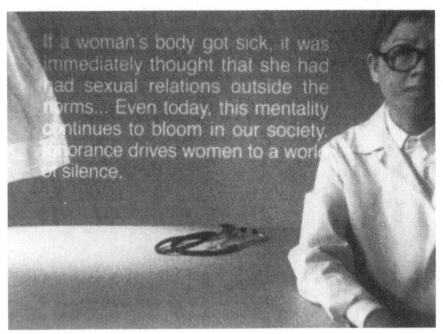

Figure 3.   Surname Viet Given Name Nam.

nomic matters in "underdeveloped" or "developing" contexts among members of overdeveloping nations. It is as if, by some tacit consent, "Third World" can/must only be defined in terms of hierarchical economic development in relation to "First World" achievements in this domain. And, it is as if the presence and the sight of imported Western products being "misused" in non-Western contexts remain highly compelling and recomforting to the Western viewer on imag-inary foreign land. The incorporation (if not emphasis) of recognizable signs of Westernization even in the most remote parts of Third World countryside is binding; for, exoticism can only be consumed when it is salvaged, that is reappropriated and translated into the Master's language of authenticity and otherness. A difference that *defies while not defying* is not exotic; it is not even recognized as difference; it is simply no language to the dominant's ear (only sheer charlatanism—a "mother's first [at-tempt]"; a something that infuriated the men asking: "What is it!?" "What can you *do* with such a film?"). Any film that fails to to display these signs of "planned poverty" in its images and to adopt the *diagnostic* language of economic-deterministic rationale, is immediately classified as "apolitical." The devices set up by the Master's liberals to correct his own mistakes thus become naturalized rules, and no matter what the context is, these rules exercise their universal power.

The political is hereby *not* this "permanent task inherent in all social existence" which, as Michel Foucault suggests, "cannot be reduced to the study of a series of institutions, not even to the study of all those institutions which would merit the name 'political'," but pertains to "the analysis, elaboration, and bringing into question of power relations and the 'agonism' between power relations and the intransitivity of freedom."[16] *The political becomes compulsively instead "the legislative, institutional, executive mirror of the social."*[17] In this exclusive realm of politics by politicians, the political is systematically de-politicized. The more "self-evident" the location of politics, the easier it is to claim knowledge, to gain control and to acquire territory. The progressive "First World" thus takes as much pride in its "Third World" underdeveloped as the church used to take pride in its poor. (As it has been astutely pointed out, the humanitarianism advocated through all the "feed the poor" images of Africa and the "do good" messages of the television missionaries may ease the consciences of the rich, but what they hide are precisely the ties between world hunger and imperialism.)[18] Not only must all films related to the Third World show the people's poverty, but whatever they put forth in their critical stance vis-a-vis oppression should not depart from the Master's image of progress, for it is only in terms of progress—more particularly acquisitive, quantified progress—that he conceives of "revolution" and transformation.

A woman viewer:—In dealing with socialist Vietnam, why don't you show what has been acquired through the Revolution?
The woman filmmaker:—The women in the film wouldn't have spoken as they did without the Revolution.
The viewer:—. . . True, but I mean real acquisitions, real attainments . . . something tangible! Do you understand me?

Poverty and class. Even the notion of class is commodified. Again, it is almost exclusively in the context of films on and by people of color that middle class viewers become suddenly over(t)ly concerned with the question of class—more as a classifying term, however, than as a way of rethinking production relations. Class, which is reduced to a fixed and categorized meaning in its common use among the viewers mentioned, has apparently never been their preoccupation in contexts other than the one that concern "their" poor. (For they do not seem to have any qualms going to the movies whose dominating attractions are the love stories of the Western petty bourgeoisie; nor are they disturbed every time they switch their television sets on, whose visual symbols and chatter are governed by the myths of the upwardly mobile and the tastes of the very affluent.)

[The] attachment to the new insures that television will be a vaguely leftist medium, no matter who its personnel might be. Insofar as it debunks traditions and institutions . . . television serves the purposes of that larger movement within which left and right (in America, at least) are rather like the two legs of locomotion: the movement of modernization. . . . Television is a parade of experts instructing the unenlightened about the weather, aspirins, toothpastes, the latest books or proposals for social reform, and the correct attitudes to have with respect to race, poverty, social conflict, and new moralities (Michael Novak).[19]

The mandatory concern for class in the exclusive context of films on and by Third World members *is in itself a class issue*. The complexity of the problem often goes unnoticed as the class bias many of us project onto others is often masked by the apparent righteousness of these "correct attitudes" popularized in relation to race and poverty. The tendency to identify Third World with mere economic poverty is always lurking below questions such as: "The film is beautiful. But some people look as if they have starched their clothes for the camera. Why do they dress so well?" (concerning a documentary shot in villages of Senegal); or else: "I am surprised to see how beautiful the women are. Here [in the U.S.], they would have been fashion models. You have obviously selected them!" Such tendency is further recognizable in the way the difference in dress codes is often ignored. While among progressist middle-class women it is important to signal publicly, through the very casual way one dresses, that one is downwardly mobile, the situation is rather the reverse in the working class. "Most black women don't dress like this [in slacks and shirt]," observes Julia Lesage, "nor do most trade union women, if they are gathering in public for a meeting. Many, if not most, women in the U.S. cherish a notion of dressing up in public or dressing up out of respect for other people. . . . [Blacks] do not have a legacy of pride in dressing down."[20] Nor do most Asians in the U.S. or elsewhere (including in post-Mao China); especially when it is a question of appearing on camera for the thousands of (respected) others, and of "saving face" for one's own family and community. Thus, in a film where both Asian middle-class and working-class women are featured, a woman viewer remarks for example: "All the women in the film are middle class. Can you talk about this?" The woman filmmaker: "Oh! . . . How do you see them all as middle class?" The viewer: "Aren't they?! . . . the way they dress! . . ." Whose middle class is it finally? In refusing to situate its own legacy in dress codes, hence to acknowledge the problem of class in dealing with class, middle-class spectatorship believes it can simply evacuate class content from its safe observer's post by reiterating the objectifying Look—the Spectacle's totalitarian monologue.

So gay a color . . . in mourning. Not too long ago (1986), in an issue of the weekly *Figaro-Magazine*, one read in large bold letters the following title of a feature article by a famed French reporter who is said to have spent twenty years covering the war in Vietnam: " *'Mon' Viet-nam d'aujourd'hui, c'est la désolation*" (" 'My' Vietnam Today Is a Desolation"). Vietnam: a sacred territory and an ideal subject for generalized colonialism. A widely unknown people, but an exceptionally famed name; all the more unforgettable as every attempt at appropriating it through the re-justification of motives and goals of the war only succeeds in setting into relief the political vacuum of a system, whose desperate desire to re-deploy its power and to correct its world image in a situation of bitter "defeat" unfolds itself through the supremacy of war as mass spectacle. Every spectator owns a Vietnam of his or her own. If France only remembers its ex-colony to expatiate forever on it being the model of a successful revolutionary struggle against the largest world power, America is particularly eager to recall its predecessor's defeat at Dien Bien Phu and Vietnam's ensuing independence from French colonialism, whose desperate effort to cling to their Asian possession had led to the American involvement in the war. It is by denouncing past colonialism that today's generalized colonialism presents itself as more humane. North and South Vietnam are alternately assigned the roles of the Good and the Bad according to the time, to suit the ideological whims of the two foreign powers. And the latter carefully take turns in siding with the "winner," for it is always historically more uplifting to endorse the "enemy" who wins than the "friend" who loses.

Yes, we defeated the United States. But now we are plagued by problems. We do not have enough to eat. We are a poor, underdeveloped nation. . . . Waging a war is simple, but running a country is very difficult (Pham Van Dong).[21] For general Western spectatorship, Vietnam does not exist outside of the war. And she no longer exists since the war has ended, except as a name, an exemplary model of revolution, or a nostalgic cult object for those who, while admiring unconditionally the revolution, do not seem to take any genuine, sustained interest in the troubled reality of Vietnam in her social and cultural autonomy. The more Vietnam is mystified, the more invisible she becomes. The longer Vietnam is extolled as the unequal model of the struggle against Imperialism, the more convenient it is for the rest of the world to close their eyes on the harrowing difficulties the nation, governed by a large post-revolutionary bureaucracy, continues to face in trying to cope with the challenge of recovery. (Even when the possessive pronoun "my" is liberalistically bracketed), whose Vietnam is the Vietnam depicted in Hollywood films as well as in the daily news and television series that offer "fresh action from Vietnam into our living rooms each evening" (Time-Life Books brochure on *Vietnam: A Television History*) and claim to deliver "the entire story of what really happened in Vietnam" in a few hours for VCR owners? Whose Vietnam is the one presented in *The Vietnam Experience* book series, "the definitive work on the Vietnam conflict . . . the whole explosive story . . . the whole astonishing truth. . . . More colorful than any novel, more comprehensive than any encyclopedia"? Whose conflict triumphantly features in "The TV war"? Whose experience finally does Time-Life Books' posters herald in its large, bold title-letters as being exclusively that of: "The Men, The Weapons, The Battles"?

Contrary to what has been affirmed by certain Vietnam experts, America's concept of its own "exceptionalism," which is said to have nurtured the roots of American intervention in the war, did not die on the shores of Vietnam. It is still well and alive even in its most negative aspects. Vietnam as spectacle remains passionately an owned territory. Presented through the mediation of the dominant world forces, she only exists within the latter's binarism; hence the inability to conceive of her outside (or rather, in the gaps and fissures, in the to-and-from movement across the boundaries of) the pro-communist/anti-communist opposition. Every effort at challenging such reductive paternal bilateralism and at producing a different viewing of Vietnam is immediately recuperated within the limit of the totalized discourse of red is red and white is white. Not every Vietnam anti-war demonstration effort was based on an advocacy of socialism, or on an elaborate questioning (instead of a mere moral condemning) of imperialism. Nor was it based on an extensive interrogation of the territorial and numerical principle of the war machine whereby the earth becomes an object. It is interesting to note the extent to which common reactions presented as oppositions to the government's stance often involuntarily meet the latter's ultimate objective in its foreign interventions, which is that of defending and promoting a specific lifestyle—the world of reification. Thus, despite the anti-war denotation of such a comment as: "It seems like we're always getting pulled in by other people's problems. We've got enough problems of our own to deal with," what is also connoted is a certain myopic view of America's "goodwill," which reduces the rest of the world to "beggars" whose misery does not concern us because *We have our own* beggars here at home.

While in Vietnam, Party officials readily acknowledge the severity of their economic crisis and even feel the urge recently to publicly declare that "only when we no longer refuse, out of fear, to admit our own failures and oversights, only when we can squarely face the truth, even if it is sad, only then can we learn how to win" (Secretary General Nguyen Van Linh, October 1988); while in Vietnam, women reject the heroic-fighter image the world retains of them, and vocally condemn the notion of heroism as being monstrously inhuman,[22] numerous foreign sympathizers continue to hold fast to an image of an exemplary model of revolutionary society and to deny the multifacet problems the regime has been facing. Thus, all reflections on socialist Vietnam which do not abide by a certain socialist orthodoxy, positively embrace the system, and postulate the validity of its social organization, are crudely distorted as they are forced into the mold of hegemonic worldview and its lifelong infatuation with binary classifications: pro-communist/anti-communist, left/right, good/bad, victory/failure. *"I am not a Marxist!" exclaimed Marx in despair of his disciples.*[23] In fact, it is imperative that socialist Vietnam remains "pure" and that is continues to be unconditionally praised, for, through past denunciations of "America's most controversial war," America can still prove that it is not entirely wrong, that "the Vietnam failure" should be attributed to a guilty government but not to "the American people." The West's friendliness and benevolence toward its Others often consists of granting itself the omnipotent rights to counteract its government and to choose, as circumstances dictate, when to endorse or when to detach itself from its institutions, while members from the Third World are required to stand by their kinsmen—government and people alike—and urged to show the official seal of approval "back home" wherever they go, in whatever enterprise they undertake.

The Commodity contemplates itself in a world it has created. And this world it has created is *boldly* that of "The Men, the Weapons, the Battles." To say that the spectacle is always masterly owned and that it aspires to genderlessness is to indulge again and again in redundancy. But repetition is at times necessary, for it has a function to fulfill, especially when it does not present itself as the mechanical recurrence of sameness, but rather, as the persistence of sameness in difference. If in Dogon rituals, men also "have their periods" and their days of "impurity," no such reversal seems to be tolerated in a male-centered context where the concept of gender is irremediably reduced to a question of sexual difference or of universal sex opposition. And since in such opposition, priority is always given to literal reading and to the validation of "evidences" (essences), rather than to the interrogation of representation, the tools of (gender) production are bound to remain the Master's (invisible) tools. (Thus, reacting to a film in which women's sufferings have been commented upon by numerous women viewers as being "very intense and depressive," a male viewer blurted out, after having uneasily tried to put forth a lengthy weasel-worded question he has embarked upon: ". . . The subject of the film is so partial . . . Don't you think it overshadows the rest of the issues? . . . I mean, how can one make a film on Vietnam, where there is so much sufferings [sic] and focus on women?" A number of women in the audience express their approval; others hiss.) While the male-is-norm world continues to be taken for granted as the objective, comprehensive societal world, the world of woman subjects (subjectivities) can only be viewed in terms of partiality, individuality, and incompleteness. The tendency is to *obscure* the issue of women's oppression or of women's autonomy in a relation of mutual exclusiveness rather than of interdependency. The impetus of the positivist project is first and foremost to supply answers, hence the need to level out all forms of oppression into one. *Not only has the question of women's liberation traditionally been bypassed by revolutionary organizations in the Third World (as it has in the West), but (again this applies to groups in the West) it has also become a target for hostility from the Left . . .* (Miranda Davies).[24]

In the society of the male-centered spectacle, gender will always be denied, even and especially when the spectacle exalts feminism (heroic workers who are also good mothers and good wives). For what the humanism of commodity markets is not two, three, but one, only One feminism. One package at a time in a policy of mutual exclusion. *To deny gender, first of all, is to deny the social relations of gender that constitute and validate the sexual oppression of women; and second, to deny gender is to remain "in ideology," an ideology which . . . is manifestly self-serving to the male-gendered subject* (Teresa de Lauretis).[25] The dogmatic, hence genderless mind has never been eager to ask why, for example, the bright red flowers of the Kapok tree are associated with menstruation and death in a context where, apparently, "bad blood" is identified with dark, coagulated blood? As mentioned earlier, "impurity" is the interval in which the impure subject is feared and alienated. It is the state in which the issue of gender prevails, for if red defies all literal, male-centered elucidation, it is because it intimately belongs to women's domain, in other words, to women's struggles. To say this is simply to recognize that the impure subject cannot but challenge hegemonic divisions and boundaries. Bound to other marginalized groups, women are often "impure" because their red necessarily exceeds totalized discourses. In a society where they remain constantly at odds on occupied territories, women can only situate their social spaces precariously in the interstices of diverse systems of ownership. Their elsewhere is never a pure elsewhere, but only a no-escape-elsewhere, an elsewhere-within-here that enters in at the same time as it breaks with the circle of omnispectatorship, in which women always incur the risk of remaining, endlessly, spectators, whether to an object, an event, an attribute, a duty, an adherence, a classification, or a social process. The challenge of modifying frontiers is also that of producing a situated, shifting and contingent difference in which the only constant is the emphasis on the irresistible to-and-fro movement across (sexual and political) boundaries: margins and centers, red and white. It has often been noted that in Chinese ink painting, there is a "lack of interest in natural color." One day, someone asked a painter why he painted his bamboos in red. When the painter replied "What color should they be?", the answer came: "Black of course."

NOTES

1. In Wit and Humor from Old Cathay, trans. J. Kowalis (Beijing: Panda Books, 1986), 63.
2. A sentence borrowed from Paul Elaurd's poem "La Terre est bleue" in Capitale de la douleur (1926, rpt, Paris: Gallimard, 1966), 153.
3. Irwin R. Blacker, The Elements of Screen-writing. A Guide for Film and Television Writing (New York: Collier Books, 1986), 48.
4. From Arthur Rimbaud's poem "Voyelles," in Rimbaud; Complete Works, trans. W. Fowlie (Chicago: University of Chicago Press, 1966), 121.
5. In China After Mao. A Collection of Eighty Topical Essays by the editors of Beijing Review (Beijing: Beijing Review, 1983), 115.
6. Antonio Gramsci. Selected Writings 1916–1935, ed. D. Forgacs (New York: Schocken Books, 1988), 321.
7. Jean Baudrillard, In the Shadow of the Silent Majority (New York: Semiotext(e), 1981), 105.
8. Guy Debord, Society of the Spectacle (1967 reprinted by Detroit: Black & Red, 1983), 82.
9. Raoul Vaneigem, The Revolution of Everyday Life, trans. D. Nicholson-Smith (London: Left Bank Books & Rebel Press, 1983), 23.
10. Johannes Itten, The Elements of Color, trans. E. Van Hagen (New York: Van Nostrand Reinhold, 1970), 86.
11. For more information, see Geneviève Calame-Griaule, Ethnologie et language. La Parole chez les Dogon (Paris: Institut d'ethnologie, 1987), 136:246.
12. Discussion of the symbolics of red among the Dogon is based on the above book by G. Calame Griaule.
13. In Foucault Live. Interviews 1966–84, trans. J. Johnston, ed. S. Lotringer (New York: Semiotext(e), 1989), 99–100.
14. G. Debord, 53.
15. Roland Barthes, The Rustle of Language, trans. R. Howard (New York: Hill & Wang, 1986), 63.
16. Michel Foucault, "The Subject and Power," in Art After Modernism. Rethinking Representation, ed. B. Wallis (New York: The New Museum of Contemporary Art and M.I.T. Press, 1984), 429–30.
17. Jean Baudrillard, The Silent Majority, 18.
18. See Julia Lesage, "Why Christian Television Is Good TV," The Independent, May 1987, 18.
19. Michael Novak, "Television Shapes the Soul," in Television: The Critical View, ed. H. Newcomb (New York: Oxford University Press, 1982), 343; 346.
20. Julia Lesage, "Christian Television," 15.
21. Quoted in Stanley Karnow, Vietnam. A History (New York: Penguin, 1983), 27–28.
22. See interviews with Thu Van and Anh in Mai Thu Van. Vietnam, un peuple, des voix (Paris: Editions Pierre Horay, 1982).
23. Quoted in Marxism and Art ed. Maynard Solomon (Detroit: Wayne State, 1979), 12.
24. Miranda Davies, ed., Third World Second Sex. Women's Struggles and National Liberation (London: Zed, 1983), iv.
25. Teresa de Lauretis, Technologies of Gender (Bloomington: Indiana University Press, 1987), 15.

Travelling Sounds:
Whose Centre,
Whose Periphery?

Iain Chambers

The discussion that follows is a part of a far wider debate on the relations between the apparent globalization of contemporary cultural languages and the evidence of micropowers and local histories revealed in the mutable constructions of identities in what Heidegger once defined as the `epoch of homelessness.' This essay forms part of a work, *Migrancy, Culture, Identity* (Routledge, 1993), which attempts to explore the question of migrancy. As both cultural history and metaphor, the theme of migrancy is deployed to reconsider the complexity of cultural powers exposed in the current decentering of the cultures and languages of the West.

Rock music in the 1980s and the 1990s is clearly the sound of an established, largely Anglo-American, hegemony. It not only occupies radio, television, clubs, restaurants, pubs and discotheques, but also accompanies our work, shopping and travel. It is the sound score of our time. But it is a hegemony that has simultaneously created the conditions for an international sonorial network that has subsequently encouraged a proliferation of margins, an emergence of other voices. In this context the sounds of the periphery, of the 'Third World', the so-called 'world music' phenomenon, can be considered not simply as a commercial ploy directed from the centre, but also as a cultural, economic and historical shift that disputes the very nature of the centre-periphery distinction. This is to suggest a break with the unilateral casuality, economism and political positivism that has tended to dominate the debate on cultural imperialism and neo-colonialism. It means to re-open that space, abandoning old indications and listening to new voices.

To write the story of 'World Music' is to face the same dilemma as that facing:

the Third World intellectual: such a person cannot afford politically to accept the 'truths' provided by colonial history, for this is a history written by oppressors from the First World; nor is there any longer an indigenous, native discourse and intellectual position, given the history and impact of colonialism on the

Iain Chambers teaches at the Istituto Universitario Orientale, Naples, Italy, and is the author of *Border Dialogues: Journeys in Postmodernity (1990).*

colonized, and given that the Third World is now a resistant and resisting effect or projection of the First World. The problem is how to speak a language of the colonizer which nevertheless represents the interests and positions of the colonized? If the subaltern can speak, what language is able to articulate, to speak or adequately represent the subaltern's position?[1]

For obvious reasons I won't attempt to write that history. What I will try to do is to suggest a cultural economy of music able to address an ethics of difference that interrogates this bipolarity and intimates how we might fruitfully move beyond such a dualism.

Youssou N'Dour and Ruichi Sakamoto playing together in New York; Cheb Khaled at the Place du Bastille in Paris; Les Têtes Brûlés in Naples: are these simple examples of the centre pillaging the periphery, bringing home exotic sounds from the edges of the empire? Are we merely passive witnesses to the structures of capital imposing its institutions and organization on new territories; the final triumph of the commodity as it takes over our ear? Or is there also something more subtle, more complex involved? The latter perspective would suggest the need to overcome the limits of simple bipolarisms, and think in terms of the extensive consequences of historical and cultural differences that, while clearly existing, are, at the same time, increasingly drawn into a common frame. This would suggest that the sounds of `world music' function not simply as a stereotypical `other' that confirms and closes the circle of ethnocentric identification — those exotic embellishments requested for refurbishing the rock soundtrack. They also offer a space for musical and cultural differences to emerge in such a manner that any obvious identification with the hegemonic order, or assumed monolithic market logic, is weakened and disrupted by the contingent contacts of musical and cultural dialogue.

Further, the very conditions of this contact, sustained by the simulaneous electronic reproduction of the same sound in multiple locations and contexts, disrupts the existing hierarchies running outwards from the centre towards the periphery, and scrambles the narrow historicism of pre-existing chronologies. I can take `North Africa' as a musical motif and, working backwards in time, play in successive order the African ethno-beat sounds of Dissidenten (Berlin) and Kunsertu (Sicily), an example of contemporary raï music sung by Chaba Fadela, a traditional piece for the Arab lute from the Maghreb, and conclude in a folk club in London's Soho in the late 1960s, where I first heard this possibility, with a guitar piece by Davey Graham. However, this is not necessarily a historical or autobiographical reconstruction. It is not simply a question of travelling back in time. For these sounds are also contemporary and co-terminous possibilities, moving to diverse tempos, overlapping in the contexts and contaminations permitted by the electronic media. We are talking here of a sort of sidereal or transversal movement in which liminal regions are put in contact. What it underlines is the increasingly unstable concept of `authenticity' in the world of musical and cultural nomadism.

The international medium of musical reproduction underlines 'a new epoch of global culture contact.'[2] Modern movement, whether through migration, the media or tourism, has dramatically transformed both musical production and publics, and intensified cultural contact. It is often argued that this inevitably leads to a flattening out of the globe, now reduced to a single economic and cultural order. Apart from the simplistic determinism of that argument, details on the ground betray the verdict.

In West Africa, in Senegal, internationally renowned Youssou N'Dour continues to release cassettes destined to circulate in bootleg form in the local markets of Senegal and Gambia, while simultaneously being distributed on Virgin CDs elsewhere in the world.[3] Different publics, different markets, different distribution, sometimes different mixes and sounds, these are the cultural signatures of difference. And, to echo Jacques Derrida, such differences represent both real distinctions and the impossibility of arresting the sense of such differences in any one of those sites. N'Dour's music both marks, and is marked by, difference and defers the possibility of an unequivocal sense.

In the Occident we have inherited an authoritative testimony that has always regarded such cultural fragmentation and mobility with horror. Intent on conserving the timeless sanctuary of the unique and singular expression of the work of art against the dispersive movements of industry, urbanization and capitalism, it has fought an endless rearguard action against modernity. In repudiating the discontinous tempos and cultures of the city, commerce and capital, this critical tradition has also sought radical alternatives in the assumed continuities of folk cultures, `authentic' habits and `genuine' communities. This nostalgia for rooted identities characterizes so much modern cultural theory and critical thought: from Romanticism to Raymond Williams. But this desire for a sense of belonging and community, accompanied by an antipathy for urban life, is also invariably shaped by the ethnic disposition of 'earth and blood'.[4] These days to go elsewhere to find that 'authenticity', now that local roots, histories and traditions in the West are apparently dispersed and destroyed, only perpetuates the mirror phase of that infantile drive: to get back to the beginnings, no longer our own, but that of an 'Other' who is now requested to carry the burden of representing our desire.[5] It is as though we could ignore the processes and mediations — imperialism, neo-colonialism, capitalism, the Western media — that has brought those alternatives into our world, and has simultaneously shaped and distributed them.

To query this particular critical drive is to contest the presumed destining of the West. It is to query a projection and protection — 'when the spiritual strength of the West fails...the joints of the world no longer hold', that ultimately links Marx's support for the 'progressive' effects of British imperialism in India to Heidegger's paean to the destiny of the German people.[6] And it links us in the West to the assumed destiny of the world that modern imperialism iterates not only in terms of territorial conquest and economic mastery, but in the very articulation and dissemination of knowledge. It is this imperial setting that `is the true defining horizon, and to some extent, the enabling condition of such otherwise abstract and groundless concepts like "otherness" and "difference".[7] Notice that Edward Said refers here to both a horizon and an 'enabling condition'. The presence of the West does not simply lead to a state of subjection involving the unilateral cancellation of subaltern identities and cultures, but also produces a *milieu* that provides the syntax in which differences represent an interruption, a questioning and an opening.[8] This suggests, as Said goes on to say, the 'idea of a collective as well as a plural destiny' in the epoch of post colonialism.[9] Here the 'Empire' not only 'writes back to the centre' (Salman Rushdie), but 'sounds off' as musics are played back to and through the metropolis in the very process of decentring the 'West'. This proposes, in the anthropologist James Clifford's words, 'a new marking of "the West" as a site of ongoing power *and* contestation, of centrality *and* dispersal'[10] Such a decentring, the subsequent break-up and deconstruction of the dualism of centre and periphery, and with that of the associated poles of 'falsity' and `authenticity', invariably takes us elsewhere. As a minimum, to 'see Others not as ontologically given but as historically constituted would be to erode the exclusive biases we so often ascribe to cultures, our own not least.'[11] It also takes us beyond an obvious opposition and expression based on a naive nationalism which, 'for all its obvious necessity, is also the enemy.'[12]Speaking of postcolonialism, Kwame Anthony Appiah writes: '...its *post–* , like that of postmodernism, is also a *post–* that challenges earlier legitimating narratives.'[13] Beyond the schema of economic imposition and cultural monopoly we need to begin to think in terms of contamination and hybridity in the circulation of cultures; a two-way, however unequal, trade, for which there is no 'authentic', untouched, non-contaminated 'Africa':

> ...there is clear sense in some postcolonial writing that the postulation of a unitary Africa over and against a monolithic West — the binarism of Self and Other — is the last of the shibboleths of the modernizers that we must learn to live without.[14]

This involves an inevitable weakening in the trope of 'authenticity'. The idea of the pure, uncontaminated 'other', as individual and as culture, has been crucial to the anti-capitalist critique and condemnation of the cultural economy of the West in the modern world. This perspective invoked its own surreptitious form of racism in the identification by the privileged Occidental observer of what should (a further ethnocentric desire and imperative) constitute the native's genuine culture and authenticity. The observed, the other, was once again spoken for and defined, and reproduced as a domesticated difference within the imperialist ordering of the world. The other had no voice, was not allowed to speak and define her or his own sense of being in the contemporary conditions of existence.

Now, to refuse the binarism that separated worlds, cultures and arts, and to choose to move in the traffic between worlds, caught in the sights, sounds and languages of hybridity, where there is neither the 'authentic' nor the 'false', does not mean that there are not real differences of experience, of culture, of history.[15] But to talk of differences, even radical and incommensurable ones, in economic and political terms, in their embodiment in ethnicity, gender and sexuality, is to talk, however, of an understanding of the making of identities in movement, under, and in, processes. To talk of 'authenticity' has invariably involved talking of tradition as an element of natural conservation and not as `element of freedom': as though peoples and individuals existed outside time and the languages of change.[16] It is to freeze them in the anthropological gaze, as though they do not experience movement, transformation, and the disruption that the anthropologist represents: the West.

We discover that there is no recovery of the unequivocal, 'no place for such absolutism of the pure and authentic.'[17] Perhaps we can draw inspiration from so-called Third World musicians and artists, forced to constantly construct their identities on the move between different worlds, and begin to entertain the idea of 'homelessness' and migrancy as the 'irrevocable condition of...world culture.'[18] It serves to underline a central distinction between music as the site of 'authenticity' and an associated closure of community and a complete 'identity', and music as a source of difference, where unicity and ethnocentricity is constantly contested and opened up.[19]

All this suggests that it is perhaps no longer useful to speak solely in terms of the clash between blocs of cultural power, between imperialist hegemony and subaltern movements, or to reduce critical judgement to the morality of threatened 'authenticities', co-option and sell-outs. It means, rather, to talk of a 'politics of transfigurations', of 'atonal ensembles', and an ethics of difference, in which common sounds, languages, syntaxes, materials and institutions are occupied and articulated in diverse directions.[20] If rock music is a global linguistic institution, a communicative practice, it stands in analogous relationship to other worldly languages, offering both a shared grammar and network, and a shifting historical-cultural syntax, contingent meanings and a contextual sense of identity. It is both held in common and differentiated. It is a material that is inhabited and marked in different ways; it is rewritten, becomes somebody else's space, somebody else's inscription. This is not to deny the real differences in power that are encountered, nor the defeats and dead-ends, nor the fact that not everyone finds a voice or a space here. But it is to insist on this opening.

The 'Third World' is changing rapidly in many different ways. It was always a portmanteau concept into which many radically different types of society and culture were crammed and, as the relations between the core and the periphery change and a new world system begins to emerge, it will open up yet new fields of difference. Cultures within the peripheries will change at different rates and in different directions. However, we can be sure that these changes will take place along the triple axes of migration, urbanization and cultural contact. The choice between an authentic nationalism and a homogenizing modernity will become more and more outmoded. Questions of cultural identity, both in the core and the peripheries, become more complex as we begin to understand that there is no single model of a hybrid or composite culture, but many different possibilities. One advantage of the linguistic paradigms — creole, vernacular, esperanto, etc. — is that it can provide us with a precise sense of the range of options available.[21] This brings me back to the hegemony of rock music, to the desert of homogeneity. After all Simon Frith informs us that rock is dead, and I tend to agree.[22] But if white, Anglo-American rock has now stumbled into Death Valley, and can only rehearse the aesthetics of its disappearance, for others its exhaustion may mark new beginnings. For if, as Jean Baudrillard insists, the desert is the place of the empty repetition of dead meanings and abandoned signs, it is also the site of infinity, of the endless unfolding of languages (Jabès), of that boundless space that signals an excess of meaning and calls for movement. An excess, as Emmanuel Lévinas argues, that permits others to exist, that permits others to exist apart and irreducible to ourselves. So the Occidental metaphor of emptiness and exhaustion — the desert — perhaps also holds the key to the irruption of differences, the temporary apprehension of the sublime, and that continual deferring and ambiguity of sense involved in the travelling of sound and peoples who come from elsewhere, but who are now moving across a landscape that we also recognise and inhabit: modernity or post-, advanced capitalism, the industries and networks of trans-national communications, the city, the end of the millennium.

A final footnote. In Gurinder Chadha's film *I'm British But...*there is a suggestive reworking of the centre-periphery question.[23] On a roof top in Southall, south London, a group of British Asian musicians are performing in the Bhangra style a song lamenting their Punjab homeland while down in the streets other Asians are observing and in some cases dancing to the sound. In this doubling of a scene from twenty years previously — the Beatles playing 'Get Back' on the roof top of the Apple offices — the Western stereotype is successfully mimicked and displaced into another sense of history, of identity, of centre.

NOTES

1. Elizabeth Grosz, `Judaism and Exile: The Ethics of Otherness', New Formations, n.12, Winter 1990, p.78.
2. Peter Wollen, `Tourism, Language and Art' New Formations, n.12, Winter 1990, p.43.
3. See Lucy Duran, `Key to N'Dour: roots of the Senegalese star', Popular Music, vol.8, n.3, October 1989.
4. Heidegger uses the phrase `earth and blood' in his notorious `The Self-Assertion of the German University: Address Delivered on the Solemn Assumption of the Rectorate of the University Freiburg', delivered in 1933. In the post-war aftermath, however, he was forced to think in terms of `homelessness'; see Martin Heidegger, `Letter on Humanism', in Basic Writings (New York: Harper & Row, 1977).
5. On contemporary black culture and the burden of representation, see Kobena Mercer, `Black Art and the Burden of Representation', Third Text, n.10, Spring 1990.
6. The quote on the `spiritual strength of the West' comes from Heidegger's 1933 rector's address, quoted in Arnold I. Davidson, `Symposium on Heidegger and Nazism', Critical Inquiry 15, Winter 1989, p.412.
7. Edward Said, `Representing the Colonized: Anthropology's Interlocutors', Critical Inquiry 15, Winter, 1989, p 217.
8. This idea of the milieu and its syntax comes Bhiku Parekh's `Britain and the Social Logic of Pluralism', quoted in Alan Durant, `From the Rushdie Controversy to Social Pluralism', New Formations, 12, Winter 1990, p.149.
9. Edward Said, op. cit. p.224.
10. James Clifford, `Notes on Travel and Theory', in Inscriptions 5, 1989, p.179.
11. Edward Said, op. cit., p.225.
12. ibid.
13. Kwame Anthony Appiah, `Is the Post- in Postmodernism the Post in Postcolonial?,' Critical Inquiry, 17, Winter 1991, p.353.
14. ibid., p.354.
15. The complexity and vitality of this traffic was graphically underlined for me in the Spring of 1990. At the Hayward Gallery in London there was `The Other Story', an exhibition of Asian, African and Caribbean artists in post-war Britain. While in Harlem at The Studio Museum there was the exhibition of nine contemporary African artists entitled `Changing Traditions'.
16. The idea of tradition as `an element of freedom' comes from Hans-Georg Gadamer, Truth and Method (New York: Crossroad, 1984), p.250.
17. David Morley and Kevin Robins, `No place like Heimat: image of home (land) in European culture', New Formations, n. 12, Winter 1990, p.20.
18. Richard Kearney, quoted in Morley and Robins, ibid., p.20.
19. Line Grenier, `From "Diversity" to "Difference"' New Formations, n.9, Winter 1989.
20. On the `politics of transfigurations', see Paul Gilroy, `It Ain't Where You're From, It's Where You're At...', Third Text, 13, Winter 1990/91; for `atonal ensembles', see Edward Said, `Figures, configurations, transfigurations', Race & Class, 32(1), 1990.
21. Peter Wollen, op.cit., p.57.
22. Simon Frith, Music for Pleasure (Cambridge: Polity Press, 1988)
23. Gurinder Chadha, I'm British But... (London: British Film Institute, 1988)

Ruin and The Other: Towards a Language Of Memory

Teshome H. Gabriel

As I am from Africa, where our heritage is one of story-tellers, it is appropriate for me to start by relating a story to you:

SHHHH!!

The story has to do with a female American cultural anthropologist who was studying the Beng culture in a rural West African village on the Ivory Coast. The Beng are a little known ethnic group who appear to understand best those things which are invisible. Every morning, the cultural anthropologist went out with them to study their work habits, their farming, their social organization and their cosmological systems. Her husband, who was an aspiring writer, would take his typewriter, pens, pencils and papers, and sit at a small clearing in the village pulling his beard, rubbing his chin, waiting for inspiration for his work. During the course of his work, he would continuously be distracted by people coming over to touch his hair, and whispering among themselves in groups gathered around him. He made his annoyance at such distractions known, until one day an elder visited him at the small clearing where he worked.

The elder asked the writer what he was doing. "Writing a story," the writer responded. The elder's immediate response was: "But you don't *write* stories, you *tell* stories." "In any case," the elder continued, "is this work inspired by the spirits?" A bit startled by the question the aspiring American writer said: "No." "Well," said the elder, "what is the story about, anyway?" The American responded: "It is about a man who lost his shadow." "Ahh," said the old man, "the spirits were responsible. They took the man's shadow away because he was a witch."[1]

Here, then, is a classic clash of two cultures: One, oral based, steeped in its own tradition and another, print culture, with its separate orientation. One day soon after,

TESHOME H. GABRIEL teaches film and television at UCLA. He is the author of *Third Cinema in the Third World: The Aesthetics of Liberation* and several essays on nomadic aesthetics, memory, and identity. This paper was first delivered in Nov. 1992 at a Seminar organized by the Center for Cultural Studies at Rice University.

the writer and his wife were invited to see a noted woman diviner along with the villagers. In a very quiet, solemn atmosphere, the woman diviner put down white powder, red cloth, some black pebbles and small statues, and started to mumble. Then she began to speak, healing people who were sick, revealing the causes of illness, who is bewitching whom, advising others on matters pertaining to the village, and discussing impeding crises which might develop if left unattended.

That night, around a campfire, the writer asked how the woman was able to do all that he had seen that day. An old woman explained that when she puts the white powder, red cloth, black pebbles and statuettes in front of her, they invited the spirits. Initially she mumbles until she is able to clear the voices of the spirits. Then, she is able to start speaking to them. "You see," the old lady explained, "we are people of oral tradition." The diviner listens to the voices of the spirits who tell her what to say. She is simply a transmitter of the voices, not an inventor of the voices. Startled, the American writer explained to the old woman that, "it sounds a bit like what a writer does. We hear voices too." "Yes," said his wife, suddenly excited, "voices try to tell him their stories. And that's what he writes down. When he gets on his typewriter, with his paper, pens and pencils laid all around, he too is waiting for voices — they are what he uses to draw the voices to him." "So, you too are like us," the old lady responded, "you also listen to voices."

The next day, the writer was back at the small clearing with his typewriter. This time, he was not being bothered by anyone, but noticed that many people were standing nearby looking at him. Now they were able to see the spirits. "Don't interrupt him," they exclaimed, "he is listening to voices. If he's interrupted, the spirits will leave and their stories will not be told. Shhhh!!"

I tell this simple story to highlight the point that in quite a few cases, it is such intangibles, such minutia of voices, which surge out from where silences dwell. It is here that a healthy cross-cultural understanding between peoples, races, cultures can occur. My hope in this paper is to make silences speak to reach a level of cognition. I attempt this partly because it is perhaps here where we may find the fabrics for a meaningful dialogue. Let me explain it in another way: in how waves work and how nodal points come about. When two competing musical waves come in contact they produce a new sound, and correspondingly, moments of silence. We know this in our own personal experience when we try to angle a speaker in our rooms to get maximum sound. We also suppose that at some location in the room there will be very little or no sound. It does not mean there is no sound at all but that sound is intelligible from that position. The nodal point where the space of silence is located is where we find interesting stories. I also believe that these points of silence have existed throughout histories and throughout cultures. I am referring here to things that one cannot comprehend, cannot see, and things that do not appear to exist but that we know they exist. Here is where the trick of the story-teller and the poet lies. The question then becomes, not whose voice but which voice do we listen to?

SPELLING TASTE

Let me give you another instance. This pertains to a problem of interracial understanding, where a simple word and its spelling created a difficulty in white-black communication. This example occurred in the media's reportage of the Los Angeles riots in late April and early May In the *Los Angeles Times*, there was a story about the burning and looting, noting how some of the stores in South Central Los Angeles had put up signs indicating black ownership, most of which did not get burned. In reporting the story, the writer pointed out that some of the signs spelled out "B-L-A-K OWNED." instead of B-L-A-C-K.

Although perhaps not intended by the writer, he touched upon a certain impression, based on racial codes, regarding the poor education of blacks, implying that those store owners didn't even know how to spell "black". Had he only asked anyone in the neighborhood, he would have understood that this was actually a code within the community: To differentiate between the two major black gangs, the "Crips" and the "Bloods," the spelling of the word "black" without the "c" ("c" stood for Crips) was in fact an indication of being in Blood turf, where Crips are unwelcome.

I suppose that if the journalist had asked why they posted that particular sign, he would have received an answer. But in failing to do that, he fell into a racial stereotype which he may have not intended. Of course, no one would volunteer to write or to call the *L.A. Times* to explain the situation, as the code is one which operated within the community, and thus *the Times* failure to understand it was not unexpected. Both institutions can be seen to have their cultural codes—the community a code which differentiates local power groups, the *Times* a code which differentiates and characterizes racial groups.

In a way, the reporter writes and reads for the specific "taste" of his readership - in doing so he is also reinforcing it. Ironically, we are all the losers in such failure of crosscultural communication; that is, the failure to communicate was our collective loss.

SCREENING THE WORD

Another instance, which appears minor but profound in its implications, was evidenced a few years ago at U.C.L.A. when we hosted an Australian film series, cosponsored by the Australian Film Commission.

I happened to have been one of the advisors and was shown the list of films and categories under which they were to be screened. One of the categories was "aboriginal films," coming under the title of "Savage Cinema." I was shocked and surprised at this kind of open bigotry. We subsequently called the Australian film commission about the offensive nature of this title. They responded that they too had been astonished, but that the word "savage" was used at the request of the aborigines themselves. Little did anyone know that the (ab)Origines were screening the word "savage" and reclaiming historical ruin, as a kind of privilege — as an emblem.
Let me try to clarify this concept of historical ruin as privilege by relating to you two more anecdotes. I need to do this to be able to discuss, in the second part of this presentation, the implication of a few of the concepts I have touched on.

FLICKERING BETWEEN FRAMES

A student of mine from New Zealand was doing a dissertation on Maori representation in the cinema a few years ago, selecting from among the most racist of Maori depictions to present to the Maoris for their reaction. He was able to find an excellent example from one of the earliest films depicting Maori society in the most racist of terms. He was gently advised by the people of the New Zealand film industry that his selection was unwise to show to the Maoris owing to its extreme stereotyping and misrepresentation.

Nevertheless, he went ahead and showed the film to the Maori community. To everyone's astonishment, the Maoris "loved" the film. They were excited to see their ancestors, their costumes, rituals, the traditional sites of ceremonies, etc. The film's racist overtones were simply discarded as an "excess" that they had no need for. Here, it seems, the Maoris disregarded what had been so visible to the white New Zealanders, focusing instead on those aspects that reinforced their cosmology. For them, the film was no more than a confirmation of what they already knew.

What we see here is that, though this film, like many others, purports to tell a history, to build a history — a fixed history, when a different reading is applied to it, it immediately falls into ruin. The film has no vital relationship to history, but rather to memory which, it seems, is always a ruin — scattered, buried and invisible. The experience of seeing the film becomes, therefore, a continuation and, indeed, an excavation, of the archeology of one's culture, of one's cultural memory.

IMPRINT IN THE SAND

A last example: Among native American Indians there is a custom where in Healing ceremonies an elaborate sand painting is done, with meticulous detail and a great deal of meditation invested in it. This elaborate sand painting is then erased when it is finished, and a healing ceremony proceeds. The painting is a living history in the form of prayer. In this instance, we are being reminded that History does not live in the object, but lives in the culture. That the object has to be destroyed in order to be remembered is part of that culture. The sand painting cannot be objectified and cannot be preserved, like the marble and bronze monuments of Western history. To live, it must be ruined; it must become a memory. The central idea here is that what has been erased, made invisible, ruined, is also history. Any attempt to restore it or preserve it is paradoxically an attempt to erase history.

LIVING AMONG THE RUINS

Indeed, do we not, in restoring ruins, always engage in the erasure of history, of our cultural memory? What I am proposing, then, is that we must learn to live in the midst of ruin not literally, of course, but figuratively — i.e., amidst invisible ruins.

To live amidst the invisible ruins of cultural memory does not mean that we ourselves are ruined or lost. Rather it is these ruins which preserve, indeed constitute, our identities. All too often, oppressed peoples have defined themselves strategically as ruined, their identities have been tampered with or lost. There is a large difference between living among ruins and being ruined oneself. To live among ruin is to live on the margins; it is not necessary to be marginal. There is a qualitative distinction between the marginality that is imposed and the marginality that one consciously chooses[2]. It is to live in, as Bell hooks says, "a space of radical openness," — a space that allows a sense of cultural identity, cultural memory, to be opened — not closed, preserved or fixed.

Indeed, ruins can be shared in a way that preservations can not. To restore a building, to preserve it, is to close it off, to make its walls and roots solid, to surround it with fences to protect it. We ask: protect it from what, from whom? Ruins, on the other hand, can be gotten into; they do not exclude, even though they may have been excluded, condemned and marginalized.

To live among ruins, then, is to exhibit a particular kind of identity, a particular kind of subjectivity — to recognize that we are various forms of subjectivities — that we never reach the "ends" of the subject, the end of our path: we are more like nomads. This subjectivity among the ruins and on the margins entails a sensitivity to the invisible, the ephemeral, to the spirits of one's past, to the ghosts of one's own memory. Was this not precisely the way in which the Beng defined their identity? Was it not the ghosts of their past that the Maoris saw flickering between the frames of a racist film? The sand paintings of the Native Americans, like all prayers, are ephemeral; they slip into ruin, into memory, but they do not cease to exist. They remain, hovering and invisible; and it is around just such ineffable memorials that the Native Americans define themselves.

There is, I believe, a lesson here for notions of Black and other minority identities. The struggles to define a black, or African-American, or Chicano identity (or others) have too often been seen as attempts to overcome a lack of identity, an identity as oppressed and victimized, by achieving a fixed identity: as though "the Black subject" were a bronze statue to be built and preserved, fenced off and defended against vandals and thieves. This is not simply a question of "essentialism" vs. "relativism" It is a question of a fixed, visible essence — the bronze statue — versus a more ephemeral — dare I say, more spiritual — essence — the sand painting, the spirits of the ancestors, cultural memory itself. It is these ephemeral ruins that we must learn to live among in order to define ourselves.

FLOATING SPACES/EPHEMERAL IMAGES

One way that people in the contemporary world talk about ruins is in terms of displacement. Nowadays, prior positions are increasingly regarded as empty structures, which can be occupied by floating subjectivities. We are thus dealing then with comprehensive and multiple spaces - spaces that are fragmented and overlapping, spaces that are always in flux. There is a global complexity that has never been the case before. There appear to be new dynamic forces shaping events that cross cultural boundaries. One such dynamic force is Television.

Television is helping to erase the formal division between the real and the imagined. This Television does to conceal the fact that it itself is made of ruins. Both in its news functions and as an institution, Television often seems to depend on disasters and ruins.

Recall that Rodney King in the first 1992 trial, was not called to the witness stand, that he did not appear on his own behalf? It was his personal ruin — his video stand-in and the hospital photographs of his bruised face, that appeared in his defense. The lack of King's body in the trial froze history in that it is not King's healed body which appeared but the wounded body of the past. This translation of King's body into the body of evidence forces history to loop back to the time of the beating, resurrected as the simulacrum of history, appearing as evidence, and as the reduction of King's body to a mute collection of wounds, that is, to a mute collection of ruins.

Television also tends to breakdown the dimensions of space and time. It takes images occurring in different places and times and it creates a news narrative out of them, which is constructed with a sense of continuity and coherence. Television is a major part of the process of present day transformation in shaping events and operating under simultaneity. It is truly baffling that a war can be fought and the major actor is **CNN!**

One account of this transformation process is worth stating here: CNN's shaping of events and its ability to operate immediately — across the world — changes our sense of spatiality and of times. It alters our notion of spaces, our shifting and multiple identities. A very revealing example was that of an elder Jewish lady who was watching CNN's coverage of the Gulf War while laying in bed in the Fairfax District of Los Angeles. Live satellite broadcasting showed that at that moment, an Iraqi scud attack was being launched on Tel Aviv. Upon hearing the sirens go off in the live report from the Israeli city, she immediately called her relatives there to be sure they were awoken to the impending danger. Her call actually woke them up, and they thanked her and immediately donned their gas masks.

The tightening of the time gap equally tightens the space gap. This illusion of intimate closeness enhanced by TV, this warping of the time/space differential into pure information gives a sense of immediacy to the universe previously felt only by religious ascetics living perpetually in the spirit world, as with the Beng people in West Africa where everything was a reflection of the Spirit.

Today, it is the ephemeral "spirits" of television and popular culture generally around which people define themselves, identify themselves. Indeed, as R. L. Rusty and James Wiltgen have recently noted in the journal *Strategies*, this same kind of "spirit" can be seen in the ghost of Elvis Presly, whose multiple, multiform appearances bespeak of an invisible point of contact for diverse peoples.[3] Elvis has become a kind of ruined and ghostly Sphinx, haunting the collective memory. That is, he has ceased to exist in the "real" world, he is purely figure, symbol — he is pure spirit. Elvis may be in that sense America's most famous ruin. As such, he is a great tourist attraction, but also, as a sign, he is always in transit

EXPEDITIONS INTO NOMADIC DISCOURSE

What do I mean by ruin? A ruin is not a frozen relic. I am not referring to a past stored in ruins, but a ruin that is mobile, shifting, nomadic. The following apt observation by Manners and Gorgeous speaks, I believe, directly to this notion of ruin as nomadic, as opposed to a notion of "preservation" that attempts to "freeze" the past, to "set it in stone."

"The Nazis,... to prove to the world that they were not barbarians but the legitimate offspring of [the] Greeks, determined not to bomb the Akropolis; doing so would have meant descending to the level of Venetians, Turks, Frenchmen, and Englishmen in their defiling of the origin. The Nazis would not repeat this mistake; they chose to preserve the Spirit in its full Hegelian splendor. Not bombing the Akropolis becomes indeed the necessary flip-site of the German occupation of Greece: as with the neutron bomb, killing villagers and communists is considered more provident than destroying buildings and monuments."[4]

Here, preservation serves to fix a history in which the Nazis become the inheritors of ancient Greek culture. To do so, however, they must repress any "non-Aryan" elements from this history, a repression which Martin Bernal (author of *Black Athena*) has convincingly observed even in contemporary Classical and Art historical studies. Ruin, on the other hand, would allow a multiplicity of histories to converge and diverge at a particular site. Thus, the notion of ruin implies a fluidity and mobility of discourses.

Let me now apply this notion of ruin and preservation to narrative. Narrative takes events separated in time and space and strives to make them continuous. Cultural narratives are essentially attempts to preserve, to restore. Narratives and historiographies are about a past that is no longer there; that perhaps never was there (e.g. the Aryan past cited above). Narratives, then, always rely on the suppression of Otherness. In this regard poetry, which always deals with fragments, is unabashedly dependent on the concept of ruin. Narrative is less evocative of ruins than poetry or the poetics of film. Both are essentially dependent on ruins. Both deal with emotion, loss, the past, relying not so much on full or completed narratives but on collections of fragments. In this way, film and poetry can be considered as the archetype of a new kind of discourse which define the states of voice and image fragmentation. Thus they occupy the site of the ruin — a marginalized discursive space that might best be described as nomadic.

Here, nomadism refers to a state of mind with reference to a style of thinking and of signification. Moving through time and space along a varying path, this form of discourse rejects fixed positions. It is a form of discourse that does not accept the notion that there is only one narrative or one truth. The nomadic sensibility, as a form of discursive strategy, thus acknowledges and accepts undifferentiated histories and narratives. Because Narratives are subject to ever- changing articulations and meanings, they too are always nomadic and transient. The issue here is therefore how narratives are transformed and how they become "set." And when a narrative becomes "set," when it is "preserved," the question becomes: whose story is being preserved and whose is being erased?

The narrative-as-ruin partakes of the technique that makes things *invisible*. A good illustration is what happens in magic shows. The intention of the performer in a magic show is to create the illusion that the natural laws of reality have been suspended in order to induce in the audience a primitive fascinating with the magician's ability to control and create objects. Though the magician appears to be working miracles, all of the tricks are, in fact, accomplished through techniques which depend on speed, dexterity, and distraction. The magician draws the attention of the audience away from the site of the trick by producing activities elsewhere. This elsewhere is imperceptible by the innocent participant. Because the audience has been watching the magician's hand flourishes and other such distractions, and is, at the same time, ignorant of the technique of the trick, the process of the trick proceeds invisibly. In this manner we can ascertain that the interest of any narrative, always reside elsewhere.

What is invisible in a story is always the key site of the discourse of nomadism. The nomadic intervention in discourse attempts to shift the reading and viewing of a given text elsewhere, towards the margins, towards that silent space of ruin where various narratives encounter other narratives, where a marginal narrative can rewrite a dominant narrative and where several narratives overlap. The ruin is thus revealed to be that site of discourse where multifarious identities, memories, nostalgias, stories and experiences reside. These were once a source of personal sustenance, but now they disappear, like ghosts, into the mythic other as forms of personal and social imaginaries. Thus, ruin is best understood, as a field of mediation, that is, as a metaphor for an expedition into memory.

INEFFABLE MEMORIALS

Let me tie these points together by ending as I began, with a story except this time I want to reach deep into the recesses of my own memory:

Over twenty years ago John Adair and Sol Worth, authors of *Through Navajo Eyes*, were engaged in an experiment with young Navajo who had not seen or used a motion picture camera before.[5] Their experiment was to find out whether film grammar was intrinsic to the apparatus or culturally learned. In other words, they were interested in finding out, what kind of filmic grammar would emerge, if you taught someone only the mechanics of filming with a motion picture camera and rudimentary editing techniques. When the filming had been completed, all the students screened their rushes. One particular shot in one film by a young Navajo especially struck me and it has since remained sealed in my memory. What follows is therefore my recreation, from memory, of a conversation about that particular shot that I presume took place between Sol Worth and the student.

Sol Worth   : Why did you include this shot of the empty
                 clearing on the ground?
Navajo boy : Well, it is important.
Sol Worth   : But, there is nothing there, it is just dirt.
Navajo boy : Yes, but there was a snake there.
Sol Worth   : I don't understand, there is nothing
                 now!.
Navajo boy : But, it does not really matter, the snake was
                 there before.

For the young boy, it was n ot necessary to shoot the actual snake but to film instead the actual image framed in his memory because the image nested in his memory was more valid than the profilmic event. Indeed, to the young Navajo the snake does not have to be there; the site still marks the place of meaning for him.

What I told you thus far is drawn from my memory of reading the cited book some 12 years ago. After I wrote these thoughts as herein described, I reread the book and the passage that triggered my memory. No sooner had I thought I spotted memory than I lost it. What I found in the book was very different from what I remembered. First, there was no dialogue between Sol Worth and the Navajo boy. Indeed, there was only a short description that served as a caption to a blurry image of the ground that I had completely forgotten. In other words, what I had remembered turned out to be not the text I thought I remembered but the image which had eclipsed it. What

I had remembered was what I had read into the image and not what I had read *into* the text.

I now realize that in memory there is always a built-in ruin. Just as the Navajo student insisted on his memory-image, I too favor my remembered version. After all, when something is turned into an image, isn't something sapped out of it, leaving behind the thing itself as ruin?. For in the ruins of my memory, I — like that young man — had constructed an important, if shifting, narrative. This is not to say that my version is more true than what was actually in the book. Truth, is neither interior, nor exterior or objective. Telling "truth" is not telling it as one actually saw it but as one sees fit to tell it. Truth is constructed between these two tellings, in the ruined in-between site of memory. It is a site that is always elsewhere: enigmatic, shifting, nomadic. Yet, what is the relationship between ruin, memory and the image? The link is no more than an imprint in the sand — those shifting sands upon which lie the ruins among which we live. To live among ruins is therefore to live in a perpetual state of rehearsals — in a state of continuous screening of memory-images and memories of even those things, events, and peoples, who are long forgotten.

***

[I am grateful to Randy Rutsky for his constructive criticism and insightful remarks on this paper. I would also like to thank David Russell, Scott Cooper and Stathis Gourgouris for their helpful suggestions and technical assistance.]

NOTES

1. Philip Graham, "A Writer in a World of Spirits: A view into veiled worlds of creativity and the Beings who live there," *Poets & Writers* magazine, Vol. 17, #3, May/June 1989.
2. bell hooks, *Yearning:* Races, Gender, and Cultural Politics,(South End Press, Boston, MA, 1990), pp 22.
3. R.A. Rusty and James Wiltgen, "Marx After Elvis: Politics/Popular Culture," *Strategies*: A Journal of Theory, Culture and Politics, No. 6, pp. 3 and *passim*.
4. Marilyn Manners & Stathis Gourgouris, "On the Road to Ruin and Restoration," *Strategies*, No. 3, 1990, p. 231
5. Sol Worth & John Adair, *Through Navajo Eyes*,(Indiana University Press, Bloomington, London, 1972). See Photo. #5 in the Photographic Section between pages 134 & 135.

Bibliographic Essay

"What's in a Name?":
Film Culture and the Self/Other Question

Martin Blythe

Names, once they are in common use, quickly become mere sounds, their etymology being buried, like so many of the earth's marvels, beneath the dust of habit
—Salman Rushdie, *The Satanic Verses*, p. 217.

INTRODUCTION

Growing up in raingreen New Zealand, I thought the most attractive names and stories were those set in distant desert lands. My early reading took in the magic of *The Arabian Nights*—Sheherezade, Sinbad, Aladdin; the caravan trails along the Silk Route—Samarkand, Bokhara; John Buchan's *Greenmantle* and Rider Haggard's "Africa." The Norse and Germanic legends—Siegfried, Tristan and Isolde, the Valkyries and Valhalla—seemed chilly and fatalistic by comparison. It was only in the desert tales that I found the powers of transformation, rejuvenation, illusion, irony, the power to strike down absolutes, archetypal trickster figures and magicians, messengers and thieves—rather than the immovable and implacable Father or Mother.

I suppose in retrospect the discovery that my childhood reading was constituted in part by a legacy of British imperial writing has not interfered with my pleasurable memories of such stories. However, it has alerted me to the "Fall" of other genres when I have encountered them in the social sciences, history, anthropology, and so on. My choice of the Fall metaphor may seem a little grand, but I always did think there was little intrinsic difference between the popular and academic writing of the British/European imperial era and the American/European writing of the present. Both have constantly confirmed the links between power and knowledge described in the jeremiads of Michel Foucault (1979, 1980) and Edward Said (1979, 1983, 1985).

Some stories were always a lot more persuasive than others, of course—the double helix, l'annee duree, postmodern implosion—but that was nevertheless the limit of their appeal, as stories. Clearly not everyone will share my view here, but "outside" of these stories there seemed to be no objective referent that I could see other than an inchoate and amorphous reality which allowed itself to be shaped

Martin Blythe *is a New Zealander with a Ph.D. in Film & Television from UCLA. He currently works in International Publicity at Walt Disney Studios.*

according to the scientific principles applied to find it, as in Thomas Kuhn's *The Structure of Scientific Revolutions* (1962) and Jean Baudrillard's essay "The Masses" (1985). Consequently, I now find it very difficult to overlook other writers' motives for writing within their chosen institutional, philosophical, and ethical frameworks.

FILM THEORY AND HISTORY DISCOVERS THE OTHER

My reasons for opening in this way have to do with what I perceive to be the relative decline of film theory as a specific genre of writing. It is precisely in that it can now be perceived *as* a genre, with its own imported narratives and myths (auteurist, psychoanalytic, Marxist, feminist, structuralist), and its own syntaxes and vocabularies, that its Fall can be tracked.

During the 1970s and early 1980s, film theory (and film culture) constituted a kind of Self, assimilating other intellectual trends for its own growth. I am not trying to imply anything shameful here—any academic or popular movement might be described the same way—but sooner or later film theory threatens to become the "canon," the "tradition." In the mid-1980s, a degree of self-consciousness set in among those influenced by literary theory and cultural studies which has as yet barely touched the hierarchy within conservative institutions like the American/ Canadian Society for Cinema Studies. The introduction of the terminology of Self/ Other, center/margins, postcolonialism and postmodernism, essentialism and pluralism, and so on over the last ten years amounts to what might once have been called an "intervention" into this world and the new jargon was useful and timely. Marxist *Screen*-speak, the empiricist historians, and the psychoanalytic-feminist alliance had by the mid-1980s clearly begun to demonstrate the kind of "Terroristic Terminology" that Charles Newman identifies, in *The Postmodern Aura* (1985), with an age of postmodern literary "inflation." Quite predictably, an impasse for film theory and film history soon resulted, since words and concepts like "voyeurism," "scopophilia," "economy," "power," "commodification," "male hysteria" and "the Classical Hollywood Cinema" constructed yet new versions of the Fall. It was a Fall because the genre confirmed in its own texts what the writers diagnosed in the society at large—a perversion or failure of vision on the one hand and a totalitarian/ monolithic institutional enemy on the other. There was no way out except self-implosion or Oedipal blindness.

With one or two exceptions, however: nowadays it is possible to read of "the Other" as another new cliche being fitted out for size. What exhilaration to wash up on new shores like Robinson Crusoe, to follow new footprints, to consume new sexual fantasies—China, Japan, India, Australia, Brazil . . .

Yet to invoke these terms, Self/Other and so on, is to recall just what many literary theorists were trying to do in the 1970s and 1980s—make our sensitivity to language at least as important as our attention to history, and to remind us that it is vital to understand how and why we name ourselves and others and our world in the way we do. Indeed the significance for me of Roland Barthes' *S/Z* (1974 in English) was in the way it confirmed my suspicions that (mis-)reading as an activity is such a subjective experience that writing "authoritatively" about anything can never be anything more than a dubious pretense. And this is to hold on to the equally dubious (but practical) distinction between writing and reading which Barthes (like Jacques Derrida) was at pains to break down. The key fable for intellectual hubris, then, would have to be The Emperor's New Suit of Clothes.

In other words, if there is male hysteria or voyeurism supposedly running rampant within the culture, it is important to ask why such writers produce these pathological diagnoses. There is nothing inherently wrong with any of these words/concepts, but academic writing does so often beg the question as to *why* they are being used in the first place, and, too, they are so closely tied up with the writer's own particular subjective experience of the world. Furthermore, once the canon is established, there is a natural tendency to reify the terminology as if it possessed an ontology. The Word. Thus we all become voyeurs, we all have selves and Others, we are all centers with margins, subjects and objects.

THE GEOGRAPHY OF THE IMAGINATION

I like to call this terminology "the geography of the imagination." Now consider some analogies from the geography of the world, which is of course really no different from the geography of the imagination.

It seems to surprise many French people that the English call the body of water they share between them the "English Channel." The French have a much more elegant name—they call it "La Manche," which literally means "The Sleeve." Nobody else in Europe calls it by its English name either. Moral: to name is to "own," and to own is to forget origins. In his study of Africanist writing, *Blank Darkness* (1986), Chris Miller has written "Place-names . . . are as charged with significance as any words can be; yet their absence from dictionaries and relegation to encyclopedias (when the two genres separated) shows the purely referential status they are given. A map is all that is needed to 'define' a place-name" (p. 8).

The Welsh have the dubious distinction of inheriting someone else's name for them. The words *Wales* and *Welsh* derive from *Walh* or *Wealas* which literally meant "foreigners" to the Anglo-Saxon invaders who pushed the Celts/Britons back into what is now called Wales. To many of the Welsh themselves, however, their country is still *Cymru* and they are the *Cymry*. Indeed they call their Film Commission Film Cymru. In a world dominated by the English language, who would know that the Greeks call their country Ellás or Elláda, the Hungarians theirs Magyarország, the Albanians Shqipëri, the Indians Bharat, the Japanese Nihon, and so on? Moral: to be named is sometimes to take the name bestowed by an Other.

Naming (i.e., Self/Other relations) is deeply imbedded in all genres, from fantasy to political economy, travel writing to history, ethnography to literary theory. For example, Tolkien's *The Lord of the Rings* can be read as a modern allegory of the Christian Salvation Myth set in the period between Celtic and Medieval England. Tolkien (who was a philologist) has his elves speak something like Welsh; the dwarves sound Norse; the Orcs' names evoke the Westerner's horror of the Turkic and Mongol hordes who swept through Eastern Europe after the disintegration of the Roman Empire; and the Shire might as well be rural England. Moral: all naming is geographically and culturally centered.

And then there are the more pejorative names like "savagery" and "civilization," "cannibalism," and "barbarism." In the New Zealand film *Utu* (1983), set during the 1860s, some of the early sequences show Maori warriors shooting up the crockery, heaving a grand piano off a second stor(e)y balcony, chopping off the head of the local Minister of the Church, and generally offending British sensibilities. Local reviewers reacted by criticizing what they took to be the negative stereotyping of Maori people. Wrote one, these Maori were shown "reverting to savagery" so that the British authorities would be justified in crushing the rebellion. Not only did those reviewers fail to understand the clever way the film resolves the circle of violence, they assumed that what we see on screen *is* savagery. My own reading of these scenes was that they were ironic and parodic, and that savagery, like anything else, is in the eye of the beholder. But the main point I want to get at here is that the reviewers found it extraordinarily easy to match these concepts to images they saw in the films. The Word blocks further thought. Moral: names set up an aesthetic which relies upon visual imagery for its force, whether this be romantic, horrific, comedic, or whatever. So, to restate my question. Is there any inherent difference between the principles behind the names discussed above and the structural oppositions of the Western academic disciplines: center and margins, Hollywood, Europe and the Third World, postmodernism and postcolonialism, material and spiritual, Self and Other, and so on? I think not. As Thomas McEvilley has argued, while savaging the 1984 "Primitivism" exhibition at the Museum of Modern Art, the classifications are basically still "tribal" at heart. In *Artforum* he writes: "The need to co-opt difference into one's own dream of order, in which one reigns supreme, is a tragic failing. Only fear of the Other forces one to deny its Otherness" (p. 59). (Also see Hal Foster's essay on the exhibition in *Recodings*, 1985). Hayden White's 1978 essay "The Noble Savage as Fetish" and Bernard Smith's *European Vision and the South Pacific 1769–1850* of 1960 are also relevant here.

To continue in the ethnographic mode, Michel de Certeau has also pointed out the resemblance between writing and cannibalism—because writing builds up a Self by cannibalizing the texts of Others (1986). In other words, if one defines other texts as "the Other," film theory and film history is really another form of consumption rather like ethnography or tourism and travel writing. For critiques of this phenomenon in the latter genres, see the contributors to James Clifford and George Marcus's anthology *Writing Culture*, and the issue of *Critical Inquiry* edited by Henry Louis Gates, Jr., *'Race,' Writing and Difference* (1985).

PROBLEMS OF TIME AND SPACE

Few studies of Self and Other are as eloquent as the early chapters of Lévi-Strauss's *Tristes Tropiques* (1955 in French; 1973 in English), at once so much more fascinating than his other more specialized works. Lévi-Strauss goes immediately to the paradox of perception and interpretation that goes with any cross-cultural context; the more one is able to recognize of an "authentic" cultural Other, the less there is of that Other surviving within the present. "I have only two possibilities: either I can be like some traveller of the olden days, who was faced with a stupendous spectacle, all, or almost all, of which eluded him, or worse still, filled him with scorn and disgust; or I can be a modern traveller, chasing after the vestiges of a vanished reality. I lose on both counts . . ." (p. 51 in my 1984 edition). To live in the future one would recognize more but see less; to live in the past one would see more but recognize less.

However, Lévi-Strauss has dramatized a fascinating but purely imaginary problem. Only with the geography of the imagination is it possible to have the luxury of imagining this time and space in which an authentic Other might exist. This is because (as far as I know) human beings only ever live in a constant present. The very idea of an on-going history which would allow for Lévi-Strauss's then/now dichotomy relies on the historical imagination for its very existence, and the idea of a historical or temporal reality unfolding around us is a cultural fiction (see Baudrillard's *Simulations*, 1983).

Lévi-Strauss is only able to resolve his dilemma by allowing time to pass, after which the "evanescent forms" have "crystallized into a sort of edifice which seems to have been conceived by an architect wiser than my personal history" (pp. 51–2). This edifice recalls Walter Benjamin's description of historiography as the imaginative reconstruction of ruins to their original glory. Yet it is only the tricks of memory and illusion that render the "historical problem" manageable at all. And as Alexander Cockburn tartly put it, "History may be irrevocable, but there is always the self to be discovered" (1984, p. 66).

I think this self-awareness is implicit in Roland Barthes' *Empire of Signs* (1982), an at-once ironic and imperial meditation on "Japan" as a Western sign system. On the other hand, Noel Burch's *To the Distant Observer* (1979) does not seem so aware of this double play when staking out Japanese cinema as an alternative to Hollywood. Perhaps Scott Malcomson, in an essay for *Screen*, "The Pure Land Beyond the Seas," is right to take them both to task for their "pursuit of authenticity" and the "Japanese essence," but not on the grounds that he, Malcomson, possesses a superior understanding of Japanese aesthetics and history. Still, Malcomson's criticism holds good for many other writers, including Fredric Jameson, who produces "magical realism" in films from Venezuela and Colombia as "a possible alternative to the narrative logic of contemporary post-modernism" (1986, p. 302).

IDENTITY AND DIFFERENCE

There seems to be an obvious moral here for film historians and theorists who prefer to believe that their writing is more than mirages, that even if it is rhetorical it does traffic in truth. For Derrida, Lévi-Strauss was engaged in "the anthropological war"—"the essential confrontation that opens communication between peoples and cultures, even when that communication is not practiced under the banner of colonial or military oppression" (Derrida, 1984, p. 107). In other words, all writing, all naming, all systems of classification—including those used by ethnic or foreign nationals writing for Western universities—impose a "violence of the letter" upon the designated Other.

Again, one may feel that Derrida's metaphors of war and violence are exaggerated, but writing is easily translated into psychological warfare, especially in a colonial context. This was one of Frantz Fanon's key themes in *The Wretched of the*

Earth (1963) and *Black Skin, White Masks* (1967), written against the background of Algeria's war of independence from the French. In the former book he wrote: "Because it is a systematic negation of the other person and a furious determination to deny the other person all attributes of humanity, colonialism forces the people it dominates to ask themselves the question constantly: 'In reality, who am I?'" (p. 250).

This question, "Who am I?" is generally converted into the abstract Third Person within academia so as to ask "What is the subject's identity?" or "How is the subject positioned within the social?" Such terms—whether personal, sexual, cultural, religious—have been key concepts whenever colonialism and nationalism have cast things into a state of flux, including the liberal democracies of the West during the late '60s and early '70s. But "identity" is also an opposite of "difference"—to *have* an identity is to know what one is *not*. Ever since the Integration Myth began losing its sway during the '60s, the need to reaffirm identity has gradually given way to calls for difference—from Black and Feminist America to the recent separatist movements within the USSR, Yugoslavia, Sri Lanka, India, China, and elsewhere. Most of these were justified on the grounds that "We were here first" or that "National frontiers are arbitrarily imposed right across ethnic or tribal lines."

The trouble with such terms is that they involve prescriptions and proscriptions about socially acceptable behavior. To *be* American is a national definition which is supposed to transcend cultural and ethnic differences. To be Kurdish or Palestinian is to be practically deprived of a national identity altogether. To *be* Black (loosely a cultural definition) is not so far removed from being *a* Black (a racial/biological definition). Things change but the language still belongs to the geography of the imagination)—the names are rhetorical before they are anything else.

Thus, the posing of a Self or Identity or Subject or Center—no matter that some poststructuralists and postmodernists have banished it by fiat—is probably a necessary response to inequities in the power relationships that organize a social order. It seems proper to me that minorities and "the oppressed," a classification that I will have to skate past, should adopt essentialist positions ("I am Navajo," or "I am oppressed," etc.), and that the powerful (including academics) should adopt pluralist positions. There is nothing inherently wrong with minorities or feminists or anyone else who can lay claim to being "Othered" adopting essentialism.

Indeed it surprises me that essentialism is so often roundly condemned in academic writing as either hypocritical or downright wrong. See, for example, the essays in the *Screen* issue titled, "The Last 'Special Issue' on Race?" (Mercer, Fusco, et al., 1988). I find it difficult to read such criticism without reacting against the elitism and legalism it endorses (see Teshome Gabriel's objections in "Colonialism and 'Law and Order' Criticism" in *Screen* (1986). In my view, essentialist or pluralist positions are only alternative writing strategies which are relative to each other. For example, "Latin" or "Hispanic" American writers can rhetorically invoke a Latin or Hispanic cultural essence as an offensive/defensive frontier against Anglo cultural hegemony here in California. However, if it is done by some claim to prior occupation of the land, then this runs straight into the counter-claim that the Indian peoples were here before them and thus the charge of hypocrisy is invited. A pluralist argument (i.e., Latin culture is not adequately represented within mainstream media) would probably be more appropriate but it would lack the immediacy and power of the essentialist argument. (See Richard Rorty's related argument on the "connoisseurs of diversity" and the "connoisseurs of love," 1986.)

If essentialism so offends the sensibilities of the contributors to *Screen*, then this only goes to show that they are repressing yet another form of essentialism—that there is only one correct way to discourse on race and culture. Thus they prove that the process is circular: to proclaim pluralism, relativism, oppositionality or anything else instead is just to promote the newest form of essentialism. This is a conjuring trick which signals a pretense to moving away from essentialist thinking while actually moving back toward it. As I argued earlier, authoritarian criticism usually doubles the very thing it identifies as the enemy.

DECONSTRUCTION AND THE THIRD WORLD

Does this sound like my attempt to preserve an olympian detachment? In my own writing I still favor a deconstructive approach. For a while I was using Gregory Bateson's (and R. D. Laing's) notion of the "double bind" as a convenient metaphor for the rhetorical "knots" one can find oneself in (Blythe, 1988). It is a metaphor which also appears in the writing of Derrida, Gayatri Spivak, and others. Whether we like it or not, the academic naming process places the people one is writing about—the "Other"—in a double bind over how to respond, so deconstruction is self-conscious about what its own function is, what terms it should use, what theoretical positions to take. Barbara Johnson, for example, writes: "It was not clear to me what I, a white deconstructor, was doing talking about Zora Neale Hurston, a black novelist and anthropologist, or to *whom* I was talking. It was as though I were asking her for answers to questions I did not even know I was unable to formulate" (1985, p. 278). I believe there are analogies here to the juridical concept of "le differend" adopted by Jean-François Lyotard (1984), and to the familial version of the Oedipus Complex attacked by Gilles Deleuze and Felix Guattari in *The Anti-Oedipus* (1977).

The main danger of all such concepts, of course, is that they soon turn into cliches when worked to death by other academics and graduate students. Double binds, deference, simulations, etc. begin to pop up everywhere. Recent rumors suggest that New York art gallery owners have become intoxicated by Baudrillard's giddy whirl of the simulacra.

The use of these names, these metaphors, in reference to the Other—"developing," "spiritual," "national," "neocolonial," "postcolonial," etc.—is only tenable, in my view, when used with a (self-) deconstructive intention in mind. It is at least in part a question of politeness. Not that my writing this will make the least bit of difference to an academic consensus that would never accept that authoritative writing is just a pose. But it is worth insisting on some form of ethics, because it enables us to establish degrees of legitimacy.

Consider the term "Third World" (excuse me if I now drop the quotation marks). Are there qualitative differences between its use by a white Western academic, or a Third World academic working in the First World, and a Third World academic in the Third World? Does it depend upon who one wishes to address? Shiva Naipaul has ridiculed the term outright as "an artificial construction of the West" with "a bloodless universality which robs individuals of their particularity" (1985). Gayatri Spivak has been particularly critical of the way Western feminists have reproduced the narratives of imperialism by assigning Western women's texts a central place from which Third World women's texts can be "recovered, interpreted and curricularized" (1985). Teshome Gabriel (1982), Roy Armes (1987), and the contributors to a Jim Pines/Paul Willemen anthology (1989), on the other hand, have defended a limited use for the term whereby the Third World, like Third Cinema, is unified only to the degree to which it maintains a difference from First World/Hollywood aesthetic and political norms.

In short, the reason there are degrees of legitimacy (never fixed of course) is that there are degrees of power and position. Obviously there is an enormous difference in the power exercised by a popular First World writer and the storyteller fabulist in a Third World village. I find myself relatively sympathetic to writers from other cultures who seek to engage with Western discourses in/on its own terms. They are automatically placed in a defensive position (as an Other) by virtue of their choice to write *in* English and *against* a tradition, a canon, an archive, with its "rules"—and rules are set up to resist or cannibalize intruders. This is basically the starting point for Edward Said's essay on "Intellectuals in the Postcolonial World" (1986), and a similar argument underlies Mario Vargas Llosa's piece, "The Radical Romance of Latin America" (1984). For an alternative strategy, read any interview with a "non-Western" intellectual statesman (e.g., Walid Jumblatt or Lech Walesa in *Playboy*); direct questions are answered with parables that simultaneously refuse *and* answer the questioner. Direct questions presuppose their answer, usually in a digital (Yes/No) form; parables incorporate a moral code and the activity of question/response into the equation.

RHETORIC AND THE WORD

What then is the situation for dissident intellectuals living in the centers of empire, especially those who are foreigners? I have already implied that their outsider status gives them a certain legitimacy on national and cultural matters. There are some writers—Salman Rushdie and V. S. Naipaul, for example—who go to great lengths to differentiate their Selfs from those whose existence is there to make them feel like "Others" in the first place. Rushdie writes in praise of a "migrant sensibility" while at the same time satirizing Britain's "Raj Revivalism" (1985), while Naipaul seems to have been everywhere in the world! Such shifting offensive and defensive stances make for highly charged relations between a writer and a reader, in keeping with the tenets of modernism, and these writers have been suitably rewarded with the official keys to the kingdom of the Arts.

But Rushdie is also enough of an insider within the self of Islam (where Naipaul is not) to toy with its canons and traditions in a way that the vast majority of his Western readers can only guess at. As the controversies over *The Satanic Verses* proved beyond all doubt, there is great danger walking the fine line between irony and the literal Word. It is simply impossible to write a controversial work like this and free the artistic (modernist) Self from the constraints of nation, family, and religion (as James Joyce once put it). It was a lesson Naipaul learned many years ago when he was branded an elitist, and now it is Rushdie's turn. That lesson is not whether we all have these cultural and institutional affiliations but who imposes them on whom, how and why they do so, and what names are used to achieve this. I agree with Naipaul in his most recent work that it is important that we try to break those "prisons of the spirit that men create for themselves and for others—so overpowering, so much a part of the way things appear to have to be, and then, abruptly, with a little shift, so insubstantial" (1988, p. 105).

Other writers have come to similar conclusions. Edward Said casts the concept of the "exile" in the nostalgic mode (1984). Deleuze and Guattari (1987), Bruce Chatwin (1988), and Teshome Gabriel (1988) all use the concept of the "nomad" to break with conventional historical narratives. Homi Bhabha is interested in the racial and cultural "hybrids" and "in-betweens" who mimic and mock the fixed order of things (1983, 1985). For New Zealand writer Keri Hulme (*The Bone People*, 1985) it is the biologically one-eighth Maori that enables her to call herself a "mongrel." These concepts provide for a ramshackle genre which I suppose could be useful to those not adequately represented by nation-states and their historians—Armenians, Zulu, Maori, and so on. But best of all, they provide a mythology for those who would like to make use of ideas which do not fall into the familiar categories of national, cultural, and religious identity.

I am an immigrant myself—a resident "alien" according to my Green Card—but I almost never think of myself that way. I do not spend much time thinking of myself as a "New Zealander" either, or of being "male" or "middle class." It seems to me that one of the best things about having an identity (however it comes to be determined) is that once it is taken for granted, it can be put aside, allowing you to get on with other things. Perhaps that is the best that can be said about it? All that is left, finally, is the pleasure this allows in speculating about what all these names/ words/concepts mean, where they come from, who uses them, and which ones have a bit of wild magic still left in them.

BIBLIOGRAPHY

Armes, Roy
    1987 *Third World Filmmaking and the West* (Berkeley: University of California Press).
Barthes, Roland
    1974 *S/Z* (New York: Hill and Wang, 1974; 1970 in French).
    1982 *Empire of Signs* (New York: Hill and Wang).
Bateson, Gregory
    1972 *Steps to an Ecology of Mind: Collected Essays in Anthropology, Evolution, and Epistemology* (San Francisco: Chandler).
Baudrillard, Jean
    1983 *Simulations* (New York: Semiotext(e)).
    1983 *In the Shadow of the Silent Majorities* (New York: Semiotext(e)).
    1985 "The Masses: The Implosion of the Social in the Media," *New Literary History* (Spring).
Bhabha, Homi
    1983 "The Other Question—The Stereotype and Colonial Discourse," *Screen* 24 (November-December).
    1985 "Signs Taken for Wonders," *Critical Inquiry* (Autumn).

Blythe, Martin
  1988   Ph.D. Diss. "From Maoriland to Aotearoa: Images of the Maori in New Zealand Film and Television" (UCLA).
Burch, Noel
  1979   *To the Distant Observer* (Berkeley: University of California Press).
Chatwin, Bruce
  1987   *Songlines* (New York: Viking Press).
Clifford, James and George E. Marcus, eds.
  1986   *Writing Culture: the Poetics and Politics of Ethnography* (Berkeley: University of California Press).
Cockburn, Alexander
  1984   "Bwana Vistas," *Harper's* (August).
de Certeau, Michel
  1986   *Heterologies: Discourse on the Other* (Minneapolis: University of Minnesota Press).
Deleuze, Gilles and Felix, Guattari
  1977   *Capitalism and Schizophrenia: Anti-Oedipus* (New York: Viking; 1972 in French).
  1987   *Thousand Plateaux* (Minneapolis: University of Minnesota Press).
Derrida, Jacques
  1984   *Of Grammatology* (Baltimore: Johns Hopkins University Press; 1967 in French).
Fabian, Johannes
  1983   *Time and the Other: How Anthropology Makes its Object* (New York: Columbia Press).
Fanon, Frantz
  1982   *The Wretched of the Earth* (New York: Grove Press; 1962 in French).
  1967. *Black Skin, White Masks* (New York: Grove Press; 1965 in French).
Foster, Hal
  1985   *Recodings* (Port Townsend, Washington: Bay Press).
Foucault, Michel
  1979   *Discipline and Punish: The Birth of the Prison* (New York: Vintage/Random House; 1975 in French).
  1980   *The History of Sexuality, Vol. I* (New York: Vintage/Random House; 1976 in French).
Fusco, Coco
  1988   "Fantasies of Oppositionality: Reflections on Recent Conferences in Boston and New York," *Screen* (Autumn).
Gabriel, Teshome
  1982   *Third Cinema in the Third World* (Ann Arbor: University of Michigan Press).
  1986   "Colonialism and 'Law and Order' Criticism," *Screen* (May/August), pp. 140–147.
  1988   "Thoughts on Nomadic Aesthetics," *Blackframes: Critical Perspectives on Black Independent Cinema*, ed. by Mbye B. Cham and Claire Andrade-Watkins (MIT Press), pp. 62–79.
Gates, Jr., Henry Louis
  1985   *Critical Inquiry* (Autumn).
Hulme, Keri
  1985   *The Bone People* (Auckland: Spiral, in association with Hodder and Stoughton).
Jameson, Fredric
  1986   "On Magic Realism in Film," *Critical Inquiry* (Winter).
Johnson, Barbara
  1985   "Thresholds of Difference: Structures of Address in Zora Neale Hurston," *Critical Inquiry* (Autumn).
Kuhn, Thomas
  1962   *The Structure of Scientific Revolutions* (Chicago: University of Chicago Press).
Lévi-Strauss, Claude
  1984   *Tristes Tropiques* (Harmondsworth, Middlesex: Peregrine Books; 1955 in French).
Lyotard, Jean-François
  1984   "The Differend, the Referent, and the Proper Name," *Diacritics* (Fall).
McEvilley, Thomas
  1984   "Doctor Lawyer Indian Chief," *Artforum* (November).
Malcomson, Scott
  1985   "The Pure Land Beyond the Seas: Barthes, Burch and the Uses of Japan," *Screen* (May–August).

Mercer, Kobena

    1988 "De Margins and de Centre," *Screen* (Autumn).

Miller, Christopher

    1986 *Blank Darkness: Africanist Discourse in French* (Chicago: University of Chicago Press).

Naipaul, Shiva

    1985 "The Illusion of the Third World," *Harper's* (September).

Naipaul, V. S.

    1988 "How the Land Lay," *New Yorker* (June 6).

Newman, Charles

    1985 *The Post-Modern Aura: The Act of Fiction in an Age of Inflation* (Evanston: Northwestern University Press).

Pines, Jim and Paul Willemen

    1989 *Questions of Third Cinema* (BFI).

Rorty, Richard

    1986 "On Ethnocentrism: A Reply to Clifford Geertz," *Michigan Quarterly Review* (Summer).

Rushdie, Salman

    1985 "Outside the Whale," *American Film* (January-February).

    1985 "The Location of Brazil," *American Film* (September).

    1989 *The Satanic Verses* (New York: The Viking Press).

Said, Edward

    1979 *Orientalism* (New York: Vintage).

    1983 *The World, the Text and the Critic* (Cambridge: Harvard University Press).

    1984 "The Mind of Winter," *Harper's* (September).

    1985 "Orientalism Reconsidered," *Race and Class* Vol. XXVII, No. 2.

    1986 "Intellectuals in the Post-colonial World," *Salmagundi* (Spring-Summer).

    1987 "Kim, The Pleasures of Imperialism," *Raritan* (Fall).

Smith, Bernard

    1960 *European Vision and the South Pacific 1769–1850* (London: Oxford University Press).

Spivak, Gayatri

    1985 "Three Women's Texts and a Critique of Imperialism" *Critical Inquiry* (Autumn).

Todorov, Tzvetan

    1985 *The Conquest of America: the Question of the Other* (New York: Harper and Row).

Vargas Llosa, Mario

    1984 "The Radical Romance of Latin America," *Harper's* (November).

White, Hayden

    1978 "The Noble Savage as Fetish," *Tropics of Discourse: Essays in Cultural Criticism* (Baltimore: Johns Hopkins Press; originally 1978).

Review Essay

Eurocentrism, Afrocentrism, Polycentrism: Theories of Third Cinema

Robert Stam

Roy Armes. *Third World Filmmaking and the West.* Berkeley: University of California Press, 1987.

Jim Pines and Paul Willemen, eds. *Questions of Third Cinema.* London: BFI, 1989.

For a long time, the various "Third World" and "Third" cinemas which collectively form the majority cinema in the world were largely ignored by standard film histories as well as by cinema studies curricula. When not ignored, Third World cinema was treated with condescension, as if it were merely the subaltern "shadow" of the "real" cinema of North America and Europe. Recently, however, a veritable explosion of theory and scholarship on Third World Cinema has given us a cornucopia of texts: Teshome Gabriel's pioneering *Third Cinema in the Third World: The Aesthetics of Liberation*, full-length books on Cuban, Argentine, Brazilian, and Indian Cinema, and valuable collections such as John Downing's *Film and Politics in the Third World*, Michael Chanan's *Twenty-Five Years of the New Latin American Cinema*, Julianne Burton's *Cinema and Social Change*, Coco Fusco's *New Latin American Cinema*, and Mbye B. Cham's and Claire Andrade-Watkins's *Blackframes*, along with the ongoing work of those journals regularly featuring work on Third World Cinema (notably *Cineaste, Jump Cut, Film Quarterly, Framework, Screen, The Independent, Black Film Review, Quarterly Review of Film Studies, Camera Obscura, Discourse* and others).

This work intervenes at a precise juncture in the history of the third world and of third cinema. The two decades since the heady days of the early radical third-worldist formulations (Rocha, Solanas-Getino, Espinosa) have witnessed a number of very complex developments, both positive and negative. On the one hand, what was once called the period of "third world euphoria" has given way to the "crisis of existing socialisms," the frustration of the hoped-for "tricontinental revolution" (with Ho Chi Minh, Frantz Fanon, and Che Guevara as key symbolic figures), the realization that the "wretched of the earth" are not unanimously revolutionary (nor necessarily allies to one another), and the recognition that international geo-politics and the global economic system have obliged even socialist regimes to make some kind of peace with transnational capitalism.

ROBERT STAM, *is Associate Professor in the Cinema Studies Department at New York University. He is the author of* The Interrupted Spectacle, Reflexivity in Film and Literature. *His* Subversive Pleasures: Bakhtin, Cultural Criticism and Film *was published by Johns Hopkins in 1989. Forthcoming is* New Vocabularies in Film Semiotics *(with Robert Burgoyne and Sandy Flitterman).*

On the other hand, these years have also witnessed ongoing anti-colonial struggles, from central America to Southern Africa and the Phillipines. In terms of the cinema, we have seen a notable increase in third world film production (especially in Asian countries), the diversification of aesthetic models (as filmmakers partially discard a didactic model in favor of a "politics of pleasure"), the emergence of audio-visual media giants in Mexico and Brazil (Brazil's Rede Globo is now the fourth network in the world), the rise (and occasionally the decline) of centralized, state-sponsored film production in both socialist and capitalist countries (Cuba, Algeria, Mexico, Brazil), and the appearance of First world nations (notably Japan, Canada, France, Holland, Italy, and Germany) as sources of funding for Third World filmmakers. Severe IMF-provoked "austerity" crises and the collapse of the old developmentalist models, meanwhile, have led to the "dollarization" of film production and consequently to the rise of co-productions, while oppressive political conditions have engendered the forced or voluntary exile of prominent Third World filmmakers, leading to a kind of diasporic third-world cinema within the first world (Raul Ruiz, Parviz Sayad, Hanif Kureishi).

These years have also witnessed an increasingly sophisticated debate concerning Eurocentrism, Afrocentrism, and multi-culturalism, as well as a kind of terminological crisis swirling around the concept of a "Third World" and consequently of "Third World Cinema." In his response to Fredric Jameson's "Third World Literature in the Era of Transnational Capitalism," Ai jaz Ahmad argues that the "three worlds" notion suppresses a multiplicity of significant differences among and within the advanced capitalist countries as well as within the Third World.[1] At the same time, the tripartite scheme masks real continuities between the diverse worlds. The experience of colonialism and imperialism, in this sense, exists on both sides of the global divide. A first-world country like the United States, for example, is marked by colonialism, not only in the form of the living remnants of genocide and slavery, but also in the shape of the refugees generated by what one might call "colonial karma" (thus Mexico, conquered in the 19th century by the United States, sends its residents back to the conquered territories as "illegal aliens") as well as in all the ways that everyday life in the United States interweaves first and third world destinies (tax dollars for repression in Central America, drugs from Columbia, shirts made in Taiwan). The notion of the "three worlds," in short, not only flattens heterogeneities, masks contradictions, and elides differences, but also obscures similarities. The first-world/third-world struggle takes place not only *between* nations but also *within* nations.

Roy Armes's *Third World Film Making and the West* and Jim Pines/Paul Willemen's *Questions of Third Cinema* form especially welcome additions to the general resurgence of writing on Third Cinema. Taken together, they make an excellent introduction to the field. The goals of the two texts are in many ways complementary; while the former concentrates on the cinematic practice of third world countries, the latter focusses on the theoretical implications of "third cinema." Both books assume that the concept of the "Third World" retains heuristic value, at least, as a convenient name for the "imperialized formations" (including those *within* the first-world). While the Armes book implicitly defines Third World Cinema as the ensemble of films produced by Third World countries (including those produced even before the very idea of "Third World" was current), *Questions of Third Cinema* prefers, generally, to speak of "Third Cinema" as an organizing category for an ideological project, i.e., those films adhering to the political and aesthetic program of third cinema, films usually, but not necessarily, produced by third world peoples themselves. As long as it is taken not as an "essential" pre-constituted entity, but rather as a collective project, something to be forged, it seems to me the notion of "Third World Cinema" retains important tactical and polemical uses for naming a politically-inflected cultural practice. In purely classificatory terms, we might envision concentric circles of denotation for "third cinema": 1) a core circle of films produced by and for third world people (no matter where those people happen to be physically located) and adhering to the principles of third cinema, defined by Teshome Gabriel as "that cinema of the Third World . . . opposed to imperialism and class oppression in all their ramifications . . ."; 2) a wider circle of the cinematic productions of third world peoples (whether or not the films adhere to the principles of third cinema, and irrespective of the period of their making; and 3) a final circle, somewhat anomalous in status, at once "inside" and "outside," consisting of those films made by first or second world people in support of third world peoples and adhering to the principles of third cinema. (That many films are hybrid and fit but awkwardly into any single category is taken as a given.)

Third World Film Making and the West is the first attempt, to my knowledge, to survey the vast film production of the Third World in all periods. Extremely ambitious, Armes's project covers a significant slice of history, a wide geographical-political area, and ventures into areas as diverse as culture, politics, economics, and literature as well as film. Part One outlines the social, cultural, and economic context of Third World Cinema; Part Two sketches its theory and practice; Part Three explores in detail specific national and regional industries; and Part Four offers focussed essays on prominent Third World auteurs. The book is ordered by a number of shaping questions and preoccupations: the nature of social structures as shaped both by the force of tradition and the impact of colonialism; the emergence of Western-educated elites as ruling groups and as prime movers in cultural production; the problems of defining "nation" and "national culture"; the relevance of national cultural traditions to cinematic production; the role of US-dominated distribution companies; the strengths and limitations of cinematic realism; the struggle against the material conditions inherent in underdevelopment; the relation of politicized auteur-filmmakers to antecedent popular film traditions; the challenge to a politicized anti-Hollywoodean cinema confronting an audience shaped by western concepts of entertainment; and the potential of revolutionary cinematic forms growing directly out of the oppositional culture of the oppressed.

Underlying much of Armes's analysis is a critical version of the "dependency analysis" advanced by such economists as Andre Gunder Frank, Immanuel Wallerstein, and Samir Amin. Dependency analysis argues, to borrow Pierre Jalee's words, that it "is not the imperialist countries which aid the Third World but the Third World which aids imperialism." (Brazilian economist Fernando Enrique Cardoso once defined "dependency" as "what you call imperialism if you don't want to lose your Ford Foundation Grant.") Dependency Theory assumes that the causes of underdevelopment must be sought in the pattern of economic relations between the dominant powers and their client states, that the free-enterprise model tends to worsen existing inequalities, and that imperialism is aided by an "accomplice" national elite. In his analysis, Armes privileges economic explanation, seeing cinema as part of a continuum of economic and industrial practices and situating Third World cinemas in the context of an international economy of film production which has always kept First World film interests in a position of strength and Third World producers at a disadvantage. Hollywood and its European counterparts (for example COMACICO and SECMA in Francophone Africa), Armes shows, came to dominate distribution through much of the Third World, simultaneously stifling its Third world competitors and enriching itself thanks to Third World box office receipts.

The dominant First World cinema has also played a clear *ideological* role in relation to the Third World by justifying political domination and economic exploitation. The cinema, according to Tunisian critic Ferid Boughedir, conspired in the falsification of reality whereby the colonizer was a technician, a man of progress, from a superior culture and civilization, while the native was a primitive, incapable of technical progress or of mastering his passions, the next best thing to a wild beast. . . ." As a result of this First World cinematic hegemony, many Third World people came to identify, if only partially and ambiguously, with European and North American stars and values. In Ethiopia, as Haile Gerima recounts, children were led to identify with Tarzan and against their own African brothers and sisters on the screen.

Armes is especially effective in clarifying the contextual factors which helped shape particular Third World Cinemas: the enlightened system of government support which has animated the "New Indian Cinema"; the importance of the world-wide Chinese communities in providing a base of support for the flourishing Hong Kong film industry; the role of the French government in financing African films which, ironically, denounced French colonialism itself. Throughout, Armes foregrounds the pathologies and stresses engendered by colonialism as a system designed exclusively for the efficient extraction of wealth, a system creating severe distortions in the cultural sphere: the systematic elision of national history in colonial schools, the self-inferiorization of the colonized, the calculated promotion of compromised self-serving elites.

It would be unreasonable to expect any one author to have the cultural or linguistic competence to deal in depth with all of Third World cinema, given the fact that the cultural differences within the Third World, and even within a single country such as India, are often more profound and significant than those which differentiate First World countries. Armes deals with this challenge in two ways. First, he relies on knowledgeable critics from the countries themselves—Ferid Boughedir on African cinema, Chidananda das Gupta on Indian Cinema, Agustin Sotto on Filipino Cinema. (Indeed, one of the many services performed by *Third World Film Making and the West* is to introduce First World readers and spectators to major Third World film critics.) Secondly, Armes adopts a policy of selectivity which discreetly privileges certain kinds of films: those which have won international prizes, or an international audience, or which have at least enjoyed a substantial audience at home. Although Armes cites a number of landmark documentaries such as *Battle of Chile* and *Hour of the Furnaces*, he seems to favor "accessible" feature fiction films in the realist mode, while speaking disparagingly of "esoteric" and "hermetic" films that "fail to find an audience." The author of a book on Italian cinema, Armes at times seems to see Third World cinemas through the grid of neo-realism, regarded both as a concrete influence on filmmakers (Ray in India, Chahine in Egypt, and Dos Santos in Brazil) and as First World analogues in situational, class, and aesthetic terms. This grid is useful up to a point, but it leaves little room for Third World traditions favoring modernist, anti-realist, or avant-garde expression. Glauber Rocha's self-aware modernism, as a consequence, gets reduced to mere "stylistic originality" rather than being seen as a conscious and systematic attack on the "populist" style of dramatic realism shared by Hollywood spectacle as well as neo-realist style social drama. Armes makes no mention, furthermore, of experimental or avant-garde movements such as Brazil's aggressive "udigrudi" (Underground) movement, with its call for an "aesthetic of garbage," and a "dirty screen" as the only appropriate strategies for a marginalized Third World country. With regard to the Phillipines, Armes mentions the work of Lino Brocka, Mike de Leon, and Ishmael Bernal, similarly, but there is no mention of the stylistically more audacious work of Kidlat Tahimik, whose witty films, for example *The Perfumed Nightmare*, constitute ironic fables satirizing the impact of the First World on villages in the Phillipines.

Third World Film Making and the West is premised on exteriority; i.e. it takes a self-acknowledgedly ethnocentric approach to its subject, announcing itself as "written from a Western standpoint, with all the implicit assumptions that this carries." Despite this auto-critique, if it is that, and despite Armes's sincere attempt to avoid the worst effects of such ethnocentrism, the book reveals how difficult it is, for first world critics (and perhaps for any critic) to completely divest themselves of first-world intellectual baggage. The notion of the 'West" in the title, for example, already carries with it a long sedimented history of ambiguous usage, having more to do with politics than with geography, going back, as Raymond Williams points out in *Keywords*, to the West-East division of the Roman Empire, the East-West division of the Christian Church, to the definition of the West as Jewish/Christian and the East as Moslem/Hindu/Buddhist, to the World War II division into "Western" and "Eastern" "fronts," and finally to the postwar division of Europe into the West (the capitalist societies and their allies) and the Marxist East (seen as the defenders of an alien ideology). Despite his citation of Third World arguments against eurocentrism, Armes at times inherits the negatives associated with this problematic term "West." Latin Americans, for example, would probably be surprised to learn that their culture and cinema are "non-Western." (Some of the contributors to *Questions of Third Cinema* also show confusion on this point.) Most Latin Americans, whatever their ethnic heritage, speak as a first language a European tongue (Spanish, Portuguese, English); many are European in origin; and, they are physically located in the West, in societies where European modes remain hegemonic. The point is that the misnamed "Latin" America—some clumsy amalgam like "Indigeno-African-European America" would be more appropriate—is irrevocably hybrid, a cultural site at once western and non-western." The "West" and "Third World" cannot, therefore, be posited as antonyms, for in fact the two worlds interpenetrate in a space of "creolization" and "syncretism."

Armes also repeatedly characterizes technology per se as "Western," an idea indirectly flattering to First World narcissism. Quite apart from the historical existence of non-European sciences and technologies (the Egyptian origins of western science, African agriculture, Chinese gunpowder, and Aztec architecture, irrigation, plumbing, and even brain surgery), Armes underestimates the inter-dependence of First and Third worlds. While no one denies that the cutting edge of technological development over the last centuries has mainly centered in Europe and North America, this development was very much a joint project facilitated by the exploitation of the Third World. If the industrial revolutions of Europe were made possible by the Third World—Great Britain's industrial revolution, for exam-ple, was partially financed by infusions of wealth generated by slave labor in Brazilian mines—then in what sense is it meaningful to speak only of "Western" technology and industry? Whose goals does it serve to posit a kind of essence, by which technology, no matter where it appears, is always "Western?" The equation of "West" and "technology," in sum, militates against the anti-colonialist thrust of most of the book.

Armes tends to depict First World-Third World exchange as a one-way street, in which the third World filmmaker is dependent not only on "Western-originated technology" but also on "formal structures of narrative derived from the West . . ." This formulation, which transfers the notion of dependency from the economic to the cultural sphere, ignores the extent to which some third world traditions draw on formal structures not derived from the West, as in the case of African films influenced by the oral tradition, Indian films deriving from Hindu legends, Bra-zilian films building on Amazonian folktales. Without denying the largely uni-directional nature of the flow of mass-mediated culture and information between First and Third worlds, moreover, it is important to insist that in broad cultural terms the flow also moves the other way, whence the impact of African art on European modernist painting, the dynamizing presence (often uncredited) of Afro-Brazilian polyrhythms within North American music, or the influence of Asian forms (Kabuki, Noh drama, ideographic writing) on European theatre and film. It "was the impact of surrealism," Armes writes, "that liberated the Carribean and African poets of Negritude from the constraints of a borrowed language," but was it not also African and Asian art which liberated the European modernists by provoking them to question *their* culture-bound aesthetic? Armes in this sense underestimates the cultural permeability between dominant and dependent cul-tures. The "Western" center penetrates the periphery, certainly, but the periphery also penetrates the center in a kind of criss-crossing ripple effect. Thus First World capitals such as New York and London are becoming Africanized, Latinized, Asiafied. The old compartmentalizations, in other words, are becoming increas-ingly irrelevant.

Despite the general stress on "Western influences," Armes occasionally fails to discern that influence where it is present. He speaks of the "enormous difficulty" created by the lack of a "critical methodology" for dealing with the mass of commercial Arab, Asian, and Latin American films since the 1930s, citing the example, among others, of the Brazilian chanchadas, the musical comedy films made in Rio de Janeiro from the thirties through the fifties. In fact, however, it is often precisely the commercial traditions that are most westernized. The cinematic and narrative codes of the chanchadas, for example, are largely modeled on American musical comedies and are therefore not particularly inaccessible for the First World spectator or critic. The 1976 anthology-film of chanchadas, *Assim Era*

Atlantida (The Days of Atlantida Film Studio) was explicitly modeled on *That's Entertainment*. Many chanchadas either plagiarized Hollywood films or explicitly parodied them; *Matar ou Correr (To Kill or to Run,* 1954) spoofs Fred Zinneman's *High Noon*, for example, and *Nem Sansao nem Dalila (Neither Samson nor Delilah,* 1954) parodies the Cecil B. De Mille Biblical spectacular. Although the films require some minimal knowledge of Brazilian cultural codes, they are otherwise quite susceptible to the kinds of analysis already applied to the Hollywood musical by Richard Dyer, Jane Feuer, Rick Altman, and others. Nor is it true that such films have "given birth to virtually no accompanying critical writing or theoretical speculation of the kind Hollywood has provoked, only to reactions of a thoroughly negative kind." While it is true that the practitioners of Cinema Novo, as part of an oedipalized revolt against the commercial "cinema de papa," made dismissive generalizations about the antecedent tradition, it is also true that since the early seventies, critics such as Paulo Emilio Salles Gomes, Jean-Claude Bernardet, and Joao Luiz Vieira have praised the chanchadas for their narrative power, their witty and incisive political critiques, and above all for their strong links to popular culture and the popular audience.

Although Armes does pay some attention to the question of national culture (the painterly influences on Hindi "mythologicals," the links between theatre, religious ritual, and film in Nigeria), he also at times employs eurocentric terminology. He describes Brazil's African-derived religions as "primitive" and "semi-pagan," language which most Brazilian intellectuals have long since abandoned as ethnocentric. At times, Armes seems to imply that countries such as Brazil lack a viable national culture, as in the following sentence: "The lack of a local tradition that could serve as a 'useful past' has had a determining impact on the development of Brazilian culture." While Armes is right to point out the complexity of an identity still being forged, his formulation slights all the ways which Brazilian culture, both popular and erudite, is constituted by the shifting intersection of European and non-European "local" (indigenous, Afro-Brazilian) elements. In his discussion of Brazilian modernism, for example, Armes stresses the "strong European influence" and the "impetus derived from abroad," missing the paradox that Brazilian modernism was "anthropophagic," devouring imported cultural products as the raw material for a new synthesis, one which attempted to turn the imposed culture back, transformed, *against* the colonizer.

The same kind of eurocentrism also surfaces in more indirect ways. Armes contrasts "local" films with those achieving a "truly international standard," and merely "regional filmmakers" with "filmmakers of international stature," a dichotomy premissed, ultimately, on a Eurocentric assumption of the "universality" of its own values. This idealization of the West also inheres in certain binarisms indirectly flattering to the First World reader or spectator. Armes describes Guney's films as "un-Western" because in his films "women are stolen and abused, seduced and abandoned, sold, killed, or driven to suicide." But even if one acknowledges that patriarchy in a country such as Turkey is particularly brutal and relentless, does not a phrase such as "un-Western" have the effect of letting the phallocentric West—the unending scene of rape, prostitution, wife-beating, and other forms of violence against women—off the hook?

My quibbles are not meant to detract from Armes's immense achievement in

Third World Film Making and the West. On the whole, the book succeeds in its ambitious task, treating the complex reality of Third World cinema with the respect and informed attention it deserves. A veritable cornucopia of information about the diverse Third World cinemas, the volume has the signal virtue of alerting First World film enthusiasts and scholars to the fact that Third World cinema is not the sporadic and marginalized phenomenon it is often assumed to be, but an inseparable part of world cinema. From a global perspective, Armes is able to see filmic and cultural currents washing over whole continents or regions. Scrupulously honest, the book never takes a narrowly promotional or idealizing attitude toward the Third World. Its calling attention to the cinemas of Asia, Africa, and the Middle East, furthermore, is a salutary corrective to the traditional privileging of Latin American Cinema in most antecedent discussions of Third World cinema.

Questions of Third Cinema, which emerged out of a three-day conference within the Edinburgh International Film Festival in 1986, makes an excellent companion volume to *Third World Filmmaking and the West,* since it is strong precisely in that area—theory—where the Armes volume is relatively weak. Like the Armes volume, *Questions of Third Cinema* too has its orienting questions. What is the signification of "Third Cinema" and "Third World Cinema?" What is the role of theory and its relationship to oppositional cultural practice? Is theory elitist? Can it be appropriated for third world purposes? Is theory necessarily first-world? Is there a Third Cinema aesthetic or only a plurality of aesthetics? Or is the very notion of "aesthetics," as Clyde Taylor argues, irremediably racist and elitist?

Questions of Third Cinema brings the debates concerning "Third World Cinema" to a new level of theoretical sophistication. Whereas the pioneer studies of Third World Cinema tended to limit their theoretical references to such figures as Fanon, Solanas-Gettino, Espinosa, Rocha, Althusser, Mattelart, Eisenstein, Vertov, and Brecht, we now find a widely expanded range of references to a globally-minded constellation of thinkers. Fanon, Solanas, Espinosa, Rocha, and Brecht remain strong presences, but they are now joined by Edward Said, Gayatri Spivak, Cornell West, Piere Bourdieu, C. L. R. James, George Mosse, Stuart Hall, and Ngugi Wa Thiong. *Questions of Third Cinema* carries out the goals of the 1986 Edinburgh Manifesto, which argued that "the complexity of the shifting dynamics between intra and inter-national differences and power relations has shown simple models of class domination at home and imperialism abroad to be totally inadequate" and which called for a sophisticated approach to questions of domination/subordination, centre/periphery, and resistance/hegemony. Indeed, *Questions of Third Cinema* constitutes a radical negation of the binarism that makes the first world the locus of theory and the third world the locus of unreflecting experience. The authors reject the positing of third world cinema and theory as antonyms, a dichotomy which indirectly recapitulates the first-world's view of itself as head/brain/control center, and the third world as body/raw material/i.e., as the unreflected "raw" to the West's "cooked" (not-so-nouvelle) "cuisine." *Questions of Third Cinema* radically interrogates such ethnocentric prejudices, suggesting that in fact it might be first-world theory that is exhausted, and elitist Western aesthetics that are at an impasse.

In his response to Jameson, Ai jaz Ahmad makes the point that whereas the first Capitalist and the second Socialist worlds are usually defined actively, in terms of their systems of production, the third world is defined passively, as having had a certain "experience," as having "suffered" and "undergone" colonialism. One of the signal virtues of *Questions of Third Cinema* is that it strives to give a positive, rather than a merely reactive, content to the concept of the "third world." Much as Albert Memmi rejected Sartre's vision (in *Anti-Semite and Jew*) of Jews as merely the projection of their enemies, insisting that there is a Jewish history and identity quite apart from the paranoid imaginings of anti-semites, so the contributors to the volume, notably Haile Gerima, Teshome Gabriel, and Clyde Taylor, emphasize commonalities forged in oppression, the reality of a vibrant third world resistance culture displaying its own creative differences. They stress the presence of a fighting community (Haile Gerima), the centrality of oral traditions (Teshome Gabriel, Manthia Diawara), and a distinct attitude toward "spirits, magic, masquerades, and rituals [which] . . . still constitute knowledge and provide collective security and protection from forces of evil" (Teshome Gabriel). Gabriel exposes the culture-bound inadequacy of first-world theories based on psychoanalysis for a third world cinema which "relies more on an appeal to social and political conflicts as the prime rhetorical strategy and less on the paradigm of oedipal conflict and resolution." Although one can quibble about specifics, this foregrounding of positive differences can serve as an antidote to psycho-analytic imperialism, as well as to a certain kind of left colonialism which scans a vast and variegated third world horizon to find only passive victims. Although anti-imperialist, this miserabilist and victimological approach remains eurocentric by implying that life in the third world is reducible to a pathological response to Western penetration. This inverted form of narcissism, rather than claiming that everywhere "we" (the first world) have brought "them" civilization, instead claims that everywhere we have brought Diabolical Evil, and everywhere their enfeebled societies have succumbed to our insidious influence. The vision remains Promethean, but here Prometheus has brought not fire but the holocaust, reproducing what Barbara Christian calls the "West's outlandish claim of having invented everything, including Evil."[2]

Clyde Taylor, in another essay, rightly detects neo-colonialist overtones in certain left denunciations of third world "particularism," denunciations which usually mask first world particularisms dressed in universal robes. "Consideration of the sensory/organizational pleasure of the dominated," Taylor writes, "is disallowed or devalued in aesthetic analysis," since the interpretations of the dominated are "debased by animalized sensitivity, bruised with rage, discolored by pain and protest, and thereby rendered unrepresentative." The eurocentric "white liberal" is thus always surprised by the "unaesthetic" and "non-objective" rage of the oppressed. Recent responses to a pro-Palestinian essay by Edward Said in *Critical Inquiry* provide a telling illustration of Taylor's point. William Philips, in *Partisan Review*, laments Said's abandonment of the "rules and courtesies of academic discourse" to write like a "street fighter" whose "anger breaks into his prose."[3] Anger is thus seen as inherently unbecoming in intellectuals, who are presumed to view the world with olympian detachment and reckoned to weigh all sides with dispassionate equanimity. The idea that anger might be a rational and coherent response to an oppressive situation is simply ruled out of bounds, and a major literary scholar-theorist, in the name of "civility," is treated as if he were a juvenile delinquent. (Objectivity, Fanon reminds us, is always wielded against the native.)

The intrinsic identification of Bakhtinian categories with difference and alterity, I have argued elsewhere, their built-in affinity for the oppressed and the marginal, makes them especially appropriate for the analysis of oppositional and third worldist cultural practices.[4] Although Bakhtin did not specifically address himself to all oppressions, he staked out a conceptual space for them, as it were, in advance. Although Bakhtin does not speak directly to Third World concerns—indeed the very concept was non-existent at the time he was writing—his broadly-formulated denunciation of "sociohierarchical inequality" and all forms of "inequality among people" is eminently well-suited to them, offering a corrective to certain Eurocentric prejudices, including those within Marxist thought. One can even discern a kind of "match" between Bakhtinian categories and the call-and-response dialogism, the polyrhythms, the multi-accentuality, and the breakdown of performer/spectator boundaries associated with the polycentric aesthetic of "Afrocentric" culture. A number of the contributors to *Questions of Third Cinema* (notably Paul Willemen, Teshome Gabriel, Clyde Taylor, and Trin T. Minh-ha) make productive use of Bakhtin, here regarded not as a fashionable new guru, but rather as the source of suggestive conceptual categories—"dialogism," "heteroglossia," "chronotope"—capable of illuminating the issues being theorized within Third Cinema. (Kobena Mercer, in an essay included in *Blackframes*, also deploys Bakhtinian categories with flair and intelligence.) Paul Willemen, for example, uses Bakhtin to conceptualize the "dialogic" relation between intellectuals and "the people" as jointly engaged in bringing about social change. He deploys Bakhtin's notion of the chronotope as the "time-space articulations characteristic of particular, historically determined conceptions of the relations between the human, the social, and the natural world." Bakhtin, for Willemen, helps us de-binarize the discussion of third cinema. In words that resonate richly for the analysis of all complex cultural relations, Willemen quotes the Bakhtin of *Speech Genres*: "[the] dialogic encounter of two cultures does not result in merging or mixing. Each retains its own unity and open totality, but they are mutually enriched." Willemen avoids the innocuous pluralism typical of certain liberal appropriations of Bakhtin, however, by recalling Bakhtin's emphasis on the *unequal* power relations between discourses, considerations which lead us "far from the post-modern or the multiculturalist free play of differences, the republican carnival of voices, towards a politics of otherness as the precondition for any cultural politics."

While Willemen's introductory essay disclaims any simple identity between "third cinema" and "third world cinema," in fact the book as a whole reveals considerable slippage between the two concepts. Willemen develops a programmatic and polemical view of third cinema as a cinema of research and experimentation, equidistant from both mainstream and auteurist cinema. Willemen distinguishes between "counter-cinema" as a prescriptive aesthetics—i.e., do the opposite of what dominant cinema does— and third cinema, with its openness to the historical variability of aesthetic strategies. Third Cinema is opposed to emotional manipulation and aimed at an "analytically informed understanding of the social formation and a desire to change it in a socialist direction." Willemen cites with approval Teshome Gabriel's characterization of the defining trait of Third Cinema as "not so much where it is made, or even who makes it, but rather, the ideology it espouses and the consciousness it displays." Gabriel's formulation, as Willemen points out, avoids an originary notion—by which third world cinema

would refer to any film produced in the third world by a third world filmmaker—
and instead ties it to a political program and vision.

Although the very concept of third world cinema would seem to be premised on a
kind of international coalition of nationalisms, *Questions of Third Cinema* only
sporadically engages the crucial question of the "national." And to avoid the
question of the national and slide directly towards an international aesthetic, as
Willemen warns, eliminates "the defining characteristics of third cinema itself: the
aim of rendering a particular social situation intelligible to those engaged in a
struggle to change it in a socialist direction." Indeed, it might be argued that
precisely because of the third world's neo-colonized status, its intellectuals/
filmmakers have necessarily been concerned with the ramifications of nationalism.
Hollywood filmmakers enjoy the luxury of being "above" petty nationalist concerns only because they can take for granted the projection of a national power
which facilitates the making and the dissemination of their films. In the Third
World, in contrast, national power rarely provides a quiet substratum of confidence;
rather, national powerlessness generates a Sisyphysian struggle to conquer an
elusive "authenticity" to be constructed anew with every generation. Haunted by
the spectre of cultural colonialism, of being too servile toward the dominant model,
third world cinema has been habitually evaluated in terms of its contribution to
"development" and "national liberation."

The concept of the national, however, is hardly unproblematic. Historically,
nationalism has always oscillated between its progressive and regressive poles
depending on the political character of the power bloc which mobilizes nationalism
to constitute its own hegemony. Many of the early discussions of nationalism,
furthermore, took it as axiomatic that the issue was simply one of expelling the
foreign to "recover" the national, as if the nation were a kind of "heart of the
artichoke" to be found by peeling away the outer leaves. The simple elimination of
foreign influences, it was assumed, would automatically allow the national culture
to emerge in all its plenitude and glory. But this originary idea of the national is
fraught with problems, since it 1) elides the realities of class, camouflaging possible
contradictions between different sectors of the third world society, 2) fails to
provide criteria for distinguishing exactly what is worth retaining in the national
tradition (a sentimental nationalism was always liable to valorize patriarchal social
institutions—Sembene mocks such valorizations in *Xala* by having his neo-
colonialized black elite defend polygamy in the name of "l'Africanite!"). 3) Even
apart from the question of class, every country is characterized by heteroglossia;
nations are at once urban and rural, male and female, elite and non-elite. The nation
as unitary subject inevitably muffles the "polyphony" of social and ethnic voices
characteristic of heteroglot culture. 4) The precise nature of the national "essence"
to be recuperated, finally, is almost always elusive and chimerical. Some nationalist
purists locate this essence in an organic past—e.g., prior to the colonizer's arrival—
or in the rural interior of the country, or in a prior stage of development (the pre-
industrial), or in a non-European ethnicity. But things are never so simple. A
country such as India, for example, constitutes an infinitely complex and shifting
overlay of cultural traces, inscribed in what Homi Bhabha calls "the perverse
palimpsest of colonial identity." The historical experience of the African diaspora,
similarly, is marked by what Stuart Hall calls "profound discontinuity," the result of

a "long and discontinuous series of transformations."[5] National collectivities must therefore be envisioned, for Hall, along a double axis of similarity and difference, continuity and rupture. They must be seen as "imagined" communities, in Benedict Anderson's apt phrase, just as many of the traditions valorized by nationalism must be seen as what Hobsbawm calls "invented traditions."[6] Any definition of nationality, then, must be selective, must take class into account, must allow for racial difference and cultural heterogeneity, and must be dynamic, seeing "the nation" as an evolving, imaginary "productive" construct rather than an originary essence.

An altered philosophical conjuncture has also subtly undermined the idea of the national. The structuralist and post-structuralist attack on the "centered subject," while on one level seeming to promise an undermining of old hierarchies, on another casts doubt, by extension, on the nation as the noble protagonist of a collective epic, as a trans-individual cogito or Sartrean "self-writ-large." The deconstructive assault on all that is "originary" by implication calls into question the idea of an "originary" nation. The old utopia of "authentic" national culture, in such a context, comes to seem a meaningless and hopelessly nostalgic chimera. In *Questions of Third Cinema*, it is Homi Bhabha, above all, who advances the post-structuralist critique of the nation as unified subject. Speaking in the voice of the theoretically sophisticated post-colonial deconstructionist, he begins his essay "The Commitment to Theory" by rejecting the view of theory as necessarily constituting the "elite language of the socially and culturally privileged" inevitably situated "within the Eurocentric archives of an imperialist or neo-colonialist West." Bhabha rejects the binarism of theory versus politics, arguing in post-structuralist fashion against "dualistic counter-myths of racial purity." While acknowledging that Anglo-American hegemony pervades the mass media as well as academic institutions, Bhabha doubts that the new languages of theoretical critique simply "reflect" hegemony. The interests of Western theory are not necessarily collusive with the hegemonic rule of the West as a power bloc. We must distinguish, Bhabha argues usefully, between the institutional history of critical theory and its conceptual potential for change and innovation. What is the function of a committed theoretical perspective, Bhabha asks, once the cultural and historical hybridity of the post-colonial world is taken as a given?

Political positions, Bhabha points out, are not simply identifiable as progressive or reactionary, bourgeois or radical, prior to the act of critique or outside the terms and conditions of their discursive and textual address. There is no simplistic opposition between ideological miscognition and revolutionary truth, but only the ambivalent juxtaposition, the "interstitial" and "invaginated" mingling of the factual and the fantasmatic. Political referents and priorities (the people, class struggle, anti-racism), Bhabha continues, are not "there" in some primordial, naturalistic sense. Nor do they reflect a unitary or homogeneous political object. The agents of political change are "discontinuous, divided subjects caught in conflicting interests and identities." The objects and subjects of political change only make sense as they come to be constructed in the *discourses* of feminism or Marxism or the Third Cinema. Bhabha therefore favors a politics of address, of the sign, seeing politics as a struggle of identifications and a "war of positions." The problem, for him, is whether such split subjects and differentiated social movements, displaying ambivalent and divided forms of identification, can be represented by a collective will.

The non-unitary nature of culture, Bhabha argues, requires us to imagine a "third space of enunciation," which would challenge notions of historical identity of culture as a homogenizing, unifying force authenticated by the original Past and kept alive in the national tradition of the People. "It is that Third Space, though unrepresentable in itself, which constitutes the discursive conditions of enunciation that ensure that the meaning and symbols of culture have no primordial unity or fixity; that even the same signs can be appropriated, translated, rehistoricized and read anew." While conceptually exhilarating, Bhabha's approach also provokes a tinge of doubt. The reader begins the essay with a thrill of expectancy, looking forward to deconstructing identities and transcending binarism, but finishes it with a severe case of post-structuralist vertigo, as so many identities have been deconstructed and so many binarisms transcended that certain crucial distinctions seem lost. Talk of all identities, even of conflicted, multiple, heterogeneous, discontinuous identities, comes to seem problematic. While recognizing the need for solidarity, the theoretical "grounds" of solidarity seem pulled out from underneath our feet.

Trin T. Minh-ha, in her poetical-theoretical ruminations on "representing the other," meanwhile, argues that the colonialist attitude has moved from obnoxious exteriority—i.e., overt hostility to the third world other—to obtrusive interiority. Now the colonialist probes the secrets of the other without ever relinquishing his own. While white Europeans confidently make films about the Goba of the Zambesi or the Tasaday in the Phillipine rain forest, the Third World filmmaker who presumes to speak about another Third World people is seen as somehow illegitimate. Like Bhabha, Minh-ha too questions originary notions, such as the assumption that only Asians can make films about Asians, Africans about Africans, etc. In such cases, she asks provocatively, what defines the insider as opposed to the outsider? Skin color? (yellows never film blacks?). Language? (only Yoruba speakers can film the Yoruuba?). Nation? Political affinity? What about those with hyphenated identities and hybrid realities? Trin T. Minh-ha, like many of the contributors to *Questions of Third Cinema*, undercuts the inside/outside opposition. There is no third world, to cite her widely quoted aphorism, without its first world, no first world without its third.

Haile Gerima, speaking in the urgent voice of the activist-filmmaker, emphasizes the community both as source of support and as audience. He salutes his own adopted Afro-American community as one of "never-ending struggle" that has "repeatedly rebelled and insisted on challenging and dismantling the oppressive aspects of the USA." Gerima calls for triangular cooperation between 1) the audience/community, 2) the filmmaker/storyteller and 3) the activist/critic, all engaged in constructive dialogue and motivated by a desire to effect the transformation of a given society in a collective, communal cinema language." He invokes a practical, concrete, multi-pronged program, involving cultural awareness organizations, film appreciation clubs, and collective production and distribution of film. Gerima sees a double role for third cinema, combining communitarian celebration and demystificatory critique, on the one hand catalyzing revolutionary uplift of third world masses, and on the other demsytifying the "superiority" of the developed countries, bringing the West down into the "human orbit." Gerima also delineates the human costs, for Afro-Americans, of making films within a racially polarized environment, where African-American artists are "choicelessly engaged in responding to the very abnormal ills of that society." The "allegorical" role projected onto black people results in tremendous pressure on beginning film-makers, who do not enjoy the luxury of growing from film to film. A kind of split personality emerges: a dissembling self that acquiesces in the typically "ignorant racist statements of people sitting in powerful positions" and an activist self which passes judgment. Gerima ends with an eloquent plea for a truly self-representational cinema, something "we owe to our ancestors, who left us monumental footprints from the Nubian and Axum all way to the Zimbabwean civilizations. . . ." If we do not at least try, Gerima warns, we will "be tried by the oldest skeletons of humanity for the crime of neglect and betrayal of our history."

Gerima compares the status of third world people in commercial cinema to that of the fly on the planet: "hovering over garbage, hunting for leftovers, predetermined from creation to be miserable, identity-less." While interesting for those obsessed with overpopulation, flies are a danger and threat to the privileged "developed" society: "You can't count them. They don't have names. Who cares to speak their language? . . . who takes their life seriously? . . . who goes to see flies talk and debate about love and hate, their desires and dreams of changing the world?" Gerima also exposes the implicit racism of pseudo-humanist entertainments like *Missing*, dedicated to illustrating "the human value of the European American" while simultaneously devaluing third world people, where the "stars of the West [play] our experiences for us." (The view that third world people cannot "star" in the realm of cinematic representation, even in their own stories, as in the case of *Mississippi Burning*, one might add, exists on a continuum with the prejudice that third world people also cannot "star" within the realm of political representation.)

Hamid Naficy's "Mediaworks Representation of the Other: The Case of Iran," meanwhile, mingles a theoretical introduction deploying a politicized psycho-analytic approach with thorough empirical research on a specific issue of represen-tation. He inventories the processes of what he calls, on the analogy of Freud's "dreamwork," "mediawork:" 1) domestication of the oppositional and subcultural other; 2) stereotyping; 3) framing via teasers, intro, promos; 4) scheduling designed to instill specific habits of consumption; 5) the setting of agendas for national political and cultural debates; 6) the use of classical Hollywood style which itself "carries" an ideology; and 7) the replication of a panoptic regime. In his shrewd analysis of "crisis journalism," Naficy clarifies the processes by which a few American hostages came to dominate the national consciousness by disseminating images which marked the American imagination: turbaned mullahs, veiled women, raised fists, shouting mobs, and blindfolded American hostages, all as part of what he calls the "commodification of the Iranian threat." Naficy examines a discursive continuum that includes the news, entertainment shows (Johnny Car-son's Ayatolla jokes), T-shirts, and popular music ("A Message to Khomeini"), along with feature films such as *Final Option* (1983) and *Threads* (1984), and TV docu-dramas such as *On Wings of Eagles* (1986).

Questions of Third Cinema features major essays by two important theorists of third cinema: Teshome Gabriel and Clyde Taylor. In "Towards a Critical Theory of Third World Film," Gabriel develops a vision of Third Cinema in the spirit of Glauber Rocha on Cinema Nova: "Wherever there is a film-maker prepared to stand up against commercialism, exploitation, pornography and the tyranny of technique, there is to be found the living spirit of New Cinema." Drawing on Fanon, Gabriel posits three "phases" of Third World film: 1) unqualified assimilation (where the danger is alienation; 2) remembrance (where the danger is romanticization), and 3) combat, where film explores the lives and struggles of third world peoples in a spirit of service and militancy. Gabriel makes provocative generalizations about the manipulation of time and space in Third World Cinema. Here one can agree with the thrust of the analysis while arguing over specifics. One might ask, for example, as Ai jaz asks of Jameson, whether it is possible to find a unifying aesthetic for all non-European cultures, or, in this case, for all third world cinemas. In his introductory article, Willemen finds Gabriel's homogenization of the third cinema chronotope into a single aesthetic family "premature" in its attempt to define a common chronotope for films as diverse as those of Ritwik Gatak, with their intricate interweaving of historical, biographical, natural, and emotional rhythms, and the allegorical farcical strategies of films like those of Joaquim Pedro de Andrade. Gabriel's analysis is suggestive, however, in its attempt to posit correlations between cinematic technique and ideology/culture. Gabriel extends the tradition of Afro-centric critique of Western modes, in the spirit of W. E. B. DuBois's contrast (in *The Souls of Black Folk*), between the communalizing ethos of Afro-American culture and the exacerbated individualism of the white middle-class male ethos. Gabriel offers a deep critique of a certain West—not the totality of the West but undeniably a real tendency within it—implicitly scoring the West's possessive individualism, its time-is-money, success- and-visibility-above-all values, most recently incarnated in the yuppie lifestyle. The western ethos here critiqued— puritanical, Manichean, utilitarian, productivist—was proleptically encapsulated, I would add, in Occidental literary heroes such as Robinson Crusoe, the archetype of the self-sufficient home-economicus, with his armored ego and neurotic obsession with cannibals. Clyde Taylor touches on this same cultural contrast between first-world individualism and third-world communalism in the opening epigraphs of his essay, where he pits Descartes "I think therefore I am"— the philosophical locus classicus of the western autonomous self-determining ego—against the dialogic communalism of a Xhosa proverb: "A person is a person only because of other people." Such broad cultural dichotomoies work, of course, only when not rigidified into Manichean absolutes. The kernel of dialogical communitarianism is hardly absent from the first world, nor is the germ of possessive individualism unknown in the third.

Gabriel's "Third Cinema as Guardian of Popular Memory" brings additional cultural substance to the concept of "third cinema." Gabriel speaks of "the wretched of the earth" as "the subjects and the critics of Third Cinema," as those who have always "smelled history in the wind" and who serve to "give history a push and popular memory a future." Citing Med Hondo's *West Indies* as a hero-less "carnival of cinema," Gabriel evokes the possibilities of a multi-generational and trans-individual autobiography focussing on a "collective subject"; (Solanas's *Los Hijos de Martin Fierro* provides another example). Art in Africa, Gabriel points out, does not form an autonomous realm of activity but is rather an integral part of everyday life, with daily functions both sacred and profane; there, aesthetics are not self-justifying but rather a function of "critical spectatorship." Gabriel's schema of contrasts between dominant and third cinema, meanwhile, is more useful as an extrapolation of tendencies than as literal-minded description. Third cinema, Gabriel rightly points out, tends to be less psychologistic, but that fact might have as much to do with the dissemination of Brechtian ideas in the Third World as it has to do with the communitarian values of oral cultures. Both first and third world traditions are heteroglossic, many-languaged; and both traditions interpenetrate each other. The schematic use of angle for political commentary, cited by Gabriel as typical of Third Cinema, for example, is common to Orson Welles and Glauber Rocha; indeed, it is Welles that Rocha cites in such films as *Land In Anguish*. (From another perspective, one might see Welles's work, especially in the never-released *It's All True*, as foreshadowing certain features of Third Cinema.)

To link non-Western cinema with oral tradition, meanwhile, is effective with some but not all traditions, working especially well, as both Gabriel himself and Manthia Diawara show, for the African film tradition, and, as Clyde Taylor has tellingly demonstrated elsewhere, for the Afro-American film tradition.[7] That there are an infinity of mediations between the oral traditions and their re-elaboration in film is a point made beautifully in Manthia Diawara's impeccably argued "Oral Literature and African Film: Narratology in *Wend Kunni*." Apart from providing a concise survey of the literature on the oral tradition in Africa, Diawara shows the limitations of antecedent approaches which tended to restrict their efforts to documenting the traces of oral literature in film (presence of the griot, heroes and heroines borrowed from the oral tradition) rather than register the transformation effected by the cinema in the narrative points of view. Rather than be "faithful" to the oral tradition, the oral tradition is deployed in a *transformative* way. In *Wend Kunni*, "orality is the subject of the film because it incorporates an oral rendering of the tale which it also subverts." Diawara rigorously enumerates the diverse myth-kernels in the film in terms of Proppian-Greimasian "functions," revealing the various ways that the myths are subverted for feminist and revolutionary purposes. Combining close textual analysis, theoretical sophistication, and acute cultural sensitivity, Diawara demonstrates that while the griot's narrative is concerned with the restoration of traditional order, the filmmaker points to the hopeful possibility of a new order. In the oral tradition a woman who defies the elders' advice to remarry would probably be considered a witch, but in the film, the "witch" is in fact shown to be a harmless soul with a sick son and a missing husband. The film thus practices what Diawara calls the "subversive deployment of orality;" the "deterritorializing" of the story transforms its semantic value in favor of the subversive activities at work in the film.

In "Black Cinema in the Post-aesthetic Era," Clyde Taylor extends and radicalizes Gabriel's quasi-anthropological critique of the Western ethos and aesthetic. Taylor gives us a whirlwind tour of Occidental racism, tracing its roots to ancient class divisions between the aristocracy and the lower orders, through a Renaissance humanism which projected "the new European man as man-in-general," to Neoclassicism, where standards are set by the "bourgeois gentleman in good health," to Kantian notions of ideal, non-practical art as the putative object of disinterested contemplation. The Western tradition, from classical Greek ocular metaphors and Cartesian rationalism, encourages the observing, classifying, and ordering of physical characteristics of human bodies. After this propitious beginning, Taylor widens his attack into an assault on "aesthetics" as complicit with the Western organization of knowledge and visually centered racism. To say "Western bourgeois aesthetics," for Taylor, "is to be tautological." While provocative, Taylor's gesture strikes me as decidedly mixed in its effects. It has, first of all, a number of salutary aspects. First, it calls for a deep rather than a superficial critique, of questioning not individual judgments of taste and value but rather the very categories in which we think. In the Afro-centric tradition, Taylor unashamedly relates art to use, against a high-bourgeois Kantian tradition of art as useless and disinterested beauty, an idea linked, as Bourdieu points out, to class values and tastes. Secondly, Taylor relativizes the question of aesthetic pleasure, exposing its social and even racial dimension. To Marx's "Who profits?" Taylor adds "Whom does it please? For whom is it beautiful? What ends does this specific pleasure serve?" Third, Taylor's critique questions the separating off of art and aesthetics, its constitution as an autonomous realm of classification. Taylor's provocative formulations fly in the face of the formalist fetishization of art-as-object, a fetishization exemplified in Kirstin Thompson's astonishing claim, in *Breaking the Glass Armor*, that "all cultures seem to have art, and they all recognize the aesthetic as a realm apart."[8] While all societies display an aesthetic sense, they do not necessarily "have" art in the Western sense, nor does art necessarily form a "realm apart." Thompson's formulation is inadequate not only to the many third world cultures which interweave art with ritual, magic, and everyday practicality, but also even to the Western tradition, where the constitution of art as an autonomous realm is a relatively recent, and even then a contested, development. The ritual theatre of the Greeks, for example, clearly linked song, dance, and theatrical speech to magical, religious, and political practices, and even in the Renaissance tradition art was seen as *utile* (useful) as well as *dulce* (sweet).

In other respects, however, Taylor's demonization of aesthetics seems ambiguous and even counter-productive. The jettisoning of aesthetics seems to implicitly discourage the idea of formal research favored not only by first world theorists like Brecht but also by many third world and third cinema practitioners of the arts. (That Taylor himself recognizes the value of formal and aesthetic approaches is of course demonstrated in his own work on independent Afro-American cinema, where he posits an aesthetic in which musicality and oral tradition, for example, form essential elements.) It strikes me as more productive, therefore, to attack the generating ideational matrix, the classifying and hierarchizing impulse that creates the separating off of aesthetics from politics and ethics, rather than to denounce aesthetics per se. We might speak, therefore, of politicizing aesthetics, or subverting aesthetics, rather than eliminating aesthetics altogether. Taylor's proposed substitutions for aesthetics—in a recent Conference he mentioned "magic" and "ethics"—bring as many new problems as they solve, since "ethics" might easily lead into a quagmire of Platonic or Christian moralizing, while a "magical" discourse easily gives way to mysticism and mystifications.[9] While art has magical and ethical dimensions, it is not reducible to either. To say that art is "specific" is not to suggest that it is "autonomous."

Although I am deeply sympathetic to Clyde Taylor's attack on Euro-centrism, then, I do not equate "Eurocentric" with "European" or "aesthetics" with "Western aesthetics." Euro-centrism needs to be questioned from without and from within, the two interrogations hopefully being mutually self-reinforcing. I therefore prefer Taylor's formulation in another essay, where the issue is posed not as one of condemning first world thinkers en bloc but rather of discerning "which [Western thinkers] and their ideas bring aid to the enterprise of liberating consciousness."[10] The cultural heterogeneities of the West cannot be reduced to the "competition of western male elites." The fact is that the West has known many aesthetics including an aesthetic of "grotesque realism" which inverts and transforms the very notion of the beautiful, turning conventional aesthetics on its head, not to abolish aesthetics, but rather to locate a new kind of popular, convulsive, rebellious "anti-canonical" beauty, one which dares to bring out the grotesquerie of the powerful, and the latent beauty of the popular and the "vulgar." Bakhtin's oxymoronic carnival aesthetic, in which everything is pregnant with its opposite, I would argue, implies an alternative logic of nonexclusive opposites and permanent contradiction that transgresses the monologic true-or-false thinking typical of Western rationalism. One can thus discern another "anti-canonical" tradition *within* the West, one which would go from Greek Dionysianism—and Greece, as Bernal demonstrates in *Black Athena*, represents an amalgam of African, Semitic, and Greek-European elements— through Roman saturnalia, to the grotesque realism of medieval "carnivalesque" fictioners (Chaucer, Rabelais) to Shakespeare, to Jarry and Surrealism on to the counter-cultural art of the sixties. There one might find inklings of what Bell Hooks has called "an aesthetic of agency, of empowerment, an aesthetics of strange and oppositional beauty."[11] Why not build on what is progressive and revolutionary, what is counter-hegemonic and anti-colonialist in these movements, rather than simplistically lump them together in an anti-colonialist "mark of the plural?" It is also important, I think, to recover the anti-colonialist strain (however ambiguous) within the Western tradition—Montaigne's anti-European inversions of the cannibalist trope in "Des Cannibales," the denunciation of colonialism in Swift's *Gulliver's Travels*, the ironic inversions of civilized/savage in Conrad's *Heart of Darkness*? We might call attention, for example, to the anti-colonialist Diderot, who acerbically mocked fashionable Europe's capacity to shed narcissistic tears over factitious sentimental dramas while withholding all empathy toward the millions of real-life black victims of slavery. Rending this tradition actual and productive strikes me as an important strategy, at least for Euro-Americans, for critiquing Western racism and colonialism from within, a way of fulfilling Malcom X's injunction to sympathetic whites to fight racism within the white community rather than paternalistically try to "help" or advise blacks.

Recently, Cornell West has called for Afro-American intellectuals to be aware of, and participate in, but also keep their distance from the postmodernism debate, seen as a parochial form of occidental navel-gazing. The precursor term "modern," West points out, was not only used to devalue the culture of oppressed peoples but also failed to illuminate the internal complexities of these cultures.[12] Taylor cites Paul Gilroy to make the point that the Afro-American "take" on movements such as modernism and post-modernism is distinct. While for whites, the aesthetics of modernism may have centered on a "detachment if not revulsion from the human," Gilroy argues, for the African diaspora, "constituted for several centuries in a 'milieu of dispossession,' modernity raised a different set of issues centering on the need to recover and validate black culture and reincarnate the sense of being and belonging which had been erased from it by slavery" (p. 110). The same point, I would suggest, could be made about post-modernism. The post-modernist discourse argues that the lines between center and margin have been erased, that the category of nation has become irrelevant. Within the global village of transnational capitalism, some postmodernists argue, the traditional privileges of Western patriarchal culture have been annulled, as all cultures get caught up in the meaningless whirl of mass-mediated simulacra. Baudrillard's account of the implosive collapse of boundaries in a mass-mediated global society, exhilaratingly apt in its metaphorical rendering of the "feel" of life in the simulacral world of the postmodern, remains painfully inadequate to the experience of the peripheralized. For if postmodernism has spread the feel of first world consumerist culture around the globe, it has hardly deconstructed the unequal relations of power between the metropolitan and the marginalized countries.

The postmodernism debate, as both Taylor and Cornel West point out, does not seriously acknowledge the distinctive cultural and political practices of oppressed peoples. Much of postmodern theory constitutes a very sophisticated example of what Anwar Abdul Malek calls the "hegemonism of possessing minorities," in that its denial of the reality of marginalization is a luxury only those not marginalized can afford. The neutralization of the radical differences of the marginalized elides the fact that some groups cannot help seeing the world through their own irreducible marginality. Thus the center proclaims the end of its privileges just when the periphery begins to lay claim to them. "Surely it is no coincidence," writes Elizabeth Fox-Genovese, "that the Western white male elite proclaimed the death of the subject at precisely the moment at which it might have had to share that status with the women and peoples of other races and classes who were beginning to challenge its supremacy."[13] Thus thinkers from the center, blithely confident in national power and international projection, denounce peripheral nationalism as atavistic and passe. Metropolitan writers announce the "death of the author" just as peripheral writers begin to win an international audience, and metropolitan filmmakers call for the "fin de cinema" just as third world nations begin to create viable film industries.

At the same time, the idea that movements such as modernism and post-modernism grant *no* place to third world "others" needs to be nuanced and complicated when one moves to a global cultural perspective. First of all, on an aesthetic level, an Afro-American cultural phenomenon like jazz is defiantly modernist, musically translating and transforming what Stuart Hall would call the "radical discontinuities" of diaspora life. Indeed, third world culture generally can be seen, as many Caribbean and Latin American theorists have argued, as the proleptic site of postmodern, neologistic culture. Secondly, from still another perspective, some avant-garde movements linked to modernism, such as surrealism, were not only vehemently anti-colonialist, but were also concretely inspired by what we would now call third world cultural forms: Leger, Cendrars, and Milhaud based their staging of "La Creation du Monde" on African cosmogony; Bataille wrote about pre-Columbian art and Aztec sacrifices; Artaud fled France for the Mexico of the Tarahumara Indians, and the avant-garde generally cultivated the mystique of voodoo and African art.

A wholescale denunciation of all modernism en bloc allows no place, more importantly, for anti-colonialist *third world* modernisms. In the 1920s, the Brazilian "anthropophogic" modernists called for the "de-Vespucciazation" of the Americas—

the reference is to Amerigo Vespucci—and the "de-Cabralization" of Brazil—referring to Pedro Cabral, Brazil's Portuguese "discoverer." Their *Cannibalist Review* described colonialism as a "descent into slavery" and lamented that Brazilians continue to be "slaves of the Occident . . . and of a rotting European culture." They denounced "the importers of canned consciousness" and the "colonial mentality." Against this servile mentality, the modernists proposed "the unification of all efficacious revolts tending in a human direction," offering as their own counter-utopia the model of indigenous, matriarchal society, without armies, police or social hierarchy, a culture characterized by a "sensibility learned in harmony with the earth."[14] What is perhaps needed at this juncture, then, is a high-flying synthesis of all of the alternative liberatory cultural aesthetics: the "anthropophagic" aesthetic of the Brazilian Modernists and Tropicalists, Henry Louis Gates's Exu-signifying-monkey aesthetic, Kobena Mercer's "diaspora aesthetic," Solanas/Getino's "third cinema," Rocha's "aesthetic of hunger," Gabriel's "nomadic aesthetic," and Espinosa's "imperfect" aesthetic.

Questions of Third Cinema is not without its practical and theoretical tensions, between those who see themselves as academics/theoreticians and those who see themselves as filmmaker/activists, and between those who speak a discourse of truth and authenticity, emphasizing the recovery of identity and organic community, and those who speak a poststructuralist discourse of fractured identities and discontinuous subjects. In the end, however, these tensions are creative, contributing to a jazzistic spirit of antagonistic collaboration. The differences of view emerge less from substantive political differences than from differences of location and positionality, of discursive environments, generated by a situation in which different voices speak from necessarily distinct positions, whether as filmmakers concretely depending on community support, or as postcolonial academics speaking in a situation where subversion can *also* be theoretical and at times even rarefied and abstract. It is normal that filmmakers, absorbed in the quotidian hustle of filmmaking, should find academic debates somewhat remote and quasi-irrelevant, and just as normal that those who swim in academic discourse like fish in water should find the work of the filmmakers under-theorized. It is normal that post-colonials working in the first world would speak of multiple and superimposed palimpsestic identities, of hybridity and syncretism, and just as normal that those filmmakers and theorists who see a community under threat, for whom the very idea of identity is an indispensible tool for liberatory mobilization, should speak with more urgent voices of the need to nourish and stimulate the memory and activism of the community. *Questions of Third Cinema* never arrives at a facile consensus, but in the end there is not a single voice in the book that does not enrich the debate, add a nuance, an accent, an intonation, the lack of which would have impoverished the whole.

NOTES

1. See Fredric Jameson, "Third World Literature in the Era of Multinational Capitalism," *Social Text* 15(Fall 1986), 65–68, and Ai jaz Ahmad, "Jameson's Rhetoric of Otherness and the National Allegory," *Social Text* 17(Fall 1987), 3–25.

2. From Work-in-progress presented at the "Gender and Colonialism" Conference hosted by the English Department at University of California Berkeley, October, 1989.

3. See William Phillips, "Intellectuals, Academics and Politics," *Partisan Review*, Vol. LVI, No. 3(1989).

4. For more on Bakhtin and third world cultural questions, see Robert Stam, *Subversive Pleasures: Bakhtin, Cultural Criticism and Film* (Baltimore: Johns Hopkins, 1989) and Kobena Mercer, "Diaspora Culture and the Dialogic Imagination: The Aesthetics of Black Independent Film in Britain," in Mbye B. Cham and Claire Andrade-Watkins, eds., *Blackframes: Critical Perspectives on Black Independent Cinema* (Cambridge: M.I.T. Press, 1988).

5. See Stuart Hall, "Cultural Identity and Cinematic Representation," *Framework* No. 38(1989).

6. See Benedict Anderson, *Imagined Communities: Reflexions on the Origins and Spread of Nationalism* (London: Verso, 1983), and E. J. Hobsbawm and Terence Rogers, eds., *The Invention of Tradition* (Cambridge: Cambridge University Press, 1983).

7. See Clyde Taylor, "Decolonizing the Image: New U.S. Black Cinema," in Peter Steven, ed., *Jump Cut* (New York: Praeger, 1985).

8. See Kirstin Thompson, *Breaking the Glass Armor* (Princeton: Princeton University Press, 1988), p. 9.

9. Taylor suggested "ethics" and "magic" as alternatives as a member of a panel at the recent "Show the Right Thing" Conference on third world programming held at New York University (September 1989).

10. See "Edinburgh Festival 1986—A Reply: Eurocentrics vs. New Thought at Edinburgh" *Framework* 34(1987).

11. From a talk given at the "Show the Right Thing" Conference concerning the exhibition of third world film, held at N.Y.U. (September 1989).

12. See Cornel West, "Black Culture and Postmodernism," in Barbar Kruger and Phil Mariani, eds., *Remaking History* (Seattle: Bay Press, 1899).

13. Elizabeth Fix-Genovese, "The Claims of a Common Culture: Gender, Race, Class and the Canon," *Salmagundi*, 72(Fall 1986), p. 121.

14. These modernist pronouncements are collected in Maria Eugenia Boaventura, *A Vanguarda Antropofagica* (São Paulo: Attica, 1985), pp. 91–100.

Review Essay

Setting Up the Stage: A Decade of Latin American Film Scholarship

Ana M. López

Barnard, Tim, ed. *Argentine Cinema*. Toronto: Nightwood Editions, 1986.

Burton, Julianne. *Cinema and Social Change in Latin America: Conversations With Filmmakers*. Austin: University of Texas Press, 1986.

Burton, Julianne. *The New Latin American Cinema: An Annotated Bibliography*. New York: Smyrna Press, 1983.

Chanan, Michael. *The Cuban Image: Cinema and Cultural Politics in Cuba*. London: British Film Institute, 1985.

Chanan, Michael. *Twenty-five Years of the New Latin American Cinema*. London: British Film Institute, 1983.

Fusco, Coco, ed. *Reviewing Histories: Selections from New Latin American Cinema*. Buffalo, NY: Hallwalls, 1987.

Johnson, Randal. *Cinema Novo X Five: Masters of Contemporary Brazilian Film*. Austin: University of Texas Press, 1984.

Johnson, Randal. *The Film Industry in Brazil: Culture and the State*. Pittsburgh: University of Pittsburgh Press, 1987.

Johnson, Randal and Robert Stam, eds. *Brazilian Cinema*. Rutherford, NJ: Associated University Presses, 1982 (paper edition, University of Texas Press, 1988).

King, John and Nissa Torrents, eds. *The Garden of Forking Paths: Argentine Cinema*. London: National Film Theater, 1988.

Mora, Carl J. *Mexican Cinema: Reflections of a Society, 1896–1980*. Berkeley: University of California Press, 1982.

Schnitman, Jorge A. *Film Industries in Latin America: Dependency and Development*. Norwood, NJ: Ablex, 1984.

Usabel, Gaizka D. de. *The High Noon of American Films in Latin America*. Ann Arbor: UMI Research Press, 1982.

ANA M. LÓPEZ, is associate professor in the Department of Communication at Tulane University and a Fulbright Fellow in Brazil (Universidade Federal Fluminense), 1989–90. She has published widely on Latin American film and her The New Latin American Cinema *is forthcoming from the University of Illinois Press.*

I. BEFORE THE 1980s

Until the 1980s it was nearly impossible to find an English-language book-length study or more than one or two monographs dedicated to the Latin American cinema.[1] Since then, as the above list of books attests, things have changed. Written by respected North American and British intellectuals, and published by solid academic presses, the texts above suggest that the English-language study of Latin American cinema has finally bypassed its journalistic infancy and achieved academic respectability.

Although the cinema has a long history in Latin America, North American and British scholars did not begin to notice the films of the Southern continent until the formally and politically innovative films of the 1960s made their way north. Inspired by the continuity of the 1959 Cuban revolution and fueled by the political turmoil throughout the continent in the 1960s and 1970s, North American and British (not to mention French) intellectuals—many of whom had also only recently discovered the cinema as an area of serious inquiry—discovered a formally seductive and politically inspiring cinematic "Other" down south in the New Latin American Cinema. Inspired by the apparent radical difference of this kind of Latin American filmmaking (and stimulated by the visibility of key films in cosmopolitan centers like New York and London), the English-language Latin American film bibliography began with essays. As Julianne Burton's excellent annotated bibliography, *The New Latin American Cinema*, attests, only a few anthologies of articles and interviews dealing with Latin American cinema had been published before 1980, whereas close to 150 articles (of varying length, depth, and rigor) had appeared in film and non-specialized journals. Unlike other national cinemas, which were introduced into English-language scholarship via translations of "master" histories written by nationals (for example, the German cinema, which was studied through the histories of Kracauer and Eisner), the various Latin American cinemas first became known ahistorically, through "contemporary" events reported in brief, non-analytical, articles providing, above all, political evaluations.

Many of these articles—for the most part, interviews with filmmakers and filmmaking collectives, brief reviews of individual films, and/or summary introductions to the "new" emerging national cinemas—were journalistic in nature, filled with inaccuracies and contradictory information, and marred by the authors' often inadequate knowledge of Latin America and/or of film analysis/history. Others, especially those published in journals like *Jump Cut*, *Cineaste*, and *Framework* (UK)—which early on committed themselves to political filmmaking and analysis—although introductory in nature, served to foment an interest in the new Latin American cinemas and to encourage other kinds of scholarly work in the field. In fact, many of the texts listed above include works first published in these journals.

Overall, this first decade of Latin American film scholarship was plagued by problems that continue to haunt serious researchers today: difficult access even to contemporary films, scarcity of reliable historical data, lost and/or destroyed earlier film traditions, and unverifiable secondary sources. Not surprisingly, the same international forces that marginalize national cultural production in order to support the hegemony of First World audio-visual material throughout most Latin

American (and other Third World) countries have also made the study and diffusion of Latin American cinema a nearly impossible task in the United States, Britain, and Canada. However, this hardly justifies the often abysmal neglect of research in some of these early works. Barely (if at all) acknowledging the excellent critical and historical work produced by indigenous scholars in either Spanish or Portuguese, English-language writers often (and in spite of political sympathies) approached the Latin American Cinema as Columbus approached the Continent: as discoverers, colonizers, and appropriators.

The most visible marks left by the scattered and often cooptive nature of the first decade of English-language Latin American film scholarship have been, on the negative side, a somewhat journalistic focus on contemporary filmmaking (the most recent films and latest developments), most evident in the proliferation of interviews and reviews that still constitutes a large percentage of today's Latin American film bibliography, and, on the positive side, a commitment to radical politics. Most of the authors and editors listed above are deeply *engagé* with their material. Without compromising their intellectual integrity, the best of these works are proudly partisan while simultaneously engaging the political and aesthetic issues at stake in contemporary Latin American filmmaking.

However, the intellectual/political commitment to radical politics of many authors/editors has sometimes also distorted the focus of this scholarship. Most interested in the political engagement of the New Latin American cinema of the 1960s and 1970s, scholars have tended to focus on these theoretically rich practices while, in some cases, ignoring and/or relegating to brief introductory comments the many decades of political and aesthetic struggles/experimentation that led to them, thereby limiting the historical importance of these practices. In fact, if there is an impulse characteristic of a large part of published work on Latin American film, it is the desire to delineate the field in broad sweeps, identifying and heralding in endless series the countries, films, and filmmakers of contemporary importance, rather than to contribute to an understanding of the critical and theoretical engagement of these works with their historical context.

II. SCHOLARLY RESEARCH IN THE 1980s

Since 1980, one or two books on Latin American cinema have been published every year. They range from an annotated bibliography (by Julianne Burton) to an extensive study of the work of five Brazilian Cinema Novo directors (Randal Johnson's *Cinema Novo X Five*), and include a large number of anthologies as well as single-author works.

The anthologies, although pedagogically useful, often suffer from excessive ambitions. Attempting to cover all of the Latin American cinema or all of a single national cinema, they tend to gather previously published work (some of dubious quality) in haphazard fashion, without any effort to maintain a coherent approach or to offer more than a panoramic vista of the field. The multi-national vastness of the field, the complicated historical determinants of each national cinema, and the theoretical complexity of the very concept of a New Latin American Cinema, are often used as justifications for the unevenness and heterogeneity of the anthologies, but these are ultimately only weak excuses for poorly thought-out collections. In fact, none of the English-language anthologies with a broad Latin American perspective published to date can serve as primers to the history of Latin American cinema as does the useful, albeit uneven, collection of original essays in *Les Cinemas de l'Amerique Latine*.[2] And, among those with a national focus, only one, *Brazilian Cinema*, succeeds as a coherent introduction to a national cinema.

Anthologies—especially those of interviews and manifestos which focus on the New Latin American Cinema—are often also justified politically as an attempt to reflect the political/theoretical engagement of the editors, filmmakers, and films in the formal structure of the scholarship. Arguing for the need to avoid coopting or colonizing the "voices" of the filmmakers or of other scholars, editors often attempt (with varying degrees of success) to efface themselves in order to assert a more collaborative and non-authoritarian scholarly practice. There is undoubtedly a need and a place for interviews and manifestos within Latin American film scholarship, but not at the expense of historical research or of work which critically engages with and contextualizes the interviewees and their films, manifestos, and theoretical positions. Furthermore, giving up one's critical voice to let others speak is, instead of a "politically correct" position, a theoretical cop-out, a refusal to engage with the productive contrast engendered by the encounter between a "first world" academic and "third world" texts. Such a position is ultimately not much different from that of the classic, "disinterested" academic observer and his/her pretense of "objectivity."[3] It is only when the anthology is used as a *collaborative* forum (for example, Johnson and Stam's *Brazilian Cinema* discussed below) to generate a productive, critical engagement among authors and between authors and texts that it succeeds conceptually.

The single-authored texts vary broadly in scope and method and are far more difficult to assess *en masse*. Overall, however, they attest to the value of extensive, intensive research and to the diversity and liveliness of contemporary English-language Latin American film scholarship. Where they are flawed, they point out interesting new directions, historical lacunae, and theoretical conflicts for the many young researchers currently initiating work in the field. For, if anything, the future of Latin American film scholarship now lies with a new generation of scholars who, trained in film studies, sensitive to Latin American culture and politics, and enmeshed in Third World theory and cross-cultural studies, have recently completed or are now working on dissertations.[4]

In order to facilitate the presentation of more detailed analyses of each of these recent publications under review here, I have schematically organized the texts according to their scope. I shall discuss, first, those texts which approach *all* of the Latin American cinema and, later, those texts focused on one national cinema, on a country by country basis.

III. COVERING THE CONTINENT

To even attempt to survey all of the Latin American cinema within the covers of one book is a daunting task, which few have either attempted or done well. Although at first glance the motivations for such an undertaking might seem to be derived from a first world colonizing impulse inherent in the term "Latin America" itself (as many have argued, hardly more than a convenient historiographical fiction), in fact contemporary Latin American filmic and theoretical practice asserts the importance of the dialectic between the Latin American and the national as a crucial socio-political imperative. And it is precisely the desire for Latin American *and* national subjecthood that promotes the development of the New Latin American Cinema which is the subject of most of these recently published books with a continental perspective.

The most extensive of the anthologies with a Latin American focus is Burton's collection of interviews with fiction and documentary filmmakers and (in an effort to avoid an auteurist bias) with others who are normally "behind the scenes" (a producer/distributor, a film critic, the head of the Cuban Film Institute (ICAIC), an actor, and a media activist). The twenty interviews included provide a fascinating discursive portrait of the personalities, experiences, and theoretical positions of some of the key figures of the New Latin American Cinema. As they respond to their various interviewers, these individuals also provide an interesting, tapestry-like version of the complexly interwoven history of contemporary filmmaking in Latin America. If there is one thread that unites these formally and stylistically varied interviews, it is, as Burton herself acknowledges in the introduction, each individual's recounting of a national filmmaking history and his or her "commitment to the film medium as a vehicle for social transformation and the expression of a national and regional cultural autonomy" (p. xiv). And, it is by comparing and contrasting the different individuals' responses to their national socio-political conditions through the cinema and their versions of national cinematic history that one can sense the solidarity between the national and the Latin American that has so often been cited as a key characteristic of the New Latin American Cinema.

However, this work has to be performed by the reader, for, although the anthology makes these comparisons possible, they remain largely implicit rather than explicit. Although Burton seems to acknowledge the problematic nature of the interview by carefully annotating the source (interviewer, place and date of interview and other pertinent data) and the publication history of each of the texts included (an important gesture that few make), she does not interrelate the interviews in her brief biographical introductions nor does she interrogate the form itself any further. Here, as is often the case in interviews, it is assumed that the interview format allows the "voice" of the interviewee to be heard directly, as if the process of questioning, transcribing, translating, editing, and selecting of interviews did not always implicate a multiplicity of voices in each and every publication of an interview. In fact, what is potentially most exciting about the interview is that, at least in theory, it is dialogical, juxtaposing and mingling two voices in its typical question and answer format. But when constantly deferring to the answerer and assuming the "objective" stance of a reporter or ethnographer, the interviewer diminishes this potential and fails to incorporate his/her own otherness into the text. When a "first-world" interviewer seeks answers from a "third-world" filmmaker, the resulting interview should/could also take up the challenge of difference and otherness rather than elide it under the guise of a nevertheless unattainable objectivity.

This lack of self-reflexivity and/or formal theoretical engagement is exacerbated by the heterogeneity of the interviews themselves. Of the twenty pieces, one is an essay by Bolivian filmmaker Jorge Sanjines (who is well-known for his avoidance of publicity and interviewers), twelve were conducted by Burton herself, and eight (previously published) by various others. The need to include the Sanjines piece as well as the interviews by others is understandable in a work that aspires to present a picture of all Latin American cinema. It would not be easy, for example, to justify the exclusion of such crucial filmmakers as Glauber Rocha, Nelson Pereira dos Santos or Raúl Ruiz from such a text. However, *this* multiplicity of voices and approaches, when compounded by the fact that Burton's own interviews—half of which were previously published in journals—also vary greatly in style further complicates the unity of the text. Most distressing, however, are the six interviews which are edited without questions so as to give the appearance of a seamless monologue by the interviewee. Here, the interviewer has consciously erased him/herself from the encounter and, in a sense, masquerades as the other whose voice we are told to listen to, severely putting into question the epistemological validity of the text.

These criticism, however, should not diminish the general importance of Burton's anthology. First of all, it gathers a number of crucially important interviews that were previously published but difficult to obtain: Burton's own excellent interviews with ICAIC personnel (Tomás Gutiérrez Alea—by far the most incisive and informative of her interviews—Humberto Solas, and Julio García Espinosa) and with the Chilean filmmaker Patricio Guzmán; Randal Johnson's interview with Brazilian filmmaker Nelson Pereira dos Santos (the most self-reflexive and conversational of the interviews); and Ian Christie and Malcolm Coad's interview with Chilean filmmaker Raúl Ruiz. Furthermore, several of the interviews also provide information not available elsewhere in English. For example, in his interview, Fernando Birri discusses his trajectory throughout Latin America and Europe after leaving Argentina (and the Documentary School in Sante Fe which he founded) in 1963, thus clarifying what otherwise seemed to be an inexplicable hiatus until his reappearance at the first International Festival of the New Latin American Cinema in Havana in 1979. Similarly, the interviews with Mario Handler and Walter Achugar (both Uruguayan, the former a filmmaker, the latter primarily an alternative film distributor) provide further information about the significance of the 1957 and 1958 film festivals sponsored by the SODRE cultural organization in Montevideo for the development of documentary filmmaking in Latin America.

Obviously such an anthology cannot possibly include interviews with *all* the significant figures of the New Latin American Cinema, but there are some unfortunate omissions. The Argentine cinema, for example, is only represented by Fernando Birri. Interviews with either Fernando Solanas or Octavio Getino—former members of the collective Grupo Cine Liberación, directors of *The Hour of The Furnaces* (1968), and currently quite active in Argentine cultural politics—would have been a welcomed addition. Similarly, some of the interviews included seem less relevant than others. For example, the interview with Helena Solberg Ladd (a Brazilian living in the US who has specialized in documentaries about Latin America for North American audiences), although quite interesting and informative, does not have the significance, for a historical understanding of the New Latin American Cinema, of the pieces with Nelson Pereira dos Santos or Tomás Gutiérrez Alea.

Above all such minor criticisms, however, this anthology is a welcomed addition to the Latin American film bibliography. It is pedagogically useful and, for the time being, clearly obviates the need for any other collection of interviews with "key" Latin American filmmakers. One simply hopes that in future works, Burton—an excellent scholar and tireless pioneer and promoter of Latin American film scholarship—will trust her own voice, analyses, and commitments enough to publish her own texts.

Michael Chanan's *Twenty-five Years of the New Latin American Cinema* is, unfortunately, difficult to obtain in the US, for it makes an excellent companion volume to Burton's interviews. Published by the British Film Institute and Channel Four Television, this slim pamphlet of forty pages was designed as a dossier to accompany Chanan's Channel Four-sponsored documentary *New Cinema From Latin America: I Cinema of the Humble II The Long Road*. It gathers, in addition to an excellent (albeit brief) historical/theoretical introduction by Chanan, six of the most important manifestos/theoretical statements about the New Latin American Cinema (several previously unavailable in English; only one previously anthologized) which lay out the scope of the movement and its theoretical development: Fernando Birri's "Cinema and Underdevelopment," Glauber Rocha's "The Aesthetics of Hunger" and "Down with Populism," Fernando Solanas and Octavio Getino's "Towards a Third Cinema," Julio Garcia Espinosa's "For an Imperfect Cinema," and Jorge Sanjines's "Problems of Form and Content in Revolutionary Cinema." These texts provide an excellent introduction to the theoretical concerns of various Latin American national cinemas (the Argentine, Brazilian, Cuban, and Bolivian contexts). Furthermore, as theoretical investigations of film practices, they serve to clarify the specificity of the New Latin American Cinema's theoretical engagements and the basis for its unity: its refusal of cinemas of emotional manipulation and of prescriptive aesthetics and its endorsement of cinematic work that promotes a critical understanding/engagement with social practice.

As with the Burton anthology, although one cannot demand all-inclusiveness of such a collection, had Chanan included two or three other documents the pamphlet would have been nearly perfect as an introductory text. The most glaring omission is the manifesto by Chilean filmmakers in support of Allende's Popular unity program, already anthologized by Chanan himself in his *Chilean Cinema*.[5] In addition, the inclusion of Tomás Gutiérrez Alea's "The Viewer's Dialectic"[6] and of some of the never translated manifestos of the anti-Peronist Argentine collective Grupo Cine de la Base,[7] would have provided an interesting contrast to the Espinosa article that exemplifies "Cuba," and the Birri and Solanas and Getino pieces that do the same for "Argentina." Such a small text cannot possibly accomplish the kind of extensive documentation provided by the recent 3-volume (1,473 pages) Mexican publication, *Hojas de Cine: Testimonios y documentos del nuevo cine latinoamericano*. However, these small additions would have broadened the scope and enriched the utility of this otherwise excellent collection.

The last of the anthologies with a Latin American focus to have been published this decade, Coco Fusco's *Reviewing Histories: Selections From New Latin American Cinema*, is by far the least useful. From a practical standpoint, the text is first of all marred by an utterly unreadable typeface that barely distinguishes between upper and lower-case letters. Although this may seem petty, it is nearly impossible to read more than one piece at a time due to the inevitable eye-strain. More substantially, however, the collection's central flaw is that it is a small text that tries to do it all, covering the entire continent and all of the New Latin American cinema, and ends up accomplishing little. As Fusco explains in the introduction, this anthology, like Chanan's, was also designed to accompany an exhibit of Latin American films. However, unlike Chanan's, this anthology has neither a theoretical nor a critical rationale to exist independently. It is obvious, given the haphazard mix of interviews, critical analyses of films, and manifestos, that the selection of texts was determined primarily by the availability of films for exhibition in the New York area rather than by their relative importance. There is no other reason to explain, for example, the representation of Argentina only by three pieces dealing with Solanas and Getino's *Hour of the Furnaces* and one brief interview with the directors of *Las Madres: The Mothers of the Plaza de Mayo* (1986). The volume does include some excellent texts—among them most of the theoretical manifestos included in the Chanan's *Twenty-Five Years* (the Solanas and Getino, The Sanjines, the Espinosa) plus the Popular Unity manifesto, Alea's "The Viewer's Dialectic," and Rocha's "The History of Cinema Novo"—and critical analyses—particularly Robert Stam's "*The Hour of the Furnaces* and the Two Avant Gardes," originally published in *Millenium Film Journal*. However, other pieces are so much less informative and/or insightful that one wonders why they were included at all. Osvaldo Sanchez Crespo's brief analyses of the Cuban films *The Last Supper* (Tomás Gutiérrez Alea) and *One Way or Another* (Sara Gómez), for example, are neither well written nor critically acute and their inclusion is particularly surprising given that these films have been well analyzed elsewhere.[8]

Ultimately, although the collection may have served well as extended program notes accompanying a touring film exhibit, on its own it fails to accomplish its self-acknowledged goal of promoting a "historical perspective" to give "a sense of dimension to contemporary Latin American cinema" (p. 7). Fusco's gamble, "at the risk of confusion . . . [to have] purposely chosen to emphasize the heterogeneity of responses to New Latin American Cinema's central questions [p. 7]" does not pay off.

The two single-authored texts that deal with the Latin American Cinema as a whole—Gaizka S. de Usabel's *The High Noon of American Films in Latin America* and Jorge A. Schnitman's *Film Industries in Latin America: Dependency and Development*—differ greatly from the anthologies because neither one of them focuses on the New Latin American Cinema. To some degree eschewing political commitment as well as aesthetic preoccupations, both texts are couched in the language of socio-scientific historical research and detail various kinds of institutional determining forces affecting the development of the cinema in Latin America: for Schnitman, the relationship among the state and Latin American film industries in the context of dependent, unequal relations with the media metropolises, and, for Usabel, the history and impact of United Artists' distribution practices in Latin America between 1919 and 1951.

It might seem odd to include the Usabel book—a history of the activities of a Hollywood studio in Latin America—in an assessment of Latin American film scholarship. However, its importance lies in the recognition that throughout Latin America the cinema was and/or is synonymous with either Hollywood or Europe

and that studying the history of the cinema in Latin America also involves recognizing the important influence of foreign distribution and its effects on consumption
practices. Unfortunately, however, Usabel's text—originally a University of Wiscon-
sin, Madison doctoral dissertation—does not fulfill the promise inherent in its
topic.

High Noon is the result of painstaking archival research of the United Artists
collection in Madison. Usabel discloses many fascinating details of the daily
activities of a Hollywood distributor in Latin America. How UA determined where
to open subsidiaries in Latin America ("where American enterprise was strongest"
(p. xvi), how those subsidiaries were staffed and managed (dictatorially by the
central office in New York and with little concern for the "native" employees), and
how the corporation related to the different national governments (via diplomatic
intercessions, meddling with national politicians, and outright bribery) are carefully recounted and substantiated by extensive references to letter files and other
corporate documents. In fact, one gets the sense that every single tidbit of "raw"
information available in these files was cross-referenced and included in the final
text, regardless of its informational value. And that is precisely the principal
problem with the text: tiresomely, most of it reads like a chronological regurgitation
of undigested data. Although Usabel attempts to analyze a cross-cultural phenomenon, the text is uninformed by cross-cultural politics and/or theory and his
approach, essentially empiricist, claims simply to objectively chronicle, rather than
critically analyze, the activities of UA in Latin America. For example, in his
conclusion, Usabel criticizes UA's policies in Latin America because of their "ignorance of Latin American culture, indifference toward its future, and greed for its
resources and revenues" (p. 255). However, immediately following, he hides behind
the veil of historical objectivity and cites "on the credit side," ameliorating factors:
UA provided some employment "in countries that were severely depressed," UA
"promoted Latin American films" by distributing them through its network, and,
finally, UA brought to Latin Americans "the most popular stars of all screens and of
all times . . . that transported them from a difficult reality into a fantasy of glamor
and delight" (p. 255). All three "positive" factors seem rather strained, if not
dubious. The few jobs UA created in its Latin American subsidiaries hardly dented
each nation's depressed economies (furthermore, UA employees were, according to
Usabel's own account, notoriously underpaid, constantly suspected of thievery,
and treated without respect). UA did not distribute Latin American films such as
Allá en el Rancho Grande (1939), Mexico's most popular *comedia ranchera*, in order to
promote continental understanding or the national cinema industry, but in order to
reap profits from their popularity with little investment at risk (in fact, seriously
undermining the national industry's ability to continue producing). Finally, the
notion that UA should be thanked for perpetuating an alienated escapism is, to say
the least, surprising.

If this conceptual critique of *High Noon* seems unsubtle is is because the text itself
is unsubtle and ideologically naive. However, this is not intended to undermine the
importance of Usabel's research and the utility of the text as a reference source. *High
Noon* presents much information that is difficult to obtain elsewhere (for example,
little known details of Hollywood's Spanish-language productions in the 1930s and
UA's distribution of Latin American films throughout the continent) and should

thus prove invaluable for scholars interested in cross-cultural analysis of the Latin American cinema before the 1950s.

Jorge Schnitman's *The Film Industries of Latin America* should be hailed as the first substantive history of Latin American filmmaking. His text is not, however, a standard, narrative history, for it is concerned, almost exclusively, with the economic and political/institutional determinants that have influenced the development (or lack thereof) of filmmaking industries in Latin America. In fact, the text's explicit institutional bias is simultaneously its most interesting characteristic and, because the institutional analysis is conducted primarily in economistic terms, its principal flaw. Film is, after all, a cultural phenomenon, and its cultural ramifications need to be analyzed alongside economic and political forces. It is disturbing that in a work of film history of more than 125 pages, only a handful of film titles are mentioned and few films are discussed in any detail that is not economic in nature.

Schnitman invokes a cross-cultural perspective, but only insofar as he argues that it is impossible to consider the history of Latin American filmmaking without reference to the international power of the Hollywood industries and its ramifications at national levels. Theoretically, the need for this contextualization of film-related activities is explained via an appeal to dependency theory defined as "a conceptualization of the consequences for peripheral societies of the changes in capitalism as a world system" (p. 11). Although this definition of the otherwise much-maligned socio-scientific concept of dependency is reasonable and even attractive, the contextualization that Schnitman goes on to present does not fulfill its theoretical promise. In two separate sections of the book, Schnitman summarizes the economic and institutional history of international film production before and after sound and these subsections then serve as the "context" for the discussions of Latin American film production in each of these periods. This kind of contextualization by juxtaposition ends up not illustrating much and suggesting that a direct correlation between international events and the specific history of film production in Latin America cannot be established (in fact, precisely the opposite of what Usabel's *High Noon* painstakingly demonstrates). Furthermore, Schnitman's dependence on secondary sources and, given his broad scope, necessarily abbreviated descriptions also undermine the significance of his cross-cultural analysis.

The text's institutional approach also results in an excessive emphasis on the importance of developing "industrial" film production in Latin America. Schnitman analyzes the abortive attempts to establish film industries in Argentina, Mexico, and Brazil (in the 1930s, 1940, and 1950s, respectively) in the context of global capitalism and dependence as clear evidence of the deleterious effects of dependency and as yet another manifestation of the "import substitution" policies that were encouraged by state-protectionist measures. However, he fails to recognize both the complex interplay of internal forces of dependence and the ideological and cultural significance of the alternatives to industrial filmmaking that were as much an effect of dependence as the failed industries. He is careful not to propose that industrialization based on the Hollywood model should be the ideal for Latin America, but his conclusions concerning state protectionism clearly indicate that he favors the development of national, state-aided industrial systems of production. Thus when he attempts to discuss the practices of the New Latin American Cinema his text is at its weakest, for in most cases these filmmakers rejected industrial models in favor of alternative models of production, distribution, and exhibition, and his historiographical/analytical method has difficulty evaluating their relative values and varied strategies.

IV. EMPHASIZING THE NATIONAL

In comparison to the texts that attempt to deal with *all* of Latin America's filmmaking history, problems, and achievements, works that focus on a specific national cinema face a relatively simpler task. Once the scope of the work is restricted to a traditionally defined nation-state (that is, without taking into considerations such factors as exile and, occasionally, shifting frontiers) the challenge becomes less monumental, although by no means simple.

1. Brazil

Through the industrious scholarship of Randal Johnson and Robert Stam in *The Brazilian Cinema* and of Johnson's own *Cinema Novo X Five* and *The Film Industry in Brazil*, the cinema of Brazil, the largest and most populated country of Latin America, is also the best documented Latin American cinema. Markedly different in scope and methodology, these three texts clearly illustrate not only what excellent scholarship can accomplish but also how much more work remains to be done for other Latin American national cinemas. Both Johnson and Stam are respected academics and scholars and their work on the Brazilian cinema will long serve as an example for future scholars of Latin American national cinemas.

The jointly-produced *Brazilian Cinema* is, according to its editors, not an anthology, but a "mosaic" "developed as a collective project by Brazilian and American scholars" rather than a collection of already-available material (p. 9). The book is organized into four parts: a thirty-five page historical introduction by Johnson and Stam, a collection of thirteen theoretical statements and manifestos, thirteen analyses of important films produced between 1963 and 1978, and a final section entitled "Special Topics and Polemics" which groups nine essays on issues as varied as parody in the Brazilian *chanchada*, women in Brazilian cinema, the documentary, the avant-garde, and the image of Brazil in Hollywood cinema. Most of the essays included, with the exception of the theoretical statements in Part II, were written expressly for this volume and thus share, as the editors claim, "within the limits of ideological nuance and personality differences, a common view of the Brazilian cinema" (p. 9). Furthering the unity of the text, each of the sections is introduced by the editors, who also preface each of the theoretical essays and the essays of the final section with brief, contextualizing paragraphs that succinctly position the debates and the authors of the essays in a broad cultural context. This highlighting of the interrelationships among authors, theoretical positions, and debates central to the development of the Brazilian cinema from the Cinema Novo of the early 1960s until the late 1970s (such as the nature of a popular cinema, for example) lends the text a great intertextual richness that complements the importance of the pieces collected.

The critical analyses in Part III, each dedicated to one film, sustain this comparative tone. Here are included excellent analyses by the editors themselves (on *Vidas Secas, São Bernardo, Macunaima, Lesson of Love, Xica da Silva, Land in Anguish,* and *The Fall*) which prove their critical acuity, as well as sensitive and theoretically interesting pieces by Ismail Xavier (on *Black God White Devil*), Roberto Schwartz (on *The Guns*), and Elizabeth Merena and João Luiz Vieira (on *Hunger for Love*).

Part IV, although still strong, is, comparatively, the weakest section. Dealing with a miscellany of issues, the focus of the text is somewhat diluted here, especially given the unfortunate inclusion of the last two pieces: Elice Munerato and Maria Helena Darcy de Oliveira's impressionistic and not very well thought out account of the role of women in Brazilian filmmaking and Sergio Augusto's chatty and unsubstantial description of "Brazil" according to Hollywood. although concluding with Augusto's discussion of U.S. representations of Brazil lends the book a kind of elegant structural symmetry (since the Part I introduction begins with an assessment of the similarities and differences between Brazil and the United States), it is nevertheless unfortunate that the overall quality of the collection could not be sustained.

It is also unfortunate that the editors chose the all-encompassing title of *Brazilian Cinema* for this work. Despite the historical introduction and inclusion of several essays dealing with films from earlier eras (Maria Rita Galvão on the history of the Vera Cruz studio in the 1950s and João Luiz Vieira on parody in the *chanchada* films of the 1930s and 1940s, for example), most of the text is devoted to Cinema Novo and its aftermath in the 1970s. Certainly, such a focus is justified in this, the first book-length study of Brazilian film to have been published in English, since the Cinema Novo and post-Novo films of the late 1970s are the most familiar to North American audiences. However, a less all-encompassing title would nevertheless have been preferable.

These minor criticisms aside, *Brazilian Cinema* is a well-designed and admirably well-executed introduction to one of the most important cinematic moments in the history of Latin American cinema and should serve as a model for similar enterprises.

Further contributing to our knowledge of the Brazilian cinema, Johnson's two single-authored books present surprisingly different approaches to the study of national cinemas. *Cinema Novo X Five* is basically an auteurist study that analyzes in detail the films of five Cinema Novo directors, while *The Film Industry in Brazil* is an institutional history of the relationship between the cinema and the Brazilian state. Although methodologically different, Johnson's *oeuvre* is, however, consistent: the seeds for the institutional analysis of *The Film Industry* are already visible in the introduction of *Cinema Novo X Five*, suggestively entitled "Cinema Novo, the State, and Modern Brazilian Cinema." Despite his great critical skills, especially his ability to analyze the transformation of literary works into films, Johnson has become more interested in teasing out the complex relationship between culture and the ever more prescient Brazilian state. It is thus *The Film Industry* that, notwithstanding the achievements of *Cinema Novo X Five*, represents the culmination of his scholarly enterprise.

In *Cinema Novo X Five*, Johnson argues that by focusing only on five of the many filmmakers involved in the Cinema Novo movement he can demonstrate the movement's significance without the reductiveness of unifying arguments that highlight only a narrow set of similarities. This, in fact, his text achieves. By relating the diversity among Joaquim Pedro de Andrade, Carlos Diegues, Ruy Guerra, Glauber Rocha, and Nelson Pereira dos Santos, both to shifting socio-political forces and to the evolution of their theoretical positions, Johnson succeeds in demonstrating the fluidity of Cinema Novo as "the spirit of modern filmmaking in Brazil, a disposition to create a strong national cinema, a process of cinematic discovery and creativity" (p. xi). The book's otherwise worrisome auteurism is overcome by this overarching structure as well as by the specific discussions of the films and theoretical pre-occupations of the five directors. Johnson excels at drawing out the connections among films, relating them to the evolution of each director, and linking them to their socio-cultural context. Informed by continental and Brazilian intellectual thought and acknowledging previous analyses by Brazilian, French, and American critics, his discussions of individual films are always illuminating. The only discordant note in this text, when read today, is its optimism about the future of the Brazilian cinema. Written at the peak of the national and international popularity of the Brazilian cinema in the early 1980s, this book could not possibly predict the deep economic and cultural crisis of the mid to late 1980s which the subsequent *The Film Industry* tackles.

After the critical fluidity and rhetorical elegance of *Cinema Novo X Five*, the socio-scientific methodology of *The Film Industry of Brazil* is surprising. Ensconced within an intellectual tradition that privileges political/economic analysis rather than textual studies, *The Film Industry* mobilizes a different set of intellectual and primary sources: political economists, cultural sociologists, and government documents rather than literary theorists. As an institutional history, this text also suffers from some of the problems of Schnitman's *The Film Industries of Latin America*, namely that few films are mentioned in other than economic terms. However, in the context of Johnson's *oeuvre* and, given the non-prescriptive nature of Johnson's text, this is here a much less serious flaw. First of all, Johnson's access to and manipulation of primary sources lends his text an authority that Schnitman's lacks. Secondly, whereas Schnitman's continental scope leads him to generalizations and to over-emphasize the impact of external forces of unequal development, Johnson, although inspired by the same impulse (and intellectual influences) as Schnitman, focuses on one nation and is able to deal with external factors in one chapter and then devote his text to the far more subtle and difficult to pinpoint internal effects of dependence.

The Film Industry describes how, over the last fifty years, the state has become an indispensable component of the Brazilian cinema. Tracing the haphazard, reactive rather than designed, development of state policies to protect and support the film industry, Johnson clearly explains the causes for the industry's current and most severe crisis. The State's cinema policies have been marked by a "dual struggle for hegemony" (p. 5) on the one side—different factions within the industry (cultural vs. commercial) have struggled to define the nature of state support—while, on the other, the state itself has struggled to create a consensus over the goals and nature of national culture. Thus, while on some levels, the state's support of the industry, especially after the creation of a state agency for the cinema (Embrafilme) has led to remarkable achievements (increased production, technical quality, thematic and creative diversity, international success), it has proved unable to reconcile its cultural and economic responsibilities. For example, although Embrafilme has helped the Brazilian cinema gain a larger share of its own market, other state policies, especially those related to the exhibition sector, have contributed to a "drastic decline in the dimensions of that market" so that "the Brazilian cinema now receives a larger slice of a much smaller pie" (p. 196).

Extremely detailed and specialized, Johnson's book is hardly an introductory text to the Brazilian cinema. It is, however, a vivid example of the efforts of sustained research and an evolving scholarly interest in a field rich with possibilities and still largely unexplored.

2. Argentina

Although historically as significant, the Argentine cinema has yet to receive the kind of scholarly attention that has been lavished on the Brazilian. To date only two anthologies—Tim Barnard's *Argentine Cinema* and John King's and Nissa Torrents's *The Garden of Forking Paths*—have appeared, and neither of them is a U.S. publication. Although in the U.S. the Argentine cinema has not had the contemporary visibility of the Brazilian, within Spanish America it and the Mexican cinema are the best known industries and this scholarly lacunae is surprising.

Both of the published anthologies were organized to accompany retrospectives of Argentine cinema and suffer from the lack of planning and internal coherence that characterizes such work. Barnard's is a curiously split text. Lavinshly illustrated, it includes some excellent material: an interview with Fernando Birri (by Julianne Burton, reprinted in her *Cinema and Social Change*), a detailed account of the effects of official censorship by Alfonso Gumucio Dagrón, a very suggestive (and previously untranslated) reassessment of the concept of "Third Cinema" by Octavio Getino, and a report on the state of the industry in 1985 (after the start of "democratization") produced by SICA, the official film industry union. However, it also inexplicably includes two pieces by/about Jorge Luis Borges' influence on the Argentine cinema that seem to function only as guarantors of cultural value, for they are otherwise neither relevant nor informative. As Barnard admits in his foreword, "no attempt [was] made to maintain a thematic unity between the articles" (p. i). And, I must add, no attempt was made to be comprehensive or representative. There is simply too much that is not covered either in the text or in Barnard's own historical overview of *all* of the Argentine cinema that serves as an introduction (for example, the important "nuevo cine" movement of the 1950s and 1960s, the ethnographic tradition, the anti-Peronist filmmakers of the late 1960s and 1970s, the complex politics of the second Peron presidency, etc.). Most surprisingly, even the post-1983 period, ostensibly the best known by English-speaking audiences (given that many important films have been widely distributed and even aired on cable TV), is barely glossed over in less than seven pages.

The King and Torrents anthology, although a slimmer volume, is somewhat more representative and coherent. The editors were interested in outlining the social and cultural context for the development of filmmaking in Argentina since the 1950s and thus included a social history of Argentine filmmaking between 1955–76 (by Ana López), an assessment of the period 1976–83 (by Nick Caistor), and a reevaluation of the period 1955–83 in the light of developments since the mid-1980s (by Nissa Torrents), as well as three interviews with important, yet little known figures (the writer Beatriz Guido whose novels were often adapted to the cinema; Maria Luisa Bemberg (*Camila, Miss Mary*), the only female director of the 1980s; and Bebe Kamín, a contemporary director). However, the coherence of the text as a socio-cultural introduction (rather than a collection of critical analyses or manifestos) is marred by the inclusion of a worthless ten-page list of films, directors, and titles by Jorge Miguel Couselo that pretends to be a narrative history of Argentine filmmaking from "sound to the sixties" and by an interesting, but out of context, analysis of Carlos Gardel's movie career by Simon Collier. Nevertheless, more than the Barnard anthology, which attempts to do too much with too little material, the King and Torrents book provides us with a suggestive set of essays that indicate many directions for future research.

Both of these texts "introduce" the complexity of the Argentine cinema to English-speaking audiences, but much careful research and publishing still need to be done before Argentine cinema scholarship finds a niche in the U.S.

3. Mexico

If the lack of focus and depth of our only accounts of Argentine cinema is disheartening, the state of English-language Mexican cinema is devastating. That the most popular and numerous Latin American national cinema is represented only by Carl J. Mora's *Mexican Cinema: Reflections of a Society, 1896–1980* is simply scandalous.

Ostensibly a social history of the Mexican cinema, Mora's book is really little more than a narrative listing of films and plot summaries interspersed with rabid commentary against "leftist" sympathizers who have, Mora claims, consistently tried to distort the "real" function of the cinema—to entertain and, therefore, be successful at the box-office—with unsuitable political propaganda (p. 2). Part of a Mexican family once living in New York, Mora heralds his "bicultural" sensitivity as a prerequisite to writing such a history for American audiences (p. xi). However, his text, with its annoying insistence on the benevolent paternalism of the U.S. towards Mexico, its refusal to acknowledge the complexity of sound/image relations, its assertion of the box-office as *the* arbiter of value, and its simple-minded politics fails to display any sensibility, much less a "bicultural" one.

Mora is not a scholar and this, despite hundreds of pedantic footnotes, is not a scholarly book. How else to explain the inclusion of the following passage in a book which claims to be a history of Mexican cinema from 1896 to 1980?

Any attempt here to analyze meaningfully all the important Mexican films made in 1971–76 is impossible. The choice of the few films discussed [five] is dictated entirely by the fact that this writer happens to be familiar with them and does not imply that, in his judgment, they were superior to others. Also, to discuss thoroughly the complex cinematic, cultural, and literary influences operative on Mexican filmmakers is too extensive an undertaking . . . (p. 121).

Mora *does* love movies, Mexican and Hollywood alike, but indiscriminately. He is unable to recognize, for example, the importance of studies of trans-cultural influence and is able to dismisses them blithely with knee-jerk anti-Marxism and irrelevant facts:

The influence of the Hollywood movie has been consistently denounced by Marxist film historians, especially with regard to the Latin American film industries. Yet it is interesting to note that up to 1972, Chiang Ch'ing, Mao Tse-tung's widow, lovingly viewed again and again Greta Garbo's *Queen Christina* (p. 244, note 23).

Although Mora's book makes extensive use of reputable and well-respected histories and critical work by Mexican scholars like Emilio García Riera and Jorge Ayala Blanco, the history presented is nevertheless curiously off-balanced and, paradoxically, ahistorical. Always privileging the most "popular," slighting experimentation, state protectionism, and of course, any obvious political intentionality, Mora manages, for example, to almost dismiss the significant influence of Eisenstein's brief stay in Mexico (p. 36–7).

Hopefully, the Latin American film bibliography in English will soon be enriched by an adequate history of this exciting, and often unfairly maligned, national cinema.

4. Cuba

Thankfully the Cuban cinema has received the almost undivided attention of the tireless Michael Chanan for almost a decade, for the result of his research, *The Cuban Image*, is simply the most interesting history of a Latin American national cinema yet published in English. *The Cuban Image* is actually more than a historical account of national filmmaking, it is also a book of cultural analysis that offers rich digressions on topics as varied as the roots of syncretism, the image of Fidel Castro, and the nature of film as commodity and art. Chanan knows Cuba, Latin American intellectual thought, and the Cuban cinema well, and his rich accounts of political/cultural debates, skillful summaries of the theoretical work of Latin American writers/filmmakers, witty prose, and wide-ranging research make this book a delight to read.

Chanan's is an innovative, highly personal, approach to the writing of history that freely mixes film analysis with economic, political, social, and all other possible intellectual debates. Although the text maintains a basic chronological structure, Chanan also ingeniously uses the films themselves to illustrate and explain various historical moments of Cuban society—for example, his use of *Viva la Republica* (Pastor Vega) and *La Primera Carga al Machete* (Manuel Octavio Gómez) to talk about the Spanish-American War in chapter 2 and his use of *Polvo Rojo* (Jesus Díaz) to describe Cuban society immediately after the 1959 revolution—and to introduce and conclude the book. His conversational writing style, although sometimes disconcertingly colloquial, nevertheless adds to the pleasure of reading the text.

Chanan is openly and proudly *engagé* (he calls his book "a partisan history" (p. 7), and the text benefits from his commitment (and Cuba's commitment to his enterprise). However, his engagement and desire to argue "against claims that the Cuban cinema has declined" (p. 4) lead him to overemphasize the "glory" years of the Cuban cinema (1960s), to discuss the troublesome 1970s very selectively, and to omit the 1980s altogether, thus avoiding the discussion of the causes of ICAIC's contemporary difficulties. In fact, one gets the sense that Chanan (like the ICAIC until 1988[9]), resolutely closes his eyes in order not to see what is apparent to everyone else: that the Cuban cinema in the late 1970s and 1980s, despite the achievements of some films, has indeed declined artistically and ideologically.

Chanan also avoids asserting his own critical voice when he analyzes films, relying either on contemporary critiques or on the analyses of other Latin American critics. Although the effort to analyze Latin American culture from within rather than as an outsider is commendable, one misses here the critical acuity that he so freely displays elsewhere, especially in his insightful descriptions of some films (for example, his discussion of *For the First Time* which opens the book). When coupled with his reluctance to deal with the ICAIC's difficulties in the 1970s and 1980s, one wonders whether Chanan is simply hiding behind others' voices in order to avoid controversy.

Despite these serious limitations, *The Cuban Image* is the most accomplished history of a Latin American national cinema in print because of its intellectual rigor, broad scope, deftly interwoven contextualizations, and wealth of information. It will undoubtedly be the definitive text on the Cuban cinema for many years to come.

V. CONCLUSION: THE 1990s

Hopefully this brief survey of a decade's scholarship has demonstrated some of the achievements as well as the flaws of contemporary English-language Latin American film scholarship. That almost half of the books here reviewed are (more or less successful) anthologies says much about the state of Latin American film scholarship. Ostensibly "easy" to put together, an edited book is actually far more difficult to produce successfully than a single-authored text. Hardly aspiring to be more than samples of information, the less accomplished anthologies reviewed here lay bare the problems of the edited book format: the inevitable arbitrariness of the process of soliciting, selecting, and editing contributions; the emptiness and uselessness of discrete pieces that are not intertextually contextualized; the need for a clear framing device that, determined by the particular theoretical commitments of the editors, locates the pieces within a well-defined overall project. Missing from most Latin American cinema anthologies is precisely what is indispensable in an edited book: a productive dialogue between an unmistakable editorial voice and the individual contributors.[10]

Anthologies are also problematic because of market concerns. That so many have appeared says as much about the still developing English-language Latin American film scholarship as about the concerns of the publishing industry. Justified by appeals to "essential" qualities of the material itself—its newness, politics, marginality—and by the growth of Latin American studies in general, these "quickie" publications help to fill publishers' catalogs, often taking the place of textbooks, but do little to develop the field or, in the long term, to sustain the interest of the publishing industry.

In order to overcome this introductory stage, Latin American film scholarship in English should assert its own complexity and the peculiarity of its position. Scholars need to reject the journalistic tendency to "introduce" material and "celebrate" achievements in order to take on the challenge of their own otherness. The encounter between "first world" academics and "third world" culture should not be conceived of as a guided tour through exotic lands, but as a way of temporarily inhabiting another culture, of assuming "difference" as the basis for all cultures. Latin America is no longer limited to the geographical mass south of Texas; it is firmly within the "North" as well—inhabiting inner cities, working the land, echoing in popular music, present in television screens. Therefore, the study of Latin American film (and culture) should entail a recognition of the multiplicity of all cultures, including our own.

For such work to be more readily produced (and in order for "first world" scholars to be able to assume such a position) the work of Latin American film scholars must be circulated. There is an urgent need for translations of "classic" works of Latin American film history and criticism as well as of the work of contemporary Latin American film scholars.[11] The history of almost every Latin American national cinema has been chronicled by indigenous historians. Although these texts vary in approach and rigor, the best of them—for example, Emilio García Riera's work on the Mexican cinema, Domingo di Núbila's exhaustive historical chronicle of the Argentine film, Paulo Emilio Salles Gomes and Jean Claude Bernardet's work on Brazilian film history—need to appear in English in order for the field to have a sense of its own history.[12] It is not necessary for every researcher who writes about Latin American cinema in English to assume that she must start from scratch. But, unless these "master" histories become readily available, it is not possible for authors to assume that their readers have any prior familiarity with the material. Nor is the English-language publishing market likely to support the publication of more specialized texts.

Although much remains to be done, undoubtedly Latin American film scholarship is much richer now than it was in the 1970s. With the energy of new generations of scholars, producing and guiding the interests of the publishing industry, one can only hope that the 1990s will witness the publication of so many texts that a decade's review such as this will be an impossible undertaking.

NOTES

1. The few books published up to 1980 are (in alphabetical order): Michael Chanan, ed., *Chilean Cinema* (London: British Film Institute, 1976), an anthology of interviews and brief articles; Michael Chanan, ed., *BFI Dossier # 2: Santiago Alvarez* (London: British Film Institute, 1980), an anthology designed to accompany an Alvarez retrospective in London; Michael Myerson, *Memories of Underdevelopment: The Revolutionary Films of Cuba* (New York: Grossman, 1973), a reconstruction—from the English subtitles—of the script of Tomás Gutiérrez Alea's *Memories of Underdevelopment* and the last part of Humberto Solas' *Lucia*; Zuzana Pick, ed. *Latin American Filmmakers and the Third Cinema* (Ottawa: Carleton University Film Program, 1978), a mimeographed anthology of articles translated from *Cine Cubano*; and, Beatriz Reyes Navarro, *The Mexican Cinema: Interviews with Thirteen Directors* (Albuquerque: University of New Mexico Press, 1976), a series of uninformative interviews.
2. Edited by Guy Hennebelle and Alfonso Gumucio-Dagrón (Paris: L'Herminier, 1981), this text collects

twenty-six commissioned essays which detail the history of film in each Latin American nation, paying attention to economic, political, sociological, cultural, and aesthetics factors. Although the quality of the essays varies widely, with the historical synopsis of some contributions excessively marked by the political commitment of the authors (in particular, Octavio Getino's Peronist history of Argentine cinema in the 1970s), this collection remains the most encyclopedic resource on Latin American film to have been published anywhere.

3. Such is the position of Roy Armes in his recent *Third World Filmmaking and The West* (Berkeley: University of California Press, 1987) reviewed elsewhere in this issue.

4. Among the many young scholars working on Latin American cinema are Ismail Xavier, João Luiz Vieira, Catherine Benamou, Deborah Mistron, John Ramírez, Charles F. Berg, and others. Their recently completed or forthcoming dissertations, when (hopefully) published in the next decade, will significantly alter the shape of the field.

5. Michael Chanan, *Chilean Cinema* (London: British Films Institute, 1976).

6. First published as *Dialéctica del Espectador* (Havana: Ediciones Unión, 1982) and later translated and published in two parts of *JumpCut*.

7. Especially, "Grupo Cine de la Base, 1969," formerly only available in mimeograph, but recently reprinted in *Hojas de Cine: Testimonios y Documentos del Nuevo Cine Latinoamericano, Vol. I* (Mexico City: Dirección General de Producciones y Medios de la SEP, 1988).

8. See, for example, Dennis West's analysis of *The Last Supper*, "Slavery and Cinema in Cuba: The Case of Gutiérrez Alea's *The Last Supper*," *The Western Journal of Black Studies* 3, no. 2 (1979): 128–133 and Julia Lesage on *One Way or Another* in *"One Way or Another"* Dialectical, Revolutionary, Feminist," *JumpCut*, no. 20 (1979): 20–23.

9. In 1988 the ICAIC recognized its crisis and undertook an extensive reorganization which resulted in the creation of three completely independent production units, each headed by a director with a recognizable style (the dialectical Tomás Gutiérrez Alea, the stylized and operatic Humberto Solas, and the more popular/commercial Manuel Pérez).

10. The best available model for successful anthologies is the format of the excellent "Readers" published by the British Film Institute. See, for example, Christine Gledhill, ed., *Home is Where the Heart is: Studies in Melodrama and The Woman's Film* (London: BFI, 1987).

11. See the brief selected bibliography of Spanish-language book-length studies for further references.

12. For a survey of some of the principal tendencies in Latin American film historical writing see my "A Short History of Latin American Film Histories," UFVA *Journal of Film and Video*, 37, no. 1 (1985); 55–69.

SELECTED BIBLIOGRAPHY

This bibliography presents a selection of some of the most important research on Latin American film published in languages other than English, with particular emphasis on Spanish and Portuguese book-length studies. It is organized by nations. When the topic/importance of a text is not obvious from its title, the citation is followed by a brief, explanatory annotation. For further information about texts published before 1983, see Julianne Burton's annotated bibliography briefly reviewed in this essay.

GENERAL: LATIN AMERICA
Frías, Isaac León, ed.
 1979 *Los años de la Conmoción, 1967–1973*. Mexico City: Dirección General de Difusión Cultural de la UNAM. A collection of interviews from the Peruvian journal *Hablemos de Cine*.
Getino, Octavio
 1987 *Cine Latinoamericano: Economia y Nuevas Tecnologias Audiovisuales*. Havana/Mérida: Fundación del Nuevo Cine Latinoamericano, 1987.
 1982 *A Diez Años de "Hacia un Tercer Cine"*. México: Filmoteca de la UNAM.
Gumucio Dagrón, Alfonso
 1979 *Cine, Censura y Exilio en América Latina*. La Paz, Bolivia: Ediciones Film/Historia.
Henebelle, Guy and Alfonso Gumucio Dagrón
 1981 *Les Cinemas de l'Amerique Latine*. Paris: L'Herminier.

274   A. M. Lopez

Hijar, Alberto, ed.
1972   Hacia un Tercer Cine. Cuadernos de Cine #20. Mexico City: UNAM.
Hojas de Cine: Testimonios y Documentos del Nuevo Cine Latinoamericano, vols. I–III
1988   Mexico City: Dirección General de Producciones y Medios de la SEP.
Martínez Torres, Augusto and Manuel Pérez Estremera
1973   Nuevo Cine Latinoamericano. Barcelona: Editorial Anagrama.
Micciche, Lino
1981   America Latina: Lo Schermo Contesso. Venice: Marsilio.
Toledo, Teresa
1990   Diez Años de un Festival. Madrid: Sociedad Estatal Española del Quinto Centenario, forthcoming. Complete credits of films and biographical information of all the participants at the Festival Internacional del Nuevo Cine Latinoamericano since 1979 compiled at the Cuban Cinematheque. Should prove an invaluable resource for Latin American film scholars.

ARGENTINA
Birri, Fernando
1964   La Escuela Documental de Santa Fe. Santa Fe: Editorial Documento del Instituto de Cinematografia de la Universidad del Litoral.
Couselo, José Miguel
1969   El Negro Ferreyra: Un Cine por Instinto. Buenos Aires: Freeland.
Di Núbila, Domingo
1959   Historia del Cine Argentino. 2 vol. Buenos Aires: Edición Cruz de Malta.
Dos Santos, Estela
1971   El Cine Nacional. Buenos Aires: Centro Editor de América Latina.
Getino, Octavio
1984   Notas Sobre el Cine Argentino. México: Edimedios.
Mahieu, Agustín
1966   Breve Historia del Cine Argentino. Buenos Aires: Universitaria.
1974   Breve Historia del Cine Nacional: 1896–1974. Buenos Aires: Alzamor Editores.
Solanas, Fernando and Octavio Getino
1973   Cine, Cultura y Descolonización. Buenos Aires: Editorial Siglo XXI.

BOLIVIA
Dagrón, Alfonso Gumucio
1982   Historia del Cine en Bolivia. La Paz: Editorial los Amigos del Libro.
Sanjines Jorge y Grupo Ukamau
1979   Teoria y Práctica de un Cine Junto al Pueblo. Mexico City: Siglo Veintiuno.

BRAZIL
Avellar, Jose Carlos
1982   Imagem e Som; Imagem e Ação. Rio de Janeiro: Paz e Terra, 1982.
Bernardet, Jean Claude
1979   Cinema Brasileiro: Propostas para uma História. Rio de Janeiro: Paz e Terra.
1978   Trajectoria Crítica. São Paulo: Polis.
Galvão, Maria Rita
1981   Burguesia e cinema: O Caso Vera Cruz. Rio de Janeiro: Civilização Brasileira.
Galvão, Maria Rita and Jean Claude Bernardet
1983   Cinema: Repercussoes em caixa de eco ideólogica (As ideias de "nacional" e "popular" no pensamento cinematografico brasileiro). São Paulo: Editora Brasiliense/Embrafilme.
Gerber, Raquel
1982   O Cinema Brasileiro e o processo político e cultural (de 1950 a 1978). Rio de Janeiro: Embrafilme.
Gonzaga, Adhemar and Paulo Emilio Salles Gomes
1966   70 Anos de Cinema Brasileiro. São Paulo: Editora Expressão e Cultura.
Ortiz Ramos, José Mario
1983   Cinema, Estado e Lutas Culturais: Anos 50/50/70. Rio de Janeiro: Editora Paz e Terra.
Ramos, Fernão
1987   Cinema Marginal (1968–1973). Rio de Janeiro: Brasiliense/Embrafilme.

Rocha, Glauber
  1963 *Revisão Crítica do Cinema Brasileiro*. Rio de Janeiro: Civilização Brasileira.
  1981 *Revolução do Cinema Novo*. Rio de Janeiro: Alhambra/Embrafilme.
Santos Pereira, Geraldo
  1973 *Plano Geral do Cinema Brasileiro: Historia, Cultura, Economia e Legislação*. Rio de Janeiro: Editor
       Borsoi.
Salles Gomes, Paulo Emilio
  1980 *Cinema Trajetoria no Subdesenvolvimento*. Rio de Janeiro: Paz e Terra/Embrafilme.
Xavier, Ismail, Jean-Claude Bernardet and Miguel Pereira
  1985 *O Desafio do Cinema*. Rio de Janeiro: Jorge Zahar.

CHILE
Bolzoni, Francesco
  1974 *El Cine de Allende*. Valencia: Fernando Torres Editor.
Godoy Quezada, Mario
  1966 *Historia del Cine Chileno*. Santiago: Ediciones Fantasia.
Guzmán, Patricio
  1977 *La Batalla de Chile*. Pamplona: Peralta Ediciones/Ediciones Ayuso.
Ossa Coo, Carlos
  1971 *La Historia del Cine Chileno*. Santiago: Editorial Nacional Quimantú.
Sempere, Pedro and Patricio Guzmán, eds.
  1977 *Chile: El Cine Contra el Facismo*. Valencia: Fernando Torres Editor.
Vega, Alicia, ed.
  1979 *Revisión del Cine Chileno*. Santiago: Aconcagua/CENECA.

COLOMBIA
Martinez Pardo, Hernando
  1978 *Breve Historia del Cine Colombiano*. Bogotá: Editora Guadalupe.
Valverde, Umberto
  1978 *Reportaje Crítico al Cine Colombiano*. Bogotá: Editorial Toronuevo.

CUBA
Argramonte, Arturo
  1966 *Cronología del Cine Cubano*. Havana: Ediciones ICAIC.
Fornet, Ambrosio
  1982 *Cine, Literatura y Sociedad*. Havana: Editorial Letras Cubanas.
Garcia Espinosa, Julio
  1979 *Una Imagen Recorre el Mundo*. Havana: Editorial Letras Cubanas.
Gutiérrez Alea, Tomás
  1982 *Dialéctica del Espectador*. Havana: Ediciones Unión.
Micciche, Lino
  1981 *Teorie e Pratiche del Cinema Cubano*. Venice: Marsilio.
Porter, Miguel, ed.
  1975 *Cine y Revolución en Cuba*. Barcelona: Fontamara.
Valdes Rodríguez, Jorge
  1966 *Cine en la Universidad de la Habana*. Havana: Empresa de Publicaciones MINED.

MEXICO
Ayala Blanco, Jorge
  1968 *La Aventura del Cine Mexicano*. Mexico City: Ediciones Era.
  1974 *La Búsqueda del Cine Mexicano: 1968–1972*. 2 vols. Mexico City: UNAM.
de los Reyes, Aurelio
  1973 *Los Origines del Cine en México: 1869–1900*. Mexico City: UNAM.
García Riera, Emilio
  1969–74 *Historia Documental del Cine Mexicano*. 8 vols. Mexico City: Ediciones Era.
García Riera, Emilio and Fernando Macotela
  1984 *La Guia del Cine Mexicano*. Mexico City: Editorial Pátria.

Reyes de la Maza, Luis
  1968   *Salón Rojo (Programas y Crónicas del Cine Mudo en México)*. Mexico City: UNAM.
Sánchez, Alberto Ruy
  1981   *Mitología de un Cine en Crisis*. Mexico City: Premia.

NICARAGUA
Dagrón, Alfonso Gumucio
  1981   *El Cine de los Trabajadores*. Managua: Central Sandinista de Trabajadores.

URUGUAY
Hintz, Eugenio, ed.
  1988   *Historia y Filmografía del Cine Uruguayo*. Montevideo: Ediciones de la Plaza.

Index